MANUAL
for
EAR TRAINING
and
SIGHT SINGING

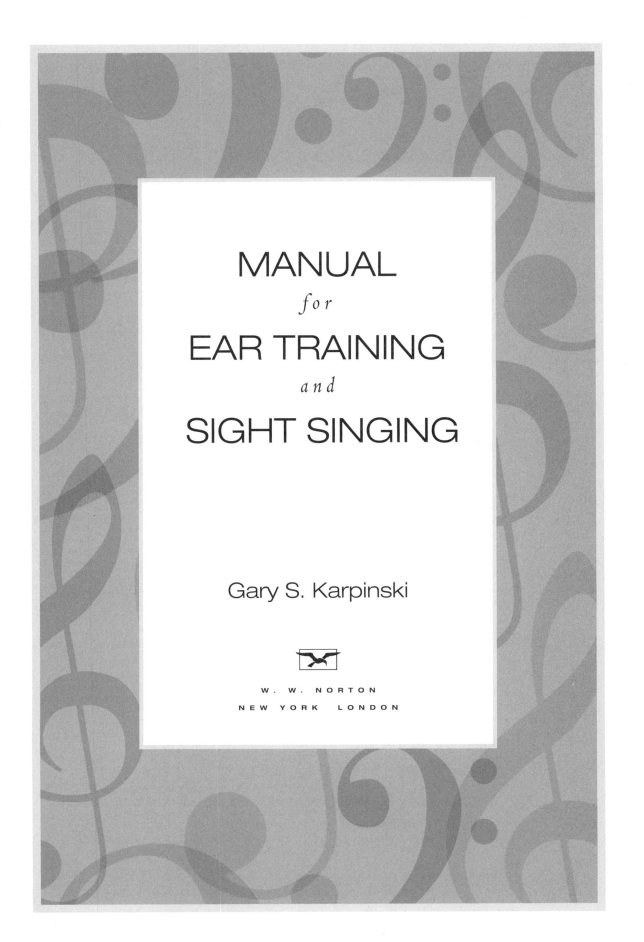

MANUAL

for

EAR TRAINING

and

SIGHT SINGING

Gary S. Karpinski

W. W. NORTON

NEW YORK   LONDON

Manufacturing by Quebecor World
Composition by A-R Editions, Inc.
Book design by Chris Welch

Editor: Maribeth Anderson Payne
Project Editor: Allison Courtney Fitch
Associate Editor: Allison Benter
Managing Editor—College: Marian Johnson
Production Manager: JoAnn Simony

ISBN-10: 0-393-97663-7
ISBN-13: 978-0-393-97663-2

W. W. Norton & Company, Inc., 500 Fifth Avenue, New York, N.Y. 10110
www.wwnorton.com
W. W. Norton & Company Ltd., Castle House, 75/76 Wells Street, London W1T 3QT

7 8 9 0

To Jean,
who was there at the beginning,
with all my love

CONTENTS

TO THE STUDENT

This is not a reference book. You will not be able to open it to any chapter and find a quick answer to a question about music. This book is not *about* music, it is a book that helps you *do* musical things well.

This book works very much like a cookbook. If you want to taste a cake, you don't merely read a recipe. Instead, you follow the recipe's instructions and *make* a cake so that you can taste it. Similarly, if you merely read this manual, you'll get as much satisfaction as you would from only reading a recipe. But if you follow this manual's instructions, you'll make music.

You don't need any previous training in music theory or music reading to begin using this manual although, in most cases, it will help. More advanced music students will find the manual to be helpful at the beginning of their college-level music training, since they often have an incomplete or merely intuitive understanding of the material covered in it. As you progress through the book, you will need to study some written music theory alongside your work. This is not a harmony text but an aural-skills manual.

The earliest chapters of this book are designed to develop your fundamental aural skills without particulars such as clef, key, and meter sign. To this end, the book employs what is referred to as "protonotation"—vertical and horizontal lines to represent meter and rhythm, combined with scale degree numbers and solmization syllables to represent pitch. Don't be too eager to jump directly into using real music notation during these early chapters. Use your work with protonotation as an opportunity to hone your basic aural skills. You'll have plenty of time to work with real music notation after that.

The two skills developed in this manual are music reading and music listening. Music reading involves more than just looking at music; you must understand what every symbol on the page means and produce the sounds they represent. You are asked to sing those sounds because singing requires that you imagine the proper sounds before you make them. This is fundamental to good music reading: You must have a precise idea of how a piece will sound before you perform it. As a performer, this makes it possible for you to control not only the rhythms and pitches, but also the subtler elements of intonation, expression, phrasing, and so on. As a music student, you will find that the ability to read music without having to sound it on an instrument is invaluable. A music student must strive to become as literate a reader of music as an English student is a literate reader of English. Fluent music reading is a necessary and indispensable skill for performers, students, teachers, conductors, coaches, composers, arrangers, musicologists, music therapists, and many others. Music listening is perhaps an even more complicated process. Yet

xii   Manual for Ear Training and Sight Singing

music is *sound* (notation is merely a set of instructions about how to make sound). To be a good musician, to truly live in music, your ability to hear and understand sound is crucial. Through using this manual you will become a much better music listener. You will be able to focus your attention more specifically, remember more, understand more, and translate that understanding into music notation.

This manual will help you to hear the music you see and see the music you hear, and this will make reading and listening to music richer, more productive, and more enjoyable experiences.

TO THE INSTRUCTOR

Manual for Ear Training and Sight Singing is the first textbook that treats aural skills with the same breadth, depth, and attention to detail found in most harmony textbooks. Each chapter focuses on a specific concept or skill and explains how to think about it, how to hear it, and how to perform it.

This book integrates ear training and sight singing, and addresses most topics in terms of both disciplines. Students benefit from studying each skill or concept using the same approach to both listening and reading. The bulk of the listening work appears at the ends of chapters in the form of dictations, transcriptions, and other exercises, which are correlated with the *Instructor's Dictation Manual* and the accompanying Student Recordings CD-ROM. The end of each chapter also includes a list of corresponding excerpts in the *Anthology for Sight Singing*.

Approach

The structure and content of this book have been shaped in large part by recent research in music cognition and perception. Knowledge about pulse perception informs discussions of meter. Studies of tonic inference affect instructions on how to understand pitches while listening. Research on short-term musical memory controls the length of dictations and transcriptions, the recommended number of listenings, and instructions for extracting memorable segments for processing. Concepts of holistic perception influence approaches to harmonic listening. Discoveries about perceptual streaming determine choices for two-part and bass-line dictation and transcription.

Several important advances in the study of music theory and analysis have also helped mold this book. Discoveries about the nature of meter and hypermeter are incorporated into every discussion of temporal organization in music. These discussions treat meter primarily as an experiential phenomenon in which metric principles are derived from what listeners and performers hear and feel in music. Likewise, Heinrich Schenker's theories have influenced certain crucial aspects of how this book approaches pitch. For instance, both harmony and voice leading play important roles in the listening and singing exercises in this manual. Similarly, the *Manual* helps students read and hear certain melodic figures through understanding the notion of structural pitches.

Advances in music theory pedagogy have also informed this project. A good deal of persuasive research has demonstrated the importance of tonally functional thinking, specifically in terms of scale degrees and their characteristic functions, so the methods and organization of pitch materials in this book have been directly affected by scale-degree thinking. On the other hand, because so many studies have shown that there is very little carryover between success in interval training and achievement in tonal aural skills, this book downplays interval work in favor of functional approaches. Nonetheless, because intervals are useful tools at certain points in the curriculum (establishing collection and tonic, for example) and in navigating certain complex tonal passages (and, of course, atonal music), interval training appears at several points throughout the book. In addition, research on categorical perception of rhythm and meter guides the order and presentation of temporal elements. Thus, for instance, all compound meters are presented together, all half-beat syncopations (regardless of beat unit) appear in the same chapter, and so on.

Because this book was developed on the basis of recent research, a few of the features in these pages might look a little strange to some readers. For example, although it has been a common practice to give students multiple cues before playing a melodic dictation, this manual provides only the clef, tonic, and bottom number in the meter sign for most dictations. Instructors and students who are used to a starting pitch, a starting rhythm, and various key-defining warm-ups might be disturbed by their absence, but eliminating these cues ensures that students learn to infer tonic, scale degrees, pulse, and meter early on in the curriculum. Readers are encouraged to work with the techniques presented in this book, and to consult the author's *Aural Skills Acquisition* (Oxford University Press, 2000) to answer questions about the underlying methods.

Once the *Manual* progresses beyond the earliest stages, it features real music as much as possible. Concepts are presented and skills developed using excerpts from various styles and genres. Abstract exercises are always presented in service of the real music that follows.

Most important, this *Manual* is not simply a collection of items for mere testing; it does not offer long lists of intervals and chords for identification, nor does it simply present a body of melodies for dictation and sight singing. This book conveys *methods* by which students—through study and practice—will be able to improve their listening, reading, and performing skills.

All the materials in this book have been developed over twenty-five years of teaching and research and have been tested in the classroom by various instructors over many semesters. The *Manual* is a dynamically evolving project, so instructors and students are encouraged to contribute comments and suggestions. There is even a form for comments available at the publisher's Web site at wwnorton.com/college/titles/music/karpinski/comment.htm.

Organization

Several important learning sequences guide the order of materials in this book. Pitch materials are organized by tonal function, beginning with diatonic melodies that skip only among members of the tonic triad and then adding skips to certain prefix neighbors, melodies that outline other diatonic chords, chromaticism, and so on. Simple duple and triple meters are introduced first, followed by quadruple meters, compound meters, and later more advanced metric concepts and skills. Rhythms begin with notes of one beat and longer, followed shortly by half-beat notes, and then a succession of shorter divisions and tuplets are introduced as the book progresses. The primary triads are introduced gradually over the first thirty chapters, but once harmonic listening and singing are introduced in earnest, the book presents a full panoply of diatonic chords followed later by chromatic harmony and modulation.

An important feature of the *Manual* is that it enables both teachers and students to focus on very specific musical elements. Separate chapters are devoted to individual features such as the supertonic chord, melodic sequence, hemiola, and so on. Similarly, this book focuses on particular musical skills. Significant passages are devoted to listening skills such as pulse-level perception, inference of the tonic, and extractive musical memory. Likewise, practical advice is offered on specific performing skills such as conducting and establishing a key.

This *Manual* is restricted mostly to tonal music. Although a couple of late chapters (73 and 76) brush against and venture slightly past the limits of the tonal system, tonal music is the driving force behind (and the limiting factor for) the materials here. Indeed, atonal aural skills are worthy of another entire book, and Chapter 76 makes some recommendations for further study in this area. Similarly, this book focuses on metric music, leaving the ametric music of pre- and post-common-practice-period music and the music of non-Western cultures outside its purview.

Dictation constitutes the majority of the listening activities in this book. This is because dictation has been proven to be the one exercise that can develop a more complete spectrum of listening skills than any other. Dictation hones focused listening, short-term musical memory, extractive memory, pulse inference, meter perception, categorical rhythmic understanding, tonic inference, scale degree perception, melodic chunking, holistic perception, and notation. In addition to dictation, the *Manual* offers other listening exercises: Transcription exercises can be found throughout the book (particularly in the middle to late chapters), affording students the opportunity to work at their own pace with longer, more contextual excerpts. Pulse-graph exercises that ask students to produce graphic representations of pulse levels appear in various chapters that present new metric and rhythmic concepts. Other listening assignments—such as charting harmonic rhythm, identifying common-tone functions, and mapping musical forms—appear as needed. Error detection is introduced in Chapter 4, and suggestions are made for continuing work on this important skill throughout the curriculum.

Curriculum

Fundamentals

The musical materials in the first eleven chapters of this *Manual* are pointedly restricted in terms of pitch, meter, and rhythm. These early restrictions afford students time to develop certain fundamental aural skills while unencumbered by the complexities of more difficult musical content or of music notation itself: This book does not introduce full-fledged music notation until Chapter 9 and music does not appear in keys other than C major until Chapter 11. The fundamental skills developed during these early chapters include short-term melodic memory, extractive listening, perception of pulse and meter, identification of rhythmic durations, inference of the tonic, and identification of scale degrees. Instructors whose students are well-grounded in these fundamentals may choose to omit early chapters and begin with Chapter 9, 10, or 11.

Essential vs. optional chapters

Many, but not all, of the chapters in this book are sequential—new chapters rely on the skills learned from previous chapters. But some of the chapters deal with tangential issues that are not necessary for further study in the book. In this way, instructors wishing to make adjustments may think of two kinds of chapters: *essential* and *optional*. All essential chapters should be covered in order to ensure that students are adequately prepared for all new pitch and rhythm skills they will encounter, but some or all of the optional chapters may be omitted (or taught at other times). Here is a table of essential and optional chapters:

Essential	Optional
	1–10*
11–12	
	13
14	
	15
16–20	
	21
22	
	23–24
25–28	
	29
30–47	
	48–50
51–63	
	64–65
66–76	
	77–78

* Chapters 1–10 may be considered optional only for those students well-grounded in the fundamentals.

Instructors may choose to move certain of the optional chapters elsewhere in the curriculum rather than eliminate them. For example, the chapters on the modes (49 and 50) may be moved earlier (to coincide with work on the minor mode) or later (to coincide with work on closely related modulation). However, instructors should be aware that some singing and dictation materials, when moved earlier in the curriculum, might bring with them other elements of rhythm or pitch not yet covered at that point. A quick perusal of these materials before making such a move will reveal which sight-singing excerpts and dictations to eliminate.

Two-year sequence

The *Manual*'s seventy-eight chapters are appropriate for a two-year sequence in aural skills. The charts below show how the chapters may be used in various curricula. (Note that any of these plans may be streamlined by omitting some or all of the optional chapters listed above.)

A Comprehensive Curriculum

Semester	Chapters
1	1–19
2	20–46
3	47–61
4	62–78

This plan reaches the minor mode in semester 1 and covers diatonic harmony in semester 2, chromatic harmony in semester 3, and modulation in semester 4. The challenging aspect of this plan is the scope of semester 2, which covers twenty-seven chapters—arduous, but achievable.

Quarter	Chapters
1	1–14
2	15–29
3	30–46
4	47–58
5	59–67
6	68–78

This plan covers basic melodic materials in quarter 1, further melodic materials in quarter 2, diatonic harmony in quarter 3, applied chords in quarter 4, other chromatic chords in quarter 5, and modulation in quarter 6. The challenging aspect of this plan is the scope of quarters 2 and 3, which cover thirty-two chapters—somewhat difficult, but manageable.

A Curriculum Beginning after Fundamentals

Semester	Chapters
1	11–29
2	30–46
3	47–61
4	62–78

This plan focuses on melodic materials in semester 1 and covers diatonic harmony in semester 2, chromatic harmony in semester 3, and modulation in semester 4.

Quarter	Chapters
1	11–22
2	23–34
3	35–46
4	47–58
5	59–67
6	68–78

This plan focuses on melodic materials in quarters 1 and 2, diatonic harmony in quarter 3, applied chords in quarter 4, other chromatic chords in quarter 5, and modulation in quarter 6.

A Curriculum from Fundamentals through Chromatic Harmony

Semester	Chapters
1	1–16
2	17–35
3	36–51
4	52–65

This plan stops short of the minor mode in semester 1 and covers further melodic materials in semester 2, diatonic harmony in semester 3, and chromatic harmony in semester 4. The disadvantage of this plan is the elimination of chapters 66–78; the curriculum never reaches modulation.

Quarter	Chapters
1	1–11
2	12–23
3	24–35
4	36–46
5	47–58
6	56–65

This plan covers basic melodic materials in quarter 1, further melodic materials in quarters 2 and 3, diatonic harmony in quarter 4, applied chords in quarter 5, and other chromatic chords in quarter 6. The disadvantage of this plan is the elimination of chapters 66–78, the curriculum never reaches modulation.

This book contains many more exercises than could be reasonably mastered by most students in a two-year sequence. Instructors will want to choose which scales, sequentials, chord progressions, and other exercises to assign, and save the remaining ones for practice and testing later. Likewise, the dictation, transcription, and other listening materials on the Student Recordings CD-ROM will likely prove sufficient for most lectures, assignments, and testing. (Nonetheless, even more dictation materials beyond those recorded on the CD-ROM are provided at the ends of most chapters in the *Instructor's Dictation Manual* for additional work in class.) The lists of corresponding excerpts from the *Anthology for Sight Singing* at the ends of the chapters are typically far too long to assign in their entirety. Once again, instructors are encouraged to assign selected excerpts and hold the others in abeyance for sight singing later.

Coordination with written theory curricula

The *Manual for Ear Training and Sight Singing* is intended for use as part of a core curriculum in music, in which written theory progresses alongside aural training, either in separate courses or in a single comprehensive course. However, the learning sequences for acquiring aural skills are different from those for learning written theory. The difference is most significant at the early stages of development. Therefore, the earliest chapters of this manual are designed to develop students' aural skills in an environment unhampered by the particularities of music notation. The complexities of many theoretical concepts are delayed until students' skills are sufficiently well established to incorporate those concepts in performing and listening activities.

This means that students' studies in written theory—particularly in harmony—can be coordinated with this manual in at least two different ways: (1) studies in written theory can proceed from the earliest days, so that students encounter concepts in the theory classroom well before they must apply these concepts in real time in aural skills; or (2) several months of preliminary studies in rudiments, counterpoint, figured bass, or other fundamental disciplines can precede the study of written harmony, and harmony work can begin about the time Chapter 25 of this manual is reached in aural training. In addition, for those instructors wishing to skip the early chapters on fundamentals, beginning work in this manual with Chapter 11 will accelerate closer coordination between aural skills training and written work in harmony.

Even at later stages, there are differences between traditional sequences for learning written theory and the skills-based learning sequence contained in this manual. Perhaps most noticeable is the treatment of modulation, which often appears much earlier in written curricula. Since modulation presents some of the most difficult challenges in tonal aural-skills training, it appears relatively late in this book.

Solmization

The *Manual for Ear Training and Sight Singing* refers to scale degrees in two ways: (1) with careted numbers ($\hat{1}$, $\hat{2}$, $\hat{3}$, etc.); and (2) with movable-do solmization (*do, re, mi,* etc.). The text combines these symbols, separating them with a slash ($\hat{1}$/*do*, $\hat{2}$/*re*, $\hat{3}$/*mi*, etc.).

For the most part, the book uses a parallel, functional approach to movable *do* (including *do*-based minor), with two exceptions: *la*-based solmization is used in

Chapter 17, when the natural minor mode is introduced, and in Chapter 49, when the modes are introduced. This approach is a logical extension of the diatonic collection students have been working with since the beginning of the book. But readers should make no mistake—this is not a *la*-based-minor book. Although the book uses relative solmization for certain limited purposes, its approach to functional tonality associates only one scale degree number and syllable with the tonic: $\hat{1}$/*do*. The other syllables (and any chromatic inflections) derive therefrom. This ensures that similar tonal functions in parallel keys will retain similar labels (for example, $\hat{5}$/*sol*–$\hat{7}$/*ti*–$\hat{2}$/*re* for the dominant triad in both major and minor).

Protonotation

The earliest chapters in this book use a notational system called "protonotation." Although it might seem a bit strange at first, protonotation has been used successfully by many instructors in a variety of settings for more than twenty years. This system uses vertical lines to represent pulses and meter, horizontal lines to represent rhythms, and scale degree numbers and syllables to represent pitches. The purpose of this symbology is to represent these features in a generic way without regard to how they might be notated in any specific meter sign, clef, or key. Using protonotation, this book presents concepts and skills in a universal way so that students can easily grasp the musical essence of the topic at hand, and then apply what they've learned in various specific contexts. Protonotation also allows students to represent what they hear, remember, and understand in dictation and transcription before they learn to notate it in any particular meter, clef, and key. Readers should not think of protonotation as a kind of shorthand, however. When dictation and transcription are working smoothly, students should strive to flow directly from hearing, remembering, and understanding into actual music notation. Nonetheless, readers will find that protonotation serves very well when addressing new skills and concepts, and when isolating notation from other stages in the listening process.

Familiar Tunes

In some chapters, exercises ask students to work with specific "familiar tunes." These melodies have been selected to develop students' facility with specific new features of pitch or rhythm. However, we should recognize that not all students will find all or even some of these tunes "familiar." Students who were not raised in the United States, for example, will have a cultural heritage that contains a very different set of familiar tunes. These familiar-tune exercises are quite helpful but not essential, so students' unfamiliarity with any of them will not prevent them from proceeding through the book. Alternatively, instructors may choose to make recordings of certain of these "familiar" melodies available for students to memorize.

Octave Designations

When a specific pitch in a specific octave must be referenced, this book uses the method adopted by the International Standards Organization. This method works like this: Start with C four octaves below middle C (a convenient starting point, since this pitch is at the lowest limits of hearing for most humans). Call that pitch

C0 ("C-zero"). Number the next higher pitch D0, the next E0, and so on, through B0. Call the next pitch C1 (the C an octave above C0). Continue with D1, E1, and so on. Number each new octave starting with C2, C3, and so on. As a point of reference, it is helpful to remember that middle C is C4. There are several other widely-used systems for designating specific octaves—see "Pitch nomenclature" in *The New Grove Dictionary of Music and Musicians,* 2nd edition (New York: Grove, 2001) for a summary and concordance.

Recordings

Nearly every chapter in this book includes listening exercises. Each exercise is numbered using a double-number scheme, in which the first number represents the chapter and the second represents the exercise. For example, number 42.12 is the twelfth listening exercise in Chapter 42. These exercises (the instructions for which are printed at the end of each chapter) correspond to the materials on the Student Recordings CD-ROM. None of the answers is printed in this book; instead, instructors have access to the music notation and other answers in the accompanying *Instructor's Dictation Manual.* In this way, listening exercises may be used for take-home assignments, quizzes, and other graded activities. Instructors may also choose to provide students with the answers to certain exercises so that they can work more independently. Nearly all of the recordings were performed by faculty and students at the Department of Music and Dance at the University of Massachusetts, Amherst.

Instructor's Dictation Manual

The music for over 600 dictations, transcriptions, and other listening exercises at the ends of chapters is printed in the *Instructor's Dictation Manual,* the recordings for which are on the Student Recordings CD-ROM. The *Instructor's Dictation Manual* also provides answers for various other listening activities, such as pulse graphs, error detection, and cadence identification. In addition, more than 130 unrecorded dictations and transcriptions are printed in the *Instructor's Dictation Manual* (labeled with letters rather than numbers), so that instructors will have extra materials for practice and testing for which students have no recordings.

Coordination with the
Anthology for Sight Singing

The *Anthology for Sight Singing* contains more than 1200 excerpts from music literature, carefully selected and graded to follow a learning sequence that parallels the one in this *Manual for Ear Training and Sight Singing.* The materials in this manual are closely coordinated with the *Anthology.* Beginning with Chapter 9, most chapters in the *Manual* include lists of corresponding excerpts from the *Anthology* appropriate for sight singing and preparation. Students who read a chapter in this *Manual* and prepare the exercises at the end of that chapter will be well equipped to begin singing the corresponding melodies in the *Anthology.*

ACKNOWLEDGMENTS

I am deeply indebted to Suzanne LaPlante, former Music Editor at W. W. Norton & Company, who approached me nearly ten years ago asking if I would be interested in applying my research in aural skills acquisition to the task of creating a textbook. She was a crucial guide during the earliest stages of formulating what could be done and how best to do it. When she decided to leave publishing, I could have asked for no better outcome than to have Maribeth Payne take her place. This was truly a fortuitous development, bringing me together again with the capable, knowledgeable, and experienced editor of my earlier book, *Aural Skills Acquisition*. Her sharp eye and keen ear, coupled with a welcome ability to tighten even the most intractable prose without sacrificing substance, helped make this a much better and more practical book. I also owe thanks to Allison Benter, former Associate Music Editor, who spent endless hours tightening and improving the manuscript. In addition, she helped navigate the difficult process of copyediting with a level-headed grace that any author would deeply appreciate. One of the trickiest parts of making a book is "production"—turning a manuscript into the pages you see before you. For making this process a painless, constructive, and pleasant one, I thank Courtney Fitch, Assistant Music Editor, who cheerfully acted as my advocate right down to the wire. JoAnn Simony, Senior Production Manager, skillfully oversaw all aspects of this process. For producing the software interface for the accompanying Student Recordings CD-ROM, I am grateful to Steve Hoge, Multimedia Editor. Imogen Howes, Music Intern, assisted efficiently and effectively with the glossary. Marilyn Bliss proved she's one of the best in the business by producing such excellent indexes.

Over the years, I have had the privilege to work with some outstanding colleagues who have used these materials in various stages of development and offered many excellent suggestions to improve them. Sigrun Heinzelmann, who is one of the best aural-skills teachers I know, recommended many excerpts, offered many suggestions and corrections, and provided several original ideas that I incorporated in these pages. Jane Hanson located several additional excerpts and suggested important corrections as well. Brent Auerbach, Hali Fieldman, and Mark McFarland also gave me helpful advice.

I'm very grateful to the many colleagues who answered my requests for information and opinions along the way. To Andrew Davis, Timothy Johnson, Tim Koozin, Stefan Kostka, William Rothstein, and Joseph Straus, thank you for your speedy and courteous replies to my sometimes obtuse inquiries.

No project of this depth and breadth could succeed without the resources of an excellent library. I am blessed to have at my disposal the Five-College Library System and its excellent staff. I am particularly grateful to Pamela Juengling, Music Librarian at the University of Massachusetts, Amherst, and to Jane Beebe, Music Librarian, and Ann Maggs, Music Library Assistant, at Amherst College.

The faculty and students in the Department of Music and Dance at the University of Massachusetts, Amherst, who performed the music on the accompanying Student Recordings CD-ROM, were selflessly cooperative and graciously accommodating. Without their musicality and professionalism, this would be a much poorer project. Greg Snedeker was highly skilled and altogether unflappable in his role as audio engineer. I am also indebted to the many developers of the Audacity audio editing software. Although there are many programs with which I could have edited the thousands of takes of these many recordings, Audacity's flexibility and ease of use made the task enjoyable.

The following individuals reviewed part or all of this project at various stages during its development. They offered many detailed suggestions that expanded and improved these books and their ancillary materials: Benjamin Broening, University of Richmond; Kate Covington, University of Kentucky; Craig Cummings, Ithaca College; Stefan Eckert, University of Oklahoma School of Music; James S. Hiatt, James Madison University; Richard Hoffman, Belmont University; Steve Larson, University of Oregon; Deron McGee, University of Kansas; Timothy A. Smith, Northern Arizona University; Barbara Wallace, Dallas Baptist University; Patrick C. Williams, University of Montana.

I owe a special debt of gratitude to Michael Rogers, Founding Editor of the *Journal of Music Theory Pedagogy* and author of *Teaching Approaches in Music Theory* (Southern Illinois University Press, 1984), who encouraged and supported me over the years. No one could ask for a better mentor or advocate. Thank you for everything, Mike.

I am most grateful to my family for their love, support, and encouragement. To my parents—who gave me so much, and who helped in so many ways to make me a musician, a scholar, and a teacher—thank you. To my wife, Jean—my friend, confidant, and champion for more than twenty-five years—I couldn't have done this without you. And to my wonderful children—who sustain me and inspire me in ways they can't yet imagine—I'm lucky you're mine. Thank you all for everything you've sacrificed so this project could come to fruition.

MANUAL

for

EAR TRAINING

and

SIGHT SINGING

THE FUNDAMENTALS OF METER AND RHYTHM

Duration in music can be understood in terms of its two primary components—meter and rhythm. In this chapter, we will seek ways to measure the lengths of notes and to write down symbols for those lengths.

Meter and rhythm do not measure time; they measure the way notes relate to one another in terms of their length. This is an important point. Meter and rhythm are relative elements—their qualities and quantities are determined internally by comparisons within a piece of music rather than externally by a device such as a metronome or wristwatch, which need only be consulted in order to determine tempo (see Chapter 15). The characteristics of meter and rhythm and of their corollaries (pulses, beats, and measures) are determined through listening directly to the music itself.

In this chapter, we'll develop a crude but effective method of writing down meter and rhythm. We'll refer to this type of notation as "protonotation" since it is not a true, full-fledged form of music notation. You are probably already familiar with traditional meter and rhythm notation, but postponing the use of this notation allows us to develop skills in hearing and reading meter and rhythm without worrying about "what kind of note gets the beat" and other notational complications.

Pulse

Sing the folk tune "Twinkle, Twinkle, Little Star." While you sing, clap steadily along with the music. You'll most likely clap one of the two following patterns (claps are shown by vertical lines):

Twin- kle,   twin- kle,   lit-   tle   star ———— ,how   I   won- der   what you   are ———— .

Both patterns represent a regularly recurring feeling of stress in the music, which is known as the **pulse.** Note that the pulse can occur at different levels in one piece of music, like the two levels shown above. Also note that each pulse occurs at a point in time—it has no duration or length.

> The **pulse** is a regularly recurring feeling of stress in music.

Primary and Secondary Pulses; Meter

In order to feel the relationship between these two levels of pulse, do this: Sing the tune and tap one pulse with your right hand while tapping the other with your left. Notice that each pulse in the top line coincides with every other pulse in the bottom line. You should feel more stress where the pulses coincide than on the individual pulses between them. Each of these stronger points of stress is called a **primary pulse.** Each of the weaker points of stress between the primary pulses is called a **secondary pulse.**

> The **primary pulse** is a pulse that regularly contains greater stress.

> The **secondary pulse** is a pulse that regularly contains less stress.

Let's rewrite the pulses so the primary pulses are larger than the secondary pulses:

Twin- kle,   twin- kle,   lit-   tle   star———— ,how   I   won- der   what you   are————.

Meter is the organization of pulses into primary and secondary levels.

When music exhibits patterns of primary and secondary pulses, the music is said to have **meter.**

Beat and Measure

A beat is the duration between successive pulses.

Since the durations between successive pulses are constant, we may use them as units of measurement. The duration between two successive pulses is, in this case, called one **beat.** (Although some books use the terms *beat* and *pulse* interchangeably, this book distinguishes between the points where stresses occur [pulses] and the durations between them [beats].) In thinking of the differences between pulses and beats, remember that pulses have no duration but beats do.

A measure is the duration between successive primary pulses.

The duration between successive *primary* pulses is also an important unit of measurement. It is called one **measure.**

Duple Meter

In **duple meter,** there are two beats per measure.

In "Twinkle, Twinkle, Little Star," we can hear and see that the pulses are grouped in pairs; each primary pulse is followed by one secondary pulse. Each measure contains two beats, creating the condition known as **duple meter.**

Rhythm

Rhythm is duration in music.

Music involves notes of various durations that occur against the steady background of the pulse. The word that describes the durations of notes is **rhythm.**

Let's figure out the rhythms to the beginning of "Twinkle, Twinkle, Little Star." If you tap the pulse and sing the music, you'll notice that each of the first six syllables (through "lit-tle") is one beat long. The following syllable, "star," lasts twice as long as the others—two beats.

We can continue this process and write out the rhythms for the beginning of "Twinkle, Twinkle, Little Star" by drawing one horizontal line for each note

Twin- kle,   twin- kle,   lit-   tle   star———— ,how   I   won- der   what you   are————.

In the drawing, the horizontal rhythm lines begin and end just short of the vertical pulse lines, but this does not mean these notes are shorter than one or two full beats. The breaks merely provide clarity, so all of the rhythm lines don't run together in one long horizontal line. The double vertical lines at the end—known as a *double bar*—indicate when the music stops.

Conducting Duple Meter

An important technique that musicians use to indicate meter is conducting. Conducting will take the place of our clapping and tapping.* When conducting duple meter with the right arm, the right hand follows this path:

Your hand should trace a backwards "J" in the air. It may help, at first, to say the words "down" and "up" at each pulse.

You should develop a feeling of pulse directly in your conducting. The point at which a pulse occurs within the beat of a conducting pattern should feel like a snap or bounce in your hand, wrist, or forearm. This point is called the **ictus.**

Conduct while singing "Twinkle, Twinkle, Little Star." Your hand should move down at each primary pulse and back up at each secondary pulse. Because the conducting pattern moves down for the first beat in each measure, that beat is called a **downbeat.** Similarly, because of the upward motion, the last beat in each measure is called an **upbeat.**

> The **ictus** is the point in each beat of a conducting pattern at which the pulse occurs.

> The **downbeat** is the first beat of a measure.

> The **upbeat** is the last beat of a measure.

Triple Meter

In duple meter, there are two beats per measure. In **triple meter,** the pulses are grouped in threes: each primary pulse is followed by two secondary pulses.

> In **triple meter,** there are three beats per measure.

The figure below shows the beginning of the folk tune "Pop Goes the Weasel" with two adjacent levels of pulse—a faster level below a slower one. Notice how the faster pulse groups into threes to form the slower pulse.

All———a- round——the cob- bl- er's bench——the mon- key chased   the wea-   sel———.

As in duple meter, primary pulses occur where the two levels coincide, and all the others are secondary. The figure below shows the first phrase, with large and small vertical lines indicating primary and secondary pulses respectively and horizontal lines indicating the rhythms.

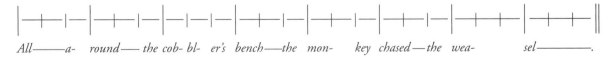

All———a- round——— the cob- bl- er's bench——the mon-   key chased—the wea-   sel————.

---

*This book gives instructions for using the right arm for all conducting patterns. To use the left arm, mirror the image of each pattern, reversing right and left directions (but not up and down).

Conducting Triple Meter

The conducting pattern for triple meter looks like this:

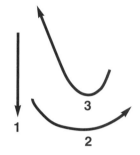

The downbeat is followed by the second beat, which moves out and to the right, and this is followed by an upbeat. It may help, at first, to say the words "down," "out," and "up" for each beat.

Sing "Pop Goes the Weasel" while conducting in triple meter.

Reading from Protonotation

We'll use the term "protonotation" to refer to the system of vertical and horizontal lines we've been using to represent meter and rhythm. So far, we've used this system to write down what we hear. We can also *read* from protonotation, conducting the meter and vocalizing the rhythms represented in the protonotation. Since this protonotation doesn't represent pitch, we should speak or intone rhythms on a neutral syllable such as "du" or "ta" on a single pitch.

Conduct and intone *only the rhythms* of "Twinkle, Twinkle, Little Star":

Before you proceed, be certain that you can perform from protonotation by conducting the meter and intoning the rhythms on a neutral syllable.

EXERCISES

1. Think of pieces of music you have in your long-term memory but which you've never seen in notation. Folk tunes, holiday songs, and children's songs are particularly good for this purpose. Perform the following tasks for each excerpt:

   a. Sing the music in your mind, without making a sound (we'll refer to this as "auralizing"—the aural analog to visualizing).

   b. Find a steady pulse in the music and clap or tap along with that pulse. Do not try to determine the meter yet.

   c. Find at least one other adjacent level of steady pulse (faster or slower).

   d. Tap the first pulse with one hand and the second pulse with the other.

   e. Identify the relationship between those two levels of pulse as duple or triple.

   f. Conduct along with the music using the appropriate conducting pattern.

   g. Write the vertical pulse lines for a short passage of this music.

   h. Fill in the horizontal rhythm lines for that same passage. What kind of rhythms do you hear that we haven't yet encountered in this chapter?

   i. Perform the rhythms of this protonotation on a neutral syllable while conducting. Have your classmates perform this protonotation as well. Do these performances sound like the original rhythms?

2. Listen to a variety of music from recordings and live performances and determine the pulses and meter for each excerpt using tasks a–g above.

3. Try to find recorded examples of music with the following rhythmic or metric characteristics:

   a. rhythm but no meter

   b. a pulse that speeds up or slows down

4. Pick one recorded example and write out vertical lines representing the fastest pulse you can tap and, above that, the next slower level of pulse. Then determine how that second pulse groups into yet another slower level and write vertical lines for that. Continue this process until you feel you've reached a level too slow to be perceived audibly. Compare your results with others'.

5. Watch a conductor at work in front of an ensemble. Observe the following:

   a. Look for duple and triple conducting patterns. Do you see any patterns other than these? (Quadruple—a pattern we will address in Chapter 4—is another common one.)

   b. Do the duple and triple patterns you see ever differ from those we learned in this chapter? If so, in what ways?

   c. What other changes occur in these patterns? Look and listen for changes in speed, size, smoothness, height, and direction. What do each of these changes convey to the performers?

   d. What additional motions do conductors make with their other hand, their body, or their face? What do these convey?

LISTENING

1. Listen to the recorded excerpts 1.1–1.5 and do the following for each:

   • distinguish and write down at least two levels of pulse from what you hear

   • determine whether those two levels form a duple or triple relationship

   • conduct along with the music using the appropriate pattern.

How many more levels of pulse can you hear?

2. Listen to the short musical fragments 1.6–1.10 and write out the vertical pulse lines and horizontal rhythm lines for each.

Learn to perform the following exercises: use a neutral syllable (such as "ta" or "du"); conduct using the appropriate pattern for each exercise; keep a steady pulse; and be certain to hold the last note out for its full value.

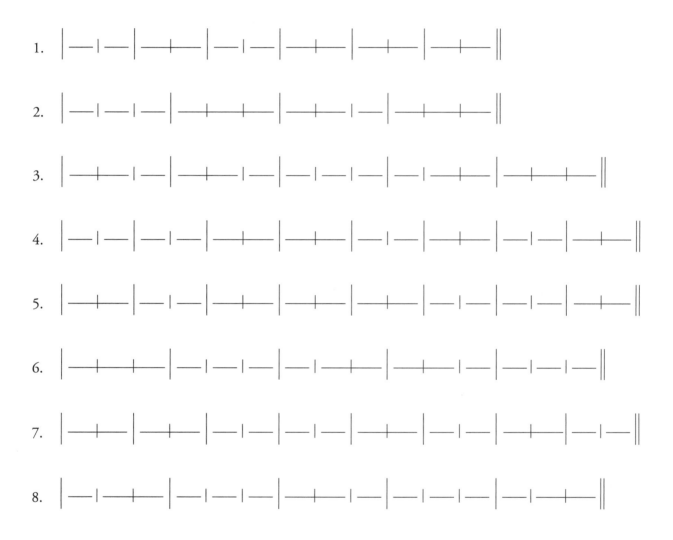

2 THE FUNDAMENTALS OF PITCH

In addition to duration, other musical characteristics can easily be measured. One such characteristic is that which we describe as being "higher" or "lower": a difference in **pitch.**

Pitch is the characteristic of sound we perceive as being higher or lower.

Determining the Relative Height of Pitches

To begin an investigation of pitch, you'll need two basic abilities:

- the ability to recognize notes of identical pitch
- the ability to distinguish a higher note from a lower note

We'll use these powers of discrimination on the folk tune "Frère Jacques." Sing the first fourteen notes of the tune ("Frè-re Jac-ques, Frè-re Jac-ques, dor-mez vous, dor-mez vous?") and think about the height (in pitch) of each note compared to the others. Which notes are the same in pitch? Which are higher or lower? Sing the tune and trace the height of each pitch with your hand in the air.

The relative up-and-down motion of pitches is called **melodic contour.** The following figure illustrates the melodic contour of the beginning of "Frère Jacques." Horizontal lines are drawn at different levels to indicate where the pitches ascend, descend, or stay the same. (Do not confuse these horizontal lines with those used for rhythm in Chapter 1.)

Melodic contour is the relative up-and-down motion of pitches in a melody.

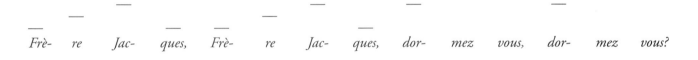

Note that some pitches are used more than once; for instance, "Frè–" and "–ques" both occur on the same pitch. There are actually only five unique pitches among these fourteen notes, and they are numbered here from the lowest to the highest:

1. Frè– and –ques
2. –re
3. Jac– and dor–
4. –mez
5. vous

Replace the horizontal lines above the syllables in the figure above with the appropriate numbers as shown in the following figure. Sing the tune for "Frère Jacques" on these numbers instead of the words.

1	2	3	1	1	2	3	1	3	4	5	3	4	5
Frè-	*re*	*Jac-*	*ques,*	*Frè-*	*re*	*Jac-*	*ques,*	*dor-*	*mez*	*vous,*	*dor-*	*mez*	*vous?*

The Major Scale and Scale Degrees

> A **scale** is a list of pitches in ascending and/or descending order.

Although there are many possible pitches, much Western music makes use of seven unique ones—two more than the five we identified above. If we arrange these seven pitches in ascending and/or descending order, we produce a **scale.**

> **Scale degrees** are the unique pitches in a scale (usually referred to by number).

When we number the seven unique pitches in a scale, each pitch is referred to as a **scale degree.** We refer to scale degrees by number (for example "scale degree one" or "the first scale degree"). This can be abbreviated as $\hat{1}$—the caret indicates "scale degree."

When you sing the notes of the scale, you'll notice that ending with $\hat{7}$ sounds incomplete. Sing the next note above $\hat{7}$ (call it "8" for now). Isolate this new note and $\hat{1}$; sing one after the other. Although there is a great distance between these two pitches, they are very much alike—so much alike that musicians call this higher pitch $\hat{1}$ as well. It's obviously higher in pitch, but it is the same in character. You can even continue above it, singing $\hat{2}$, $\hat{3}$, and so on.

Because $\hat{7}$ sounds so incomplete, musicians usually perform scales by including $\hat{1}$ at the top and bottom of the scale. We can write out the notes of a scale as follows:

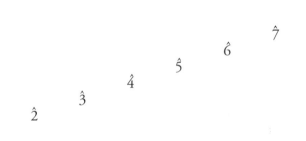

Sing this scale using numbers. The scale you're singing is called the *major scale.*

Solmization

In addition to using numbers to label the scale degrees, musicians also use syllables. The practice of singing syllables for different pitches is a traditional one that goes back at least a thousand years. It is called **solmization.**

> **Solmization** is the discipline of singing syllables that correspond to pitches (or rhythms).

Here are the scale degrees, shown with numbers, the corresponding syllables, and their pronunciation.

Scale degrees:	$\hat{1}$	$\hat{2}$	$\hat{3}$	$\hat{4}$	$\hat{5}$	$\hat{6}$	$\hat{7}$
Syllables:	*do*	*re*	*mi*	*fa*	*sol*	*la*	*ti*
Pronunciation:	"doh"	"ray"	"mee"	"fah"	"soh" [or "sole"]	"lah"	"tee"

Note that the syllables are pronounced with their Latinate vowels (A="AH"; E="AY"; I="EE").

Now return to "Frère Jacques," and sing it using solmization syllables rather than words or numbers:

do	*re*	*mi*	*do*	*do*	*re*	*mi*	*do*	*mi*	*fa*	*sol*	*mi*	*fa*	*sol*
Frè-	re	Jac-	ques,	Frè-	re	Jac-	ques,	dor-	mez	vous,	dor-	mez	vous?

Some musicians prefer to use only syllables to represent scale degrees, and others prefer to use only numbers. When this text refers to "singing on syllables," we use both numbers and syllables, separating the two with a slash; for example, Î/ *do* represents the first scale degree. If your instructor uses only numbers, simply read the number before the slash. If your instructor uses only syllables, read the syllable after the slash.

Names for Scale Degrees

Each scale degree has certain characteristics of sound that distinguish it from the others. Given its important position as the first and last note in the scale, Î/ *do* deserves special attention. This pitch has important properties as a resting tone—the note to which others in a composition seem to want to resolve (some more directly than others). This pitch is called the **tonic.**

Every scale degree has a name identifying its function (in addition to a number and syllable). Here is a list of those names:

> The **tonic** is the pitch to which all others seem to want to resolve. We often place it as the first and last note of a scale.

Î/ *do*	2̂/ *re*	3̂/ *mi*	4̂/ *fa*	5̂/ *sol*	6̂/ *la*	7̂/ *ti*
Tonic	Supertonic	Mediant	Subdominant	Dominant	Submediant	Leading tone

EXERCISES

1. To become as familiar and fluent with the syllables and scale-degree numbers as you can, sing the scale from Î/ *do* to Î/ *do*, ascending and descending, at a brisk pace, both from the bottom to top and back, and from the top to bottom and back.

2. Learn the following pitch patterns by heart. Be able to sing them at any time, in any order.

1a. $\hat{1}/do$ $\hat{2}/re$ $\hat{3}/mi$ $\hat{1}/do$		1b. $\hat{1}/do$ $\hat{3}/mi$ $\hat{1}/do$	
2a. $\hat{1}/do$ $\hat{2}/re$ $\hat{3}/mi$ $\hat{4}/fa$ $\hat{5}/sol$ $\hat{1}/do$		2b. $\hat{1}/do$ $\hat{5}/sol$ $\hat{1}/do$	
3a. $\hat{1}/do$ $\hat{7}/ti$ $\hat{6}/la$ $\hat{5}/sol$ $\hat{1}/do$		3b. $\hat{1}/do$ $\hat{1}/do$ $\hat{5}/sol$	
4a. $\hat{3}/mi$ $\hat{2}/re$ $\hat{1}/do$ $\hat{3}/mi$		4b. $\hat{3}/mi$ $\hat{1}/do$ $\hat{3}/mi$	
5a. $\hat{5}/sol$ $\hat{4}/fa$ $\hat{3}/mi$ $\hat{2}/re$ $\hat{1}/do$ $\hat{5}/sol$		5b. $\hat{5}/sol$ $\hat{5}/sol$ $\hat{1}/do$	
6a. $\hat{5}/sol$ $\hat{4}/fa$ $\hat{3}/mi$ $\hat{5}/sol$		6b. $\hat{5}/sol$ $\hat{3}/mi$ $\hat{5}/sol$	
7a. $\hat{3}/mi$ $\hat{4}/fa$ $\hat{5}/sol$ $\hat{3}/mi$		7b. $\hat{3}/mi$ $\hat{5}/sol$ $\hat{3}/mi$	
8a. $\hat{5}/sol$ $\hat{6}/la$ $\hat{7}/ti$ $\hat{1}/do$ $\hat{5}/sol$		8b. $\hat{5}/sol$ $\hat{1}/do$ $\hat{5}/sol$	

> **A sequential** is an exercise in which a pitch pattern is repeated on successive scale degrees.

3. A **sequential** is a valuable exercise in which a pitch pattern is repeated on successive scale degrees (any such repeated pattern is called a **sequence**—see chapter 62). Here is a simple sequential based on the pattern $\hat{1}/do$–$\hat{2}/re$–$\hat{3}/mi$. (Note the combination of rhythmic protonotation with syllables. We'll explore this further in the next chapter.) Sing the two parts of the sequential as one continuous exercise.

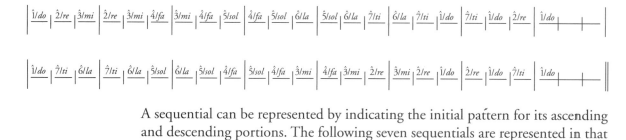

A sequential can be represented by indicating the initial pattern for its ascending and descending portions. The following seven sequentials are represented in that manner:

Sequential	Ascending	Descending
1	1̂/do 2̂/re 3̂/mi . . . ♫♫ ♫♫	1̂/do 7̂/ti 6̂/la . . .
2	1̂/do 2̂/re 3̂/mi 1̂/do . . . ♪♫♩	1̂/do 7̂/ti 6̂/la 1̂/do . . .
3	1̂/do 3̂/mi 2̂/re 1̂/do . . . ♫♫♩	1̂/do 6̂/la 7̂/ti 1̂/do . . .
4	1̂/do 3̂/mi . . . ♫♫♫♫♩	1̂/do 6̂/la . . .
5	1̂/do 2̂/re 3̂/mi 4̂/fa 5̂/sol . . . ♫♫♩	1̂/do 7̂/ti 6̂/la 5̂/sol 4̂/fa . . .
6	1̂/do 5̂/sol . . . ♩♪♩♪	1̂/do 4̂/fa . . .
7	1̂/do 3̂/mi 5̂/sol . . . ♫♫♫ ♫♫♫ ♫♫	1̂/do 6̂/la 4̂/fa . . .

Be sure to finish each half of these sequentials (ascending and descending) with a longer note on 1̂/do equal to the duration of one presentation of the pattern.

Sequentials can employ a variety of rhythms. Your instructor will specify rhythms for each sequential.

Continue to work on these sequentials as you progress through subsequent chapters in this book.

Keep the following in mind as you learn these sequentials:

- Each ascending and descending portion of the sequential ends when 1̂/do is reached on a downbeat.
- Learn each sequential entirely in your mind by thinking of the initial pattern and moving that pattern from one scale degree to the next. Do not write them out in syllables or music notation. This work will reward you with fluency in the syllables and a heightened acuity for scale degrees.
- Memorize each sequential.

4. Familiar tunes. The pitches in the following melodies belong to the scale degrees we've discussed thus far:

- Frère Jacques (finish the entire tune)
- Joy to the World (continue through "Her King")
- Row, Row, Row Your Boat
- Twinkle, Twinkle, Little Star
- Old McDonald
- Mary Had a Little Lamb
- Three Blind Mice
- Yankee Doodle (1st half)
- The First Noel (through "where they lay")
- When the Saints Go Marching In

You might not be familiar with all of these melodies, so work only with those you know well. If you don't know any of them, your instructor will have some suggestions for comparable work.

Sing some of these tunes aloud and auralize others silently in your mind. For each tune, your goal is to determine the scale degrees of its pitches and sing each tune on the proper numbers or syllables without the aid of any instrument or writing. Do the work entirely *in your mind.*

Follow these guidelines for each tune:

    a. Find the tonic (the syllable 1̂/do) recalling that it might not be the first, last, highest, or lowest note—listen for the pitch with the feeling of 1̂/do

b. Determine the syllable of the first pitch by comparing it with $\hat{1}$/*do* (isolate the starting pitch and $\hat{1}$/*do,* sing each and compare)

c. Work out the subsequent syllables

d. Memorize your familiar tunes on the proper syllables.

Some additional suggestions for this exercise (and for the listening to follow):

- Determine the contour of the melody. Trace its shape in the air with your hand or draw it on paper. Listen for and identify the difference between stepwise motion (motion between adjacent scale degrees) and motion by skip or leap (nonadjacent motion).

- If you have difficulty determining $\hat{1}$/*do,* pick *any* high note in the melody and sing down the scale from there using the pitches contained in the melody. Listen for a sense of closure and finality—as you approach $\hat{1}$/*do,* your intuition should guide you.

- If you have difficulty determining the scale degree of the first pitch, sing the starting pitch and then sing up or down the scale (using pitches contained in the melody) until you arrive at $\hat{1}$/*do.* As you do this, keep track of the number of pitches you have traversed. Count back to identify the scale degree of the starting pitch. (This technique is rather mechanical, but it will help you to get the right answer and to become more familiar with the sound and feel of various scale degrees.)

- To become more efficient and fluent at applying syllables to melodies, use your contour-identifying skills. For stepwise passages, apply the syllables in a linear fashion (this is one place where facility at scales and sequentials helps). When the music skips, calculate the scale degree of the pitch following the skip using the same techniques you use for the starting pitch. Use your knowledge of patterns such as scalar motion, repetition, and sequences only to the extent that you are certain you can identify these features by ear.

- Be meticulous about fitting the right syllables to the pitches. If you do this incorrectly for any melody, you not only get the wrong answer for that particular melody but you also begin to link incorrect syllables and scale degrees in your mind, making it that much harder to find the right ones in the future.

LISTENING

Listen to each of the short musical fragments 2.1–2.8 and figure out the appropriate scale-degree syllables for each. Here are some guidelines to help you:

a. Focus your attention while listening: you must first remember each fragment (if you don't, you can't figure out anything about it). Pay particular attention to the sound of the first pitch—latching on to the first note will help you successfully combine your contour memory with your pitch memory.

b. Find the tonic ($\hat{1}$/*do*) of the fragment.

c. Calculate the first pitch of the fragment by comparing it to $\hat{1}$/*do.*

d. Determine the proper scale-degree labels for each of the fragment's pitches.

e. Write the scale-degree syllables that correspond to the pitches of each fragment.

3 COMBINING PITCHES WITH METER AND RHYTHM

We now have two sets of symbols: those that represent meter and rhythm (the vertical and horizontal lines from Chapter 1), and those for pitches (the scale-degree syllables from Chapter 2). In this chapter, we'll combine both of those types of symbols in one system of protonotation.

To do this, we'll simply write the scale-degree numbers and/or syllables directly above each of the horizontal lines that represent rhythms. For example, the meter, rhythms, and pitches of "Frère Jacques" (see Chapter 2) can be represented like this:

| $\hat{1}$/do | $\hat{2}$/re | $\hat{3}$/mi | ↘$\hat{1}$/do | $\hat{1}$/do | $\hat{2}$/re | $\hat{3}$/mi | ↘$\hat{1}$/do | ↗$\hat{3}$/mi | $\hat{4}$/fa | $\hat{5}$/sol | ↘$\hat{3}$/mi | $\hat{4}$/fa | $\hat{5}$/sol |

Frè- re, Jac- ques, Frè- re Jac- ques, dor- mez vous, dor- mez vous?

The small directional arrows before certain syllables indicate a skip (up or down) in the melody. (If no arrow appears, the music moves by step.) You should become accustomed to seeing and using these arrows whenever the music skips. Now read from this combined protonotation and sing "Frère Jacques" on syllables or numbers while conducting in duple meter.

Do the same for "Twinkle, Twinkle, Little Star." Write vertical lines for its meter, then horizontal lines for its rhythms, then the numbers and/or syllables for the scale degrees of its pitches. As you work out the syllables for this tune, be careful and patient. Compare the sounds of the scale degrees with those of the other melodies and patterns whose pitches you've determined. Now conduct and sing "Twinkle, Twinkle, Little Star" with syllables while reading from the protonotation you just constructed.

Try singing one more in the same manner:

| $\hat{3}$/mi | $\hat{2}$/re | $\hat{1}$/do | $\hat{2}$/re | $\hat{3}$/mi | $\hat{3}$/mi | $\hat{3}$/mi | $\hat{2}$/re | $\hat{2}$/re | $\hat{2}$/re | $\hat{3}$/mi | ↗$\hat{5}$/sol | $\hat{5}$/sol |

If you performed that protonotation properly, you sang the rhythms and pitches for the beginning of "Mary Had a Little Lamb." Write out the meter, rhythms, and scale degrees for the rest of "Mary Had a Little Lamb" in protonotation.

We're now ready to use our combined systems of rhythmic and pitch notation for both dictation and music reading.

Melodic Dictation

Dictation is the process of hearing music and writing it down in notation. Taking dictation involves several steps. We'll begin with short, easily memorable fragments, 3.1–3.8, which we will write in protonotation, so those steps will be relatively simple. They will become more complex later, when we introduce longer melodies and real music notation. Here are the three primary steps:

a.   *Hear the music.* Focus your attention on the music as it sounds. This means excluding all distractions. Musicians must be able to focus their complete attention on the music at hand.

b.   *Remember the music.* Remember what you have heard, or nothing you do beyond this point will matter. One of the best tests of your memory of a melody is to sing it. You must also be able to auralize it. Develop your auralizing skills by using your mind like a tape recorder to play back the sound. Manipulate the sound in your mind by slowing it down, stopping and starting it, and comparing various pitches and rhythms.

c.   *Understand the music.* First, determine the pulse. Then, determine how that pulse is organized into meter (is it duple or triple?), and write that meter using the vertical lines of protonotation. Next, determine the rhythms of the notes in relation to the pulse and meter. Write horizontal lines representing those rhythms. Finally, find $\hat{1}$/*do,* determine the scale degree of the starting note, and work out the subsequent scale degrees (review the suggestions at the end of Chapter 2). Write the scale degrees above the rhythm lines in your protonotation.

Write your answers in protonotation—like this, for example:

Sing the following exercises on syllables while conducting. You should be able to sing them in *any* order. Observe the directional ticks and make skips accordingly.

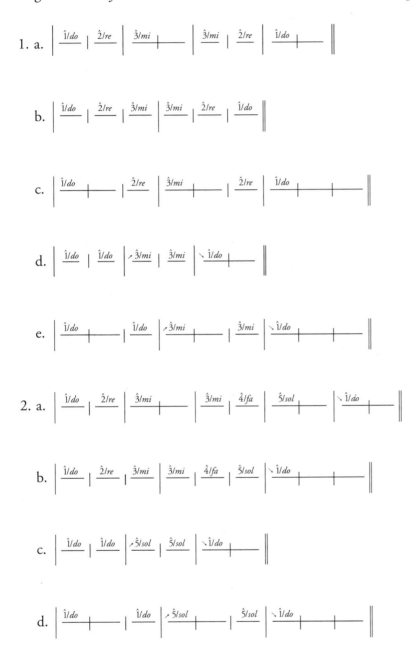

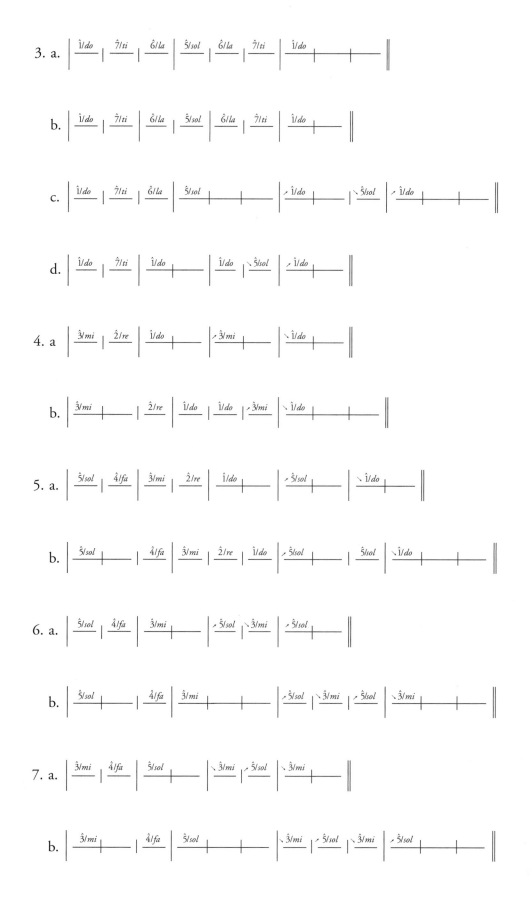

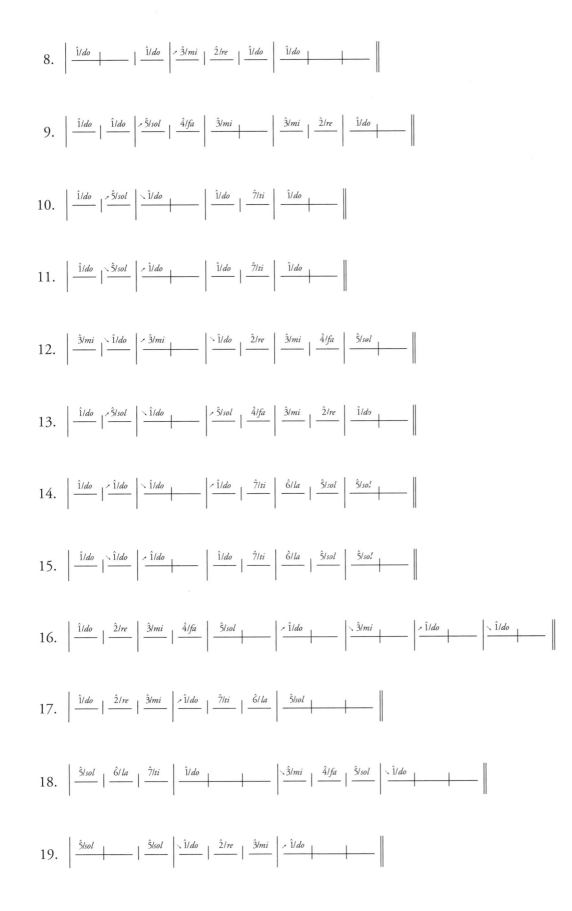

20.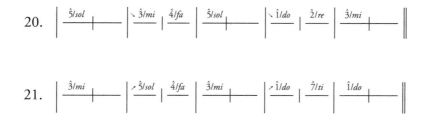

21.

4 ERROR DETECTION AND CORRECTION

One of the most important skills you will develop as a musician involves detecting discrepancies between what you hear and what the music *should* sound like, and correcting those errors as necessary. Error detection will form a thread throughout your studies. Every musician uses this skill. Some say it's the single most useful and valuable skill they have learned.

You have already done some error detection and correction in preparing and performing exercises in this book, listening to be sure that the sounds you produce match the rhythms and syllables printed on the page. This chapter will introduce the basic skills and techniques necessary for detecting and correcting errors through protonotation. Later, you will apply what you've learned here to real music notation.

Here are some suggestions to consider as you practice error detection and correction.

- Before you hear the music, auralize the notation as if *you* were performing it. This will allow you to formulate an accurate aural representation of the notation against which you can match the performance. If you don't auralize the notation, the performance can deceptively sound "correct."

- Always be ready to accept "no errors" as a possible answer. This is exactly how error detection works in real life. One can never be sure when errors will occur, if at all.

- As you phrase your response, start by specifying exactly where the error(s) occurred. Do this by giving the broadest reference first. In other words, specify measure number first, then beat number. (This becomes particularly important when working with larger excerpts. "Line 4, measure 2, beat 3, bass voice" is much easier to follow than "bass voice, beat 3, measure 2, line 4.")

- It is important that you learn to phrase your answers in words. When ensemble members, teachers, conductors, and coaches use error detection and correction, they must communicate their findings to colleagues, students, and performers clearly, using words. Therefore, your work with error detection in this book will similarly be expressed in words.

- Be specific with regard to your corrections. Compare the following:

Not specific enough	Specific
"In measure 2, beat 2, the '$\hat{4}$/*fa*' was too high"	"In measure 2, beat 2, the '$\hat{4}$/*fa*' was played as '$\hat{6}$/*la*' "
"In measure 4, the three-beat note was too long"	"In measure 4, the three-beat note was held for five beats"

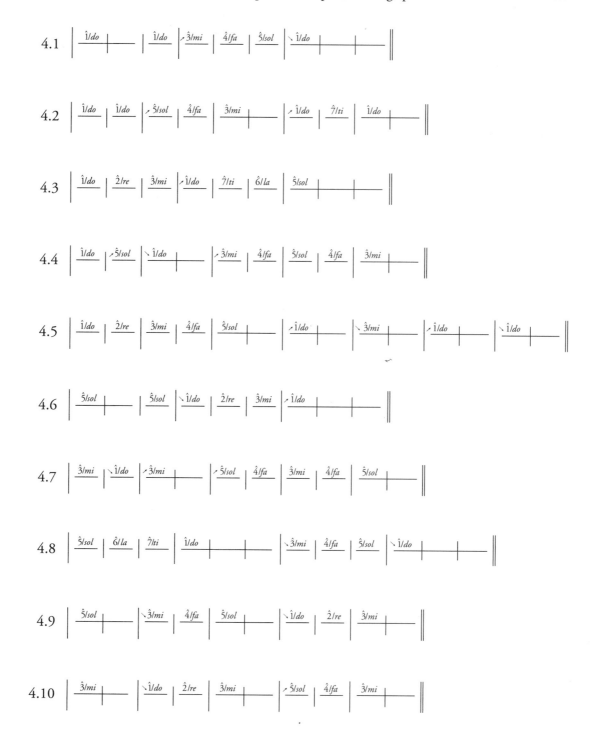

Use the following short printed melodic segments to practice error detection and correction. Some will be played by your instructor in class, and others you can practice with your classmates by playing correct and incorrect versions for each other. All are recorded on the accompanying CD. Practice error detection and correction with other protonotations in this book, and with protonotation that other students and your instructor compose for this purpose.

Study the protonotation and auralize it. Listen to the performance. Respond in the manner described in the present chapter, writing specific corrections in words.

5 MORE ABOUT METER AND RHYTHM

Duple Division of the Beat

An important factor affecting the perception of meter is the existence of more than two levels of pulse. In Chapter 1, we found two levels of pulse in "Twinkle, Twinkle, Little Star." We can also find a third, broader level of pulse.

We can shift our focus to the two broadest levels. This is neither more correct nor incorrect; it is merely another way of feeling the structure of the stresses.

Applying the techniques learned in previous chapters, we can notate the meter and rhythm of this example using those two levels, like this:

Twin- kle, twin- kle, lit- tle star ——, how I won- der what you are ————.

This approach yields some notes that are one-half beat in length in addition to the one-, two-, and three-beat notes we've seen in earlier chapters. A meter in which the beat is regularly divided in halves is called a **simple meter** (compare compound meters in Chapter 16). Sing the beginning of "Twinkle, Twinkle, Little Star" as written above, while conducting the indicated pulses.

In Chapter 1, we practiced meter and rhythm by intoning rhythms on a neutral syllable such as "du" or "ta." You may continue to do this, or you may begin to use a system of rhythm syllables known as **Takadimi.** To divide a beat in half using Takadimi, the note on the beat is called "ta" and the note on the half-beat is called "di." In this way, the Takadimi syllables for the first four measures of "Twinkle, Twinkle, Little Star" would be "Ta-di Ta-di Ta-di Ta."

> In **simple meters** the beat is regularly divided in halves.

> **Takadimi** is a system of rhythm syllables.

Quadruple Meter

Return to the three levels of pulse in "Twinkle, Twinkle, Little Star" that we identified at the beginning of this chapter. We'll label them **a, b,** and **c** as shown in the following figure.

If we think of the beat as the duration between two successive pulses on level **a,** but think of the measure as the duration between successive pulses on level **c,** then we can see (and hear) that there are now four beats per measure. This condition is called **quadruple meter.**

The conducting pattern for quadruple meter follows this path:

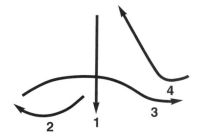

In quadruple meter, there are at least *three* different types of pulses:

1. primary pulses, where levels **a, b,** and **c** coincide, on the downbeats;
2. a medium-stress pulse in the middle of each measure, on the third beat, where levels **a** and **b** coincide; and
3. two weak pulses, on beats 2 and 4, where only pulse level **a** is felt.

We can combine those three levels of pulse into a single series of vertical lines, using lines of *three* different lengths to distinguish among the pulses:

| | | | | | | | | | | | | | | |

Twin- kle,   twin- kle,   lit-   tle   star————, how   I   won- der   what   you   are————.

Quadruple meter is fundamentally more complex than duple or triple meter in that it explicitly recognizes three adjacent levels of pulse, whereas duple and triple only recognize two.

Many pieces can be felt on more than two levels of pulse, even those notated in simple duple or triple meter. For example, "Twinkle, Twinkle, Little Star" is often written in duple meter showing only the relationship between levels **a** and **b.** (See Mozart's variations on this tune, "Ah, Vous Dirai-Je, Maman," K. 265.) Nonetheless, we can feel level **c** beyond that.

Although musicians often feel several levels of pulse, most notated meter represents only two or three levels of pulse. It is important for you to be able to recognize and perform with an understanding of pulses beyond those made explicit in notation.

Rests

When the pulse continues in a piece of music but nothing sounds, those durations of silence are called **rests.** In this book, we'll indicate rests in protonotation by leaving the duration blank within or among the pulse lines. However, when you take dictation using protonotation, you should fill in the spaces where you hear rests by using a symbol, such as a large "X." This way, you won't confuse rests with those places where you simply haven't filled in rhythms yet.

The Anacrusis

Sometimes, music actually begins before the first downbeat. Think of the pulses you feel from the following rhyme:

As **I** was **go**ing **to** St. **Ives,**
I **met** a **man** with **seven wives,**

The stressed syllables appear in bold type, and the text and meter begin *before* the first downbeat.

Auralize and perform the rhythms and meter shown below in protonotation. The music begins on the third beat of an incomplete measure. Your conducting should begin on that third beat. (Alternatively, you may silently conduct imaginary beats 1 and 2, but the music doesn't begin until beat 3 and the first real downbeat comes after that.)

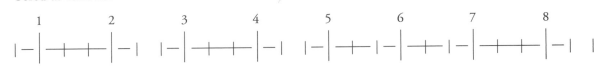

Any notes that occur *before* the first downbeat are referred to as an **anacrusis** or **pickup.** In general, when music begins with an anacrusis, most subsequent musical gestures (rhythmic groups, breathing, phrasing, etc.) tend to begin with similar upbeats. The final measure of a passage with an anacrusis usually ends at the point before another anacrusis would appear. For example, if a musical passage in triple meter begins with a one-beat anacrusis, the last measure will usually contain only two beats.

> An **anacrusis** or **pickup** is any incomplete measure of music before the first downbeat.

Another important consideration concerning the anacrusis involves measure numbering. The first measure begins with the first downbeat and it does not include the anacrusis. Thus, in our present example, the measures would be numbered as follows:

```
  1        2        3        4        5        6        7        8
|-|+++|-| |-|+++|-| |-|++|-|++|-|+++|-| |
```

We refer to the anacrusis separately as "the anacrusis," "the pickup," or even "measure 0."

LISTENING

Melodic Dictation

Listen to the short melodies 5.1–5.8 and write out the meter, rhythms, and pitches using the types of protonotation discussed in this chapter. Remember to be aware of the new possibilities introduced in this chapter—duple division of the beat, quadruple meter, rests, and the anacrusis.

The following exercises include duple, triple, and quadruple meters, with note values of one-half beat, one beat, and multiples of the beat. In addition, some of these exercises include an anacrusis and some include rests.

Prepare them using a neutral syllable or Takadimi while conducting.

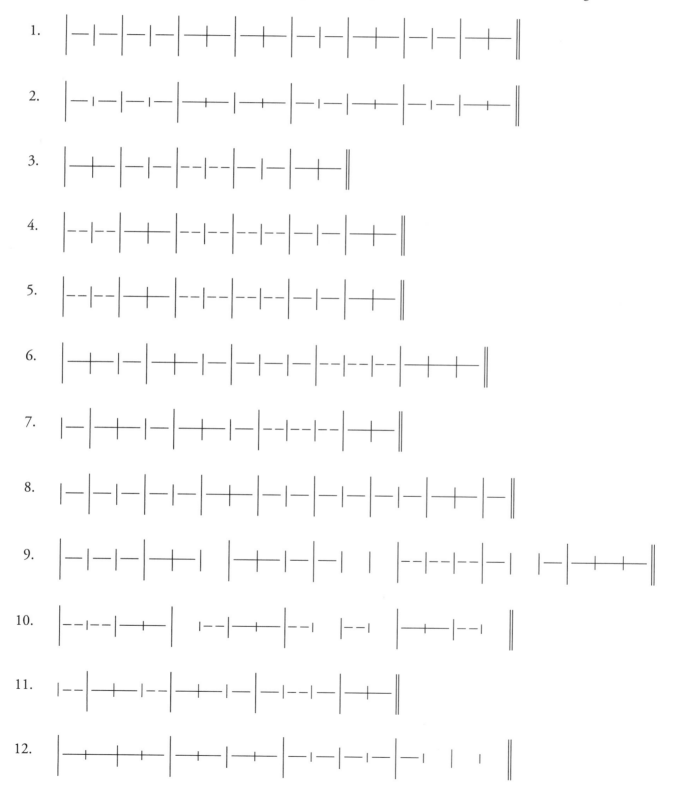

6 MORE ABOUT PITCH

We have developed a general understanding of the fact that pitches are high or low in relation to one another. Now we can observe that relationship more specifically by measuring the distance between pitches, which is called an **interval.**

> An **interval** is the distance, in terms of pitch, between two notes.

Measuring Intervals Using Ordinal Numbers

One way to measure the interval between two pitches is to count the number of scale degrees spanned by those pitches. For example, the interval from $\hat{1}$/*do* up to $\hat{3}$/*mi* spans three scale degrees ($\hat{1}$/*do*, $\hat{2}$/*re*, $\hat{3}$/*mi*), so it is called a 3rd. We use ordinal numbers for intervals (2nd, 3rd, 4th), with the following exceptions:

- the interval from one scale degree to itself (no higher, no lower) is called a unison, not a 1st;
- the interval that spans eight scale degrees is called an octave, not an 8th;
- intervals larger than an octave are called compound intervals, and they are usually referred to as a combination of an octave and a smaller interval (for example, a 14th is called "an octave and a 7th"), unless they span between nine and thirteen scale degrees, when they may also be known by their ordinal names (9th, 10th, 11th).

For now, we will focus on the quantitative measurement of intervals. In subsequent chapters, we'll also explore the qualitative aspects (major, minor, perfect, etc.).

Steps and Skips

The seconds formed by adjacent scale degrees are also called **steps.** Thus, the interval from $\hat{1}$/*do* to $\hat{2}$/*re* is a step, from $\hat{2}$/*re* to $\hat{3}$/*mi* is a step, and so on. Any interval larger than a step is called a **skip** or a **leap.**

> A **step** is the distance between two adjacent scale degrees.

> A **skip** or **leap** is an interval larger than a step.

Whole Steps and Half Steps

There are two *sizes* of steps: the **whole step** (for example, $\hat{1}$/*do* to $\hat{2}$/*re*) is larger than the smaller **half step** (for example, $\hat{3}$/*mi* to $\hat{4}$/*fa*).

You should be able to feel the difference between a whole step and a half step with your voice. Practice singing both whole and half steps above and below a single note. You should also be able to hear the difference between whole and half steps. Have someone sing or play various ascending and descending whole and half steps while you practice identifying them.

> Steps come in two sizes: the **whole step** (for example, $\hat{1}$/*do* to $\hat{2}$/*re*) and the **half step** (for example, $\hat{3}$/*mi* to $\hat{4}$/*fa*).

The Major Scale

The **major scale** consists of the following series of intervals ascending from the tonic: 1, 1, ½, 1, 1, 1, ½.

The pattern of whole and half steps shown in the figure below provides a more rigorous definition of the **major scale** (compared to its introduction in Chapter 2).

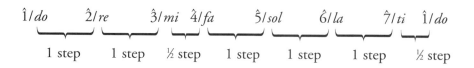

The Tonic Triad

For our present purposes, you should consider a triad as any group of three pitches that can be arranged into a stack of thirds. In the tonic triad, the lowest pitch in this stack of thirds is the tonic (1̂/*do*), and it functions as the root of the triad. Stacked above it are the third (3̂/*mi*) and the fifth (5̂/*sol*).

5̂/*sol*—fifth
3̂/*mi*—third
1̂/*do*—root

In previous chapters, the pitch patterns began on 1̂/*do*, 3̂/*mi*, or 5̂/*sol*, and all the pitch materials (with the exception of most sequentials) included skips only to 1̂/*do*, 3̂/*mi*, or 5̂/*sol*. These three members of the tonic triad will serve as points of reference for you throughout your work in tonal music. Learn their sounds well and be able to sing skips to all three of them from various places in the scale.

Skips within the Tonic Triad

Within the tonic triad, a variety of skips between the three scale degrees is possible. Here is an inventory of the skips smaller than an octave you might encounter when music outlines the tonic triad:

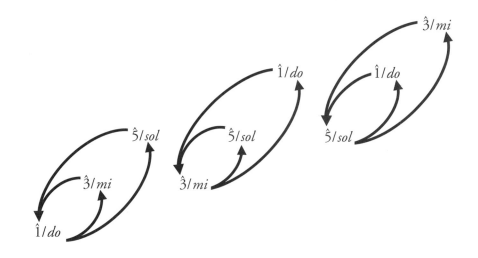

EXERCISES

1. **Know the intervals between successive scale degrees.** While singing a major scale, identify each interval you sing. Be prepared to stop on any scale degree and name the interval you just completed. For example, after singing $\hat{6}$/ *la*–$\hat{7}$/ *ti,* you would say "whole step."

2. **Know the number of scale degrees spanned by any two members of the scale.** In the following exercises, identify the number of scale degrees spanned by the two syllables. For example, $\hat{3}$/ *mi* up to $\hat{1}$/ *do* is a 6th.

   a. $\hat{1}$/ *do* up to $\hat{5}$/ *sol*
   b. $\hat{1}$/ *do* down to $\hat{5}$/ *sol*
   c. $\hat{5}$/ *sol* up to $\hat{1}$/ *do*
   d. $\hat{5}$/ *sol* down to $\hat{3}$/ *mi*
   e. $\hat{1}$/ *do* up to $\hat{6}$/ *la*
   f. $\hat{6}$/ *la* up to $\hat{1}$/ *do*
   g. $\hat{1}$/ *do* down to $\hat{2}$/ *re*
   h. $\hat{7}$/ *ti* down to $\hat{4}$/ *fa*
   i. $\hat{3}$/ *mi* down to $\hat{6}$/ *la*
   j. $\hat{2}$/ *re* up to $\hat{7}$/ *ti*

3. **Know the number of half steps spanned by any two members of the scale.** Musicians sometimes measure intervals in half steps. Calculate the total number of half steps between the two scale degrees in each of the following exercises. For example, $\hat{3}$/ *mi* up to $\hat{1}$/ *do* is eight half steps.

   a. $\hat{7}$/ *ti* down to $\hat{5}$/ *sol*
   b. $\hat{1}$/ *do* up to $\hat{3}$/ *mi*
   c. $\hat{7}$/ *ti* up to $\hat{3}$/ *mi*
   d. $\hat{2}$/ *re* up to $\hat{4}$/ *fa*
   e. $\hat{1}$/ *do* down to $\hat{6}$/ *la*
   f. $\hat{3}$/ *mi* up to $\hat{7}$/ *ti*
   g. $\hat{1}$/ *do* down to $\hat{5}$/ *sol*
   h. $\hat{7}$/ *ti* down to $\hat{4}$/ *fa*
   i. $\hat{4}$/ *fa* down to $\hat{7}$/ *ti*
   j. $\hat{2}$/ *re* up to $\hat{1}$/ *do*

4. **Be able to sing whole and half steps above and below any pitch.** Use a three-note figure that begins with one pitch, travels up or down a whole or half step, then returns to the starting pitch. Practice this three-note drill on a neutral syllable, such as "loo."

   a. For each pitch, practice this drill in this order:
      • whole step above
      • half step above
      • half step below
      • whole step below

   b. For each pitch, mix up the order of these four patterns (for example, whole step below, followed by whole step above, etc.).

   c. Repeat one of these four patterns from a different pitch each time.

   d. Sing any or all of these patterns from various starting pitches. Continue to scramble the order in which you sing them.

5. **Be able to identify whole and half steps above and below any given pitch by listening.** Ask your friends, classmates, or instructors to produce these intervals on different instruments and by singing. Identify each by size and direction. Be sure to listen for the unique quality and affect of each.

6. **Be able to sing skips to all members of the tonic triad.** Practice singing skips to $\hat{1}$/*do*, $\hat{3}$/*mi*, and $\hat{5}$/*sol*. Sing melodies and exercises from earlier chapters and, upon stopping anywhere, skip to $\hat{1}$/*do*, $\hat{3}$/*mi*, or $\hat{5}$/*sol*. Practice skips *among* members of the tonic triad (for example, $\hat{1}$/*do* up to $\hat{5}$/*sol*, $\hat{5}$/*sol* up to $\hat{3}$/*mi*, $\hat{1}$/*do* down to $\hat{3}$/*mi*, etc.). Be able to identify these skips by number (for example, 5th up, 6th up, 6th down, etc.).

ADDITIONAL ACTIVITIES

1. How do the quality and affect of intervals change when heard in different parts of the major scale? For example, how is the $\hat{7}$/*ti*–$\hat{1}$/*do* half step different from the $\hat{3}$/*mi*–$\hat{4}$/*fa* one?

2. Determine your vocal range. Start singing a scale on the lowest pitch you can sing and continue singing while counting scale degrees until you reach your upper limit. What is the interval between your lowest and highest pitches? Try this in the morning and again in the evening. Try it again when you have a cold.

3. Why are two pitches an octave apart labeled with the same syllable? They are obviously different in pitch, but somehow resemble each other enough to share an identity. What causes this?

7 NOTATING RHYTHM AND METER

The protonotation we've been working with in these early chapters has allowed us to focus on some important basic concepts and skills with as few complications as possible. But now the time has come to see how those concepts and skills work in real music notation.

Rhythmic Values

For the past several hundred years, musicians have used the symbols shown in the following table to represent relative rhythmic durations.

Name	Note	Rest
Double whole or Breve	𝅜	𝄺
Whole	𝅝	𝄻
Half	𝅗𝅥	𝄼
Quarter	♩	𝄽
Eighth	♪	𝄾
Sixteenth	𝅘𝅥𝅯	𝄿
Thirty-second	𝅘𝅥𝅰	𝅀
Sixty-fourth	𝅘𝅥𝅱	𝅁

Each note or rest in the table is worth half the value of the note above it. Theoretically, the chart could continue beyond this point, but smaller note values are hardly ever used. These notes and rests don't have any real musical meaning unless they are written in the context of a meter sign.

Meter Signs

A **meter sign** (or **time signature**) for simple meters indicates the number of beats per measure (the top number) and the note value equal to one beat (the bottom number).

The **beat value** or **beat unit** is the note value equal to one beat.

Meter signs (also known as **meter signatures** or **time signatures**) indicate the meter and the rhythmic value being used to equal one beat. Thus far, we have explored simple meters with only two, three, or four beats per measure. In simple meters, the top number in the meter sign indicates the number of beats per measure. The bottom number indicates the note value (whole note, half note, etc.) equal to one beat (the **beat value** or **beat unit**). The most common beat units in simple meters are the half note (**2**), quarter note (**4**), and eighth note (**8**). You will see others as well, however.

It's important to note that the top number in a meter sign is determined by the sound of a piece of music—the number of beats per measure is an audible result of the relationships between the primary and secondary pulses (although, as we've already seen, there is often more than one level on which to view these relationships). The bottom number is not a product of sound—it is chosen by the composer, transcriber, arranger, or editor. This means that a single rhythm and meter may be written out in different ways. Here's an example, written first in protonctation and then with three different beat values:

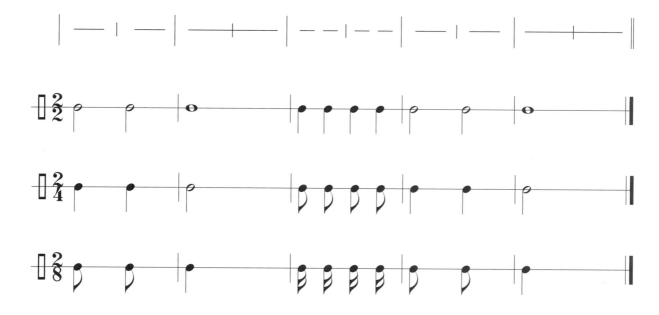

In each version of notation, the top number is **2** because the original rhythm is in duple meter (two beats per measure). The versions differ because different note values were chosen to equal one beat: the half note, quarter note, and eighth note, respectively.

None of these differences is audible—music notated using one beat value (for example, $\frac{2}{4}$) can sound just like the same music notated using another beat value (for example, $\frac{2}{2}$ or $\frac{2}{8}$). Read the rhythms of each version, using a neutral syllable or Takadimi while conducting. All three should sound exactly the same. The speed of a piece of music is determined not by the kind of beat value used to notate it but by tempo. (For more on the relationship between beat unit and tempo, see Chapters 15 and 23.)

When we notate rhythm without pitch, we use the following conventions:

- The box-like symbol at the beginning of each line means that the notes represent rhythms only.
- A single horizontal line runs through all the measures, and the noteheads are centered on that line.
- Vertical barlines mark the end of each measure.
- The double bar, consisting of one thin and one thick barline, indicates the end of a piece.

There are two symbols that work like shorthand in representing certain meter signs:

𝄴 — This symbol stands for $\frac{4}{4}$ meter. It is often erroneously dubbed "common time." (In fact, neither this nor the following symbol involves the letter "C." They both stem from the broken circle used in early music notation.)

𝄵 — This symbol translates as "alla breve," which (since the eighteenth century) means the half note equals one beat. Some call it "cut time," because the beat unit is "cut" from the quarter note to the half note. It most frequently represents $\frac{2}{2}$ meter, but it can also represent $\frac{4}{2}$ or other meters in which the half note is worth one beat.

Beams

You will encounter various uses of beams to connect groups of flagged notes. For example, the eighth notes we wrote out with flags in m. 2 of the $\frac{2}{4}$-version above might appear in either of the following ways:

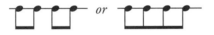

Beams can be used to convey much about musical structure. It is important that you learn to read and write beams so that they clearly convey the metric and rhythmic structure of the music. In general, you should focus on a single metric unit—usually the beat, the measure, or sometimes the half measure (in quadruple meters)—and beam consistently within that unit.

One exception to the rule of metric beaming occurs in vocal notation. In most vocal music, notes are beamed together according to the syllables in the text. Multiple notes sung on one syllable are beamed, whereas single notes (one note per syllable) retain their individual flags. Instrumentalists who are unfamiliar with vocal beaming may need extra time to decipher the metric groups it can sometimes obscure.

Three-Beat Notes: The Augmentation Dot

The **augmentation dot** is placed after a note to increase the note by half its value. For now, we will be adding dots only to notes that are originally two beats long, thereby creating three-beat notes:

> The **augmentation dot** increases a note by half its rhythmic value.

3 beats = 2 beats + 1 beat

in $\frac{3}{8}$ or $\frac{4}{8}$:   ♩. = ♩ + ♪

in $\frac{3}{4}$ or $\frac{4}{4}$:   𝅗𝅥. = 𝅗𝅥 + ♩

in $\frac{3}{2}$ or $\frac{4}{2}$:   𝅝. = 𝅝 + 𝅗𝅥

Relationships between Protonotation and Real Notation

At this point, you should strive to see, hear, and feel the relationships between protonotation and real notation of rhythm and meter. This works in both directions: (1) from protonotation into real notation (which will help in dictation and other listening skills); and (2) from real notation into protonotation (which will help in sight reading and other related skills).

EXERCISES

1. Convert the following from protonotation into real notation using the conventions described in this chapter (use a single horizontal line, centering note heads on the line). The beat unit you should use for each exercise is indicated by the symbol preceding the protonotation. As you complete these exercises, also think about the following questions:

   • What aspects of any particular protonotation cause aspects of the real notation to be predetermined?
   • What choices do you have when deciding on a meter sign?
   • After that, what other notational choices remain?

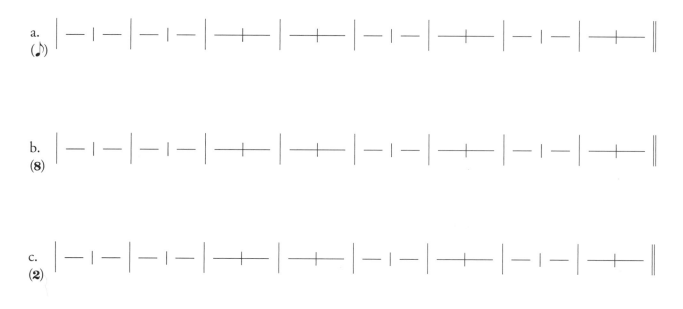

a.
(♪)

b.
(8)

c.
(2)

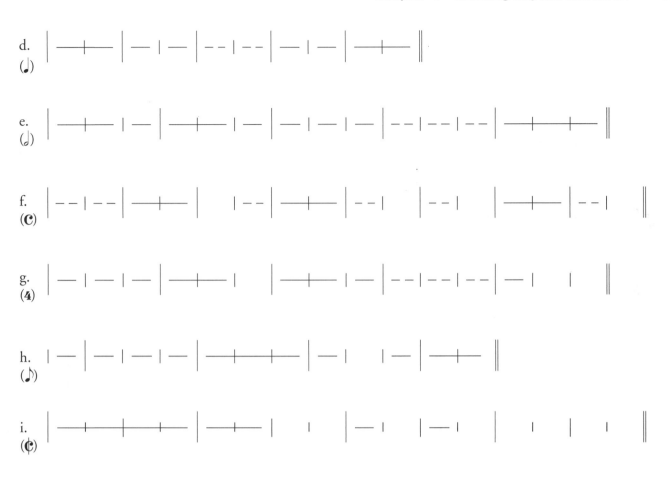

2. Convert the following from real notation into protonotation. As you complete
   these exercises, also think about the following questions:

   • What processes are involved in converting real notation into protonotation?

   • What kind of information is lost when doing this?

   • What kind of information is gained?

d.

e.

f.

g.

h.

Melodic Dictation

You can now begin to work on listening to rhythms and writing them down in real rhythmic notation. At present, we will focus on fragments short enough to remember with only one hearing.

Listen to the short fragments 7.1–7.8 and take rhythmic dictation, observing the following procedure:

- Figure out the pulses and meter
- Write those out in protonotation with vertical lines
- Fill in the rhythms using horizontal lines
- Convert your protonotation into real notation

Exercise	Bottom number in meter sign
7.1	2
7.2	4
7.3	8
7.4	4
7.5	2
7.6	4
7.7	4
7.8	2

READING AND SIGHT SINGING

As you read music, keep in mind the relationship between real rhythm notation and protonotation. Be certain that you attend to and understand the meaning of each meter sign, and properly interpret the duration of each note and rest in terms of beats. Think about how each meter and rhythm would be written in protonotation.

Read the following using a neutral syllable or Takadimi while conducting.

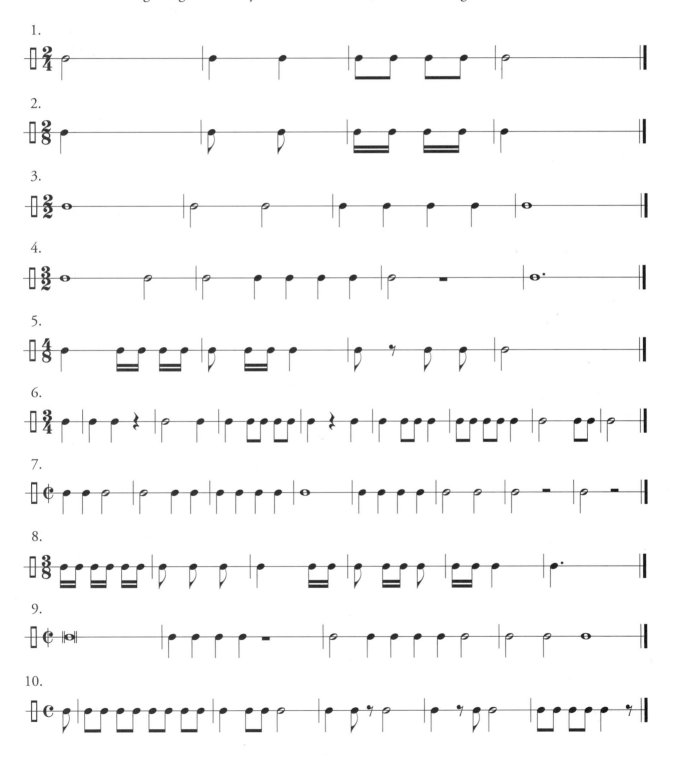

8 NOTATING PITCHES

The last chapter explained the correlation between traditional rhythmic notation and what we had previously learned about rhythm and meter. This chapter will transfer what we know about pitch into its own traditional form of notation.

Letter Names

For a very long time, musicians have been using letters in addition to syllables for representing pitches. In Western music notation, we use the letters A through G. Thus, there are two systems for labeling pitches: (1) a *fixed* method, using letter names to represent absolute pitches (C, D, etc.); and (2) a *functional* method, using numbers and/or syllables to represent the scale degrees of pitches within a key ($\hat{1}$/*do*, $\hat{2}$/*re*, etc.). For this chapter and the next, $\hat{1}$/*do* will correspond to the letter C, and the other scale degrees and letters will line up as follows:

$\hat{7}$/*ti* = B

$\hat{6}$/*la* = A

$\hat{5}$/sol = G

$\hat{4}$/*fa* = F

$\hat{3}$/*mi* = E

$\hat{2}$/*re* = D

$\hat{1}$/*do* = C

Staves and Clefs

> The **G clef** curls around the line representing G.

> In the **treble clef staff,** G is the second line from the bottom.

We can apply these letter names (and their scale degrees and syllables) to the lines and spaces of the musical staff (*pl* staves). The symbols that locate letter names on a staff are called **clefs.**

A **G clef** curls around the line for G. When the G clef is printed on a staff placing G on the second line from the bottom, the staff is then referred to as the **treble clef staff** and the clef is often called the **treble clef.**

> The **F clef** surrounds the line representing F with two dots.

> In the **bass clef staff,** F is the fourth line from the bottom.

An **F clef** has two dots that surround the line for F. When the F clef is printed on a staff placing F on the fourth line from the bottom, the staff is then referred to as the **bass clef staff,** and the clef is often called the **bass clef.**

The treble clef staff and bass clef staff can be joined together by a vertical line to create a **grand staff.** A gap is left in between the two staves to allow room for notes that fall between them. For instance, the pitch that has come to be known as **middle C** is written in the middle of the grand staff. It also happens to fall near the middle of the piano keyboard. This pitch, and others that fall above or below a staff, can be written on a **ledger line,** which is a small segment of a staff line.

Here are the letter names, scale degrees, and syllables of the lines and spaces of the grand staff, beginning on C two ledger lines below the bass clef staff and ending on C two ledger lines above the treble clef staff:

> The **grand staff** combines the treble and bass clef staves.

> **Middle C** is the C between the treble and bass clef staves, near the middle of the piano.

> A **ledger line** is a small segment of a staff line used for writing notes too high or low for that staff.

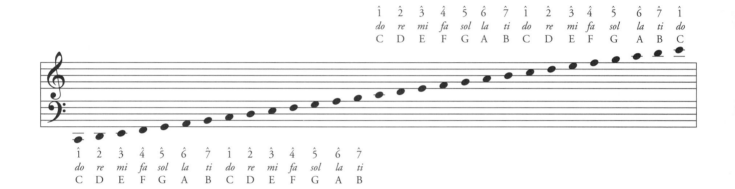

We will also encounter a variation on the treble clef called the vocal tenor clef. This variation indicates that all pitches are to be performed one octave lower than in the regular treble clef (usually to be sung by the tenor voice). It may be written in several ways:

L I S T E N I N G

Melodic Dictation

You can now begin to work on listening to pitches and writing them down in real staff notation. At present, we will continue to work on fragments short enough to remember with only one hearing.

Listen to the short fragments 8.1–8.8 and take melodic dictation, observing the following procedure:

- Identify the tonic
- Determine the scale degrees of the pitches
- Write out the pitches as syllables
- Convert this into real notation, using C as the tonic in the clef specified for each
- Use stemless noteheads without regard for durations

Exercise	Clef	Tonic
8.1	treble	C
8.2	treble	C
8.3	bass	C
8.4	bass	C
8.5	treble	C
8.6	treble	C
8.7	bass	C
8.8	bass	C

R E A D I N G   A N D   S I G H T   S I N G I N G

In order to learn to read fluently in both the treble and bass clef staves, you must be able to sing using both syllables and letter names. Sing each one of the following pitch patterns both ways. Sing the pitches in a steady rhythm, at a speed of about two notes every second. These patterns are written in various octaves, some of which will fall outside of your vocal range. Sing them in whatever octave is comfortable for your voice.

Have someone play or sing some of the "a" patterns while you write down the pitches in the staff. Remember: use your memory; find 1̂/*do;* find the starting pitch; work out all the syllables. Then, on the staff, write the pitches that correspond to those syllables.

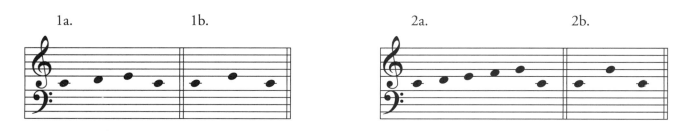

1a.   1b.   2a.   2b.

10.

11.

12.

9 COMBINING RHYTHM AND PITCH NOTATION

In order to write out real melodies, which consist of both pitches and rhythms, we must combine rhythm and pitch notation.

Translating Protonotation into Real Music Notation

Let's set a simple goal: to write the rhythms and pitches of the beginning of "Frère Jacques" in real music notation. Here it is in protonotation:

Let's write it out in the treble clef staff, starting with $\hat{1}$/*do* on middle C, in $\frac{2}{4}$ meter:

Of course, we could just as easily write it in other octaves, beginning on a different C or perhaps even using the bass clef staff. In addition, we could use another beat unit in a meter sign such as $\frac{2}{2}$ or $\frac{2}{8}$. All of these would be valid ways of notating "Frère Jacques."

Reading Real Music Notation

Each note of music notation represents two things: pitch and rhythm. The position of the notehead on the staff indicates a particular pitch, and the type of note (whole note, eighth note, etc.) specifies its rhythm. It is important to recognize that there are two systems operating in music notation: rhythm notation and pitch notation. Good music reading requires you to master each system on its own and to read both at the same time.

Melodic Dictation

In taking dictation, we'll now be writing out both the rhythms and pitches of what we hear. Review the detailed instructions at the end of Chapter 3 for these first three steps in taking dictation:

Step 1: *Hear the music*

Step 2: *Remember the music*

Step 3: *Understand the music*

The introduction of notation adds a *fourth* step to the process:

Step 4: *Notate the music*

Transfer the understanding you explicitly demonstrated in step 3 into real music notation. You have already heard, remembered, and understood the meter, beat durations, and scale degrees. Now you can notate them using the symbols introduced in Chapters 7, 8, and 9.

As you listen to Exercises 9.1–9.8, write your response for each in protonotation first, then translate that into real notation on the staff. These fragments are still short enough to remember with only one hearing.

The clef and bottom number in the meter sign are provided for each exercise. For the present chapter and the next, the tonic is always on C.

Exercise	Clef	Tonic	Bottom number in meter sign
9.1	bass	C	2
9.2	treble	C	4
9.3	treble	C	8
9.4	bass	C	4
9.5	treble	C	2
9.6	bass	C	2
9.7	bass	C	4
9.8	treble	C	8

In order to become fluent in music notation, you must do lots of reading, both prepared and at sight, combining the techniques used in the preceding chapters. The *Anthology for Sight Singing* comprises many excerpts from real music collected for this very purpose. Beginning with the present chapter, this *Manual* will provide references to excerpts in the *Anthology for Sight Singing* that are appropriate for developing the reading skills presented in each chapter.

For each of the excerpts, conduct while singing the pitches on their syllables in the proper rhythm. A few of these excerpts, like a lot of music, will be an octave or more too high or too low for your voice. In order to sing them, you must make the appropriate octave adjustments. For example, most women will probably want to take No.1 down an octave; most men will probably take it down *two* octaves. Excerpts that need to be transposed are preceded by "vocal transposition" instructions (see "Vocal Range and Transposition" in the Preface to the *Anthology for Sight Singing*).

For excerpts that have more than one part, learn all parts. Practice singing them with your classmates, and be prepared to sing them as part of an ensemble in class.

Carefully consider the scale degree of the starting note in each excerpt. Some begin on Î/*do,* but others begin on Ŝ/*mi* or Ŝ/*sol.* Start with the C-major scale in mind, and auralize the proper starting pitch before you begin.

Excerpts for reading and sight singing
from the
Anthology for Sight Singing
1–14

10 DICTATION IN LONGER CONTEXTS

We will now learn some helpful techniques for dealing with dictation melodies that are longer than the short fragments you have been working with thus far.

Extractive Memory

Many listeners—and especially most beginning aural skills students—are unable to remember new melodies longer than nine or ten notes after one listening. If you play a melody of, say, eighteen notes once and ask one of your classmates to sing it back, you'll find that most will be unable to get past the first ten notes correctly, and some will be so overwhelmed by the length of the melody that even the beginning will fail them. (If the melody contains logical groups, such as scales, chords, or sequences, some listeners can extend their memories through a process known as "chunking." Subsequent chapters will help you learn to hear such chunks.)

In order to listen to and write down longer melodies, you need to be able to extract and remember short sections (up to ten notes) of the melody after individual hearings. Initially, you must try to remember as much of the beginning of a melody as you can by extracting it from what comes after it. Whenever possible, you should aim to remember a musically cohesive section.

For example, in the melody above, the first nine notes (four measures) form a natural group, ending with the long note in measure 4. After one hearing, you should try to remember this opening section. However, some melodies will seem to go on without pause, in which case you must try to concentrate on the first six to ten notes.

Use this technique for the dictation melodies at the end of this chapter, and practice using it on the many different kinds of melodies you hear throughout your day (in class, from a nearby practice room, on the radio, etc.). See if you can sing back the opening section of any melody accurately after one hearing.

Repeated Listenings

With repeated listenings, your memory can extract successive sections of a melody. In ideal circumstances, you should be able to remember, understand, and notate the first half of a dictation after one playing, then move on to do the same for the second half after a second playing. However, this process does not always progress flawlessly; a third playing will allow you to check your work and to go back and fill in any gaps. The flowchart below shows this basic approach:

First listening:
  1. *Hear* (entire excerpt)
  2. *Remember* (first half of the excerpt)
  3. *Understand* (first half of the excerpt)
      meter and rhythm
          pulse
          meter
          rhythmic proportions
      pitch
          tonic
          scale degree of starting pitch
          scale degrees of subsequent pitches
          stepwise groups
          each skip treated as new starting pitch
  4. *Notate* (first half of the excerpt)

Second listening:
  Repeat the process above, this time remembering, understanding, and notating the second half of the excerpt.

Third listening:
  Use the last playing to fill in any missing information.

EXERCISES

Although the dictation exercises that follow will give you some opportunity to develop your short-term musical memory, you should exercise your memory as often as possible. Sing back or auralize fragments extracted from what you hear. You can practice this with all kinds of music in various situations—walking past practice rooms, listening to the radio, watching television, listening to recordings, and so forth. Make musical memory an integral part of your daily life. When you hear a melody, do one of the following:

1. Sing back or auralize the opening section (about six to ten notes), following these steps, if necessary:

   • As soon as you've heard enough of a melody to fill up your short-term musical memory (about six to ten notes), sing these notes aloud immediately, even as the rest of the melody continues to sound.

- Repeat the first step, but this time sing very quietly (*sotto voce*) so that you can focus on singing but still hear the rest of the melody at the same time.
- Auralize the opening without actually singing it while the rest of the melody is sounding.

2. Sing back or auralize the *closing* section (about six to ten notes).

LISTENING

Melodic Dictation

Listen to the pitches and rhythms in Exercises 10.1–10.8 and write them down in real music notation. To do this, work on extracting sections of the melody with each successive listening, working through the steps outlined in this chapter.

The clef and bottom number in the meter sign are provided for each exercise. For the present chapter, the tonic is still always on C.

Exercise	Clef	Tonic	Bottom number in meter sign
10.1	bass	C	4
10.2	treble	C	4
10.3	treble	C	8
10.4	bass	C	2
10.5	bass	C	4
10.6	treble	C	2
10.7	bass	C	8
10.8	treble	C	4

11 THE FIFTEEN MAJOR KEYS

So far, we have projected scale degrees into the key of C major only, so Î/*do* has always been C. There are fourteen other major keys in addition to C major. This chapter explores the effects of these other keys on sight singing and ear training.

Key Signatures and the Tonic

The tonic can be moved to various pitches. When we move the tonic to a new pitch, we say that we are in the **key** of that new pitch. For example, if we move the tonic to G, we say we are in the key of G major. In order to move the tonic from C (C major) to G (G major), you must reproduce the same pattern of whole steps and half steps (review Chapter 6) at the new pitch level. The **key signature** adjusts certain pitches by raising them (with a sharp) or lowering them (with a flat) in order to maintain the pattern of whole and half steps of the major scale. The signature for C major has no sharps or flats because the pattern for the C-major scale does not require any adjustments. G major does require an adjustment, and the key signature for this key has one sharp (F♯), which is necessary to maintain the whole step between scale degrees 6̂ (E) and 7̂ (F♯) and the half step between 7̂ (F♯) and Î (G).

> A **key** is named by the pitch where the tonic lies.

> A **key signature** moves the pattern of whole and half steps using sharps or flats and allows the tonic to be moved.

Key Signatures and Scale Degrees

Key signatures move *all* scale degrees to new pitches. For example, consider the following hymn tune ("Watt's Cradle Hymn," measures 1–4; *Anthology for Sight Singing,* No. 5) and its associated scale-degree syllables in C major:

When we move this melody up to the key of E major, the new key signature moves all of the scale degrees to new pitches as follows:

The scale-degree syllables represent the *functions* of the pitches in the prevailing key. When the key changes, the function of each pitch changes. For example, in C major the pitch B functions as 7̂/*ti,* but in E major it functions as 5̂/*sol*—it has a different label because of its different function and feeling in each key.

Key Signatures for the Major Keys

The following figure shows the fifteen major-key signatures and the tonic associated with each. It is laid out in a spiral that begins at the top with the key of C major. From there, the sharp keys progress clockwise around the spiral, and the flat keys progress counterclockwise, arranged by increasing number of sharps or flats.

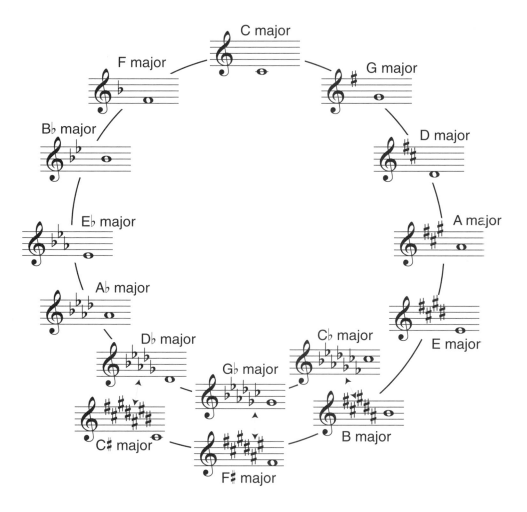

Enharmonic pitches are spelled differently but occupy the same location on the piano keyboard.

The **circle of fifths** arranges the twelve enharmonically unique keys in a circle. Each key in the circle is separated from the next by one more or one fewer sharp or flat. The tonics of the keys progress around the circle by fifths.

The ends of the spiral come together so that three sharp keys overlap three flat ones. The two keys in each of these overlapping pairs are referred to as enharmonic keys. **Enharmonic** pitches or keys are spelled differently, but they occupy the same location on the piano keyboard. For example, G♭ and F♯ are enharmonic, so the same piano key serves as the tonic for both G♭ major and F♯ major. Although enharmonic keys sound alike, they present vastly different challenges in music reading and writing.

The overlap of enharmonic keys in this figure reveals that the fifteen keys identified by note names and key signatures actually yield only twelve enharmonically unique keys. The overlap also functions to compress the spiral into a circle of twelve keys. Motion from one key to the next around the circle always encompasses the interval of a fifth (C up to G, D♭ up to A♭), so this figure is referred to as the **circle of fifths.**

The sharp, flat, or natural notes created by any given key signature are called **diatonic** pitches. All the diatonic pitches from a given key signature taken together form the **diatonic collection.**

While we're working with only *major* keys, seeing a key signature will automatically tell you where $\hat{1}$/*do* has been moved. When reading music in various major keys, your first step should be to look at the key signature to determine where $\hat{1}$/*do* is. All other pitch relationships spring from this tonal center. Most important, you should locate the members of the tonic triad ($\hat{1}$/*do,* $\hat{3}$/*mi,* and $\hat{5}$/*sol*) on the staff in your mind's eye before performing. Do this for all instances of these pitches in the range of the music you're reading. For example, if you were to read the treble-clef, E-major version of "Watt's Cradle Hymn" (above), you should visualize the following before you begin:

> **Diatonic** pitches are those created by a given key signature.

> A **diatonic collection** is all the diatonic pitches from a given key signature.

It takes time and practice to learn to read the syllables in each key and clef, especially when you realize that thirty combinations are possible (fifteen major keys in treble clef and bass clef). As shown in the following figure, however, these combinations group together according to where $\hat{1}$/*do* falls on the staff. There are only seven possible unique positions for $\hat{1}$/*do* on the five-line staff. Understanding that the lines and spaces have identical functions within each of these groups will facilitate the process of reading and listening. Of course, you will still have to be able to *think* in the various keys and clefs.

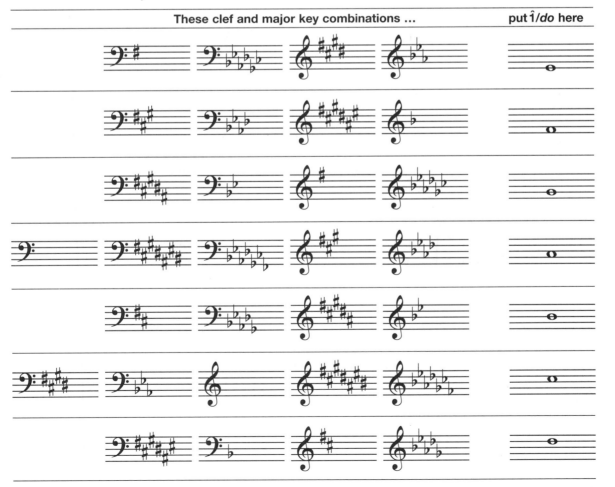

Let's look at "Watt's Cradle Hymn" to see how this principle works. As shown in the first group, there is a relationship between G major and G-flat major (in bass clef) and E major and E-flat major (in treble clef). In all of these keys, î/*do* falls on the lowest line of the staff, as well as on the fourth space. All the other scale degrees correspond to similar positions on the staff in these four keys. For instance, 5̂/*sol* appears on the third line in all four keys.

Establishing Collection and Tonic

You must learn to establish a key from only one sound: the *starting* pitch. There are several reasons for this. First, focusing on the starting pitch emphasizes the diatonic collection (the pitches that make up the scale, chords, and other patterns within a key) more than just the tonic and scale. Second, in many performance situations, such as auditions and rehearsals, only a single note is given as a cue. Third, in preparation for reading and singing music that modulates (moves to other keys), you must be able to isolate a single pitch in order to adjust the half and whole steps around it for the new key.

Fortunately, you have already learned the two skills necessary to perform this task: (1) singing half and whole steps above and below any given note, and (2) singing the melodic interval from î/*do* to 5̂/*sol*. To establish the key from the starting pitch, follow this procedure:

1. Establish the collection

   • Listen to the starting pitch.
   • If necessary, sing stepwise by whole steps to reach the nearest half step within the collection.
   • Sing the nearest half step using the three-note drill that we used when we sang half and whole steps alone (see Chapter 6).

- Sing stepwise by whole steps to reach the other half step in the collection.
- If you need to further establish the collection, sing the entire scale.

2. Establish the tonic
   - If necessary, sing by steps to reach the tonic.
   - Sing the tonic and dominant pitches ($\hat{1}$/*do*–$\hat{5}$/*sol*–$\hat{1}$/*do*).
   - If you need to further establish the tonic, sing the tonic and dominant chords.

Do not try to jump immediately to the tonic from the starting pitch. Use the stepwise procedure outlined above—establish the diatonic collection first (through its whole and half steps), then establish the tonic. You may wish to add further collection- and key-orienting patterns, but you should do them *after* following these procedures.

For a while, you should always establish the collection and tonic *out loud* before continuing so that your classmates and instructor can hear that you are indeed carrying out these important steps. After a few weeks of this kind of practice, you should begin to follow this procedure in your mind; that is, you must mentally hear the half and whole steps and tonic and dominant pitches before beginning to sing.

The chart below shows the syllable patterns you should sing to establish keys from $\hat{1}$/*do,* $\hat{3}$/*mi,* and $\hat{5}$/*sol:*

$\hat{1}$/*do*	$\hat{3}$/*mi*	$\hat{5}$/*sol*
$\hat{1}$/*do*–$\hat{7}$/*ti*–$\hat{1}$/*do*	$\hat{3}$/*mi*–$\hat{4}$/*fa*–$\hat{3}$/*mi*	$\hat{5}$/*sol*–$\hat{4}$/*fa*–$\hat{3}$/*mi*
$\hat{1}$/*do*–$\hat{2}$/*re*–$\hat{3}$/*mi*	$\hat{3}$/*mi*–$\hat{2}$/*re*–$\hat{1}$/*do*	$\hat{3}$/*mi*–$\hat{4}$/*fa*–$\hat{3}$/*mi*
$\hat{3}$/*mi*–$\hat{4}$/*fa*–$\hat{3}$/*mi*	$\hat{1}$/*do*–$\hat{7}$/*ti*–$\hat{1}$/*do*	$\hat{3}$/*mi*–$\hat{2}$/*re*–$\hat{1}$/*do*
$\hat{3}$/*mi*–$\hat{2}$/*re*–$\hat{1}$/*do*	$\hat{1}$/*do*–$\hat{5}$/*sol*–$\hat{1}$/*do*	$\hat{1}$/*do*–$\hat{7}$/*ti*–$\hat{1}$/*do*
$\hat{1}$/*do*–$\hat{5}$/*sol*–$\hat{1}$/*do*		$\hat{1}$/*do*–$\hat{5}$/*sol*–$\hat{1}$/*do*

For example, if given the pitch F♯ as the third scale degree in the key of D major, you would sing the following:

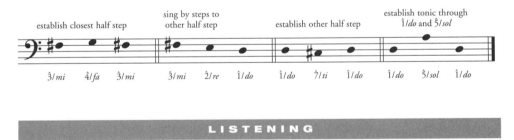

LISTENING

Melodic Dictation

Now that you understand key signatures, you can begin to take dictation in keys other than C major. Your task will be the same as it has been all along: Hear and remember a section of the music, determine where the tonic ($\hat{1}$/*do*) lies, calculate the other scale degrees from that tonic, then finally notate those pitches. The difference is that the tonic will not always be C. Obviously, you need to work to become fluent in writing out key signatures and translating scale degrees into pitches in various keys in both treble and bass clefs.

Listen to exercises 11.1–11.15. First write them in protonotation, and then transfer the protonotation into real notation on the staff, using the indicated clef, tonic, and bottom number in the meter sign for each dictation.

Exercise	Clef	Tonic	Bottom number in meter sign
11.1	bass	C	8
11.2	treble	G	2
11.3	bass	F	4
11.4	treble	D	2
11.5	treble	B♭	8
11.6	bass	A	4
11.7	treble	E♭	4
11.8	bass	E	4
11.9	bass	A♭	2
11.10	treble	B	2
11.11	bass	D♭	8
11.12	treble	F♯	4
11.13	treble	G♭	4
11.14	bass	C♯	2
11.15	treble	C♭	8

READING AND SIGHT SINGING

Prepare the following melodies, singing on syllables while conducting. Before you begin each melody, be certain to take note of its clef, key signature, and meter sign. Pay special attention to where each combination of clef and key signature places $\hat{1}$/do on the staff. Visualize the positions of $\hat{1}$/do, $\hat{3}$/mi and $\hat{5}$/sol on the staff.

For excerpts with more than one part, learn all parts. Practice singing them with your classmates, and be prepared to sing them in ensemble in class.

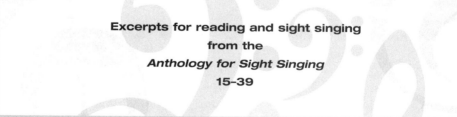

Excerpts for reading and sight singing
from the
Anthology for Sight Singing
15–39

12 TIES AND THE DOTTED BEAT

Ties

In Chapter 7, we learned how to lengthen the duration of a note by adding an augmentation dot. Another way to increase a note's value is to join it to the next note using a **tie.** A tie connects two notes of the same pitch and combines the lengths of those two notes. The second note is not played separately, but is merely added to the first. The tie tells readers to sustain the pitch through both durations.

> A **tie** joins the rhythmic values of the notes it connects.

For example, in the following melody from Haydn's Op. 77, No. 1, the first note is four beats long, but the longest single note value one can write in triple meter is three beats. Anything longer than that must extend into the following measure, so Haydn had to tie the dotted half from the first measure to the first quarter note in the next.

Joseph Haydn, String Quartet, Op. 77, No. 1 (Hob. III:81), mmt. 3, mm. 82–86 (1799)

The tie also reminds you not to rearticulate the second note. You can practice this by articulating the first note on "taah" and *gently* articulating the second note with the letter "H," so the second note in a tied pair becomes "haah," like this:

taah—   haah   taah   taah

The Dotted Beat

The opening of "My Country 'Tis of Thee" ("God Save the Queen") provides us with an example of another kind of rhythm. Work on a separate piece of paper to write out the meter and rhythms of the first sixteen notes (through "of thee I sing") using protonotation. Your answer should look like this:

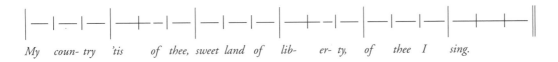

My   coun- try   'tis   of thee, sweet land   of   lib-   er- ty,   of   thee   I   sing.

Notice how the first horizontal rhythm line in measures 2 and 4 extends through the second pulse mark and ends half way through the second beat. This indicates that these notes each last one and one-half beats.

53

There are two ways to use real notation to write notes one and one-half beats long. One way to do this is to tie one note to another half its value. Another way is to add an augmentation dot to a one-beat note. The following example illustrates these two possibilities in various meters:

	One beat	+	one-half beat	=	one and one-half beats
$\frac{3}{8}$	♪	+	♪	=	♪ ♪
	♪	+	.	=	♪.
$\frac{3}{4}$	♩	+	♪	=	♩ ♪
	♩	+	.	=	♩.
$\frac{3}{2}$	𝅗𝅥	+	𝅗𝅥	=	𝅗𝅥 𝅗𝅥
	𝅗𝅥	+	.	=	𝅗𝅥.

Using dotted notes, we can write the rhythms for the opening melody of "My Country 'Tis of Thee" in the following ways (using the three common beat units):

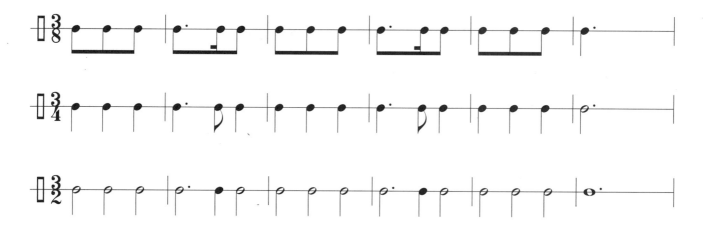

In order to understand a particular dotted rhythm, you can break it down into parts using ties, as shown below:

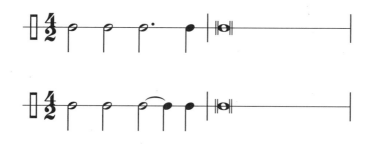

When you practice sight reading dotted beats, you can use a gently articulated "haah" when the dotted note crosses the following pulse (as we did with tied notes).

Melodic Dictation

Listen to excerpts 12.1–12.10 and write out the pitches and rhythms for each using the indicated clef, tonic, and bottom number in the meter sign.

Exercise	Clef	Tonic	Bottom number in meter sign
12.1	bass	B♭	2
12.2	treble	C♯	8
12.3	treble	D♭	4
12.4	treble	G	2
12.5	bass	E	4
12.6	bass	A♭	8
12.7	treble	G♭	2
12.8	bass	B	4
12.9	bass	E♭	4
12.10	treble	F	2

Prepare the following melodies, singing on syllables while conducting. Look for ties and dotted beats and practice them in the manner described in this chapter.

**Excerpts for reading and sight singing
from the
Anthology for Sight Singing
40–72**

13 MORE ABOUT INTERVALS: NUMBER AND QUALITY

In Chapter 6, we learned how to measure intervals by counting whole and half steps, and we used ordinal labels to describe intervals in a quantitative, though imprecise manner. Intervals with the same ordinal label are not all the same size. For example, the 2nd from C to D spans two half steps, but the 2nd from B to C spans only *one* half step. This means that there are at least two different kinds, or *qualities* of 2nds. In fact, there are several different qualities of each ordinal interval.

We express the quality of an interval by preceding its number with an adjective. For example, the interval from C to D is called a *major* 2nd, whereas the interval from B to C is a *minor* 2nd. The five adjectives used for this purpose are major, minor, perfect, augmented, and diminished.

Your work in written music theory will teach you methods of determining the precise number and quality of any interval. This chapter is devoted to working with this kind of knowledge in singing and hearing music.

Singing Intervals

The music you have been singing in previous chapters has consisted of three types of melodic motion: (1) repeated notes; (2) motion by step; and (3) motion by leap to scale degrees $\hat{1}$/*do,* $\hat{3}$/*mi,* and $\hat{5}$/*sol.*

In stepwise music, the intervals between the pitches are all 2nds. What are the qualities of these 2nds? (See the exercises at the end of this chapter for more about this.)

The number and quality of the interval of a leap depend on the pitch you depart from as well as the pitch you leap to. For example, a leap from $\hat{3}$/*mi* up to $\hat{1}$/*do* spans a minor 6th, whereas a leap from $\hat{5}$/*sol* up to $\hat{1}$/*do* spans a perfect 4th. Notice that the target pitch ($\hat{1}$/*do*) remains the same in both cases.

In tonal music, you should think much more about the scale degree of the pitch to which you are leaping rather than focusing too much on the size of the interval itself. Avoid reading tonal music in an interval-by-interval manner. Too much reliance on intervals leads to readings and performances that lack a sense of key or sensitivity to tonal relationships, which tend to come across as mechanical and unmusical.

However, you will rely on interval singing more when you begin to deal with non-tonal music. There are instances—even in tonal music—wherein the ability to sing a specific interval at any given time will come in handy. To this end, you should begin to practice singing specific intervals from any given pitch, both ascending and descending.

Hearing Intervals

All the points we just discussed about singing intervals apply in a similar fashion to *hearing* intervals. It is often helpful to be able to listen to and identify the number and quality of a specific interval regardless of its context. You should begin to practice listening to and identifying intervals, including some that are sounded in isolation, out of the context of any key or other surrounding music. Additional work should be done identifying intervals *within* a key, scale, or melody.

A special caveat applies to identifying intervals out of context. There is no audible difference between enharmonic intervals sounded out of context. For example, if you hear C up to F♯ in no particular context you would be correct in identifying it as either an augmented 4th (C–F♯) or a diminished 5th (C–G♭). Only a tonal context can make such an interval function as one or the other (an augmented 4th in G major and a diminished 5th in D♭ major).

As with intervallic singing, be careful of focusing too closely on the individual distances between successive notes when you listen to tonal music, or you risk sacrificing the tonal functions of the scale degrees and the relationships among various tonal figures.

EXERCISES

1. Identify the number and quality of the intervals from the tonic up to each pitch in the major scale. Enter your findings here:

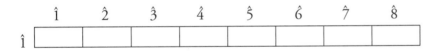

2. Identify the number and quality of all the intervals smaller than an octave between pairs of scale degrees in the major scale. Do this methodically. Keep track of your findings in tables such as those shown below:

   a. Record each interval from the scale degree on the left up to those across the top. (For now, treat the interval between identical scale degrees—for example, 1̂ to 1̂—as a unison.)

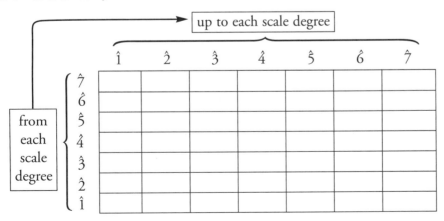

b. Keep track of how many of each quality there are for each interval number in the following table.

	Major	Minor	Perfect	Augmented	Diminished
7ths					
6ths					
5ths					
4ths					
3rds					
2nds					
unisons					

3. Review the sequentials at the end of Chapter 2. As you sing them, be prepared to name the interval (both number and quality) between successive pitches.

4. Review the melodies at the ends of all the preceding chapters. Be able to identify the intervals between successive pitches, between any pitch and the tonic, and between any two notes sounding at the same time in multiple-part excerpts.

5. Begin to work on the aural identification of intervals.

   • When listening to a melody (any melody), try to identify the last melodic interval you hear. Begin by concentrating on the last two notes of a section or phrase. Also use this procedure on familiar tunes you know well but have never seen in notation. Since you can control the speed, repeat, and stop your mental replay of familiar tunes at will, choose many melodic note-pairs along the way to identify.

   • Learn to identify the melodic interval formed between any pitch and the tonic in a tonal melody.

   • Listen to two-part music and work on identifying the intervals formed between the two parts. Begin by concentrating on long, sustained intervals and those formed at the ends of phrases.

6. Take note of how any particular interval changes its affect (or feeling) when it occurs in different scale-degree contexts.

   • For example, how does the perfect 5th formed by $\hat{1}$/ *do*–$\hat{5}$/ *sol* differ from the perfect 5th at $\hat{3}$/ *mi*–$\hat{7}$/ *ti*? The one at $\hat{4}$/ *fa*–$\hat{1}$/ *do*? What is it that gives each of these perfect 5ths a different feel?

   • How does the fact that any single interval has different functions in different scale-degree contexts affect the idea that you can learn intervals simply by memorizing certain familiar tunes (such as learning all major 6ths as the opening of "My Bonnie Lies Over the Ocean")?

One way to describe the motion in the music we have been listening to and singing is to refer to it as either **conjunct** (motion by step) or **disjunct** (motion by leap). Conjunct motion refers to motion to an adjacent scale degree, although it also includes repeated notes. Disjunct motion moves from one scale degree to a nonadjacent scale degree by skipping over the intervening stepwise pitches.

Although we have had no restrictions on the kind of conjunct motion we've encountered, the skips we've been singing and hearing have all been to $\hat{1}$/do, $\hat{3}$/mi, or $\hat{5}$/sol. (The only exceptions to this restriction have been during sequentials, whose motion has set up skips to various scale degrees by virtue of continuing their particular patterns.) In this chapter, we will begin to investigate certain ways to read, sing, and hear skips to $\hat{7}$/ti and $\hat{2}$/re.

> **Conjunct motion** is motion to an adjacent scale degree, including repeated notes. (Also called "stepwise" motion)

> **Disjunct motion** is motion that moves directly from one scale degree to a nonadjacent scale degree by jumping over the intervening stepwise pitches. (Also called motion by "skip" or by "leap")

Neighboring and Prefix Neighboring Notes

"Conjunct motion" can refer to motion in one direction (by scale), to repeated notes, or to **neighbor notes** that embellish the pitches to which they relate. For example, the following passage from Mozart's Trio in G, K. 564, includes both scalar and neighboring motion after its initial leap:

> A **neighbor note** is the scale degree immediately above or below a pitch.

W. A. Mozart, Trio K. 564, mvt. 2, mm. 1–4 (1788)

unison   skip   lower neighbor   scale   upper neighbor

The first neighboring note in the above example occurs on the third beat of measure 1, where $\hat{7}$/ti appears as a lower neighbor to $\hat{1}$/do. When, as in this case, the neighbor note is surrounded before and after by the pitch it embellishes, this condition is called a **complete neighbor-note figure.** Thus, all complete neighbor-note figures are three-note groups.

With apologies to Mozart, imagine if the first note of that three-note group were omitted as follows:

> A **complete neighbor-note figure** is a three-note group that begins with a main pitch, moves to its neighbor, and returns to the main pitch.

$\hat{7}$/ti

In this case, the $\hat{7}$/ti in measure 1 is a neighbor only to the following $\hat{1}$/do, in a two-note group known as an **incomplete neighbor.** (Here and elsewhere in this

An **incomplete neighbor-note figure** is a two-note group that either begins with a neighbor and moves to the main pitch (a **prefix neighbor**), or begins with the main pitch and moves to its neighbor (a **suffix neighbor**).

text, the note approached by skip is circled and the notes of the neighbor figure are marked with a brace.) Because the neighboring note occurs before the pitch it embellishes, this kind of incomplete neighbor is called a **prefix neighbor.** When the neighboring note occurs after the pitch it embellishes, it's called a **suffix neighbor.**

The skip in measure 1 from $\hat{5}$/*sol* to $\hat{7}$/*ti* is best viewed as a prefix neighbor to $\hat{1}$/*do*. It is often helpful to imagine a prefix neighbor as part of a complete neighboring figure—preceded as well as followed by the pitch it embellishes. Thus, if asked to sing the altered Mozart excerpt above (with the prefix neighbor), it would be helpful to hear the real Mozart (with the complete neighbor). Another useful approach is to practice the passage without the prefix neighbor in order to firmly establish the pitch following the prefix. Both approaches can help you assimilate skips, so it would be wise to learn and practice both approaches.

Skips to $\hat{7}$/*ti*

$\hat{7}$/*ti* can appear as a lower neighbor to $\hat{1}$/*do* or an upper neighbor to $\hat{6}$/*la*. At present, we will only discuss the former in order to work on skips to $\hat{7}$/*ti* in relation to the scale degree with which you are most familiar. The short melody below includes a skip to $\hat{7}$/*ti* (see measure 99, beat 2).

Anton Arensky, Piano Trio No. 1, Op. 32, mvt. 2, mm. 96–101 (1894)

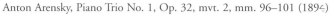

In order to auralize and perform this skip to $\hat{7}$/*ti,* it is helpful to rethink the skip using one or both of the approaches mentioned above: (1) with a complete neighboring note; and (2) without the prefix neighbor. Let's apply each of these approaches to the passage from the Arensky Trio.

We can recompose measure 99, beat 2, as a complete neighbor by changing that beat to two eighth notes—an eighth-note B♭ followed by the lower neighbor A. This places the neighboring note in a stepwise context, surrounded by a pitch you know quite well. After having learned the passage this way—internalizing $\hat{7}$/*ti* as a complete lower neighbor to $\hat{1}$/*do*—try singing the original.

We can also recompose measure 99, beat 2, by eliminating the lower neighbor entirely, which focuses our attention on the target note at its point of arrival. Once again, learn the passage this way, then return to the original.

Skips to 2̂/*re*

Skips to 2̂/*re* can appear as prefix neighbors to either 1̂/*do* or 3̂/*mi*. A skip to 2̂/*re* as a prefix to 1̂/*do* appears in measure 4 in this passage from Schubert's Sonata D. 408 (also note the skip to 7̂/*ti* in measure 2):

Franz Schubert, Violin Sonata D. 408 [Op. 137, No. 3, mvt. 3], mm. 1–8 (1816)

Once again, such a skip can be conceived as a complete neighbor, as shown in the first recomposed version of measures 3–5, or the prefix neighbor can be eliminated entirely, as shown in the second recomposed version below.

Morley's "Hard by a Crystal Fountain" includes an example of a skip in which 2̂/*re* functions as a prefix neighbor to 3̂/*mi*:

Thomas Morley, "Hard by a Crystal Fountain,"
mm. 1–7, from *The Triumphs of Oriana* (1601)

The skip to 2̂/*re* at the end of measure 2 can be conceived as an incomplete prefix neighbor to 3̂/*mi*. As before, try to hear it as a complete neighbor, or by eliminating the prefix entirely.

EXERCISES

Sequentials

Certain sequentials—when memorized in pairs—can help you to internalize skips to 7̂/ *ti* and 2̂/ *re* as prefix neighboring notes. Learn the following sequentials on syllables. Memorize the *pattern* for each, then learn it without looking at the notation. Imagine these sequentials in various keys as you sing them. Learn these sequentials in pairs—that is, learn version a of the sequential first, then learn version b. After that, sing the measures of any version b in various orders.

1.
a.

b.

2.
a.

b.

3.
a.

b.

4.

a.

b.

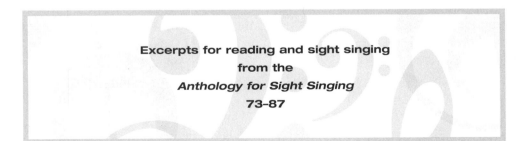

LISTENING

Melodic Dictation

Listen to excerpts 14.1–14.10 and write out the pitches and rhythms for each.

Exercise	Clef	Tonic	Bottom number in meter sign
14.1	treble	A♭	4
14.2	bass	D	4
14.3	treble	F	2
14.4	treble	A	4
14.5	bass	D♭	2
14.6	bass	C	4
14.7	treble	B	8
14.8	bass	E	4
14.9	bass	B♭	4
14.10	treble	E♭	2

READING AND SIGHT SINGING

Prepare the following melodies, singing on syllables while conducting. As you do so, identify each skip to $\hat{7}$/*ti* and $\hat{2}$/*re* (which in this chapter always appear as prefix neighbors to $\hat{1}$/*do* or $\hat{3}$/*mi*). Where possible, rewrite each skip to $\hat{7}$/*ti* and $\hat{2}$/*re* (1) as a complete neighbor and (2) by eliminating the prefix entirely. Learn to sing these rewritten excerpts, then move on to the music as originally notated.

> **Excerpts for reading and sight singing**
> **from the**
> *Anthology for Sight Singing*
> **73–87**

15 TEMPO

Although meter and rhythm are essentially relative elements whose characteristics depend on comparison of internal features, such as primary and secondary pulses, one important aspect of meter and rhythm relies on an absolute external standard. This aspect concerns the speed at which the pulses progress, or **tempo** (pl. tempi).

> **Tempo** is the speed at which pulses progress.

Musicians indicate tempo in two ways: (1) through an expressive tempo mark—a word or phrase printed above the staff indicating a general sense of speed and mood; (2) through a metronome mark indicating speed precisely in terms of beats per minute. We will examine each of these in turn.

Expressive Tempo Marks

Expressive tempo marks consist of a word or phrase printed above the staff to indicate one or both of two factors: speed and mood. In the following excerpt, the word "slowly" affects the factor of speed. We get a fairly clear sense of the appropriate tempo even though we don't know the *exact* speed.

Charles Ives, "Remembrance," mm. 1–4 (1921)

The tempo marks in the following excerpt provide additional descriptive information about the mood as well as speed:

Henry Clay Work, "No Letters From Home," mm. 1–4 (1869)

Composers sometimes use descriptive phrases such as "Mysteriously" or "Graciously" without an indication of speed. These still function as tempo marks for sensitive musicians, who adjust the speed to fit such moods.

Expressive tempo indications appear in a number of languages. Italian has been considered a kind of common language among Western musicians since the early seventeenth century, but composers indicate tempi in their individual native languages as well.

As a musician, you must become familiar with many basic tempo indications in at least four languages—Italian, German, French, and English. The following table lists some basic tempo marks in these four languages.

English	Italian	German	French
Very fast	Vivace Vivo Presto	Lebhaft Eilig	Vif Vite
Fast	Allegro	Bewegt Schnell	Animé
Somewhat fast	Allegretto	Etwas bewegt	Un peu animé
Moderately	Moderato	Mässig Mässig bewegt	Modéré
Moderately slow	Andante Andantino	Mässig langsam Gehend	Allant Très modéré
Somewhat slow	Larghetto Adagietto	Etwas langsam	Un peu lent
Very slow	Largo Adagio Lento	Langsam Breit	Lent Large

This table groups together terms that indicate generally similar speeds, but you should become acquainted with the subtle differences among these terms. For example, *Lento* literally means "slow," whereas *Largo* connotes the ideas of "large" and "broad."

Modifiers are added to basic tempo marks in some languages; for instance, "very fast" often appears as "Très vif" in French music. Superlatives can be formed from many of these terms, such as "Prestissimo" (as fast as possible). Some tempo marks denote sudden changes in tempo, like "meno mosso" (less quickly), and others indicate gradual changes, the most common being "accelerando" (speed up) and "ritardando" (slow down).

Metronome Marks

Composers and arrangers indicate the speed of a composition more exactly by using a metronome mark. A metronome is a mechanical device invented in the early nineteenth century that measures the speed or tempo of music according to the number of beats per minute. The abbreviation MM or M.M. often accompanies the metronome marking that denotes a specific number of beats per minute.* In the example below, the marking "♩ = 69" tells readers that there should be 69 quarter notes every minute. Note that this marking is combined with an expressive tempo mark.

*M. M. stands for Maelzel's Metronome, so named because Johann Nepomuk Maelzel received the first patent for the device that was actually invented by Diederich Nikolaus Winkel.

We have at our disposal a variety of metronomes, mechanical and electronic, which all operate on the same basic principle: users select a specific number of beats per minute and the device generates a pulse (audible and/or visible) at that speed.

No matter how "specific" metronome marks might seem, they serve only as guidelines for how a piece should be played. A sense of speed can be influenced by many factors beyond the sheer number of beats per minute. These factors include articulation, vibrato, dynamics, instrumentation, and even the surrounding acoustics. You should take into account the effect of all such factors on the apparent speed and mood of your performances.

Tempo and Beat Unit

As we learned in Chapter 7, music can be notated with various beat units, and the beat unit does not inherently affect the speed. Speed is determined not by the number on the bottom of the meter sign but by a metronome or expressive tempo mark. The following two excerpts provide a striking example of the relationship between the tempo and beat unit.

In the first excerpt, the eighth note serves as beat unit, but it moves at a slow pace. In the second excerpt, the half note is the beat unit, and it moves at a pace faster than the eighth note in the first excerpt. For centuries, tempo and beat unit have been completely separate parameters.

LISTENING

1. Listen to musical excerpts 15.1–15.4. Choose the tempo mark from the list below that is most appropriate for each excerpt. Use each tempo mark only once.

      Adagio   Andante   Allegretto   Prestissimo

2. Listen to musical excerpts 15.5–15.8. Without using a watch or metronome, write down a metronome mark that is most appropriate for each excerpt. Then return to each excerpt and use a watch or metronome to determine the precise tempo. Write this next to your estimated mark. Were your initial estimates within 5% of each actual tempo? (A 5% difference would be within 4 beats per minute of 80; 5 beats per minute of 100; 6 beats per minute of 120; etc.). If not, determine whether your estimates were consistently too slow or too fast, and by what percentage. Then try to adjust your perception of tempo by working with a watch or metronome while you listen, matching tempi to what you hear, so that you will become more accurate in future assessments.

READING AND SIGHT SINGING

Prepare the following melodies, singing on syllables while conducting. Translate the Italian, German, and French tempo marks into English. Write down a suitable translation of each, and write a sentence or two about how you would perform each one. Observe these tempo indications in your performances, interpreting them as appropriately as possible.

> **Excerpts for reading and sight singing**
> **from the**
> *Anthology for Sight Singing*
> 2, 7–9, 11–14, 18–19, 21–26, 29–30, 41–46, 48–49. 52–58,
> 61, 63–64, 66–67, 69–70, 73, 76, 78–79, 81, 87

Pick one to sing

Recite one of the rhythms (there on moodle)

Intervals

Sequentials

16 COMPOUND METERS

In Chapter 5 we first encountered the idea of simple meters, in which the beat regularly divides into halves. This chapter will introduce meters in which the beat regularly divides into thirds.

Compound Duple Meter

In most music, not only are the rhythms grouped into patterns within each measure, but the measures themselves also come in groups. Sing the French carol "Un Flambeau, Jeanette Isabelle" while conducting pulse level **a** in triple meter.

Pulse level **a** is represented by eighth notes and pulse level **b** is represented by measures. The meter sign $\frac{3}{8}$ directly represents the relationship between levels **a** and **b**—a simple triple meter.

In level **c,** the measures are paired—one primary measure and one secondary. If we shift the primary pulse to level **c,** we can conduct a downbeat for each pulse at **c** and an upbeat for each **b** pulse in between. We can also renotate the music, removing the barlines between pairs of measures so that each measure contains six pulses at level **a.** The meter sign therefore becomes $\frac{6}{8}$ ($\frac{3}{8} + \frac{3}{8}$).

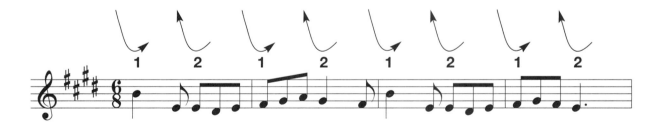

Conduct "Un Flambeau, Jeanette Isabelle" using a duple pattern (illustrated above) to show the level **b** pulse, while tapping the level **a** pulse with your other hand. We have shifted the beat to level **b** and divided that beat regularly into threes.

When reading rhythms that divide beats into three parts, you may intone them on a neutral syllable, or you may use the Takadimi system (first introduced in Chapter 5). In Takadimi, the syllable on each beat remains "Ta" while the two following triple divisions are "ki" and "da." In this way, the first two measures of "Un Flambeau, Jeanette Isabelle" would be intoned as Ta-da Ta-ki-da Ta-ki-da Ta-da.

A meter in which the beat is regularly divided into threes is called a **compound meter.** The number of beats per measure in a compound meter can be determined by dividing the top number in the meter sign by 3. When the top number is 6, as in $\frac{6}{16}$, $\frac{6}{8}$, and $\frac{6}{4}$, there are two beats per measure, and each beat can be divided into threes. We call these compound duple meters—compound because the beats divide into threes, and duple because there are two beats per measure.

You will recall that the bottom number in the meter sign of simple meters represents the beat unit (in $\frac{4}{8}$, the beat unit is an eighth note). In compound meters the bottom number represents the *triple division* of the beat (in $\frac{6}{8}$, the beat unit is a dotted quarter note, which divides into three eighth notes). To determine the beat unit in compound meters, add together three note values represented by the bottom number of the meter sign (♪ + ♪ + ♪ = ♩.).

> In **compound meter,** the beat is regularly divided into threes. In compound meters, the beat unit is equal to three of the note values represented by the bottom number of the meter sign.

Compound Triple Meter

In "Un Flambeau, Jeanette Isabelle," the beats at level **b** grouped into pairs in level **c**. Beats in compound meters may also group into *threes*, as in the Canadian folk song "Un Canadien Errant," below:

When this song is written in $\frac{3}{4}$ meter, quarter-note beats at pulse level **a** are grouped into threes at the measure level **b**. But beyond that, the measures are themselves grouped into threes at a still deeper level **c**.

If we shift the primary pulse to level **c** and conduct a downbeat for each pulse at **c** and a secondary beat for each of the two **b** pulses in between, we create triple meter. To renotate this example, we remove barlines within each group of three measures and combine $\frac{3}{4}$ + $\frac{3}{4}$ + $\frac{3}{4}$ to produce a meter sign of $\frac{9}{4}$:

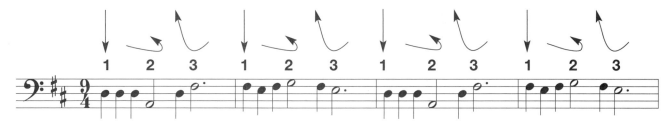

Compound triple meters, such as $\frac{9}{16}$, $\frac{9}{8}$, and $\frac{9}{4}$, contain three beats per measure, and each beat divides into threes.

Compound Quadruple Meter

Compound meters may also contain four beat units per measure. We'll start once again with a tune in simple triple meter, this time observing how the measures group into pairs of pairs. Sing the following German folk song ("Freut euch des Lebens"):

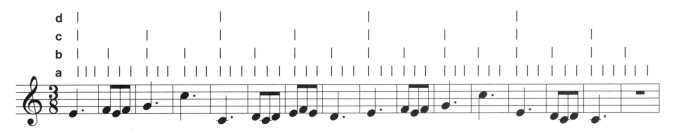

The eighth-note level **a** is grouped into the measure level **b** in threes (as shown by the simple $\frac{3}{8}$ meter sign). The measure level **b** groups into a deeper level **c** in pairs. Moving even deeper, level **c** groups into level **d,** also by pairs.

If we shift the primary pulse to level **d** and conduct a downbeat for each pulse at **d** and a secondary beat for each of the **b** pulses in between, we create quadruple meter. To renotate this example, we remove barlines within each group of four measures and combine $\frac{3}{8} + \frac{3}{8} + \frac{3}{8} + \frac{3}{8}$ to produce a meter sign of $\frac{12}{8}$:

Compound quadruple meters, such as $\frac{12}{16}$, $\frac{12}{8}$, and $\frac{12}{4}$, contain four beats per measure, and each beat divides into threes.

The process of combining simple meters to create compound meters is summarized below.

	Beat unit = ♪.	Beat unit = ♩.	Beat unit = ♩.
Compound duple:	$\frac{3}{16} + \frac{3}{16} = \frac{6}{16}$	$\frac{3}{8} + \frac{3}{8} = \frac{6}{8}$	$\frac{3}{4} + \frac{3}{4} = \frac{6}{4}$
Compound triple:	$\frac{3}{16} + \frac{3}{16} + \frac{3}{16} = \frac{9}{16}$	$\frac{3}{8} + \frac{3}{8} + \frac{3}{8} = \frac{9}{8}$	$\frac{3}{4} + \frac{3}{4} + \frac{3}{4} = \frac{9}{4}$
Compound quadruple:	$\frac{3}{16} + \frac{3}{16} + \frac{3}{16} + \frac{3}{16} = \frac{12}{16}$	$\frac{3}{8} + \frac{3}{8} + \frac{3}{8} + \frac{3}{8} = \frac{12}{8}$	$\frac{3}{4} + \frac{3}{4} + \frac{3}{4} + \frac{3}{4} = \frac{12}{4}$

Dictation Strategies

When taking dictation, you will first decide on a level of pulse you would conduct as the beat. Next, determine whether that beat is grouped into duple, triple, or quadruple meter. Then determine whether the beat divides into twos (simple meter) or threes (compound meter). Once you've made these two determinations, you need only a bottom number for the meter sign in order to write in the appropriate meter.

1. For each of the following melodies, do the following:

   • Combine measures to rewrite it in an appropriate compound meter. Change barlines and meter signatures, but not actual note values. Are there any that are not easily rewritten in compound meter? If so, why not?

   • Sing the melodies you rewrote in compound meter in the previous step. Sing while conducting, using the appropriate compound-meter conducting pattern as presented in this chapter.

Don't Change the bottom number

a.

b.

c.   "Fais do-do," French lullaby

d.

"V'la p'tit Jean qui prend sa serpe," French folk song, mm. 1–16

e.

"Im Wald und auf der Heide," German folk song, mm. 1–12

f.

2. Review all of the dictations you've done that are in triple meter, and for each, repeat the procedures outlined in exercise 1.

3. Write the following familiar tunes in compound meters using various beat units. Some of the pitch materials are more advanced than those covered in this book thus far; you may choose either to notate only the rhythms or to try your hand at the pitches as well.

- Row, Row, Row Your Boat
- On Top of Old Smokey
- Daisy, Daisy
- Pop Goes the Weasel (compare to the simple triple version in Chapter 1)
- For He's a Jolly Good Fellow
- Mexican Hat Dance
- Take Me Out to the Ball Game

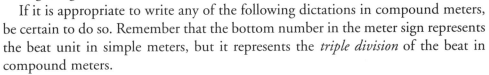

Melodic Dictation

Listen to excerpts 16.1–16.10 and write out the pitches and rhythms for each, following the given instructions.

If it is appropriate to write any of the following dictations in compound meters, be certain to do so. Remember that the bottom number in the meter sign represents the beat unit in simple meters, but it represents the *triple division* of the beat in compound meters.

Exercise	Clef	Tonic	Bottom number in meter sign
16.1	bass	G	4
16.2	bass	B	8
16.3	treble	B♭	4
16.4	bass	G♭	4
16.5	treble	F♯	8
16.6	treble	A	16
16.7	bass	E♭	8
16.8	treble	E	4
16.9	bass	C♯	8
16.10	treble	F	8

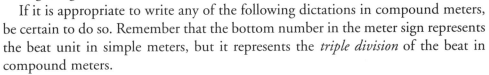

READING AND SIGHT SINGING

Prepare the following melodies, singing on syllables while conducting, using the methods described in this chapter.

**Excerpts for reading and sight singing
from the
Anthology for Sight Singing
88–108**

17 INTRODUCTION TO THE MINOR MODE: RELATIVE AND PARALLEL APPROACHES

In previous chapters, every diatonic collection and its key signature have been associated with only one tonic, and all scales have had the same intervals between their scale degrees. This chapter shows that tonic and collection can be changed independently, which results in different modes.

Tonicization

A pitch has been **tonicized** when it has been established as a tonic.

We already know about the importance of the tonic; now we will learn how a pitch *becomes* tonic. The organization of the notes in a particular composition is what establishes one of them as a tonic. When a pitch has been established as a tonic, it is said to have been **tonicized.** It is the relationships among the notes themselves that tonicizes a pitch, not the key signature.

The **dominant** pitch is a perfect fifth above (or a perfect fourth below) the tonic.

A pitch can be tonicized melodically in several ways. One of the strongest stems from the tonic-dominant relationship. The **dominant** pitch is a perfect fifth above (or a perfect fourth below) the tonic. Therefore, the fifth scale degree ($\hat{5}$) in any key is the dominant.

A **mediant** pitch is a third above (or a sixth below) the tonic.

Another, somewhat weaker, pitch relationship that can convey a feeling of tonicization involves the interval of a third (major *or* minor). A third, if emphasized, will tend to make the lower of its two pitches feel like a tonic. The pitch a third above the tonic ($\hat{3}$) is called the **mediant,** and the tonicizing force between the two pitches is called the tonic-mediant relationship.

The tonic-dominant and tonic-mediant relationships can be emphasized in many ways: a close juxtaposition of the two pitches, scalar connections, and a variety of metrically based connections, including beat-to-beat, strong-beat-to-strong-beat, and downbeat-to-downbeat connections.

The tonic-dominant relationship often works in conjunction with the tonic-mediant relationship. For example, in the following excerpt the mediant, dominant, and tonic appear on successive downbeats, thus outlining the tonic triad (review Chapter 6):

Ludwig van Beethoven, Symphony No. 9,
Op. 125, mvt. 4, mm. 92–99 (1824)

Tonicizing Minor

In Chapter 11, you learned about and memorized the relationships between key signatures and major keys. You associated each diatonic collection (the pitches yielded by a key signature) with a single pitch that, when tonicized, results in a major key. A second pitch within each diatonic collection may alternatively serve as a tonic. Consider the following melody:

"Job," Welsh carol, mm. 1–4

Notice that B on the anacrusis and D on the downbeat form a tonic-mediant relationship that is joined by the dominant (F♯) in measures 2 and 3, resolving back to the tonic in measure 4. These factors strongly tonicize B in our ears and minds. This new tonic (B) lies a minor third below (or a major sixth above) the major tonic (D), and it is known as the **minor tonic.**

> A **minor tonic** lies a minor third below (or a major sixth above) the major tonic within a given diatonic collection.

Here, the words "major" and "minor" refer to two different tonicizations within a diatonic collection known as **modes**—major mode and minor mode. From now on, we will name keys using their tonic and mode, in that order. Thus, we would say that the excerpt above is in B minor.

> **Mode** is the combination of a tonic and a diatonic collection.

Relative Keys

Every diatonic collection has one major tonic and one minor tonic. Any two keys that share the same key signature are called **relative keys** (also called relative modes).

> **Relative keys** are keys that share the same diatonic collection and, therefore, the same key signature.

Here are the scales from two relative keys—C major and A minor—written so you can see the placement of their scale degrees within the same diatonic collection:

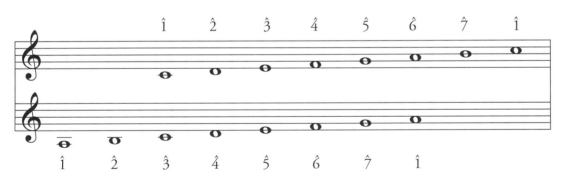

Since every diatonic collection can be used for two relative keys, you must now also memorize fifteen *minor* key signatures in addition to the fifteen major key signatures you memorized in Chapter 11. Fortunately, since the minor tonic always lies a minor third below its relative major tonic, you can use your knowledge of the major key signatures to determine their minor counterparts.

In the following figure, the keys are presented in the circle-of-fifths arrangement. The major keys (in uppercase letters) are written around the outside of the circle, and their relative minor keys (in lowercase letters) are written on the inside.

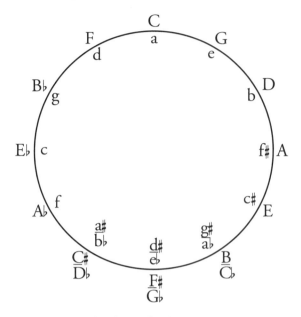

Relative Solmization

This chapter presents two methods of applying solmization syllables to minor-mode melodies: relative and parallel. In the relative approach, we leave the syllables on the pitches to which they applied in the major mode. The syllable *do* continues to represent the major tonic even while the music tonicizes the relative minor (*la*). A major tonic is always a minor third above its relative minor, resulting in a *do–la* relationship.

In the following melody, the syllable *do* remains on the major tonic (G) while this minor-mode melody tonicizes *la* (E).

"Jésus-Christ s'habille en pauvre," French folk song, mm. 1–6

When we use relative solmization, the syllable *la* becomes the first scale degree in the minor scale, or $\hat{1}$/*la*. The remaining scale degrees and syllables in the minor scale follow accordingly:

$$\hat{1}/la \quad \hat{2}/ti \quad \hat{3}/do \quad \hat{4}/re \quad \hat{5}/mi \quad \hat{6}/fa \quad \hat{7}/sol \quad \hat{1}/la$$

By leaving the syllables in their original diatonic positions, we maintain the solfege syllables of the half steps *mi–fa* and *ti–do*—both crucial, collection-defining intervals. Their scale degree functions change from $\hat{3}$–$\hat{4}$ and $\hat{7}$–$\hat{1}$ in the major mode to $\hat{5}$–$\hat{6}$ and $\hat{2}$–$\hat{3}$ in the minor mode.

Parallel Keys

We can also compare major and minor keys that share the same *tonic* but use different diatonic collections. These are called **parallel keys** or parallel modes.

If we compare the two excerpts below, we see that the first uses the diatonic collection with no sharps or flats and the second uses the diatonic collection with three flats. The first is in C major, and the second is in C minor.

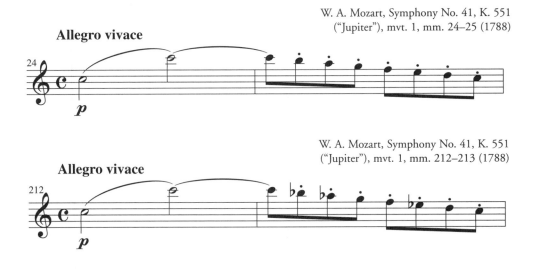

W. A. Mozart, Symphony No. 41, K. 551
("Jupiter"), mvt. 1, mm. 24–25 (1788)

W. A. Mozart, Symphony No. 41, K. 551
("Jupiter"), mvt. 1, mm. 212–213 (1788)

Parallel major and minor keys share the same tonic, and all their corresponding scale degrees share similar functions. Compare the scale degrees in parallel major and minor keys:

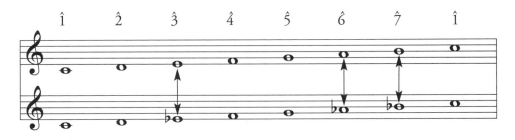

Scale degrees $\hat{1}$, $\hat{2}$, $\hat{4}$, $\hat{5}$ are the same in both modes; however, scale degrees $\hat{3}$, $\hat{6}$, and $\hat{7}$ are each a half-step lower in the minor mode than in the major mode. This is true of all parallel major and minor keys. Although scale degrees $\hat{3}$, $\hat{6}$, and $\hat{7}$ are lower in comparison to the parallel major, they are still *diatonic* pitches. They just reflect a different diatonic collection, the one used for the minor mode (indicated by the key signature).

Parallel Solmization

Just as focusing on relative keys leads to relative solmization, focusing on parallel keys leads to parallel solmization. Parallel keys share the same tonic and other scale-degree functions, so you can label the tonic $\hat{1}$/*do* in both parallel major *and* minor.

> **Parallel keys** share the same tonic but not the same diatonic collection.

In this way, many of the same functions carry the same labels (for instance, the tonic-dominant relationship is still called $\hat{1}$/*do*–$\hat{5}$/*sol*). Scale degrees $\hat{1}$, $\hat{2}$, $\hat{4}$, and $\hat{5}$ are the same in parallel major and minor keys, so their solfege syllables are the same.

Scale degrees $\hat{3}$, $\hat{6}$, and $\hat{7}$ are different in the minor mode, so their syllables are altered. Their initial consonants are the same as the syllables for their parallel major counterparts, but the vowels are changed to indicate that the pitches are a half step lower. All three syllables use the vowel "E" (pronounced "AY"): $\hat{3}$/*me*, $\hat{6}$/*le*, and $\hat{7}$/*te*. Thus, the syllables for parallel major and minor scales look like this:

| parallel major: | $\hat{1}$/*do* | $\hat{2}$/*re* | $\hat{3}$/*mi* | $\hat{4}$/*fa* | $\hat{5}$/*sol* | $\hat{6}$/*la* | $\hat{7}$/*ti* | $\hat{1}$/*do* |
| parallel minor: | $\hat{1}$/*do* | $\hat{2}$/*re* | **$\hat{3}$/*me*** | $\hat{4}$/*fa* | $\hat{5}$/*sol* | **$\hat{6}$/*le*** | **$\hat{7}$/*te*** | $\hat{1}$/*do* |

The minor-mode melody we discussed under "Relative Solmization" can now be represented using syllables for the parallel minor mode:

"Jésus-Christ s'habille en pauvre," French folk song, mm. 1–6

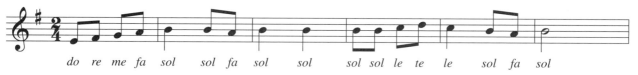

do   re   me   fa   sol   sol   fa   sol   sol   sol   sol   le   te   le   sol   fa   sol

EXERCISES

The following exercises will help you become fluent with the minor syllables.

Relative Solmization

1. Sing the diatonic minor scale from $\hat{1}$/*la* to $\hat{1}$/*la,* ascending and descending, at a brisk pace. Learn it at least two ways: (1) bottom to top and back, and (2) top to bottom and back.

2. Learn the following relative-minor pitch patterns by heart. Be able to sing them at any time, in any order.

Relative minor	
1a. $\hat{1}$/la $\hat{2}$/ti $\hat{3}$/do $\hat{1}$/la	1b. $\hat{1}$/la $\hat{3}$/do $\hat{1}$/la
2a. $\hat{1}$/la $\hat{2}$/ti $\hat{3}$/do $\hat{4}$/re $\hat{5}$/mi $\hat{1}$/la	2b. $\hat{1}$/la $\hat{5}$/mi $\hat{1}$/la
3a. $\hat{1}$/la $\hat{7}$/sol $\hat{6}$/fa $\hat{5}$/mi $\hat{1}$/la	3b. $\hat{1}$/la $\hat{5}$/mi $\hat{1}$/la
4a. $\hat{3}$/do $\hat{2}$/ti $\hat{1}$/la $\hat{3}$/do	4b. $\hat{3}$/do $\hat{1}$/la $\hat{3}$/do
5a. $\hat{5}$/mi $\hat{4}$/re $\hat{3}$/do $\hat{2}$/ti $\hat{1}$/la $\hat{5}$/mi	5b. $\hat{5}$/mi $\hat{1}$/la $\hat{5}$/mi
6a. $\hat{5}$/mi $\hat{4}$/re $\hat{3}$/do $\hat{5}$/mi	6b. $\hat{5}$/mi $\hat{3}$/do $\hat{5}$/mi
7a. $\hat{3}$/do $\hat{4}$/re $\hat{5}$/mi $\hat{3}$/do	7b. $\hat{3}$/do $\hat{5}$/mi $\hat{3}$/do
8a. $\hat{5}$/mi $\hat{6}$/fa $\hat{7}$/sol $\hat{1}$/la $\hat{5}$/mi	8b. $\hat{5}$/mi $\hat{1}$/la $\hat{5}$/mi

Parallel Solmization

3. Sing the diatonic minor scale from $\hat{1}$/do to $\hat{1}$/do, ascending and descending, at a brisk pace. Learn it at least two ways: (1) bottom to top and back, and (2) top to bottom and back.

4. Learn the following parallel-minor pitch patterns by heart. Be able to sing them at any time, in any order.

Parallel minor	
1a. $\hat{1}$/do $\hat{2}$/re $\hat{3}$/me $\hat{1}$/do	1b. $\hat{1}$/do $\hat{3}$/me $\hat{1}$/do
2a. $\hat{1}$/do $\hat{2}$/re $\hat{3}$/me $\hat{4}$/fa $\hat{5}$/sol $\hat{1}$/do	2b. $\hat{1}$/do $\hat{5}$/sol $\hat{1}$/do

3a.	$\hat{1}$/ do	$\hat{7}$/ te	$\hat{6}$/ le	$\hat{5}$/ sol	$\hat{1}$/ do	3b.	$\hat{1}$/ do $\hat{5}$/ sol	$\hat{1}$/ do
4a.	$\hat{3}$/ me	$\hat{2}$/ re	$\hat{1}$/ do	$\hat{3}$/ me		4b.	$\hat{3}$/ me $\hat{1}$/ do	$\hat{3}$/ me
5a.	$\hat{5}$/ sol	$\hat{4}$/ fa	$\hat{3}$/ me	$\hat{2}$/ re $\hat{1}$/ do	$\hat{5}$/ sol	5b.	$\hat{5}$/ sol $\hat{1}$/ do	$\hat{5}$/ sol
6a.	$\hat{5}$/ sol	$\hat{4}$/ fa	$\hat{3}$/ me	$\hat{5}$/ sol		6b.	$\hat{5}$/ sol $\hat{3}$/ me	$\hat{5}$/ sol
7a.	$\hat{3}$/ me	$\hat{4}$/ fa	$\hat{5}$/ sol	$\hat{3}$/ me		7b.	$\hat{3}$/ me $\hat{5}$/ sol	$\hat{3}$/ me
8a.	$\hat{5}$/ sol	$\hat{6}$/ le	$\hat{7}$/ te	$\hat{1}$/ do $\hat{5}$/ sol		8b.	$\hat{5}$/ sol $\hat{1}$/ do	$\hat{5}$/ sol

5. Familiar tunes:

   • When Johnny Comes Marching Home

   • We Three Kings of Orient Are (1st 31 notes)

   • God Rest Ye Merry Gentlemen

   • Heigh-ho, Anybody Home? (Food nor Drink nor Money Have We None)

   For each tune, determine the scale degrees of its pitches so that you can sing each tune on its proper syllables. Do this work entirely in your mind, without the aid of any instrument or writing.

   Follow this process for each tune:

   a. Find the tonic, or the syllable $\hat{1}$/ *do,* recalling that it might not be the first, last, highest, or lowest note—listen for the pitch with the feeling of $\hat{1}$/ *do*

   b. Determine the syllable of the first pitch by comparing it with $\hat{1}$/ *do* (isolate the starting pitch and $\hat{1}$/ *do,* sing each and compare)

   c. Work out the subsequent syllables

   d. Memorize your familiar tunes on the proper syllables.

6. Here is the first phrase from the French folk song, "Ma mère et mon père." Play it on an instrument:

"Ma mère et mon père," French folk song, mm. 1–4

What pitch sounds like a tonic in this excerpt? What factors create that sense of tonic? How do your answers relate to the "rule" you may have heard about "looking at the last note" to figure the tonic? How do you suppose that "rule" came about?

LISTENING

Melodic Dictation

Listen to excerpts 17.1–17.10 and write out the pitches and rhythms. The instructions name the tonic for each excerpt but not the mode. You will encounter both major and minor mode. Pay special attention to which of these modes you hear for each dictation and write the appropriate key signature accordingly.

Homework

Exercise	Clef	Tonic	Bottom number in meter sign
17.1	treble	C	8
17.2	treble	C	8
17.3	treble	A	4
17.4	bass	D	8
17.5	bass	D	8
17.6	treble	F	2
17.7	bass	B♭	4
17.8	treble	E	2
17.9	treble	C♯	2
17.10	bass	F♯	4

READING AND SIGHT SINGING

Prepare the following melodies, singing on syllables while conducting. Use the solmization system assigned by your instructor.

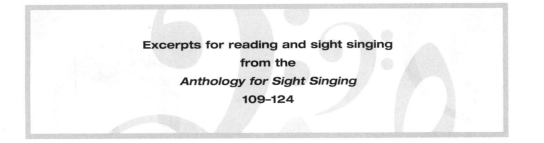

Excerpts for reading and sight singing
from the
Anthology for Sight Singing
109–124

18 CHROMATIC LOWER NEIGHBORS

Diatonic and Chromatic Lower Neighbors

The note immediately below any scale degree is known as its lower neighbor. In the major scale, $\hat{2}$/*re*, $\hat{3}$/*mi*, $\hat{5}$/*sol*, $\hat{6}$/*la*, and $\hat{7}$/*ti* have lower neighbors a whole step below them. The other two pitches, $\hat{1}$/*do* and $\hat{4}$/*fa*, have lower neighbors a *half* step below.

You can alter the interval of the lower neighbors for $\hat{2}$/*re*, $\hat{3}$/*mi*, $\hat{5}$/*sol*, $\hat{6}$/*la*, and $\hat{7}$/*ti* by raising them to create "artificial" half steps. These raised pitches, which are not part of the prevailing diatonic collection, are called **chromatic** pitches.

> A **chromatic** pitch is not part of the prevailing diatonic collection.

Solmization of Chromatic Lower Neighbors

To show that a scale degree has been raised chromatically by a half step from its diatonic position, we place an up arrow (↑) before its scale-degree number (for example, ↑$\hat{1}$). To reflect this change in the syllables *do, re, fa, sol,* and *la,* we change their vowels to "I" (pronounced "EE"). (*Mi* and *ti* are already a half step below their upper diatonic neighbors.) Thus, the scale-degree numbers and syllables for chromatic lower neighbors in the major mode are ↑$\hat{1}$/*di*, ↑$\hat{2}$/*ri*, ↑$\hat{4}$/*fi*, ↑$\hat{5}$/*si*, and ↑$\hat{6}$/*li*.

The following figure shows diatonic and chromatic syllables in ascending order. Diatonic syllables are on the left and chromatic pitches are on the right, and the arrows indicate which diatonic syllables have been inflected to create chromatic ones.

Diatonic pitches

$\hat{1}$/*do*
$\hat{7}$/*ti*

$\hat{6}$/*la* ↗ ↑$\hat{6}$/*li*

$\hat{5}$/*sol* ↗ ↑$\hat{5}$/*si*

$\hat{4}$/*fa* ↗ ↑$\hat{4}$/*fi*
$\hat{3}$/*mi*

$\hat{2}$/*re* ↗ ↑$\hat{2}$/*ri*

$\hat{1}$/*do* ↗ ↑$\hat{1}$/*di*

Chromatic pitches

Although it is certainly true that these chromatic pitches result from raising their diatonic forms by a half step, it is often more helpful to think of them as *lower neighbors*—a half step below the diatonic pitches *above* them. For now, we will focus on examples of complete neighbor-note figures, in which a diatonic pitch surrounds its chromatic lower neighbor.

Later, we'll encounter chromatic pitches in other contexts. Each of these contexts—chromatic passing tones, stepwise approaches, and leaps—will require you to think about and hear chromatics in different ways. Nonetheless, one of the most practical and musical ways to think of a chromatically raised pitch is to relate it to the note above it as a lower chromatic neighbor.

Reading and Writing Chromatics in Various Keys

In music notation, we must place the appropriate symbol in front of any diatonic lower neighbor to raise it by a half step. Any such symbol (sharp, flat, natural, etc.) that is not part of the key signature is called an **accidental.** The following examples show how a sharp, natural, or double sharp can raise a diatonic pitch chromatically by one half step.

> An **accidental** is a symbol (such as a sharp or flat) placed directly before a note, affecting its pitch.

Bb: 3̂/mi ↑2̂/ri 3̂/mi   Ab: 2̂/re ↑1̂/di 2̂/re   E: 7̂/ti ↑6̂/li 7̂/ti

EXERCISES

In the following exercises, both diatonic and chromatic lower neighbors are used. Make a clear distinction between the two.

1. Memorize the diatonic lower-neighbor sequential in both ascending order (as shown below) and descending order (1̂/do–7̂/ti–1̂/do, 7̂/ti–6̂/la–7̂/ti, 6̂/la–5̂/sol–6̂/la, etc.).

do ti do re do re mi re mi fa mi fa sol fa sol la sol la ti la ti do
1̂   7̂ 1̂   2̂   1̂   2̂   3̂   2̂   3̂   4̂   3̂   4̂   5̂   4̂   5̂   6̂   5̂   6̂   7̂   6̂   7̂   1̂

2. Memorize the chromatic lower-neighbor sequential in both ascending order (as shown below) and descending order (1̂/do–7̂/ti–1̂/do, 7̂/ti–↑6̂/li–7̂/ti, 6̂/la–↑5̂/si–6̂/la, etc.).

do ti do re di re mi ri mi fa mi fa sol fi sol la si la ti li ti do
1̂   7̂ 1̂   2̂ ↑1̂ 2̂   3̂ ↑2̂ 3̂   4̂   3̂   4̂   5̂   ↑4̂ 5̂   6̂ ↑5̂ 6̂   7̂ ↑6̂ 7̂   1̂

3. Learn to sing the three-note lower-neighbor figure below any given scale degree in various orders. Do this in both diatonic and chromatic versions.

4. Familiar tunes:
   - America the Beautiful ("Oh beautiful for spacious skies")
   - You Are My Sunshine
   - Mexican Hat Dance (both sections)
   - Take Me Out to the Ball Game
   - Beautiful Dreamer

   Each of these tunes contains at least one lower chromatic neighbor. For each tune, determine the scale degrees of its pitches so that you can sing each tune on its proper syllables. Do the work entirely *in your mind,* without the aid of any instrument or writing.

   Memorize each of these tunes on the proper syllables.

LISTENING

Melodic Dictation

Listen to excerpts 18.1–18.10 and write out the pitches and rhythms for each, following the given instructions. Listen carefully for the difference between diatonic and chromatic lower neighbors.

Exercise	Clef	Tonic	Bottom number in meter sign
18.1	bass	E	4
18.2	bass	E	4
18.3	treble	E♭	2
18.4	bass	A	8
18.5	treble	D♭	4
18.6	treble	G	8
18.7	bass	B	4
18.8	treble	C	8
18.9	treble	F♯	2
18.10	bass	F	4

READING AND SIGHT SINGING

Prepare the following melodies, singing on syllables while conducting. Carefully distinguish (in both syllable and sound) between diatonic and chromatic lower neighbor notes in your performance.

Excerpts for reading and sight singing
from the
Anthology for Sight Singing
125–134

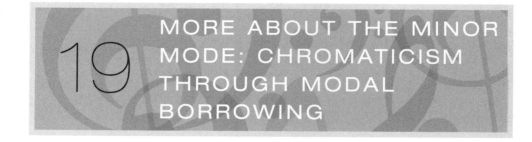

19

MORE ABOUT THE MINOR MODE: CHROMATICISM THROUGH MODAL BORROWING

More about Tonicization: The Leading Tone

We have learned about two ways to tonicize a pitch. One is to emphasize the tonic-dominant relationship, and the other is to emphasize the tonic-mediant relationship. Another pitch relationship that can tonicize a pitch is the half step. An emphasis on two pitches one half step apart tends to tonicize the higher of the two pitches. Sing or play the first four measures of the following excerpt:

Ludwig van Beethoven, Symphony No. 7, Op. 92, mvt. 3, mm. 149–155 (1812)

> The **leading tone** is a pitch one half step below the tonic.

The strong emphasis on the D–C♯ relationship tends to give D a feeling of centricity, even though these four measures lack both tonic-dominant and tonic-mediant relationships. Now sing or play the first *three* measures and stop on the C♯ at the end of measure 151. Notice how this seventh scale degree (C♯) directs our attention back to D. This feeling of leading to the tonic has given rise to a special name for a seventh scale degree that lies one half step below the tonic: the **leading tone.**

In the major mode, the leading tone occurs naturally, because the seventh scale degree is diatonically one half step below the tonic. But in the minor mode, the seventh scale degree occurs diatonically one *whole* step below the tonic. Sing or play the following D-minor excerpt.

"Is There No Balm in Christian Lands?" English hymn, mm. 1–4

subtonic   leading tone

The first appearance of the seventh scale degree (C) in this passage is a whole step below the tonic (D). (A pitch one whole step below a tonic is often called the subtonic.) However, in measure 3, the C is raised to C♯, creating a leading tone that did not exist diatonically. Functioning as a lower chromatic neighbor to D, this leading tone strengthens the tonic feel of the pitch above it.

The dominant, mediant, and the leading tone may work independently or in conjunction with one another to establish a feeling of tonic.

Modal Borrowing; Three Forms of the Minor Scale

Although the above melody is in D minor, the C♯ in measure 3 is exactly the same pitch as the leading tone in D *major*. Because the chromatic leading tone in any minor mode is identical to the diatonic leading tone in its parallel major, we often say that the chromatic leading tone has been *borrowed* from the major mode. When the pitch and function of a scale degree are borrowed from the parallel mode and produced through chromaticism, we call it **modal borrowing.** The most common form of modal borrowing occurs in the minor mode with the use of the chromatic leading tone.

Modal borrowing occurs when a pitch is borrowed from one mode and produced in a parallel mode through chromaticism.

Because it takes place between parallel modes, modal borrowing is most clearly represented using parallel solmization syllables. In this way, the leading tone will be sung as $\hat{7}$/*ti* in both major and minor modes. For example, let's begin with the diatonic form of the C minor scale, which is also widely known as the natural minor scale:

Natural Minor (diatonic)

$\hat{1}$/*do* $\hat{2}$/*re* $\hat{3}$/*me* $\hat{4}$/*fa* $\hat{5}$/*sol* $\hat{6}$/*le* $\hat{7}$/*te* $\hat{1}$/*do*

If we borrow the leading tone (B♮) from C major, we raise the seventh scale degree to ↑$\hat{7}$/*ti* and create the harmonic minor scale:

Harmonic Minor ($\hat{7}$/*te* raised to ↑$\hat{7}$/*ti*)

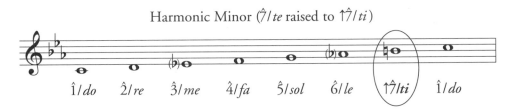

$\hat{1}$/*do* $\hat{2}$/*re* $\hat{3}$/*me* $\hat{4}$/*fa* $\hat{5}$/*sol* $\hat{6}$/*le* ↑$\hat{7}$/*ti* $\hat{1}$/*do*

Sometimes, both $\hat{6}$/*la* and $\hat{7}$/*ti* are borrowed from the parallel major, particularly in scalar passages moving up from $\hat{5}$/*sol* to $\hat{1}$/*do*. When we raise $\hat{6}$/*le* and $\hat{7}$/*te* to ↑$\hat{6}$/*la* and ↑$\hat{7}$/*ti* in the minor mode, we create the ascending form of the melodic minor scale. The only remaining pitch difference between the two parallel scales occurs on scale degree $\hat{3}$.

Melodic Minor, ascending form
($\hat{6}$/*le* raised to ↑$\hat{6}$/*la* and $\hat{7}$/*te* raised to ↑$\hat{7}$/*ti*)

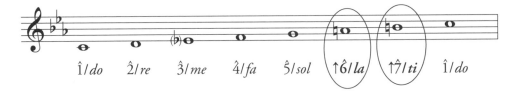

$\hat{1}$/*do* $\hat{2}$/*re* $\hat{3}$/*me* $\hat{4}$/*fa* $\hat{5}$/*sol* ↑$\hat{6}$/*la* ↑$\hat{7}$/*ti* $\hat{1}$/*do*

The melodic minor scale has conventionally assumed a different form when descending: it reverts to the natural form. (The natural and harmonic forms of the minor scale stay the same regardless of whether they are ascending or descending.) The complete melodic minor scale looks like this:

Melodic Minor, ascending and descending forms
(↑$\hat{6}$/ *la* and ↑$\hat{7}$/ *ti* when ascending; $\hat{6}$/ *le* and $\hat{7}$/ *te* when descending)

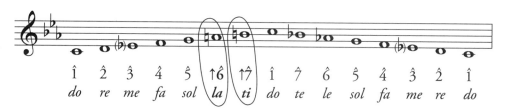

| $\hat{1}$ | $\hat{2}$ | $\hat{3}$ | $\hat{4}$ | $\hat{5}$ | ↑$\hat{6}$ | ↑$\hat{7}$ | $\hat{1}$ | $\hat{7}$ | $\hat{6}$ | $\hat{5}$ | $\hat{4}$ | $\hat{3}$ | $\hat{2}$ | $\hat{1}$ |
| *do* | *re* | *me* | *fa* | *sol* | *la* | *ti* | *do* | *te* | *le* | *sol* | *fa* | *me* | *re* | *do* |

These three forms of the minor scale—natural, harmonic, and melodic—are artificial constructions. Although some compositions seem to conform to one or another of these scale forms, other compositions do not. You will find examples of works in the minor mode that don't use any of these three scales exactly. In these places, treatment of the sixth and seventh scale degrees varies: they appear in both chromatically raised and diatonically natural positions in a variety of combinations and circumstances.

In order to approach these two scale degrees, you should remember their functions as diatonic or chromatic pitches. In the major mode, $\hat{6}$/ *la* and $\hat{7}$/ *ti* are diatonic; in the minor mode, ↑$\hat{6}$/ *la* and ↑$\hat{7}$/ *ti* are chromatic. In the minor mode the diatonic sixth and seventh scale degrees are $\hat{6}$/ *le* and $\hat{7}$/ *te;* they must be raised one half step to turn them into ↑$\hat{6}$/ *la* and ↑$\hat{7}$/ *ti.*

Establishing Collection and Tonic in Minor

The principles for establishing the collection and tonic in minor are the same as those for the major mode. Review the guidelines found in Chapter 11.

1. Establish the collection
   - Listen to the starting pitch.
   - If necessary, sing stepwise by whole steps to reach the nearest half step within the collection.
   - Sing the nearest half step using the three-part neighbor-note drill that we used when we sang half and whole steps alone.
   - Sing by whole steps to reach the other half step in the collection.
   - If you need to further establish the collection, sing the entire scale.

2. Establish the tonic
   - If necessary, sing by steps to reach the tonic.
   - Sing the tonic and dominant pitches ($\hat{1}$/ *do*–$\hat{5}$/ *sol*–$\hat{1}$/ *do*).
   - If you need to further establish the tonic, sing the tonic and dominant chords.

The important difference here is the placement of the diatonic half steps in minor. In the major mode, the diatonic half steps occur between $\hat{7}$/ *ti* and $\hat{1}$/ *do* and between $\hat{3}$/*mi* and $\hat{4}$/*fa*. In the minor mode, they occur between $\hat{2}$/*re* and $\hat{3}$/*me* and between $\hat{5}$/*sol* and $\hat{6}$/*le*.

Remember that $\uparrow\hat{7}$/*ti* is a chromatic pitch in minor. Its appearance serves *not* to establish the diatonic collection but to tonicize $\hat{1}$/*do*. Because of this, do *not* sing $\uparrow\hat{7}$/*ti* while establishing the collection. You may, however, sing $\uparrow\hat{7}$/*ti* while establishing the tonic.

The procedure for establishing keys from each of the members of the tonic triad is shown below:

$\hat{1}$/*do*	$\hat{3}$/*me*	$\hat{5}$/*sol*
$\hat{1}$/*do*–$\hat{2}$/*re*–$\hat{3}$/*me*	$\hat{3}$/*me*–$\hat{2}$/*re*–$\hat{3}$/*me*	$\hat{5}$/*sol*–$\hat{6}$/*le*–$\hat{5}$/*sol*
$\hat{3}$/*me*–$\hat{2}$/*re*–$\hat{3}$/*me*	$\hat{3}$/*me*–$\hat{4}$/*fa*–$\hat{5}$/*sol*	$\hat{5}$/*sol*–$\hat{4}$/*fa*–$\hat{3}$/*me*
$\hat{3}$/*me*–$\hat{4}$/*fa*–$\hat{5}$/*sol*	$\hat{5}$/*sol*–$\hat{6}$/*le*–$\hat{5}$/*sol*	$\hat{3}$/*me*–$\hat{2}$/*re*–$\hat{3}$/*me*
$\hat{5}$/*sol*–$\hat{6}$/*le*–$\hat{5}$/*sol*	$\hat{5}$/*sol*–$\hat{4}$/*fa*–$\hat{3}$/*me*–$\hat{2}$/*re*–$\hat{1}$/*do*	$\hat{3}$/*me*–$\hat{2}$/*re*–$\hat{1}$/*do*
$\hat{5}$/*sol*–$\hat{4}$/*fa*–$\hat{3}$/*me*–$\hat{3}$/*re*–$\hat{1}$/*do*	$\hat{1}$/*do*–$\hat{5}$/*sol*–$\hat{1}$/*do*	$\hat{1}$/*do*–$\hat{5}$/*sol*–$\hat{1}$/*do*
$\hat{1}$/*do*–$\hat{5}$/*sol*–$\hat{1}$/*do*		

EXERCISES

1. Learn the following pitch patterns by heart. Be able to sing them at any time, in any order.

1a. $\hat{1}$/*do* $\hat{7}$/*te* $\hat{1}$/*do*	1b. $\hat{1}$/*do* $\uparrow\hat{7}$/*ti* $\hat{1}$/*do*

2a. $\hat{5}$/*sol* $\hat{6}$/*le* $\hat{5}$/*sol*	2b. $\hat{5}$/*sol* $\uparrow\hat{6}$/*la* $\hat{5}$/*sol*

3a. $\hat{5}$/*sol* $\hat{6}$/*le* $\hat{7}$/*te* $\hat{1}$/*do* $\hat{5}$/*sol*	3b. $\hat{5}$/*sol* $\uparrow\hat{6}$/*la* $\uparrow\hat{7}$/*ti* $\hat{1}$/*do* $\hat{5}$/*sol*	3c. $\hat{5}$/*sol* $\hat{6}$/*le* $\uparrow\hat{7}$/*ti* $\hat{1}$/*do* $\hat{5}$/*sol*

4a. $\hat{1}$/*do* $\hat{7}$/*te* $\hat{6}$/*le* $\hat{5}$/*sol* $\hat{1}$/*do*	4b. $\hat{1}$/*do* $\uparrow\hat{7}$/*ti* $\uparrow\hat{6}$/*la* $\hat{5}$/*sol* $\hat{1}$/*do*	4c. $\hat{1}$/*do* $\uparrow\hat{7}$/*ti* $\hat{6}$/*le* $\hat{5}$/*sol* $\hat{1}$/*do*

2. Memorize each of the three forms of the minor scale. Know them by name. Be able to sing them from any given starting pitch on syllables in two ways: (a) from bottom to top and back down again; and (b) from top to bottom and back up again.

3. Do the following with at least three different major-mode melodies that you know by heart: Sing each melody aloud in the *parallel minor*. What changes do you have to make to the melody? When do you choose to borrow the sixth or seventh scale degrees from major? Why?

4. While singing each of the three forms of the minor scale, be able to identify each interval you produce immediately. For example, if stopped after singing $\hat{5}$/*sol*–$\hat{6}$/*le*, you must be able to say "half step" without hesitation.

5. Practice quickly identifying the number of scale degrees spanned by any two syllables in the minor mode (expressed as an ordinal number). For example, if given $\hat{6}$/ *le* up to $\hat{2}$/ *re*, you would say it is a 4th.

6. Practice quickly calculating the total number of *half* steps between any two scale degrees in minor. For example, given $\hat{6}$/ *le* up to $\hat{2}$/ *re*, you would say it spans six half steps.

7. In which minor keys is ↑$\hat{6}$/ *la* produced by one accidental while ↑$\hat{7}$/ *ti* is produced by a different kind? (For example, ↑$\hat{6}$/ *la* is produced by a natural while ↑$\hat{7}$/ *ti* is produced by a sharp.) What are the accidentals for ↑$\hat{6}$/ *la* and ↑$\hat{7}$/ *ti* in each of those keys? How will knowing this help you in dictation and sight reading?

LISTENING

Melodic Dictation

Listen to excerpts 19.1–19.10 and write out the pitches and rhythms for each. Pay close attention to the sounds of $\hat{6}$/ *le*, ↑$\hat{6}$/ *la*, $\hat{7}$/ *te*, and ↑$\hat{7}$/ *ti* and which accidental (if any) is needed for each in the various keys.

Exercise	Clef	Tonic	Bottom number in meter sign
19.1	bass	F	4
19.2	treble	C♯	8
19.3	bass	G	4
19.4	bass	E	2
19.5	treble	D	4
19.6	bass	G♯	8
19.7	treble	B♭	2
19.8	treble	D♯	4
19.9	bass	C	4
19.10	treble	B	4

READING AND SIGHT SINGING

Prepare the following melodies and sing on syllables while conducting. Use the solmization system assigned by your instructor.

Excerpts for reading and sight singing

from the

Anthology for Sight Singing

135–149

20 TRIPLETS AND DUPLETS

Simple and compound meters provide the most straightforward means of indicating whether the beat divides into twos or threes. A piece in which the beat divides into twos is most appropriately written in a simple meter. A piece in which the beat divides into threes is most appropriately written in a compound meter. However, music can shift between duple and triple beat divisions within a single passage, or even within a single measure. We can notate these temporary changes in beat division by using rhythmic values without altering the meter sign.

Triplets

The following rhythmic pattern illustrates a simple duple meter in which the prevailing divisions of the beat are duple, but one division is triple:

Each beat in the first measure is divided in half, but the first beat of the second measure is divided into *three* equal durations, as if that one beat were borrowed from compound meter.

We can combine the Takadimi syllables we learned in Chapter 5 for duple division of the beat (Ta-di) with those we learned in Chapter 16 for triple division of the beat (Ta-ki-da). Thus, the Takadimi syllables for the two measures above would be Ta-di Ta-di Ta-ki-da Ta-di.

In order to notate these rhythms in a simple duple meter, such as $\frac{2}{4}$, we would have to use a **triplet,** which fits three notes of equal duration in the place of two:

> A **triplet** fits three notes of equal duration in the place of two.

A triplet can be notated by including a 3 above or below the triplet (♪♪♪) or by adding a bracket (♪♪♪) or a slur (♪♪♪) to the 3. Sometimes these extra symbols are omitted, and the reader must determine which notes form triplets.

We notate triplets with the same rhythmic value that would divide the beat in half in simple meter, but we use three of those notes in the place of two. If the beat unit is a quarter note, eighth-note triplets divide the beat into three equal parts. Other beat units use their corresponding half-beat values, as shown in the following table:

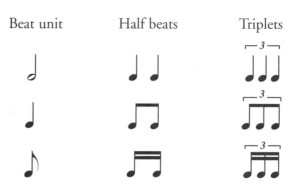

As shown in the following example, two of the three triplet divisions can be combined into one longer note, creating a note 2/3 of a beat long. It is important when performing such figures that you feel a triple beat-division underlying the corresponding beats.

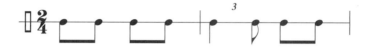

A triplet occurs as an irregular beat-division only in simple meter. In compound meters, the three-note beat division is not a triplet. You should refer to them by their actual note values (for example, "eighth notes" in $\frac{6}{8}$).

Duplets

A **duplet** fits two notes of equal duration in the place of three.

In compound meters, such as $\frac{6}{8}$, we have encountered only triple divisions of the beat. There is no rhythmic value among all those we've learned that will divide a dotted quarter note into two equal durations. The solution to this problem is a rhythmic configuration known as a **duplet,** which fits two notes of equal duration in the place of three.

The following rhythmic pattern illustrates a compound duple meter in which the prevailing divisions of the beat are triple, but one division is duple:

Each beat in the first measure is divided into three equal parts; however, the first beat of the second measure is divided into *two* equal durations, as if that one beat were borrowed from simple meter.

Takadimi syllables for this rhythm would be Ta-ki-da Ta-ki-da Ta-di Ta-ki-da. To notate these rhythms in a compound duple meter, such as $\frac{6}{8}$, we would notate measure 2, beat 1 as a duplet:

The various notational practices described above for triplets also apply to duplets. In addition, duplets are sometimes written in the following manner:

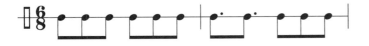

Duplets are relatively rare in comparison to triplets. Nonetheless, you must become competent at reading, performing, and hearing duplets as well as triplets.

EXERCISES

Set a metronome to a moderately fast tempo (112 is a good starting point) and practice intoning duple divisions of that pulse, then triple divisions. Work at changing from one division to the other at will.

LISTENING

Melodic Dictation

Listen to excerpts 20.1–20.10 and write out the pitches and rhythms for each. You should first determine what you think is the normative beat division—duple or triple—and write your answer in simple or compound meter accordingly. Then you should write deviations from this division as triplets or duplets as necessary.

Exercise	Clef	Tonic	Bottom number in meter sign
20.1	treble	E♭	4
20.2	treble	E♭	4
20.3	bass	G♯	8
20.4	treble	D	2
20.5	treble	C♭	4
20.6	bass	F	8
20.7	bass	F	8
20.8	treble	E	4
20.9	bass	C	4
20.10	bass	B	2

READING AND SIGHT SINGING

Prepare the following melodies, singing on syllables while conducting.

Excerpts for reading and sight singing
from the
Anthology for Sight Singing
150–163

21 INTRODUCTION TO TRANSCRIPTION

Transcription is the process of writing down music from a live or recorded performance. In this chapter, you will learn about the differences between dictation and transcription and about notating more than just pitches and rhythms.

The Process of Transcription

When taking dictation, you are given a fixed number of playings and a certain amount of time between those playings in order to notate the pitches and rhythms that you hear. When you transcribe music, you listen to a recording in order to notate a certain span of music, such as a phrase, a specific number of measures, a section, or an entire movement. In transcription (unlike dictation), *you* determine how much of the recording to play back at each listening, *you* determine the time between listenings, and *you* determine the total number of listenings.

Some transcribers prefer to listen to short fragments at each listening, while others prefer longer portions. Some take long periods of time between listenings, and others take very little time. As you work, take note of your habits and try varying these two factors (length of listening and time between listenings). Determine which changes improve your work and which ones interfere with it. The results of this process can be very illuminating.

If you find that you can work with only short fragments (fewer than seven pitches), you should try to improve the capacity of your short-term memory by trying to remember longer fragments. Listen carefully for repetitions, sequences, scalar passages, and so on. Awareness of these patterns and organizational features will not only reduce the amount of sheer memorization necessary to recall musical passages, but it will also benefit your musical life beyond dictation and transcription.

If you find that you need longer periods of time between listenings (more than a minute), you should work to improve your efficiency in understanding what you hear and translating it into notation. Pay close attention to the process you use between listenings. Narrate out loud exactly what you are doing and aim toward using the same procedure between each listening. Ask yourself the following questions:

- How am I determining meter and rhythm?
- What do I do to figure out the scale degrees of the pitches?
- How long does it take me to write out a twenty-note passage in music notation?

Work toward writing out a passage with twenty notes in less than a minute. Videotape your writing hand while taking dictation or transcription, or have someone watch you during this process and offer comments on ways of improving your efficiency.

Instrumental and Vocal Timbres

Timbre or **tone color** is the difference between notes of identical pitch, rhythm, and dynamics produced by different instruments or voices.

Musicians must be able to recognize various instruments by their sound alone, so we will include identifying instruments as part of the transcription process. First, we will focus on individual instruments playing one at a time. Later, we will work to identify different instruments playing multiple parts.

The term **timbre** (or **tone color**) refers to the distinction in sound between two different instruments playing the same pitch, rhythm, and dynamic. This is what distinguishes a flute from an oboe, a trombone from a cello, a voice from a fog horn.

Recordings, such as those accompanying this text, are valuable tools in learning how to discriminate between different timbres. However, distortion affects even the most sophisticated playback equipment, particularly in the reproduction of timbre.

Ideally, you should listen to live performances by voices and acoustic instruments as much as possible. When you attend live concerts, particularly of small ensembles, look at the instruments and voices and pay close attention to the various timbres they produce. You can also follow a score while listening to a performance, once again attending to the timbres of the various lines. You can test yourself by "blind" listenings of recordings, performers behind a screen, or live performances.

Your first step in identifying timbre is to recognize and distinguish between the four broad instrumental families of the Western classical orchestra: strings, woodwinds, brass, and percussion.

Next, you should hone this identification down to specific instruments within each of these families. For example, in the woodwind section, learn to distinguish among flutes, oboes, clarinets, and bassoons, then add other close relatives, such as the English horn and the alto clarinet. Eventually, you will also learn to identify various timbral alterations, such as flutter-tonguing and muting.

Similarly, you should learn to distinguish among human voice types, in the four broad vocal ranges: soprano, alto, tenor, and bass. Eventually you may wish to develop your ability to identify more specific voice types, such as mezzo-soprano and baritone.

Tempo Marks

Your transcriptions should also indicate the tempo, through either an expressive mark or a metronome mark. Review the discussion of tempo in Chapter 15 and be certain to include such marks in your transcriptions where appropriate.

LISTENING

A. Transcribe the recorded excerpts 21.1–21.8. For each, indicate the instrument and tempo in addition to notating the pitches and rhythms. For tempo marks, use each of the following at least once: Italian, German, French, English, and a metronome mark.

Exercise	Clef	Tonic	Bottom number in meter sign
21.1	treble	D	4
21.2	treble	C	4
21.3	treble	B♭	4
21.4	bass	D	4
21.5	treble	E	16
21.6	treble	C	8
21.7	bass	C♯	8
21.8	treble	A♭	2

Share your transcriptions with others and ask them to sing from your notation. Then have them play your transcriptions on instruments. For each performance, ask the following questions:

- Did it sound like the original?
- If not, why not?
- Were discrepancies caused by my understanding of what I heard, by my notation, or by their performance?

B. Practice the following blind tests by gathering a group of classmates together to play instruments from each of the four instrumental families. Appoint one person at a time to identify the timbre played by the others without being able to see them or their instruments. Here are some suggestions for various things they can play:

- A single, isolated note in various registers, particularly at the top and bottom of their range
- A short passage from a standard work in the repertoire of their own instrument
- A short passage from a standard work in the repertoire of another, vastly different instrument
- Special timbral effects such as muting, pizzicato, *col legno,* hand-stopping, flutter-tonguing, and so forth.

What factors seem to account most for each of the difficulties encountered in this identification process?

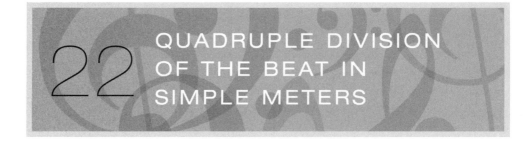

22 QUADRUPLE DIVISION OF THE BEAT IN SIMPLE METERS

In previous chapters, we divided the beat equally into twos and threes. In this chapter, we'll investigate quadruple division of the beat.

Dividing the Beat into Four Equal Parts

We have already seen how primary and secondary pulses group together in the first phase of "Frère Jacques" to create a simple duple meter, as shown in the pronotation below:

Frè-   re,   Jac- ques, Frè-   re   Jac- ques, dor- mez vous,   dor-   mez vous?

The second phrase of this song illustrates quadruple division of the beat:

Son-nez les ma- ti-   nes,   Son-nez les ma- ti-   nes,   ding- dong- ding_____ , din- din- don_____

Each of the four notes on the syllables "son-nez les ma-" receives one-quarter of the value of one beat unit. The table below shows common beat units in simple meters, the note values equal to one-fourth of the beat, and the corresponding rhythmic notation for measure 5 from "Frère Jacques":

Beat unit	1/4 value	"Frère Jacques," measure 5
		⎸– – – –⎸– –⎸
𝅗𝅥	♪	𝄴²₂ 𝅘𝅥𝅮𝅘𝅥𝅮𝅘𝅥𝅮𝅘𝅥𝅮 𝅘𝅥
♩	𝅘𝅥𝅯	𝄴²₄ 𝅘𝅥𝅯𝅘𝅥𝅯𝅘𝅥𝅯𝅘𝅥𝅯 𝅘𝅥𝅮
♪	𝅘𝅥𝅰	𝄴²₈ 𝅘𝅥𝅰𝅘𝅥𝅰𝅘𝅥𝅰𝅘𝅥𝅰 𝅘𝅥𝅯

Combining Parts of Quadruple Division

The four divisions of the beat may be combined in various groups of two and three to form six different patterns. The table below shows these patterns in protonotation, Takadimi, and rhythm notation for the three most common beat units. You must learn to auralize and recognize these six patterns as they appear in these different beat units.

Pattern	Beat unit		
	𝅗𝅥	𝅘𝅥	𝅘𝅥𝅮
Ta ka di mi			
Ta di mi			
Ta ka di			
Ta mi			
Ta ka			
Ta ka mi			

The Double Dotted Beat

When beats divide equally into four parts, augmentation dots can be used to add more than half the value of the note. When a one-beat note is followed by *two* augmentation dots, the first dot adds a half of a beat to the note, and the second dot (which is applied to the first dot) adds a quarter of a beat. This results in a note one and three-fourths of a beat long. Here is an example:

Rikard Nordraak, national anthem of Norway, mm. 19–20 (1864)

Reading Strategies

Before you begin reading any music that includes quadruple division patterns, it is essential for you to auralize a feeling of four equal divisions per beat. You should continue that feeling during your performance. For example, in order to read the following melody, you should internalize the rhythms printed below the staff:

Ottorino Respighi, "Nebbie," mm. 2–5

One of the challenges of reading music with quadruple beat divisions is the sheer increase in the number of notes per beat. You may find that the rhythms, pitches, and syllables simply come too fast. These two strategies may help: (1) control your tempi as you practice, possibly by working with a metronome for half of your practice time; (2) become more facile by practicing syllables, scales, sequentials, earlier melodies, and sight reading at progressively faster tempi.

Dictation Strategies

Learn to recognize the six quadruple patterns as separate entities. For example, if you can immediately say "that's 1+1+2," or "Ta-ka-di," you'll be able to understand and notate these rhythms much more quickly.

We have acknowledged the possibility of more than one perfectly correct answer to a dictation, depending on how various listeners assign the beat to different pulse levels. Dictations originally notated with quadruple division of the beat often elicit more than one correct response. For example, the following dictation melody can be notated correctly as shown in the two versions below:

Antonín Dvořák, Symphony No. 9 ("From the New World"), mvt. 2, mm. 7–10 (1893)

Try to get lots of practice using quadruple division of the beat in your listening and writing. If you find that you tend not to hear notes shorter than the half-beat division, try to focus on the next broader (slower) level of pulse.

EXERCISES

1. Choose four folk melodies in simple meters from previous chapters of this manual, and read and sing each. Then, change your metric focus to a broader level of pulse so that you now hear some quadruple division of the beat (similar to the discussion of "Frère Jacques" in this chapter). Rewrite these melodies using quadruple beat division. Use a variety of beat units until you become comfortable with quadruple division using several rhythmic values.

2. Practice scales (several octaves, if possible) using three different divisions of the beat: duple, triple, and quadruple. Do this to a metronome set anywhere between 60 and 100 beats per minute.

3. Relearn the sequentials in Chapter 2 with new rhythmic patterns based on a quadruple division of the beat. Repeat the pattern on each group of the sequential. For example, sequential 1 can be reworked in the following manner:

î/do 2̂/re 3̂/mi 2̂/re   3̂/mi 4̂/fa 3̂/mi   4̂/fa 5̂/sol 4̂/fa   5̂/sol 6̂/la   5̂/sol   6̂/la 7̂/ti 6̂/la   7̂/ti î/do 7̂/ti   î/do 2̂/re î/do

Invent at least two more sequentials that focus on quadruple-division patterns.

LISTENING

Melodic Dictation

Listen to excerpts 22.1–22.10 and write out the pitches and rhythms for each.

Exercise	Clef	Tonic	Bottom number in meter sign
22.1	treble	D	4
22.2	treble	F	2
22.3	bass	A♭	4
22.4	treble	B	8
22.5	treble	G	2
22.6	bass	F♯	4
22.7	bass	E♭	8
22.8	treble	G	4
22.9	bass	E	2
22.10	bass	A	4

Prepare the following melodies by singing on syllables while conducting.

Excerpts for reading and sight singing
from the
Anthology for Sight Singing
164–205

23 CONDUCTING PULSE LEVELS OTHER THAN THE NOTATED BEAT

In some cases, it is musically appropriate to conduct a pulse level other than the one indicated by the meter sign. This can mean either that we group two or more notated beats into one conducting beat, or that we divide notated beats into two or more conducted beats.

Grouping Notated Beats

When music moves very quickly, it sometimes becomes necessary to group two or even three notated beats into one conducting beat. This can occur in quadruple, duple, or triple meters.

Quadruple Meter

Look at the following excerpt and note the three levels of pulse marked above the music:

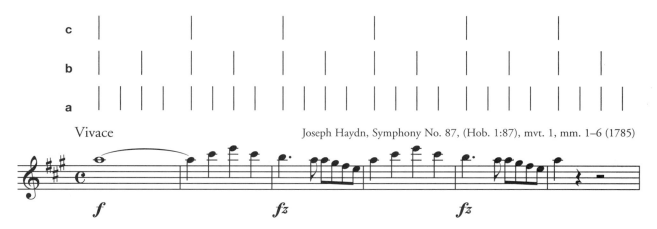

Joseph Haydn, Symphony No. 87, (Hob. 1:87), mvt. 1, mm. 1–6 (1785)

Sing this excerpt slowly and conduct each beat at level **a**. Conduct and sing this excerpt again, observing the tempo mark: *Vivace* (♩ = *180*). Conducting a quadruple pattern becomes awkward and counterproductive at this speed. Try shifting the conducted beat from the notated beat (level **a**) to the next broader level (level **b**). Thus, you would conduct the half note using a *duple* pattern as if the excerpt were in ²⁄₂ meter.

Sing this excerpt again at the same tempo (♩ = *180*), but this time conduct only two beats per measure (♩ = *90*).

Duple Meter

Some passages in simple duple meter, such as the following movement by Schubert, move so quickly that two notated beats must be grouped together in one conducting beat.

Franz Schubert, Symphony No. 2, D. 125, mvt. 4, mm. 5–12 (1815)

Rather than conducting every quarter note at a tempo of *Presto vivace*, you should shift your conducting beat up to level **b**, as if the excerpt were in $\frac{1}{2}$ meter. Sing the passage above, conducting one beat per measure. The easiest way to conduct a one pattern is to conduct straight down and then bounce straight back up again, with the single ictus at the bottom of each stroke. Variations on this motion include circular or oval-shaped patterns, but the ictus remains at the bottom of the motion.

Triple Meter

A one conducting pattern is used most frequently for fast passages in triple meters (typically $\frac{3}{4}$ or $\frac{3}{8}$) with the ictus falling at the beginning of each measure. In the example below, Beethoven specifies that the *dotted half note* should proceed at a speed of 116 per minute, even though the meter sign calls for a quarter-note beat.

Ludwig van Beethoven, Symphony No. 3, Op. 55 ("Eroica"), mvt. 3, Trio, mm. 1–7 (1803)

His markings clearly indicate that we should conduct not level **a**, but level **b**, or one beat per measure. Sing this excerpt, conducting once per measure at a tempo of ♩. = *116.*

Dividing Notated Beats

When music moves very slowly, it is sometimes easier and clearer to divide the notated beats into two or three conducting beats. Otherwise, you are conducting so slowly that a continuous sense of the pulse can be lost. Generally, this means conducting at a beat level that is *narrower* than the notated beat.

Simple Duple Meter

Let's see how this works in simple duple meters ($\frac{2}{4}$, $\frac{2}{2}$, $\frac{2}{8}$). In the following excerpt, the meter sign indicates that the quarter note is worth one beat, as shown in level **b**:

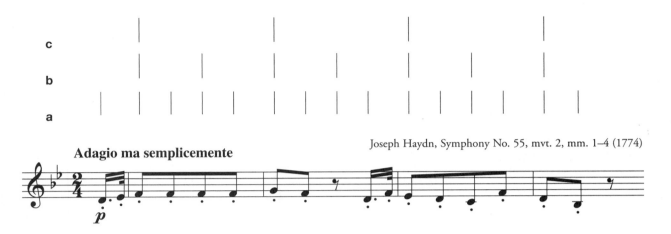

Joseph Haydn, Symphony No. 55, mvt. 2, mm. 1–4 (1774)

Adagio ma semplicemente

The *Adagio* tempo, however, moves very slowly (around ♩ = *36*), so rather than conducting the quarter note, we would move down to level **a** to conduct the eighth note.

There are two basic ways to do this in simple duple meter: (1) use a *quadruple* conducting pattern as if the excerpt were in ⁴⁄₈ meter, or (2) use a *subdivided duple* pattern. A subdivided conducting pattern, such as the one illustrated below, takes a basic pattern and divides each notated beat into two or three icti—two for simple meters and three for compound.

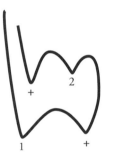

Rather than singing the excerpt from Haydn's Symphony 55 while conducting the quarter note (♩ = *36*), sing it while conducting eighth notes (♪ = *72*). Conduct four beats per measure, once using a quadruple pattern, and then again using a sub-divided simple duple pattern.

Simple Triple Meter

Simple triple meters (³⁄₄, ³⁄₂, ³⁄₈) can also be subdivided at slow tempi. The only way to conduct a half-beat pulse in simple triple meter is to subdivide the notated beat, as shown in the drawing below. (Do *not* use a six-pattern, which works for the 3+3 of compound duple but not the 2+2+2 of simple triple.)

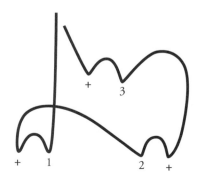

Simple Quadruple Meter

Simple quadruple meters ($\frac{4}{4}$, $\frac{4}{8}$, $\frac{4}{2}$) can also be subdivided, using a pattern similar to the one shown here:

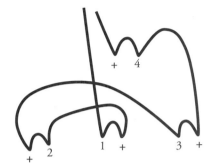

Compound Duple Meter

Compound meters can also be subdivided in slow tempi in order to keep a steady sense of the pulse. Let's remind ourselves of how compound meters work by looking first at compound duple meters ($\frac{6}{8}$, $\frac{6}{4}$, $\frac{6}{16}$). A meter sign of $\frac{6}{8}$ represents three levels of pulse: the **8** indicates the eighth-note pulse at level **a;** as part of a compound meter, the **8** also points to the dotted quarter note of level **b,** which is created by grouping together three level-**a** pulses; and the **6** indicates level **c,** which is created by combining two level-**b** pulses. These three levels are illustrated in the following example:

Adagio. ($\flat$ = *84.*)

Hector Berlioz, *Symphonie fantastique*, Op. 14, mvt. 3, mm. 20–23 (1830)

Up until now we have been conducting two beats per measure in $\frac{6}{8}$, or level **b.** The metronome mark of $\flat$ = *84* is far too slow for keeping a steady dotted-quarter-note pulse, so we need to conduct the eighth-note pulse. To subdivide patterns in compound meters, place *three* icti in the place of each notated dotted-note beat. In compound duple this results in six beats rather than two per bar, as shown below.

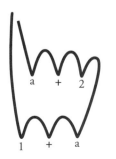

Sing the excerpt from Berlioz's *Symphonie Fantastique* using a subdivided compound duple conducting pattern.

Compound Triple Meter

Compound triple meters ($\frac{9}{8}$, $\frac{9}{4}$, $\frac{9}{16}$) can also be subdivided to create *nine* conducted beats per measure, as illustrated below:

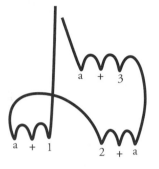

Compound Quadruple Meter

The process is the same for subdividing compound quadruple meters ($\frac{12}{8}$, $\frac{12}{4}$, $\frac{12}{16}$). Subdivide each beat into three parts as shown below:

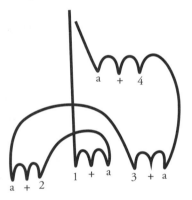

Dictation Strategies

As mentioned in earlier chapters, listeners cannot always know which levels the composer has chosen to represent with a meter sign. During dictation you will not have recourse to the original notation, so you might focus on a different pulse level than the composer. Look at each example in this chapter and consider how it might be notated differently but still correctly. Consider the meter, the tempo marking (and metronome speed), and the pulse level at which you might conduct.

For example, you could accurately notate the Schubert excerpt (on page 104) with a slower tempo and with a broader level of pulse. As notated below, the quarter-note beat combines two quarter-note beats of the original:

Allegretto

The following excerpt by Beethoven is notated in triple meter, with a metronome marking that implies subdividing each beat into two eighth-note pulses.

Ludwig van Beethoven, Symphony No. 4,
Op. 60, mvt. 2, mm. 2–4 (1806)

The passage could also be notated in duple meter, with a notated beat (and metronome marking) that makes the subdivision explicit.

What other ways of notating these excerpts would be similarly correct?

In your further dictations in this manual, pay special attention to the different pulse levels you hear. Once you choose a pulse level as the beat, think about how you might also notate it at different levels.

READING AND SIGHT SINGING

Prepare the following melodies, singing on syllables while conducting. Observe the tempo indications. Where appropriate, conduct a pulse level other than the beat indicated by the meter sign.

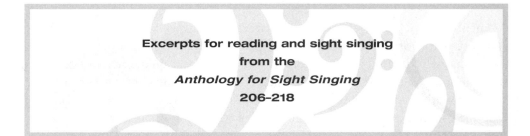

**Excerpts for reading and sight singing
from the
Anthology for Sight Singing
206–218**

24 PERFORMANCE INDICATIONS

In addition to the music symbols that represent the basic aspects of pitch, rhythm, and tempo, there are symbols that indicate dynamics, articulation, phrasing, and other features. Although studying the subtleties of these terms and symbols is a life-long pursuit, this chapter will introduce some of them and the basic principles involved in their use.

Dynamics

Dynamic markings are used to indicate aspects of volume in music. The simplest of these are *f* (*forte,* loud) and *p* (*piano,* soft). Each can be modified with the suffix *-issimo* (the most) to indicate extremes: *ff* (*fortissimo,* the loudest) and *pp* (*pianissimo,* the softest). They can also be modified with the word *mezzo* to indicate moderation by half: *mf* (*mezzo forte,* half-loud) and *mp* (*mezzo piano,* half-soft). This results in the following scale of dynamics, from softest to loudest:

pp	*p*	*mp*	*mp*	*f*	*ff*

Although *pp* and *ff* were originally intended to serve as absolute extremes, more *p*s and more *f*s have been added to these extremes, so that indications such as *ppp*, *pppp*, *fff*, and *ffff* have become possible.

Terms used to represent a gradual change of dynamics include *crescendo* (gradually getting louder), and *diminuendo* or *decrescendo* (gradually getting softer). These terms are often abbreviated as *cresc.* and *dim.* in the music, as in the example below.

SCHERZO.
Molto vivace. (♩. = 88.)   Robert Schumann, Symphony No. 1, Op. 38, mvt. 3, mm. 17–24 (1841)

When a crescendo or diminuendo lasts over a long period of time, composers often use dashed lines to indicate the length of the change:

Andante (♩ = 80)   Béla Bartók, *First Term at the Piano,* No. 11, "Minuet," mm. 13–16 (1913)

Symbolic abbreviations of these terms appear as wedges, sometimes informally called "hairpins." Wedges appear as a pair of diverging lines representing a crescendo, or a pair of converging lines representing a diminuendo:

Richard Wagner, *Rienzi*,
Overture, mm. 1–2 (1842)

Some of the other variations on dynamic indications appear in the table below. In addition, some expressive markings that apply to tempo, such as *Tranquillo* (tranquilly) and *Agitato* (agitated), affect more than merely the speed of a composition but also the mood (including such features as dynamics and articulation).

Term	Translation	Usage
al niente	to nothing	a diminuendo fading to silence
molto	much	added to crescendo or diminuendo
poco	a little	added to crescendo or diminuendo
subito	suddenly	added to *piano* or *forte*
fp	forte-piano/loud-soft	attack the note *forte*, drop immediately to *piano*

Articulation

The broad category of indications known as articulation markings incorporates a number of different types of instructions for performers.

One of the crucial roles of articulation marks regards the relationship between notes. The term *legato* ("bound") indicates that notes are to flow from one to another without detachment. The opposite of legato is staccato, which means that the notes should be short and detached from one another. The term *portato* indicates an articulation half way between legato and staccato.

Staccato can be indicated by a dot written directly above or below the notehead. A series of notes to be played legato are often grouped together under one slur. The slur may have other implications depending on the performing medium, affecting, for example, breathing for singers, and bowing for strings. Do not confuse the slur and the tie. The slur connects *different* pitches to be performed together in a legato fashion. The tie combines the rhythmic values of two successive notes with identical pitch.

The following excerpt illustrates the use of contrasting articulation (staccato and legato) along with the contrast between low and high registers and loud and soft dynamics.

Gustav Mahler, Symphony No. 5, mvt. 5, mm. 4–9 (1903)

Among the most common articulation markings are simple dynamic accents, which indicate that a note should be played louder than surrounding unaccented notes. The horizontal accent (>) indicates a relatively moderate accent. A stronger accent is indicated by ʌ (above a note) or v (occasionally, below).

Franz Liszt, *Album d'un voyageur,* II "Fleurs mélodiques del Alpes," No. 2, mm. 1–3 (1838)

Other accents indicate that a note is to be stressed, which is a more subtle aspect of articulation than simple dynamic accents. For instance, the marking *marcato* means "marked" or "stressed." The *tenuto* accent—a dash above or below the notehead—indicates that a note is to be stressed by leaning on it (more than attacking it). As its name implies, the *tenuto* is to be held for its full value (and perhaps even a little more, depending on context).

Claude Debussy, Preludes, Book II, "Hommage à S. Pickwick Esq. P. P. M. P. C.," mm. 1–6 (1913)

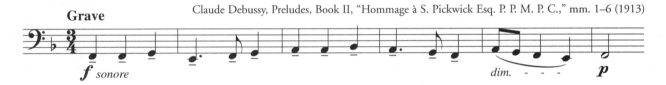

Accents often combine aspects of articulation with dynamics; for instance, the forte-piano (*fp*, mentioned above) functions in this way. In addition, the terms *forzando, forzato, sforzando,* and *sforzato* (abbreviated variously *fz, sf, sfz*) indicate a forced accent.

There are also many instrument-specific articulation markings—far too many to discuss in this manual—such as the snap pizzicato on string instruments, flutter-tonguing for winds, or the cymbal choke. (For discussions of these, see any comprehensive orchestration text.)

As we have already seen, some tempo markings affect not just speed but other elements, including articulation. Indications such as *Sostenuto* (sustained) and *Vivace legato* (fast and connected) tell as much about articulation as they do about speed.

Phrasing

When groups of notes spanning several measures or more are grouped together under a single slur, this falls under the category of phrasing. The implication of a phrase marking—subject to various stylistic and instrumental or vocal exigencies—is to play the passage as a logical whole, whatever the articulation. The phrase markings in the following excerpt connect some rather disjunct notes and span phrases longer than most could sing in one breath.

Mikhail Glinka, *Farewell Waltz*, mm. 1–8

Whereas phrase markings show which notes belong *together,* other symbols show where phrases *separate.* A break in regular beaming can indicate such a separation (although this practice does not generally apply to vocal notation, where beams are determined by text syllables). In measure 2 of the following excerpt, a break occurs between notes that would otherwise be beamed together.

W. A. Mozart, *The Magic Flute*, K. 620, "Der Vogelfänger bin ich ja," mm. 1–4 (1791)

Composers and performers use a variety of marks to separate phrases or provide breaks in the music, some of which are stronger than others. The *luftpause,* signaled by a large comma (,), indicates a strong break or pause in the music, often with a short breath, as in the following excerpt:

Carl Orff, *Carmina Burana*, No. 2, "Fortune plango vulnera," mm. 13–20 (1936)

A longer breath mark— V —is much more frequently pencilled in by performers than notated by composers. And a longer pause, which is reserved almost exclusively for the ends of phrases, is indicated by two slanted lines—//.

The *fermata* creates a break between phrases by giving performers freedom to hold a note briefly (depending upon aspects of style and performance practice). This mark can affect not only the phrasing but also the rhythm and tempo of the passage, as illustrated by one of the most famous appearances of the fermata:

Ludwig van Beethoven, Symphony No. 5, Op. 67, mvt. 1, mm. 1–5 (1808)

Reference Materials

As you encounter various performance indications that we have not discussed in this manual, you should consult musical dictionaries and books on notation in order to interpret them. From this point on, it is incumbent on you to know the meaning of every word and symbol in every piece of music you read.

EXERCISES

1. What is problematic about the dynamic markings in the following passage?

Felix Mendelssohn, Piano Trio No. 1, Op. 49, mvt. 1, mm. 1–16 (1839)

Molto Allegro agitato.

2. What is unplayable in the following passage?

3. What are the particular difficulties involved in playing legato on the piano? On the trombone?

LISTENING

1. Take "dynamics dictation" by listening to a live or recorded performance and writing down all the dynamics you hear. Try to sketch these out in order, in some proportion to the durations they span, without writing down the pitches or rhythms.

2. In later chapters, when transcribing musical excerpts, pay close attention to dynamics, articulation, and phrasing. In your notation, be as accurate as possible in using symbols to represent these features. Compare your transcriptions with the original music notation. How can you account for differences between your transcriptions and the notation?

3. Practice detecting errors in aspects of dynamics, articulation, and phrasing. Listen for discrepancies between performance and notation and write these differences in prose form. (Follow the guidelines in Chapter 4.)

READING AND SIGHT SINGING

Excerpts in this manual (and in the *Anthology*) include various performance indications that are taken directly from original sources. You should proceed to work on subsequent chapters with appropriate attention to tempo, dynamics, articulation, and phrasing.

25 THE DOMINANT TRIAD

A Triad Built on $\hat{5}$/*sol*

In addition to the tonic triad which has its root on $\hat{1}$/*do,* other triads can be built by stacking thirds on other scale degrees. One very important triad is the **dominant triad,** so named because its root is the dominant pitch, $\hat{5}$/*sol.* Thus, the pitches in the dominant triad are $\hat{5}$/*sol,* $\hat{7}$/*ti,* and $\hat{2}$/*re.* The dominant appears most frequently before the tonic: V–I.

> The **dominant triad** is a triad whose root is $\hat{5}$/*sol.*

In the minor mode, it is possible to build a dominant triad using the *diatonic* seventh scale degree ($\hat{7}$/*te*) as the third of the chord. However, for now, we will use only the *raised* seventh scale degree—the leading tone ($\uparrow\hat{7}$/*ti*)—as the third of the dominant triad in the minor mode: $\hat{5}$/*sol*–$\uparrow\hat{7}$/*ti*–$\hat{2}$/*re.* In tonal music, this is by far the most common form of the dominant triad in the minor mode.

We will label triads with Roman numerals representing the scale degree of the root, using upper case for major triads, lower case for minor. Thus, a tonic triad is labeled I or i (major or minor) whereas a dominant triad is labeled V (for now, always major).

The following melody clearly presents both tonic and dominant triads in several places. Note the circled pitches and the triads they form:

"Das Steckenpferd," German folk song

Some melodies skip around among the members of a chord. In measure 5 of the example above, the melody skips from $\hat{2}$/*re* to $\hat{7}$/*ti* to $\hat{5}$/*sol.* We have encountered skips to $\hat{7}$/*ti* as prefix neighbors to $\hat{1}$/*do,* but here the skip to $\hat{7}$/*ti* is part of a larger group of skips among the members of the dominant triad.

Skips within the Dominant Triad

The diagram below shows the skips smaller than an octave you might encounter when a melody outlines the dominant triad:

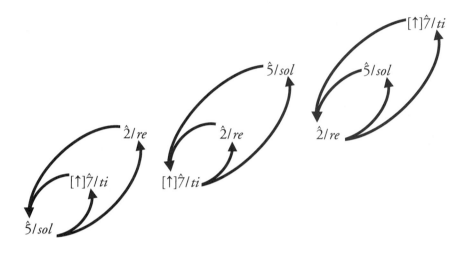

You will be able to hear, read, and perform such skips more easily if you think of them as part of the prevailing harmony and if you practice various skips among the members of particular chords.

<hr>

EXERCISES

1. Arpeggiate from tonic to dominant and back on syllables. Do each in both major and minor mode (use the major dominant triad with ↑7̂/*ti* in minor mode). Use even quarter notes with a quarter rest between chords, and keep a steady tempo.

   a. First, arpeggiate as root-position triads, in which the tonic begins on 1̂/*do* and the dominant begins on 5̂/*sol*. Leap both up and down to reach 5̂/*sol* in the dominant chord as shown below:

   1̂/*do* 3̂/*mi* 5̂/*sol* 3̂/*mi* 1̂/*do*   5̂/*sol* 7̂/*ti* 2̂/*re* 7̂/*ti* 5̂/*sol*   1̂/*do* 3̂/*mi* 5̂/*sol* 3̂/*mi* 1̂/*do*

   1̂/*do* 3̂/*mi* 5̂/*sol* 3̂/*mi* 1̂/*do*   5̂/*sol* 7̂/*ti* 2̂/*re* 7̂/*ti* 5̂/*sol*   1̂/*do* 3̂/*mi* 5̂/*sol* 3̂/*mi* 1̂/*do*

b. Then, begin your arpeggiation on 1̂/*do*, 3̂/*mi*/*me*, and 5̂/*sol* as shown below. Connect to the dominant triad using the closest possible voice leading, as indicated by dotted slurs. For instance, when you begin the tonic triad on 1̂/*do*, the closest member of the dominant triad to 1̂/*do* is 7̂/*ti*.

1̂/*do* 3̂/*mi* 5̂/*sol* 3̂/*mi* 1̂/*do*   7̂/*ti* 2̂/*re* 5̂/*sol* 2̂/*re* 7̂/*ti*   1̂/*do* 3̂/*mi* 5̂/*sol* 3̂/*mi* 1̂/*do*

3̂/*mi* 5̂/*sol* 1̂/*do* 5̂/*sol* 3̂/*mi*   2̂/*re* 5̂/*sol* 7̂/*ti* 5̂/*sol* 2̂/*re*   3̂/*mi* 5̂/*sol* 1̂/*do* 5̂/*sol* 3̂/*mi*

5̂/*sol* 1̂/*do* 3̂/*mi* 1̂/*do* 5̂/*sol*   5̂/*sol* 7̂/*ti* 2̂/*re* 7̂/*ti* 5̂/*sol*   5̂/*sol* 1̂/*do* 3̂/*mi* 1̂/*do* 5̂/*sol*

c. Do the same type of arpeggiation again from the top down.

5̂/*sol* 3̂/*mi* 1̂/*do* 3̂/*mi* 5̂/*sol*   5̂/*sol* 2̂/*re* 7̂/*ti* 2̂/*re* 5̂/*sol*   5̂/*sol* 3̂/*mi* 1̂/*do* 3̂/*mi* 5̂/*sol*

1̂/*do* 5̂/*sol* 3̂/*mi* 5̂/*sol* 1̂/*do*   7̂/*ti* 5̂/*sol* 2̂/*re* 5̂/*sol* 7̂/*ti*   1̂/*do* 5̂/*sol* 3̂/*mi* 5̂/*sol* 1̂/*do*

3̂/*mi* 1̂/*do* 5̂/*sol* 1̂/*do* 3̂/*mi*   2̂/*re* 7̂/*ti* 5̂/*sol* 7̂/*ti* 2̂/*re*   3̂/*mi* 1̂/*do* 5̂/*sol* 1̂/*do* 3̂/*mi*

I I⁶ I⁶₄ V I

2. Practice the following skips in both major and minor modes:

   • from any pitch in the dominant triad to any other pitch in the dominant triad;
   • from any pitch in the tonic triad to any pitch in the dominant triad;
   • from any pitch in the dominant triad to any pitch in the tonic triad.

3. Learn to play the I–V–I progression as block chords on the piano (or other keyboard) in all major and minor keys.

LISTENING

Melodic Dictation

Listen to excerpts 25.1–25.10 and write out the pitches and rhythms for each. Listen carefully for areas that outline or imply the dominant triad. Circle these areas and label them with the Roman numeral V.

Exercise	Clef	Tonic	Bottom number in meter sign
25.1	bass	F♯	2
25.2	treble	D♭	4
25.3	treble	A♭	4
25.4	bass	E	8
25.5	treble	B	4
25.6	bass	E	4
25.7	bass	G	2
25.8	treble	F	8
25.9	treble	B	4
25.10	bass	D	4

READING AND SIGHT SINGING

Sing the following melodies on syllables while conducting. For each excerpt, locate the places where the pitches outline a dominant chord. Spend half of your practice time accompanying yourself with block tonic and dominant chords on the piano. Use your eyes (looking for chord tones) and your ears (listening for which chord sounds best) to determine which chords belong where.

**Excerpts for reading and sight singing
from the
Anthology for Sight Singing
219–241**

26 THE C CLEFS: ALTO AND TENOR CLEFS

In addition to the treble and bass clefs, two other clefs appear frequently in both ancient and modern music: the alto and tenor clefs. They both operate on the principle of identifying where middle C falls on the staff.

Just as the G clef shows the position of G and the F clef shows the position of F, there is a **C clef,** the center of which shows the position of middle C. It looks like this:

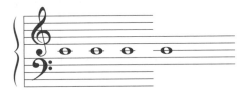

(Although it may look at first more like a "B," the symbol is indeed a fancy, stylized "C.")

> The center of a **C clef** shows the position of middle C.

The Alto Clef in Relation to the Grand Staff

On the grand staff, middle C appears on a ledger line between the staves. If we imagine that the ledger line for middle C becomes an independent staff line of its own, we can create a new five-line staff by extending that line and the two lines above it and below it, as shown below:

Then, we can center a C clef on that line on our new five-line staff:

The C clef takes on specific names depending on its location in the staff. When it is placed on the third line, as above, we call it the **alto clef,** and the lines and spaces represent the following pitches:

> The **alto clef** is a C clef placed on the third line of a five-line staff.

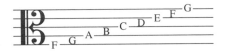

The alto clef consists of the top two lines from the bass clef staff (the alto clef's bottom two lines), a middle C line (the alto clef's middle line), and the bottom two lines from the treble clef staff (the alto clef's top two lines). As you read and write in the alto clef, think of working directly in this middle-of-the-grand-staff pitch space.

The Tenor Clef in Relation to the Grand Staff

When we extend this middle C line and use three lines from the bass clef staff and only one from the treble, middle C falls on the *fourth* line of this new staff, as indicated by the C clef:

When the C clef is placed on the fourth line, as above, we call it the **tenor clef,** and the lines and spaces represent the following pitches:

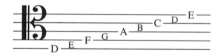

> The **tenor clef** is a C clef placed on the fourth line of a five-line staff.

As with the alto clef, it is important to think of the tenor clef as occupying space near the center of the grand staff.

Musicians sometimes refer to the C clef as a "movable" clef. Whereas it may appear that this clef can move up or down on a seemingly fixed five-line staff, the C clef stays in the same place (on middle C) and its different incarnations are a result of which five lines surround that fixed clef. This may be a bit hard to see at first, but your ability to adopt this way of thinking about C clefs will have profound effects on your fluency with them.

Key Signatures in Alto and Tenor Clefs

You should become familiar with the positions of the sharps and flats in key signatures in the alto and tenor clefs. Note the different arrangement of sharps in the tenor clef:

Uses for C Clefs

C clefs have been used for centuries, and you will encounter both alto and tenor clefs in music from the past and the present. Music of the Middle Ages, Renaissance, and Baroque eras was written using a variety of clefs. In order to read original manuscripts and printed music from these eras, you must be able to read the clefs in which they were written. Some nineteenth- and twentieth-century scores also use alto or tenor clef for certain bass-clef instruments—such as bassoon, trombone, cello, and even double bass—when their ranges extend above middle C. In modern scores, the alto clef appears most frequently in the viola part. Although viola passages in higher registers occasionally appear in treble clef, the standard clef for viola is the alto clef.

The ability to think in seven different clefs will be helpful when you learn about transposition (see Chapters 48 and 64). Practice these clefs faithfully in order to become fluent in reading them and notating them.

LISTENING

Melodic Dictation

Listen to excerpts 26.1–26.10 and write out the pitches and rhythms for each, using the indicated clefs.

Exercise	Clef	Tonic	Bottom number in meter sign
26.1	alto	C	4
26.2	alto	F	2
26.3	tenor	C	4
26.4	tenor	E	8
26.5	alto	A	2
26.6	tenor	B	4
26.7	alto	G	8
26.8	alto	E	8
26.9	tenor	F♯	4
26.10	tenor	D♭	8

READING AND SIGHT SINGING

Sing the following melodies on both syllables and letter names while conducting. Learn them on the piano and on at least one other instrument as well.

Excerpts for reading and sight singing
from the
Anthology for Sight Singing
242–265

27 SKIPS TO $\hat{4}$/fa AND $\hat{6}$/la/le AS PREFIX NEIGHBORS

In Chapter 14, we examined the differences between complete and incomplete neighboring notes. We found that $\hat{7}$/ti could occur as an incomplete prefix neighbor to $\hat{1}$/do, and $\hat{2}$/re could occur as an incomplete prefix neighbor to $\hat{1}$/do or $\hat{3}$/mi. The pitches $\hat{4}$/fa and $\hat{6}$/la/le can also appear as prefix neighbors, as this chapter will demonstrate.

Skips to $\hat{4}$/fa and $\hat{6}$/la/le as Prefix Upper Neighbors

The following excerpt from a song by Louise Reichardt shows a skip to $\hat{6}$/la as a prefix upper neighbor to $\hat{5}$/sol in measures 8–9, and a skip to $\hat{4}$/fa as a prefix upper neighbor to $\hat{3}$/mi in measures 9–10 (marked by circles and braces).

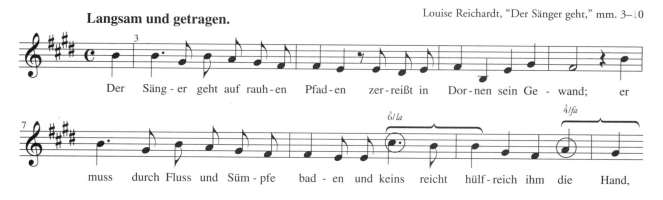

Langsam und getragen.

Louise Reichardt, "Der Sänger geht," mm. 3–10

Der Säng-er geht auf rauh-en Pfad-en zer-reißt in Dor-nen sein Ge-wand; er

muss durch Fluss und Süm-pfe bad-en und keins reicht hülf-reich ihm die Hand,

Rewrite each of these figures as we did in Chapter 14, first making them complete neighboring notes, and then eliminating the prefix neighbor. Sing these recompositions, and then sing the original. The key to all of these versions is thinking of $\hat{5}$/sol and $\hat{3}$/mi as structural points of arrival.

Skips to these prefix upper neighbors also occur in minor mode, so that $\hat{4}$/fa resolves to $\hat{3}$/me and $\hat{6}$/le resolves to $\hat{5}$/sol, as shown in the example below.

J. S. Bach, *Well-Tempered Clavier*, Book II, Fugue in F♯ minor (No. 14), BWV 883, mm. 1–4

Skips to $\hat{4}$/fa as a Prefix Lower Neighbor

In measures 5–6 of the following example, $\hat{4}$/fa appears as a prefix neighbor to $\hat{5}$/sol.

Giacomo Carissimi, Cantata *Serenata "I Naviganti" (Sciolto havean),* "Amanti, che dite," mm. 3–6 (1653)

A - man - ti, che di - te, che di - te?

Although it appears in a variety of settings, this leap to 4̂/*fa* as a prefix neighbor to 5̂/*sol* occurs most frequently in the bass voice as part of a descending leap from 1̂/*do*.

EXERCISES

1. For each of these familiar tunes, determine the scale degrees of its pitches, so that you can sing each tune on its proper syllables. Do the work entirely *in your mind,* without the aid of any instrument or writing.

   • Hark, the Herald Angels Sing

   • Happy Birthday to You

   • The Holly and the Ivy

   Memorize each of these tunes on the proper syllables.

2. The following pairs of sequentials can help you to internalize skips to 4̂/*fa* and 6̂/*la*/*le* as prefix neighboring notes. Learn these sequentials on syllables, memorizing the pattern first, then singing them without looking at the notation. Imagine these sequentials in various keys as you sing them, thinking of letter names and visualizing the appropriate pitches. Learn version (a) of the sequential first, then (b). Then practice rearranging measures of version (b).

   Create and sing other versions of these sequentials beginning and ending on scale degrees other than 1̂/*do*.

   Rework each of these sequentials in the minor mode, using the harmonic form of the minor scale. Also try them in natural and melodic minor.

1. (a)

(b)

2. (a)

(b)

3. (a)

(b)

Melodic Dictation

Listen to excerpts 27.1–27.10 and write out the pitches and rhythms for each.

Exercise	Clef	Tonic	Bottom number in meter sign
27.1	treble	A	4
27.2	bass	G	4
27.3	bass	G♭	8
27.4	treble	E♭	2
27.5	bass	C♯	8
27.6	treble	G♭	4
27.7	treble	D	4
27.8	bass	B	2
27.9	alto	C	4
27.10	tenor	D	2

Prepare the following melodies, singing them on syllables while conducting. Identify all skips to $\hat{4}$/*fa* and $\hat{6}$/*la*/*le* as prefix neighbors. Where possible, rewrite them, first making them complete neighbors, and then eliminating the prefix entirely. Practice them both ways before returning to the original.

**Excerpts for reading and sight singing
from the
Anthology for Sight Singing
266–301**

28 SEXTUPLE DIVISION OF THE BEAT IN COMPOUND METERS

The shortest rhythms we have encountered in compound meters have been one-third of a beat long. These values can be further subdivided in half, creating *six* equal parts, also referred to as sextuple division of the beat.

The Principle of Sextuple Division

Sing the following Polish folk song ("You'll Climb the Mountain") while conducting with a simple triple pattern:

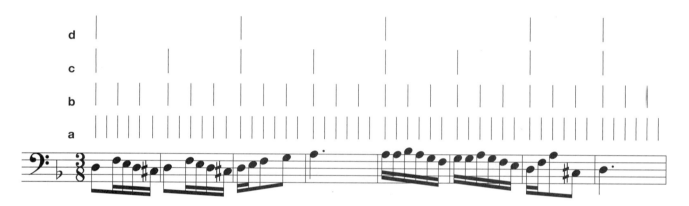

Let's examine four layers of pulse in this melody. Level **a** consists of the shortest note values—sixteenth notes—and the most rapid steady pulse. The eighth-note pulse in level **b** is formed by pairs of sixteenth notes. In level **c,** the measure is formed by groups of three eighth notes, and pairs of measures group to form level **d.** Combining two $\frac{3}{8}$ measures creates the familiar compound duple meter $\frac{6}{8}$, as shown below.

If you perform this melody in $\frac{3}{8}$, you conduct the eighth note of level **b,** and the smallest division is one-half of a beat. If you perform the same melody in $\frac{6}{8}$, you conduct the dotted quarter note of level **c,** and the smallest division becomes one-sixth of a beat. In subdividing the beat in compound meter, you create sextuple division of the beat.

Sing the Polish folk melody again, this time conducting the dotted quarter note in $\frac{6}{8}$. It is important to feel the eighth-note pulse dividing each conducting beat into three parts, so that you can subdivide those eighth notes evenly into sixteenth notes.

In the Takadimi system, sextuple division of the beat starts with the pattern for triple division of the beat (Ta-ki-da) and inserts syllables with the same vowel sounds in between to reflect the subdivision into six parts: **Ta**-va-**ki**-di-**da**-ma.

Combinations Involving Sextuple Division

Sextuple divisions of the beat combine with other beat divisions to form various rhythms. The following table shows typical combinations involving sextuple division down the left-hand column (shown in protonotation, with a single beat divided into three parts by the vertical lines), the same rhythms in Takadimi, and the music notation that represents each of those rhythms in eighth-note and then quarter-note compound meters.

pattern	Takadimi	$\frac{6}{8}$ $\frac{9}{8}$ $\frac{12}{8}$	$\frac{6}{4}$ $\frac{9}{4}$ $\frac{12}{4}$
|– – |– – |– –|	Ta va ki di da ma		
|—|– – |– –|	Ta ki di da ma		
|– – |—|– –|	Ta va ki da ma		
|– – |– – |—|	Ta va ki di da		
|—|—|– –|	Ta ki da ma		
|—|– – |—|	Ta ki di da		
|– – |—|—|	Ta va ki da		
|—+– |– –|	Ta di da ma		
|—+– |—|	Ta di da		
|—+—|– –|	Ta da ma		
|– – |—+—|	Ta va ki		

Learn to recognize these rhythms at sight. Focus on the beat and perform each of these various combinations as a unit, rather than trying to figure out each note in the group.

Similarly, work at recognizing these rhythms by ear. Learn to hear the groups in each beat as a unit that you can notate as a single pattern, rather than having to figure out each division of every beat.

EXERCISES

Write the following familiar tunes in compound meters using various beat units. Some of the pitch materials are more advanced than those covered in this book thus far; you may choose either to notate only the rhythms or to try your hand at the pitches as well.

• Silent Night
• Rockabye Baby
• My Bonnie Lies Over the Ocean
• Did You Ever See a Lassie?
• The First Nöel (through "in fields where they lay")

LISTENING

As you begin taking dictation and transcription using sextuple beat divisions in compound meters, you must pay careful attention to at least three levels of pulse: the measure, the beat, and the triple division of the beat.

If you are still using (or at least thinking in) protonotation, you may find it particularly helpful to use pulse lines to represent all of these levels. So, for example, the pulse-grid for compound duple meter would look like this:

$$| \; | \; | \; | \; | \; | \; | \; | \; | \; | \; | \; | \; | \; | \; | \; |$$

Using a pulse-grid that marks each of the triple beat divisions in compound meter makes it much easier to be specific about where (when) the sextuple divisions fall.

Melodic Dictation

Listen to excerpts 28.1–28.5 and write out the pitches and rhythms for each.

Exercise	Clef	Tonic	Bottom number in meter sign
28.1	bass	E	8
28.2	treble	A	8
28.3	treble	D	8
28.4	alto	B	8
28.5	tenor	F♯	16

Melodic Transcription

Transcribe excerpts 28.6–28.8. Take as many listenings and as much time between them as necessary, but be certain to write down as many aspects of the performances as you can, including timbre, tempo, articulation, rubato, and so forth.

Exercise	Clef	Tonic	Bottom number in meter sign
28.6	treble	C	4
28.7	bass	D	8
28.8	treble	B♭	8

READING AND SIGHT SINGING

Prepare the following melodies, singing on syllables while conducting. Conduct the beat level but establish and maintain the internal feel of the triple beat divisions and the sextuple divisions within them.

**Excerpts for reading and sight singing
from the
Anthology for Sight Singing
302–322**

REPEAT SIGNS

Repetition occurs at many different levels in music, from individual beats or measures to large sections. These repetitions may be indicated by a variety of symbols.

Repeat Bars

Among the simplest of repeat signs is the *repeat bar*, which appears facing either to the right or to the left, as shown below in "Twinkle, Twinkle, Little Star":

"Twinkle, Twinkle, Little Star," European-American folk song

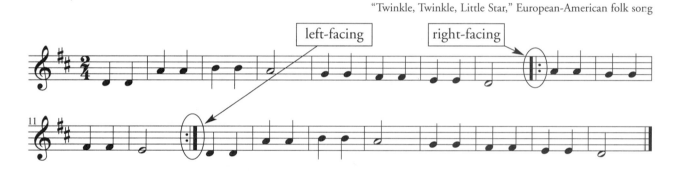

If the first repeat bar you encounter is a right-facing one, you will continue through it until you reach a left-facing one. Then you will return to the right-facing one, repeat the entire section, and move on. If the first repeat bar you encounter is a left-facing repeat bar, you will return to the beginning of the piece (or movement), repeat the entire section, then move on.

Multiple Endings

When a section of music repeats but with a different ending the second time through, it is often notated with *first* and *second* endings. You read the first pass directly through the first ending to the repeat bar, return to the beginning of the section, read the second pass up through the measure immediately before the first ending, then jump directly to the second ending and continue from there. The following short folk song is written using first and second endings:

"V'la p'tit Jean qui prend sa serpe," French folk song

Da Capo, Dal Segno, Fine, and Coda

The phrase *Da Capo* (abbreviated *D.C.*) means "from the top" (literally "from the head"). It instructs you to return to the beginning of the piece, even if this requires jumping over other repeat signs. It is often used in ABA forms with the term *Fine* ("end") printed at the end of the A section. The phrase "*Da Capo al Fine*" ("from the beginning to the 'end'") typically appears at the end of the B section, so you read the A section (passing over the *Fine*), read the B section, then return to the beginning of the A section and stop at the *Fine*. "Twinkle, Twinkle, Little Star" exhibits a small ABA form, and it can be notated this way. Note that the B section contains its own internal repeat, which is executed before the *Da Capo* instruction.

"Twinkle, Twinkle, Little Star," European-American folk song

The phrase *Dal Segno* ("from the sign"), or its abbreviation *D.S.*, represents a similar process, but it instructs you to return to a symbol—usually 𝄋 (occasionally ⊕)—printed above an earlier spot in the music. It is also often combined with *Fine* so that you pass over the sign and *Fine* the first time. Then, upon encountering the instruction *Dal Segno al Fine*, you return to the sign and read only as far as the *Fine* mark.

"Du, du, liegst mir im Herzen," German folk song

A coda (literally, "tail") is an ending section that can be combined with these other signs in various ways. In its most explicit form, the phrase "*Da Capo al Segno e poi la Coda*" ("from the beginning to the sign and afterward, the coda") appears below a measure. When you first encounter the sign—usually ⊕ (occasionally 𝄋)—read through it. Then, when you reach the *Da Capo* instruction, return to the beginning and read only as far as the sign, then jump to the coda (which is often marked with a corresponding sign).

"V'la p'tit Jean qui prend sa serpe," French folk song

Not all such notations are so explicit. For example, many times only the words *Da Capo* are printed, leaving readers to navigate to the coda on their own. Nonetheless, the underlying principles remain the same. In your music reading, you will encounter various combinations of these indications. You can use the principles you have learned here to decode the various directions you find.

Repeated Beats and Measures

The repetition of smaller units of music can also be indicated by symbols.

Ludwig van Beethoven, Symphony No. 6, Op. 68 ("Pastoral"), mvt. 5, mm. 260–264 (1808)

In the example above, the slash (╱) instructs performers to repeat the contents of the previous beat exactly, and the symbol ✗ instructs them to repeat the contents of the previous measure exactly.* Similarly, the symbol ✗ may be placed across the barline between two measures to indicate the repetition of the two previous measures. You will find some small variations on these symbols, but their essential function will remain the same.

---

*Sometimes, if the beat contains nothing but sixteenth notes, two slashes are used, and three are used for thirty-second notes. But the single slash often applies to *all* repeated beats.

Prepare the following melodies, singing on syllables while conducting. Be certain to observe all of the repeat signs carefully in your performances.

Excerpts for reading and sight singing
from the
Anthology for Sight Singing
323–333

THE SUBDOMINANT TRIAD

A Triad Built on 4̂/*fa*

In addition to having roots on the first and fifth scale degrees, triads may also be built on the fourth scale degree, which is also known as the subdominant. A triad with a root on the fourth scale degree is called a subdominant triad. It frequently appears as a preparation for the dominant: IV–V.

In the following melody, the pitches in measure 5—G♭, B♭, and D♭—form a triad whose root is scale degree 4̂. Thus, this is a subdominant triad.

"Kein Feuer, keine Kohle kann brennen so heiß," German folk song

In the major mode, the syllables in the subdominant triad are 4̂/*fa*, 6̂/*la*, 1̂/*do* (a major triad). In the minor mode, the third is different: 4̂/*fa*, 6̂/*le*, 1̂/*do* (a minor triad). Note the minor quality of both the tonic and subdominant triads in the following excerpt:

Felix Mendelssohn, Piano Trio No. 2, Op. 66, mvt. 1, mm. 23–26 (1845)

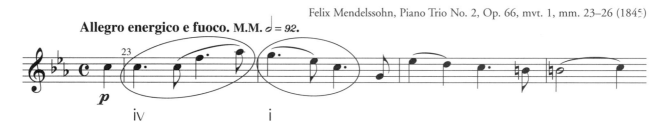

Skips within the Subdominant Triad

The following diagram illustrates the skips smaller than an octave you might encounter when a melody outlines the subdominant triad:

134

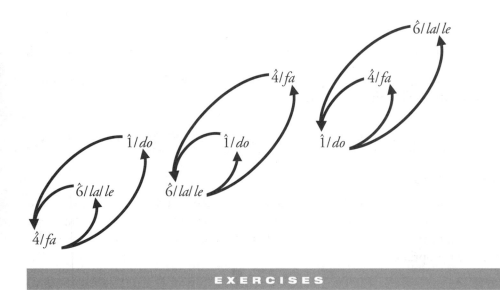

EXERCISES

1. For each of these familiar tunes, determine the scale degrees of its pitches, so that you can sing each tune on its proper syllables. Do the work entirely *in your mind,* without the aid of any instrument or writing.

   • Oh, Susanna

   • On Top of Old Smokey

   • Old Folks At Home (Swanee River)

   • Camptown Races (Doo-dah)

   • Somewhere Over the Rainbow (first "half")

   Memorize each of these tunes on the proper syllables.

2. Arpeggiate the I–IV–V–I progression on syllables in both major and minor mode (use the major dominant triad with ↑$\hat{7}$/*ti* in minor mode). Use the following rhythm for each triad: ♩♩♩♩♩𝄾

   a. First arpeggiate root-position triads (I–IV–V–I). You should be able to leap both up and down to reach $\hat{4}$/*fa* in the subdominant chord:

   (I) $\hat{1}$/*do* $\hat{3}$/*mi* $\hat{5}$/*sol* $\hat{3}$/*mi* $\hat{1}$/*do*   (IV) $\hat{4}$/*fa* $\hat{6}$/*la* $\hat{1}$/*do* $\hat{6}$/*la* $\hat{4}$/*fa*

   (V) $\hat{5}$/*sol* $\hat{7}$/*ti* $\hat{2}$/*re* $\hat{7}$/*ti* $\hat{5}$/*sol*   (I) $\hat{1}$/*do* $\hat{3}$/*mi* $\hat{5}$/*sol* $\hat{3}$/*mi* $\hat{1}$/*do*

   b. Then, arpeggiate in close voice leading from the bottom up, beginning with $\hat{1}$/*do*, $\hat{3}$/*mi*/*me*, and $\hat{5}$/*sol* as the lowest voice. (Review Chapter 25 for how to proceed with this exercise.)

   c. Do this again in close voice leading from the top down.

3. Practice the following skips in both major and minor modes:

   • from any pitch in the subdominant triad to any other pitch in the subdominant triad;

   • from any pitch in the tonic triad to any pitch in the subdominant triad;

- from any pitch in the subdominant triad to any pitch in the tonic triad;

- from any pitch in the subdominant triad to any pitch in the dominant triad.

4. Learn to play the I–IV–V–I progression as block chords on the piano (or other keyboard) in all major and minor keys.

LISTENING

Melodic Dictation

Listen to excerpts 30.1–30.10 and write out the pitches and rhythms for each following the given instructions. Listen carefully for areas that outline or imply the subdominant triad. Circle these areas and label them with the Roman numeral IV or iV as appropriate.

Exercise	Clef	Tonic	Bottom number in meter sign
30.1	treble	F♯	2
30.2	treble	B♭	8
30.3	treble	D	8
30.4	bass	F	2
30.5	bass	B	4
30.6	treble	A♭	4
30.7	bass	C	8
30.8	bass	F♯	4
30.9	tenor	E	4
30.10	alto	C	2

READING AND SIGHT SINGING

Sing the following melodies on syllables while conducting. For each excerpt, locate the places where the pitches outline a subdominant chord. Spend half of your practice time accompanying yourself with block tonic, dominant, and subdominant chords on the piano. Use your eyes (looking for chord tones) and your ears (listening for which chord sounds best) to determine which chords belong where.

Excerpts for reading and sight singing
from the
Anthology for Sight Singing
334–366

31 SYNCOPATION

Thus far, most of the rhythms we have encountered clearly articulate most of the beats within each measure. The ties and dots that first appeared in Chapter 12 can upset this regularity slightly by extending notes and eliminating articulations on certain beats. Syncopation provides another means of altering regular metric divisions by shortening notes and skipping articulations on subsequent beats.

The Metric and Rhythmic Structure of Syncopation

Study and sing the rhythms of the following spiritual:

"Who's That Yonder?" North American spiritual, mm. 1–8

In measures 7–8, the ties eliminate the articulations on the second beat of measure 7 and the downbeat of measure 8. The duration of the first note in measure 7 has been "cut short" by a half beat, so that the subsequent two notes appear a half beat early.

Musicians refer to such rhythms as **syncopation** (literally, a "cutting short" of the normal metric divisions). Syncopation begins with a single instance of cutting a beat short, creating a condition that might last for only a beat or two or for many measures. Syncopations can be notated in two ways: with ties (as above) or by combining tied notes into one note (as below).

> **Syncopation** occurs when the duration of a note is cut short, eliminating articulations on the following beat or beats.

"Who's That Yonder?" North American spiritual, mm. 1–8

Performing Syncopation

There are two useful strategies for learning to read and perform syncopation. Strategy A temporarily removes the syncopation by lengthening the first note that has been cut short. For example, in the spiritual above, if we were to lengthen the first note of measure 7 to a full beat, the subsequent notes would fall clearly on the beat:

Perform this altered version while conducting, then go back and perform the original.

Strategy B involves three steps that can be practiced using a neutral syllable, Takadimi, or pitch syllables.

1. Articulate the beat that the syncopated note skips. Below the following excerpt, we've divided each syncopated quarter note into two eighth notes.

Andantino sostenuto e cantabile   W. A. Mozart, "Io non chiedo, eterni Dei," K. 316 (300^b), mm. 22–29 (1779)

2. Soften the articulation (with an "h") for the part of the syncopation where the beat should occur.

3. Sing without any articulation of the syncopated beats, sustaining each note for its full value. This will produce the original, syncopated rhythms.

EXERCISES

1. Write out the rhythms of each of the following familiar tunes using at least two different beat units. Use ties for some and, for others, combine ties into full values when possible.

- Camptown Races (Doo-dah)
- Old Folks At Home (Swanee River)
- When the Saints Go Marching In
- Oh, Susanna
- Shoo Fly (Don't Bother Me)
- The Hokey Pokey

Melodic Dictation

Listen to excerpts 31.1–31.10 and write out the pitches and rhythms for each, following the given instructions. As you listen, tap the beat or conduct to maintain a steady sense of pulse through any syncopation.

Exercise	Clef	Tonic	Bottom number in meter sign
31.1	treble	G♭	4
31.2	bass	G	4
31.3	treble	C♯	2
31.4	bass	G	4
31.5	bass	D♭	2
31.6	treble	E♭	4
31.7	bass	D♯	8
31.8	treble	D	4
31.9	alto	F	4
31.10	tenor	A	8

Prepare the following melodies, singing on syllables while conducting. As you practice, employ one or both of the strategies for reading syncopation suggested in this chapter.

**Excerpts for reading and sight singing
from the
Anthology for Sight Singing
367–382**

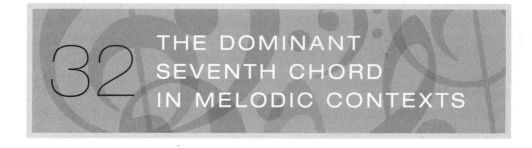

32 THE DOMINANT SEVENTH CHORD IN MELODIC CONTEXTS

In addition to outlining triads, melodies also outline seventh chords. In this chapter, we will focus on the dominant seventh chord and how it functions in melodic contexts.

The Dominant Seventh Chord as a Stack of 3rds

If you view the formation of a seventh chord as a stack of four pitches built up in 3rds, you see it as a chord with a third, fifth, and seventh above its root. A seventh chord whose root is the dominant pitch—$\hat{5}$/*sol*—is identified as the dominant seventh chord.

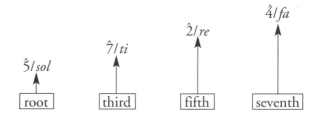

The pitches of the dominant seventh chord do not always appear melodically in a simple stack of 3rds. They can appear in any order, such as that found in the circled notes in the following excerpt:

Giacomo Puccini, *La Rondine*, "Chi il bel sogno di Doretta," mm. 1–4 (1917)

The Dominant Seventh as Passing Tone

It is often helpful to think of the seventh of a dominant seventh chord in terms of its function as a passing tone. The seventh is produced melodically by passing from the root of the chord *down* through the seventh. This motion continues beyond the seventh, resolving down and by step.

In the following excerpt, the dominant triad (B♭–D–F) is fully formed in measures 14–15, and the seventh (A♭) appears only at the end of measure 15 as a passing tone from B♭ to G.

W. A. Mozart, *Don Giovanni*, K. 527, Act I, "Ah chi mi dice mai," mm. 13–16 (1787)

The passing motion may derive from more indirect linear connections involving other intervening notes, as shown in measure 2 of the following example:

Giuseppe Tartini, Violin Sonata Op. 2, No. 4 [Brainerd e7], mvt. 1, mm. 1–2 (1743)

The dominant triad (B–D♯–F♯) is clearly outlined on beat 2, followed by a skip down to the seventh of the chord (A). Rather than thinking of the leap from F♯ down to A as a major 6th, you may find it easier to hear this A($\hat{4}$/*fa*) as a passing note from B($\hat{5}$/*sol*) at the beginning of the beat to G($\hat{3}$/*me*) in the next beat.

Skips within the Dominant Seventh Chord

Skips to each of the members of the dominant seventh chord include those we have already addressed within the dominant triad, as well as those to and from the added seventh, $\hat{4}$/*fa*. This new pitch forms six skips (three ascending and three descending) to and from the other members of the dominant seventh chord. Pay special attention to these skips in your sight singing and dictation.

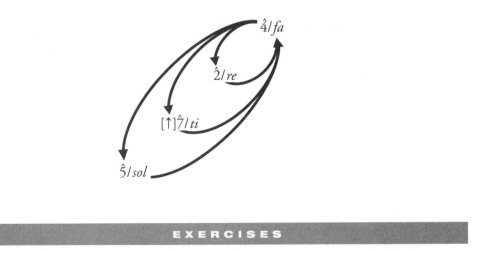

1. For each of the following familiar tunes, determine the scale degrees of its pitches so that you can sing each tune on its proper syllables. Do the work entirely *in your mind* without the aid of any instrument or writing.

- Brahms's Lullaby
- Silent Night
- Rudolph, the Red-Nosed Reindeer (through "reindeer games")

Memorize each of these tunes on the proper syllables.

2. Arpeggiate the I–V⁷–I progression on syllables in both major and minor mode (use the major third in the dominant seventh—↑$\hat{7}$/*ti*—in minor mode). Use the rhythm (♩♩♩♩♩𝄾) for each triad and (♩♩♩♩♩♩♩𝄾) for each seventh chord.

   a. First, arpeggiate root-position chords (I–V⁷–I). You should be able to leap both up and down to reach $\hat{5}$/*sol* in the dominant chord:

   (I) $\hat{1}$/*do* $\hat{3}$/*mi* $\hat{5}$/*sol* $\hat{3}$/*mi* $\hat{1}$/*do*

   (V⁷) $\hat{5}$/*sol* $\hat{7}$/*ti* $\hat{2}$/*re* $\hat{4}$/*fa* $\hat{2}$/*re* $\hat{7}$/*ti* $\hat{5}$/*sol*

   (I) $\hat{1}$/*do* $\hat{3}$/*mi* $\hat{5}$/*sol* $\hat{3}$/*mi* $\hat{1}$/*do*

   b. Then, arpeggiate in close voice leading from the bottom up, beginning with $\hat{1}$/*do,* $\hat{3}$/*mi*/*me,* and $\hat{5}$/*sol* as the lowest voice. (Review Chapter 25 for how to proceed with this exercise.) Be especially careful to sing a melodic 2nd between $\hat{4}$/*fa* and $\hat{5}$/*sol.*

   c. Do this again in close voice leading but from the top down.

3. Practice the following skips in both major and minor modes:
   - from any pitch in the dominant seventh chord to any other pitch in that same chord;
   - from any pitch in the tonic triad to any pitch in the dominant seventh chord;
   - from any pitch in the dominant seventh chord to any pitch in the tonic triad.

4. Learn to play the I–V⁷–I progression as block chords on the piano (or other keyboard) in all major and minor keys.

LISTENING

Melodic Dictation

Listen to excerpts 32.1–32.10 and write out the pitches and rhythms for each, following the given instructions.

Exercise	Clef	Tonic	Bottom number in meter sign
32.1	bass	B	8
32.2	treble	A♭	4
32.3	bass	A	8
32.4	treble	D	4
32.5	bass	B♭	8
32.6	treble	C	2
32.7	bass	E	4
32.8	treble	F	4
32.9	tenor	G♯	4
32.10	alto	B♭	8

READING AND SIGHT SINGING

Prepare the following melodies, singing on syllables while conducting.

**Excerpts for reading and sight singing
from the
Anthology for Sight Singing
383–426**

33 INTRODUCTION TO HARMONIC SINGING

You have been working with the I, IV, and V triads and the V⁷ chord in melodic dictation and singing. Now you can begin to develop a deep sense of how these chords sound, so you can recognize them when you hear them and auralize them as you read music.

Harmonic Singing

Occasionally, music moves in relatively straightforward ways among the pitches of various triads. For instance, the folk melody we examined in Chapter 25 neatly outlines some tonic and dominant triads (circled):

"Das Steckenpferd," German folk song

In other measures, it is not as obvious which triads, if any, are being implied. Sing the melody, and accompany yourself by playing tonic and dominant triads. Which chords sound best with which beats in those other measures? Notice how hearing the entire chord makes it easier to sing individual pitches from it (particularly when the music skips around).

In this and other similar tunes, you get the sense that a chord seems to *govern* a span of music, only to be displaced at a certain point by another chord. Many pieces of music—even unaccompanied single-line melodies—can imply chords that seem to govern the notes that they span. Once you sense which chord is implied, the span in turn seems to be governed by this chord.

As you sing, listen consciously for which chords govern various beats and measures. Develop your ability to auralize each new chord as it arrives (and perhaps even a bit before).

Triads and Inversions

Every triad can be sung (and heard) in three basic configurations determined by which chord member is the lowest pitch. When the root is the lowest pitch, the chord is said to be in root position. When the third is the lowest, it is in first inversion, and when the fifth is the lowest, it is in second inversion.

Any single pitch can function as the root, third, or fifth, above which three different triads can be formed. In the example below, the pitch C serves three different functions in three different triads. The numbers below each triad (the "figured bass") represent how the triads are formed by placing intervals above the lowest pitch. The first triad places a 5th and a 3rd above the C; the second places a 6th and a 3rd above it; and the third places a 6th and a 4th above it. To the right of each triad are labels showing how these pitches function as the root, third, and fifth of each triad.

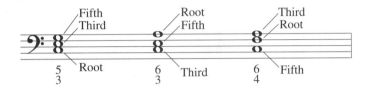

In figured bass, the first set of figures is usually omitted, so that the absence of figured bass stands for a ⁵₃ chord. The second set is usually abbreviated, so that a single 6 stands for a ⁶₃ chord. They are spelled out here for sake of clarity.

The intervals specified by these figures can appear in any octave, but as long as the same chord member remains in the bass, the inversion remains unchanged.

Names for Scale Degrees and Chords

We learned the functional names for scale degrees in Chapter 2, and these same names will be applied to chords as well. Once you determine the root of a chord, use the name of its scale degree as the name of the chord. You should learn and use these names for all the scale degrees and their associated chords. The list below expands the one in Chapter 2 by including scale degrees in the minor mode. The most significant change regards scale degree $\hat{7}$, which is named *subtonic* for $\flat\hat{7}$ / *te* and *leading tone* for $\hat{7}$ / *ti*.

$\hat{1}$ / do	$\hat{2}$ / re	$\hat{3}$ / mi / me	$\hat{4}$ / fa	$\hat{5}$ / sol	$\hat{6}$ / la / le	$\flat\hat{7}$ / te	$\hat{7}$ / ti
Tonic	Supertonic	Mediant	Subdominant	Dominant	Submediant	Subtonic	Leading tone

EXERCISES

1. Review various melodies you've sung in recent weeks, with an eye (and ear) towards which chords govern each beat or measure. Where do the chords change? Which chords work best in each spot? Are there other chords that could substitute for any of these? How is such substitution possible?

   Mark each of these melodies with appropriate symbols for the chords that seem to govern certain beats or measures. Prepare these melodies and sing on syllables while conducting. Spend half of your practice time accompanying yourself on the piano or other chord-producing instrument. This will help to get the sounds of the chords "in your ear." Spend the rest of your practice time singing the tunes while auralizing but not playing those chords. Maintain these procedures as you continue to study music in this manual and in your other pursuits as a musician.

2. The following table outlines a new sequential, the "inversion sequential," which will prepare you for singing and hearing triads in different inversions. This sequential constructs three different triads above each scale degree. For example, the triads I, vi^6, and IV$^6_4$ appear above 1̂/*do*.

																			5̂/*sol*	5̂/*sol*	5̂/*sol*
																4̂/*fa*	4̂/*fa*	4̂/*fa*			
													3̂/*mi*	3̂/*mi*	3̂/*mi*					3̂/*mi*	3̂/*mi*
										2̂/*re*	2̂/*re*	2̂/*re*					2̂/*re*	2̂/*re*	2̂/*re*		
							1̂/*do*	1̂/*do*	1̂/*do*					1̂/*do*	1̂/*do*	1̂/*do*					1̂/*do*
				7̂/*ti*	7̂/*ti*	7̂/*ti*					7̂/*ti*	7̂/*ti*	7̂/*ti*					7̂/*ti*	7̂/*ti*	7̂/*ti*	
	6̂/*la*	6̂/*la*	6̂/*la*					6̂/*la*	6̂/*la*						6̂/*la*	6̂/*la*	6̂/*la*				
5̂/*sol*					5̂/*sol*	5̂/*sol*	5̂/*sol*					5̂/*sol*	5̂/*sol*	5̂/*sol*							
		4̂/*fa*	4̂/*fa*	4̂/*fa*					4̂/*fa*	4̂/*fa*	4̂/*fa*										
3̂/*mi*	3̂/*mi*					3̂/*mi*	3̂/*mi*	3̂/*mi*													
			2̂/*re*	2̂/*re*	2̂/*re*																
1̂/*do*	1̂/*do*	1̂/*do*																			

Each group of three adjacent columns shares a single lowest pitch. The first column in each group outlines a $^5_3$ chord. The second column moves the top pitch up one scale degree to form a $^6_3$ chord. The third column moves the middle pitch up one scale degree to form a $^6_4$ chord.

Sing the inversion sequential by arpeggiating the syllables in each column, from bottom to top and back down again, using this rhythm (♩♩♩♩♩ 𝄾). Then move on to the next column. Here is how the first few columns would be performed in C major:

etc.

To sing the inversion sequential in the minor mode, you will have to make certain decisions about when to sing the diatonic seventh scale degree and when to raise it. Common usage of the chords containing 7̂ indicates that 7̂/*te* be used in all mediant chords (III, III^6, and III$^6_4$) and ↑7/*ti* be used in all dominant and leading-tone chords (V, V^6, V$^6_4$, vii°, vii°^{6}, and vii°$^6_4$).

If the end of the inversion sequential in the minor mode is too difficult at this time, eliminate the chords ii°$^6_4$ and III$^6_4$. This should make the transitions between the chromatically shifting chords containing 6̂/*le*, 7̂/*te*, and ↑7/*ti* easy enough to navigate.

Use the following four procedures in your work on the inversion sequential:

a. Memorize the inversion sequential in both major and minor modes, not by reading it from a page, but by thinking of the $^5_3$–$^6_3$–$^6_4$ process applied to each scale degree;

b. As you sing, be able to name the root and inversion of each triad you sing (for example, if stopped while singing "$\hat{4}$/ *fa* $\hat{6}$/ *la* $\hat{2}$/ *re* $\hat{6}$/ *la* $\hat{4}$/ *fa*," you should respond "supertonic first inversion" or "ii⁶");

c. When you can sing the inversion sequential from memory, practice skipping to any scale degree and singing the three inversions ($\frac{5}{3}$, $\frac{6}{3}$, $\frac{6}{4}$) in order above that pitch;

d. Finally, be able to sing any of the three inversions in any order immediately above any given scale degree.

34 INTRODUCTION TO HARMONIC LISTENING: HARMONIC RHYTHM AND CADENCES

When most musicians listen to tonal music, they are aurally and mentally aware of the chords that govern each beat or measure. This is true for music in multiple parts and for single-line music that outlines or implies certain chords. In upcoming chapters, we will investigate specific techniques for discerning the individual chords you hear. In this chapter, we will consider ways in which you can focus your harmonic listening first in a narrow way, by listening for the speed or pace at which chords change, and then in a broad way, by listening for goals of harmonic motion.

Harmonic Rhythm

> The durations governed by successive chords are called **harmonic rhythm.**

The term **harmonic rhythm** refers to the collective rhythm of chord changes, or the durations governed by the successive chords.

In the following excerpt by Schubert, each successive measure is governed by a chord different from that in the previous measure.

Franz Schubert, Impromptu, Op. 90, No. 4, D. 899, mm. 47–50 (1827?)

The harmonic rhythm of this excerpt is completely regular: one chord per measure. You can map this out on a pulse-graph like this:

In the excerpt below, the harmonic rhythm is not regular, and the chords last different durations.

Robert Lowry, "Nothing But the Blood" ("Plainfield"), Gospel hymn, mm. 1–4

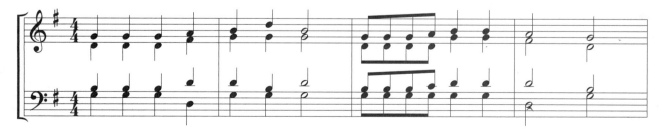

The pulse-graph of this passage shows where the chords change:

You must become keenly aware of the harmonic rhythm of whatever passage you are listening to. Knowing *when* the chords change is an important step towards identifying the chords you hear.

Tonic and Dominant as Harmonic Origins and Goals

Another aspect of harmonic listening involves paying special attention to the points of departure and goals of harmonic motion. Much tonal music is grouped into phrases (or other analogous time-spans), each of which has one chord as its point of departure and one chord as its goal.

Each of the chords that make up a phrase is important, but the opening and final chords usually serve special roles. The first chord establishes the harmonic origin of the phrase, and the last chord provides the target towards which harmonies progress.

Listening for harmonic origins and goals can help you make sense out of long passages of music, even whole movements and complete pieces. Much of the harmonic logic and rhetoric of tonal music is rooted in these harmonic anchors.

Tonic and dominant chords account for the vast majority of the harmonic origins and goals in tonal music. For example, listen to the following short phrase from the hymn "Old Hundredth":

Loys Bourgeois, "Old Hundredth," mm. 1–3 (1551)

You may not be able to identify every chord in this phrase, but your already highly developed sense of tonic should help you feel the tonic chord at both the opening and closing of the phrase. This short phrase feels complete, as it is bounded harmonically by the tonic as both origin and goal.

Listen to the second phrase of this hymn and perform the same broad listening task—where does it begin and end harmonically?

Loys Bourgeois, "Old Hundredth," mm. 4–6 (1551)

This phrase also departs from the tonic, but this time it aims for the dominant. This produces a feeling of incompleteness and gives the second phrase a sense of harmonic fulfillment yet to come.

A phrase may also begin on the dominant, although this is not as common. Listen to the opening of the third movement from Haydn's Symphony No. 100 and pay special attention to the initial and final chords in each of its four-measure phrases.

Joseph Haydn, Symphony No. 100 (Hob. I:100), mvt. 3, mm. 1–8 (piano reduction)

Moderato

The first phrase leads from the tonic in measure 1 to the dominant in measure 4, whereas the second phrase begins on the dominant in measure 5 and returns to the tonic in measure 8. In leading from the dominant to the tonic, the second phrase produces a particularly strong feeling of closure.

The following pulse-graph of these eight measures shows the phrases with two large phrase marks above and the chords of departure and arrival below.

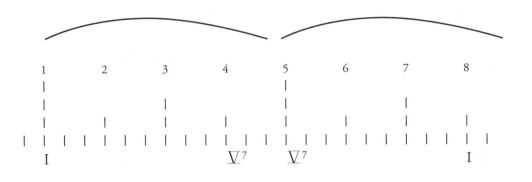

Cadences

In the above excerpt by Haydn, the ends of the phrases are clearly delineated in two ways. Metrically, each phrase completes a four-measure group built from levels of pulse as shown in the pulse-graph above. Rhythmically, they are delineated by the only rests that appear in the passage. (Such rhythmic delineation can also result from a lengthening or slowing down in the rhythm.) This metric and rhythmic punctuation coincides with the harmonic goal of each phrase.

This kind of confluence of harmonic motion and metric and rhythmic punctuation creates a very specific kind of goal in music. When these forces act together, the point of arrival is called a **cadence.***

Cadences can be classified broadly as either **conclusive** or **inconclusive.** Conclusive cadences end on the tonic. Inconclusive cadences end on some other chord.

A conclusive cadence can also be called **closed** or **full,** to contrast with one that ends with a dominant chord, which is referred to as an **open** or **half** cadence or sometimes a **semicadence.**

Deceptive cadences end on an unexpected chord, something other than tonic or dominant, although this term often applies only to the cadential progression V to vi.

> A **cadence** is created by the confluence of harmonic motion and metric and rhythmic punctuation.

> A **conclusive cadence** ends on the tonic.

> An **inconclusive cadence** ends on some other chord than the tonic.

> A **closed** or **full cadence** ends on the tonic.

> An **open cadence, half cadence,** or **semicadence** ends on the dominant.

> A **deceptive cadence** ends on an unexpected chord.

LISTENING

A. Listen to excerpts 34.1–34.5 and write out a pulse-graph for each. Beneath the graph, indicate where each chord changes.

B. Listen to excerpts 34.6–34.9 and write out a pulse-graph for each. Above the graph, draw phrase marks to show where the phrases begin and end. Below it, write the Roman numeral for each chord at the beginning and end of each phrase.

C. Listen to excerpts 34.10–34.13 and write out a pulse-graph for each. Label each of the cadences as conclusive or inconclusive.

D. Listen to excerpts 34.14–34.17 and write out a pulse-graph for each. Label each of the cadences as full, half, or deceptive.

---

*The word cadence is derived from the Latin word "cadere," which means "to fall."

35 TWO-PART MUSIC

We will now begin to focus on the skills involved in both reading and listening to more than one part at once. This chapter investigates some fundamental aspects of working with multiple parts in the simplest of contexts: two-part music.

Singing Duets

When singing one part in a two-part texture, you should pay attention to *both* parts while singing only one of them. To do this, try to develop what might be called "vertical" peripheral vision—the ability to read symbols on the page above and below where your eyes are focused. You can either focus on the part you are performing while taking in the other part with your vertical peripheral vision, or you can focus between the parts, taking in both parts from the periphery.

Your first priority is to remain synchronized with the other reader. Has either of you dropped a beat or skipped ahead? If so, can you quickly adjust to bring the parts together? You should also coordinate your performance with the other reader in terms of tempo and phrasing, adjusting them together as necessary. Coordination also includes intonation. Spend lots of time performing very slowly and adjusting your pitch to the other part and the overall tonality of the music. You should also adjust the dynamic balance between the parts. Always think about the totality of your performance together.

Playing the Keyboard while Singing

An especially effective way to develop two-part reading is to play one part on the piano while singing the other. This does not make great demands on your skills at the piano—indeed, you'll be playing only a single line on the keyboard. But, it will enable you to read and perform two parts at once. Every musician is up to this task; however, it does require more work from some than from others.

This activity does make great demands on your vertical peripheral vision. Try each of the following strategies to learn which is the most helpful for you: (1) shift your focus back and forth between the staves; (2) focus on one part while reading the other; (3) focus between the staves while reading both parts.

Look (at both parts) and *listen* (to both parts) as you sing and play.

Two-Part Dictation and Transcription

The special kind of focused listening that dictation and transcription demand often makes it difficult to divide attention between parts. You may find that you need to focus on one line to the exclusion of the other for a listening or two. Then, you can concentrate on the other part with subsequent listenings. Focusing on one line to the exclusion of another is a skill that musicians use all the time. Although we *hear* all the parts, we can learn to *listen* to one in particular. As you take two-part dictation and transcription, pay special attention to your ability to focus your attention on individual lines. What factors seem to help or hinder this process?

When focusing your attention on individual lines, you still need to pay attention to contextual cues from one part that will help guide your listening and understanding in the other. Indeed, if we were to develop nothing but our skill at attending to only one line at a time, we would miss another important aspect of multiple-part music—the delightful way lines work *together* in time and tonal space. The principles of rhythm, voice leading, counterpoint, and harmony can guide your listening. Consider how the following features are expressed by multiple parts as they move together.

Rhythm. Pay attention to the aggregate rhythm produced by the articulations of both parts together: Are the rhythms of both parts identical? If not, how do they differ? Is there a constant rhythmic proportion between the two (say, eighths against quarters)? Is one consistently busier than the other? Do they "trade" rhythmic figures?

Consonance and dissonance. Listen for the consonant and dissonant intervals formed by the confluence of the parts. Where do you hear consonances? Do you hear dissonances struck together? Do you hear other dissonances created by voice leading such as passing tones and neighbor tones (see Chapter 45)? How do these dissonances resolve?

Imitation. Does one part copy or imitate the other at a fixed distance, either at the beginning or elsewhere throughout the passage? Do they "trade" pitch or rhythm patterns?

Harmonic rhythm. Take note of the harmonic rhythm formed by the combination of the parts. Which chords do you hear, and where? Just how do the parts create these chords?

The more you think about such questions as you work, the more you will be able to remember and understand, and you will become less of a musical stenographer and more of a sensitive, musical listener.

LISTENING

Two-Part Dictation

Listen to excerpts 35.1–35.10 and write out the pitches and rhythms for each, following the given instructions.

Exercise	Clef	Tonic	Bottom number in meter sign
35.1	grand staff	G	4
35.2	grand staff	E♭	4
35.3	grand staff	D	8
35.4	grand staff	B	4
35.5	grand staff	F	2
35.6	grand staff	C	2
35.7	grand staff	E	4
35.8	grand staff	E	8
35.9	top: alto clef bottom: bass clef	B	4
35.10	top: treble clef bottom: tenor clef	D♭	4

READING AND SIGHT SINGING

Here are some duets culled from earlier material, specially selected for your work on these skills. Prepare the following duets in two different ways:

A. Prepare each individual line, singing on syllables while conducting, to be sung as a duet with a classmate or teacher.

B. Sing the upper part while playing the lower part on the piano (or similar keyboard). Then reverse parts, singing the lower part while playing the upper part.

**Excerpts for reading and sight singing
from the
Anthology for Sight Singing
12, 20, 23, 55, 143, 183, 235, 254, 290, 303, 314, 350–51, 393**

36 INTRODUCTION TO BASS-LINE DICTATION

A very important tool in harmonic listening is the ability to hear and understand the bass line. The bass line has played a central role in harmonic function in Western music for over four hundred years. It has provided the harmonic foundation for most compositional and performance practice in the Baroque, Classical, and Romantic eras, and in much pop and jazz music.

In order to perceive a bass line, you must be able to focus your attention on the lowest voice. This task often comes more easily to jazz and pop musicians, bass players, bass vocalists, keyboard players, and others who have had experience attending to bass lines. Your first responsibility is to determine how easily *you* can listen to and understand bass lines.

Bass-line dictation will help you focus your attention on the bass voice. You will listen to various multiple-part excerpts and write down the bass voice for each. Knowing that you have to write down only the bass lets you shift your attention from the upper voices (especially the melody) to the bass. Use the same attention-shifting skills you used in Chapter 35.

Once you learn to focus your attention on the bass voice, bass-line dictation simply becomes another form of melodic dictation. You can apply all your dictation skills to hearing, remembering, understanding, and notating the bass.

EXERCISES

1. Sing multiple-part music with your classmates. Take turns singing the bass part. Pay special attention to the roles the bass plays in supporting the harmonies above it.

2. Practice bass-line singbacks. Listen to a variety of recordings and performances, and sing back short phrases from the bass. These phrases should be approximately six to ten notes long. Practice working with short phrases in isolation as well as the first and last phrases from a longer section you hear.

LISTENING

Bass-Line Dictation

Listen to excerpts 36.1–36.10 and write out the pitches and rhythms of the bass line for each. (Use the bass clef for all bass-line dictations.)

Exercise	Clef	Tonic	Bottom number in meter sign
36.1	bass	A	4
36.2	bass	E♭	2
36.3	bass	C	4
36.4	bass	B♭	2
36.5	bass	B	8
36.6	bass	G	4
36.7	bass	A♭	4
36.8	bass	F	2
36.9	bass	D	8
36.10	bass	E	4

READING AND SIGHT SINGING

For the following excerpts, sing the bass part while playing the upper parts on the piano. Men should read and play all pitches as written. Women should transpose all parts up one octave.

**Excerpts for reading and sight singing
from the
Anthology for Sight Singing
427–431**

37 ROOT POSITION AND FIRST INVERSION TRIADS

In tonal music, most triads appear in root position or first inversion. Second inversion triads appear less frequently, and they have a special function in tonal music, so we reserve them for a later chapter.

Hearing Intervals above the Bass: $\frac{5}{3}$ and $\frac{6}{3}$ Position

One of the main skills you need for harmonic listening in tonal music is the ability to identify the difference between root position ($\frac{5}{3}$) and first inversion ($\frac{6}{3}$) chords by ear. If you hear a triad outside of any musical context, you can identify its position either holistically or through arpeggiation. (Within musical contexts, you can identify triads with the aid of voice leading, a topic for the next chapter.)

Holistic Identification

When you are able to identify something simply because you know what it is, not because you have analyzed or manipulated it, then you have identified it **holistically.** In general, unfamiliar things require scrutiny. But as the unfamiliar becomes more familiar, we begin to recognize it holistically.

Your ability to identify chords can work this way. For instance, once you learn the difference in sound between triads in $\frac{5}{3}$ and $\frac{6}{3}$ position, in time you may find yourself saying something like "Ah, yes . . . the old familiar $\frac{6}{3}$!" Unfortunately, there is no magic path to this kind of familiarity. Repeated exposure to and identification of chords is the only means of making them more familiar. Therefore, until you reach this level of familiarity, you must employ some other technique of identification.

Identification via Arpeggiation

Attention to the vertical arrangement of the members of a triad can lead to an identification of its inversion. To do this, arpeggiate the notes of any triad you hear and pay special attention to the intervals formed between the bass pitch and the next two members of the triad above the bass, compressing all three notes into a single octave. If the intervals—from the bass up—form two successive 3rds, the triad is in root position. If they form a 3rd followed by a 4th, the triad is in first inversion.

Here's an example. If you were to hear the triad on the left, you could arpeggiate the pitches on the right:

hear this: arpeggiate this:

> A **holistic** approach to listening is somewhat analogous to the way we easily recognize a well-known face, a familiar voice on the telephone, or the taste of a common spice. When you see a friend, you don't recognize that person by consciously thinking, "Hmmmm. Sandy hair. Dark eyebrows. Glasses. Long nose. Square chin. Must be Bob!" On the contrary, you simply see Bob and recognize Bob. Even if Bob has shaved his head and taken to wearing contact lenses, you'll still probably recognize him without apparent analytical thought.

Do not try to place the pitches in their proper octave. Leave the bass voice as the lowest of the three, then arpeggiate directly up from there. Sing the next pitch above the bass that belongs with the chord, then the remaining pitch above that. Try doing this aloud, arpeggiating through the triad members as the chord sounds. Then, try to perform the same arpeggiation by mentally auralizing the pitches without singing.*

This procedure works well on triads played outside of any musical context. When dealing with real musical passages, it works best on pieces with slow harmonic rhythm. The faster the harmonies change, the more difficult it is to arpeggiate every chord.

Harmonic Possibilities above Each Scale Degree

Your bass-line listening skills can be combined with your new skill of identifying $\frac{5}{3}$ and $\frac{6}{3}$ chords to help you develop a methodical way of identifying chords by ear.

If you know the scale degree of the bass note that supports a chord, and you know the inversion of the chord above, then you can simply deduce the root, the Roman numeral, and the figured bass label for the chord. For example, in the major mode if you hear scale degree $\hat{3}$/ *mi* in the bass and a root-position chord above it, then the harmony is iii. In contrast, if you hear scale degree $\hat{3}$/ *mi* in the bass and hear a first-inversion chord above it, then the harmony is I^6.

The following table summarizes these possibilities above all seven diatonic scale degrees in the major mode:

scale degree in bass:	$\hat{1}$	$\hat{2}$	$\hat{3}$	$\hat{4}$	$\hat{5}$	$\hat{6}$	$\hat{7}$
$\frac{5}{3}$ position:	I	ii	iii	IV	V	vi	vii°
$\frac{6}{3}$ position:	vi^6	vii$^{°6}$	I^6	ii^6	iii^6	IV^6	V^6

Construct a similar table in the minor mode. What complications do you encounter?

Before proceeding, review the inversion sequential you learned in Chapter 33.

Arpeggiating Chord Progressions

In earlier chapters, you arpeggiated the tonic, dominant, and subdominant triads in root position and in some inversions based on principles of voice leading. Now, you can begin to arpeggiate chords from Roman numeral and figured bass symbols. For now, we will restrict ourselves to progressions containing only I, IV, and V triads in root position and first inversion for these chord arpeggiations (but not for the inversion sequential).

To sing arpeggiations from chord symbols, first read the Roman numeral and figured bass of each chord to determine if the chord is tonic, dominant, or subdominant, and if the chord is in root position or first inversion. Then, identify the scale degree of the bass note and sing that as the lowest pitch. Begin the arpeggio on that pitch and use the rhythm you have used previously for arpeggios (♩♩♩♩♩𝄾).

---

*Some listeners prefer to arpeggiate both above and below the bass pitch to better identify its membership as root, third, or fifth. This is fine, but do not lose track of which pitch belongs in the bass.

For instance, if you see IV, you would recognize it as a subdominant chord in root position, with 4̂/*fa* in the bass, and arpeggiate 4̂/*fa* 6̂/*la* 1̂/*do* 6̂/*la* 4̂/*fa*. If you see IV⁶, you would recognize it as a subdominant chord in first inversion, with 6̂/*la* in the bass, and arpeggiate 6̂/*la* 1̂/*do* 4̂/*fa* 1̂/*do* 6̂/*la*.

You can read entire chord progressions in this manner. For example, you would arpeggiate the progression I I⁶ IV V I like this:

When moving from one chord to the next, always take the shortest interval between the bass pitches. For example, in moving from I to IV⁶, the shortest interval from 1̂/*do* is *down* to 6̂/*la*. You should only take the larger leap if (1) the shorter path would take you beyond your vocal range, or (2) the progression specifically asks for a certain direction (e.g., the arrow in I ∕ IV⁶ V I, indicates a skip *up* from 1̂/*do* to 6̂/*la*).

Listening to Progressions

You can now combine bass-line dictation skills with chord-identifying skills in order to take harmonic dictation. The listening materials in this chapter will contain only the tonic, dominant, and subdominant triads in root position and first inversion. Therefore, your choices will involve only six chords: I, I⁶, IV, IV⁶, V, and V⁶ (and, of course, their corresponding versions in the minor mode). Notice that each of these chords is supported by a unique bass note.

scale degree in bass:	1̂	2̂	3̂	4̂	5̂	6̂	7̂
5⁄3 position:	I			IV	V		
6⁄3 position:			I⁶			IV⁶	V⁶

Your main job will be to focus on hearing the bass line and determining the harmonic rhythm. In cases where the bass line contains non-chord tones, you will need to determine which bass notes support chords and which are non-chord. Then you can determine which of the three chords you have heard and in which position.

Write out your results in the form of a bass line with accompanying Roman numerals and figured bass symbols. For example, your written response to the harmonic dictation shown below would appear as a single bass line with chord symbols, as in the example on the next page. Your instructor may choose to have you write out the top ("soprano") voice as well.

In upcoming chapters, we will add new chords one by one, so you will have to make more judgments about the harmonies you hear. In the next two chapters, you will learn about some other listening techniques involving voice leading and triad qualities that will help you to make these judgments.

EXERCISES

1. Review the inversion sequential from Chapter 33. Create a version of the sequential in which you sing only a root-position chord followed by a first-inversion chord above each scale degree. In the minor mode, use $\hat{7}$/*te* in the mediant chord and ↑$\hat{7}$/*ti* in the dominant and leading-tone chords. Repeat the first four steps from Chapter 33 on this version of the sequential.

2. Arpeggiate the following chord progressions:

   a. I I⁶ IV V I
   b. i i⁶ iv V i
   c. I V⁶ IV⁶ V I
   d. i V⁶ iv⁶ V i
   e. I IV⁶ V I
   f. i iv⁶ V i
   g. I ╲ IV I⁶ V I
   h. i ╲ iv i⁶ V i

LISTENING

Harmonic Dictation

Listen to excerpts 37.1–37.8 and write out the bass line for each. Then supply the appropriate Roman numerals and figured bass symbols to represent each chord. Your instructor may also choose to have you write out the top ("soprano") voice as well.

Exercise	Tonic	Bottom number in meter sign
37.1	F	2
37.2	A	4
37.3	E	8
37.4	E	8
37.5	C	4
37.6	A	2
37.7	D	8
37.8	E	4

38 INTRODUCTION TO VOICE LEADING

proper introduction to voice leading must begin by distinguishing between a part and a voice. A **part** is a feature of the musical surface, a line performed as a continuity. In ensemble music, a part is just that—the notes played or sung from a single printed part (for example, "Bassoon I"; "Altos"). In keyboard music, parts are those lines separated from one another by the musical texture. A **voice,** on the other hand, is a theoretical construct. Upper voices are the abstract lines formed by the smoothest possible melodic motion from one prevailing harmony to the next.

The following musical excerpt has four parts, as indicated by the direction of the stems. As the anacrusis moves to the downbeat of the first measure, the three upper parts move to different pitches, but they actually just trade places (with some octave differences). The notes F, A, and C are common to both beats. In this sense, there are three upper *voices* that remain on those common tones.

A **part** consists of the notes played or sung from a single printed part. It is more difficult to distinguish separate parts in the notation of keyboard music than those written for single-line instruments. However, composers and editors often differentiate parts through markings such as stem direction, slurs, and dotted lines.

A **voice** is the abstract line formed by the smoothest possible melodic motion from one harmony to the next.

J. S. Bach, Chorale No. 26, "O Ewigkeit, du Donnerwort," mm. 1–2

Hearing Voice Motion above a Bass Line

One important and useful way of listening to harmony is to follow the motion of the upper voices. Since many triads are in either $\frac{5}{3}$ or $\frac{6}{3}$ position, it will be useful to listen for whether an upper voice is sounding a 5th or a 6th above each bass pitch.

The Bach example above offers an excellent opportunity to use voice leading to identify chords. In measure 1, beat 2, with $\hat{2}$/*re* in the bass, a $\frac{5}{3}$ chord would contain the syllables $\hat{2}$/*re,* $\hat{4}$/*fa,* and $\hat{6}$/*la* and a $\frac{6}{3}$ chord would contain the syllables $\hat{2}$/*re,* $\hat{4}$/*fa,* and $\hat{7}$/*ti.* The only difference is the upper voice, which could lie either a 5th or a 6th above the bass—$\hat{6}$/*la* or $\hat{7}$/*ti.* To identify by ear which of these two scale degrees is present during this beat, follow the voice that is on $\hat{1}$/*do* for beat one of the measure. Does $\hat{1}$/*do* descend to $\hat{7}$/*ti* for the second beat? Indeed it does. You could also try following the voice that is on $\hat{5}$/*sol* during the first beat. Does it ascend to $\hat{6}$/*la*? No, it can only move smoothly to $\hat{4}$/*fa.* Thus, the chord on measure 1, beat 2 consists of $\hat{2}$/*re,* $\hat{4}$/*fa,* and $\hat{7}$/*ti*—a leading tone chord in first inversion (vii°⁶).

The downbeat of measure 2 is another good example. The pitch $\hat{4}$/*fa* in the bass could support either a $\frac{5}{3}$ chord ($\hat{4}$/*fa*, $\hat{6}$/*la*, and $\hat{1}$/*do*) or a $\frac{6}{3}$ chord ($\hat{4}$/*fa*, $\hat{6}$/*la*, and $\hat{2}$/*re*). Since the previous harmony (measure 1, beat 4) is a tonic triad, we can trace the $\hat{1}$/*do* voice from that chord into the downbeat of measure 2. Is $\hat{1}$/*do* suspended into that measure, or does it move to $\hat{2}$/*re*?

You will probably find that merely *listening* to the music is often not enough to make such voice leading apparent to you. You'll need to actively *sing* the voice you are following, but don't sing too loudly and overshadow the music itself.

The diagram below illustrates the process we use to determine these chords. The chord members crucial to determining the position of each chord (the 5th and 6th above each bass note) are written above the bass line. The syllables that actually sound in the chorale are underlined, and lines show how you might follow the voices in real time. (The cadence is not marked, under the assumption that its familiar concluding V–I sound can be identified easily in a holistic fashion. If this is not the case for you, continue the voice markings through all chords.)

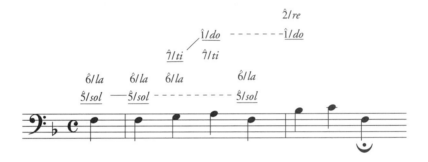

In fact, there are *two* important voices you would need to follow: one in the $\hat{5}$/*sol*–$\hat{6}$/*la* region and another in the $\hat{7}$/*ti*–$\hat{1}$/*do*–$\hat{2}$/*re* region. Many listeners find that as they first learn to follow voices, they need to concentrate on one voice-region during each listening. Try this, returning to a different voice-region on each subsequent listening.

We will call the voice leading at these important spots the *salient* voice leading. Attending to salient voice leading will make it possible for you to identify chords you can't yet identify holistically. The faster and more accurately you can take bassline dictation, the freer you will be to plan for which voices you should follow. If, after taking down a bass line, you can choose which voice(s) you should follow, you will find that identifying the salient voice leading and the harmonies that result from it are well within your grasp.

Once you learn to perceive voice leading in $\frac{5}{3}$ and $\frac{6}{3}$ triads, you will be able to extrapolate these skills into a variety of situations.

As you learn to follow voice leading, you will not only become more adept at identifying which harmonies are products of that voice leading but you will also become a much more sensitive listener in general, attending to the motion of various voices within a wide variety of musical textures.

Voice Leading as an Aid in Reading

An awareness of voice leading can also assist you in reading music. For instance, in the following excerpt by Brahms, the *part* itself skips widely; however, just below the surface of this excerpt, several *voices* are moving smoothly. An awareness of and sensitivity to these voices can go a long way towards making such disjunct music much easier to perform.

Johannes Brahms, *Waltzes,* Op. 39, No. 9, mm. 1–4 (1865)

Imagine the opening pitch D as sustaining through the first full measure; it is not displaced by the next two pitches. Only the C♯ in measure 2 displaces this D, creating a simple voice-leading event—$\hat{1}$/*do* moving to $\hat{7}$/*ti*. This C♯ is then displaced by D at the downbeat of measure 4. Similarly, the F in measure 1 moves to the E in measure 2 and resolves to D in measure 4. The A is a common tone throughout these four measures. This current of smoothly moving voices is illustrated below, first on separate staves and then directly on the melody, with dotted slurs indicating the voice leading in the latter.

Johannes Brahms, *Waltzes,* Op. 39, No. 9, mm. 1–4 (1865)

While reading such music, try to think about where the underlying voices are moving, especially when you are navigating what may at first seem to be some awkward skips.

Compound Melody

A **compound melody** is a melody in which two or more voices seem to progress as equal partners.

A melody in which two or more voices seem to progress as equal partners is called **a compound melody.** As shown in the example below, lines of a compound melody can often be heard as sounding together. The dotted slurs in the music indicate voice leading of the two voices, which are combined below as simultaneous notes.

J. S. Bach, *Well-Tempered Clavier,* Book I, Fugue in C♯ minor (No. 3), BWV 848, mm. 5–7 (1722)

In both listening and reading, recognizing a compound melody can facilitate your work.

EXERCISES

1. Be able to quickly name the syllables of chords in $\frac{5}{3}$ and $\frac{6}{3}$ position above any scale degree. Focus specifically on naming the syllables that differ between these two positions—the 5th and 6th above the given pitch.

2. Memorize the oblique-motion compound-melody sequential shown below. Learn it in the major mode (as shown) and in the three forms of the minor scale (review Chapter 19). Then learn it starting on scale degrees other than $\hat{1}$/*do*.

3. Memorize parallel-motion compound-melody sequentials based on intervals of the 3rd, 4th, 5th, and 6th (sometimes called "broken scales"). You learned the ones based on the 3rd and 5th in the exercises at the end of Chapter 2. Now you can add those based on the 4th and 6th to your repertory.

4. Listen to excerpts from a variety of different compositions. Pick a voice and sing the smooth voice leading as it progresses from one harmony to another. Start with mostly homophonic music, including Bach chorales, Gospel music, and pop music by groups that use vocal harmony, such as the Beatles and the Eagles, for example.

Voice-Leading Drills

Each of the following drills isolates a single voice between the tonic and another chord. The syllables for the two notes in the bass are supplied. For each drill, determine the salient voice leading above the bass that will help you discern the position of the second chord ($\frac{5}{3}$ or $\frac{6}{3}$). Then listen to the chord pair and identify—through the voice leading—the position of the second chord.

The first drill supplies the two choices of salient voice leading ($\hat{1}/do$–$\hat{1}/do$ or $\hat{1}/do$–$\hat{7}/ti$) and the two possible chords (I^6 or iii). Listen to the chord pair and decide which of the two voice-leading results you heard. Circle the correct result ($\hat{1}/do$ or $\hat{7}/ti$). Then circle the chord produced by that voice leading.

For the remaining drills, determine the two possible syllables that would result in chords in $\frac{5}{3}$ or $\frac{6}{3}$ position, what syllable you should trace from the initial tonic chord to arrive at either of those pitches, and the two possible chords that would result from these two different voice-leading choices. Write these possibilities in before listening. Then listen and circle the correct voice leading and resultant chord.

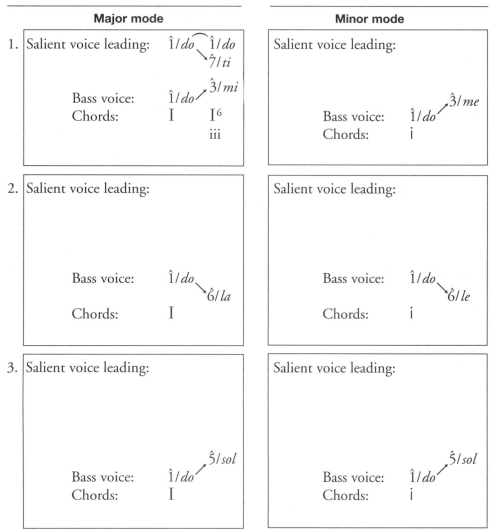

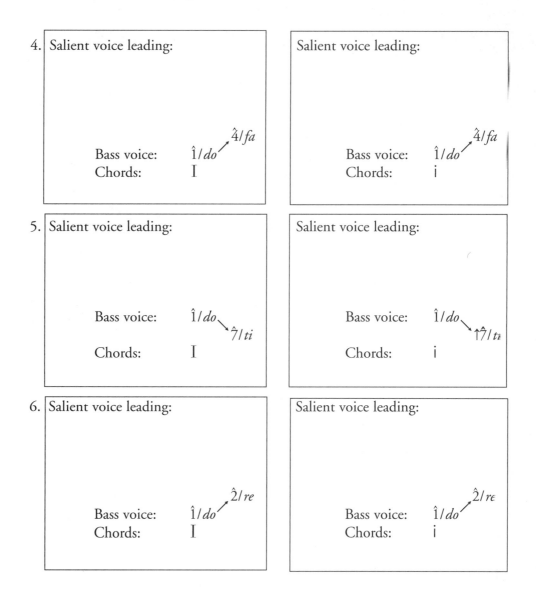

4. Salient voice leading:

Bass voice: $\hat{1}/do$ → $\hat{4}/fa$
Chords: I

Salient voice leading:

Bass voice: $\hat{1}/do$ → $\hat{4}/fa$
Chords: i

5. Salient voice leading:

Bass voice: $\hat{1}/do$ → $\hat{7}/ti$
Chords: I

Salient voice leading:

Bass voice: $\hat{1}/do$ → $\uparrow\hat{7}/ti$
Chords: i

6. Salient voice leading:

Bass voice: $\hat{1}/do$ → $\hat{2}/re$
Chords: I

Salient voice leading:

Bass voice: $\hat{1}/do$ → $\hat{2}/re$
Chords: i

READING AND SIGHT SINGING

Prepare the following melodies, singing on syllables while conducting. Mark some of the voice leading directly on the music, particularly in those spots where it will help you navigate seemingly difficult leaps.

**Excerpts for reading and sight singing
from the
Anthology for Sight Singing
432–455**

39 TRIAD QUALITIES

Just as intervals have qualities (for example, *minor* 6th, *major* 3rd), triads have qualities as well. A triad's quality is determined by the qualities of its component intervals, as shown below:

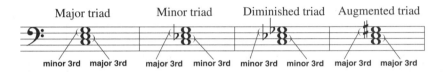

Major, minor, and diminished triads are found in the diatonic pitches in any key, but the augmented triad can be achieved only through the introduction of chromatic pitches.

Although it is easiest to learn these qualities in root-position triads, triads don't always appear in root position. In the following excerpt, a C-major triad appears in the upper part in measure 10 in root position and in the lower part in measure 12 in first inversion. Although the order of the pitches has changed, the triad remains essentially the same and retains its major quality.

George Frideric Handel, *Hercules,* HWV 60, "The smiling hours," mm. 9–13 (1744)

Allegro, ma non troppo.

As a musician, you need to be able to sing these various triad qualities and recognize them by listening.

Change of Quality through Chromaticism

You can alter the quality of *any* chord by chromatically changing one or more of its pitches. The two kinds of chromatic alteration that occur most frequently are the leading tone in the minor mode and the Picardy third.

We have already encountered the use of the leading tone (↑$\hat{7}$/*ti*) in the minor mode when we used the major dominant in the minor mode (review Chapter 25). When $\hat{7}$/*te* is changed to ↑$\hat{7}$/*ti* as the third of a dominant triad, the quality of that triad changes from minor to major and it functions as a true dominant chord. Similarly, the leading-tone triad (see Chapter 40) can be built only on the true leading tone, which, in the minor mode, requires changing $\hat{7}$/*te* to ↑$\hat{7}$/*ti*, resulting in the diminished triad ↑$\hat{7}$/*ti*–$\hat{2}$/*re*–$\hat{4}$/*fa*. You'll begin to recognize these uses of ↑$\hat{7}$/*ti* as a usual part of tonal function in the minor mode.

The Picardy third results from a chromatically raised third of a tonic chord in the minor mode at a cadence. Replacing $\hat{3}$/*me* with ↑$\hat{3}$/*mi* changes the minor tonic chord (i) to a major tonic (I♯), which produces a striking effect and lends a bright quality to the cadence. The upper-case Roman numeral indicates the chord's major quality, and the sharp following the Roman numeral indicates its raised third. (Technically, a natural sign should be used in minor keys with more than one flat. What would you do in the keys of D♯ minor and A♯ minor?)

We will encounter other chord-quality changes when we investigate chromatic harmony—especially applied chords—in later chapters.

EXERCISES

1. List all the diatonic triads in the major mode and identify each by its quality. Memorize these.

2. List all the diatonic triads in the minor mode and identify each by its quality. Memorize these.

3. Identify the chords whose quality is affected by changing from natural minor to harmonic minor and from natural minor to melodic minor. Which of these changes have composers used most frequently?

4. Arpeggiate the four triad qualities in root position starting with any given pitch. For example, if given an F♯ and told to arpeggiate a minor triad, you would sing F♯–A–C♯. Sing these on a neutral syllable and on letter names.

5. Once you have established a key, arpeggiate a root-position triad from any given scale degree. Name the quality of each triad you arpeggiate.

6. Learn to identify the qualities of triads by listening to triads played melodically (heard as separate pitches) and harmonically (with all pitches sounded at once). Work on them in two ways:

   • *Sing* the pitches that make up the triad and identify the component intervals;

   • *Listen* to the overall effect and affect of each triad and learn to recognize each triad quality as a whole.

7. Listen to a variety of compositions, particularly those that are homophonic in texture, and identify the quality of the triads you hear. Be aware that context can be very deceptive. Some listeners who can identify triad qualities in isolation have difficulty when those triads are surrounded by other chords and function within a key.

40 THE LEADING-TONE TRIAD

We have discussed triads with roots on the first, fourth, and fifth scale degrees—the tonic, subdominant, and dominant triads. A triad whose root is on the seventh scale degree when it appears as a leading-tone (on [↑]$\hat{7}$/*ti* but not $\hat{7}$/*te*) is known as the leading-tone triad. In the following melody, the leading-tone triad is outlined in measures 2–3 and measures 6–7.

W. A. Mozart, German Dance K. 605, No. 3, Trio ("Die Schlittenfahrt") mm. 1–8 (1791)

The leading-tone triad is diminished because it consists of two minor 3rds ([↑]$\hat{7}$/*ti*–$\hat{2}$/*re* and $\hat{2}$/*re*–$\hat{4}$/*fa*). In the major mode, the root is $\hat{7}$/*ti*, but in the minor mode, this triad is based on a chromatically raised root (↑$\hat{7}$/*ti*).* As a result, a leading-tone triad in the minor mode is identical to a leading-tone triad in the parallel major. In the example below, the pitches E♯–G♯–B in measure 1 form a diminished triad whose root is the raised seventh scale degree, E♯.

George Frideric Handel, *Siroe*, HWV 24, "Gelido, in ogni vena scorrer mi sento il sangue," mm. 7–10 (1728)

When writing in the minor mode, don't forget to use the appropriate accidental when you hear ↑$\hat{7}$/*ti*.

Skips within the Leading-Tone Triad

You may have already noticed that the members of the leading-tone triad form a subset of the dominant seventh chord—a chord with which you have been working since Chapter 32. So, the leading tone triad presents no new interval or scale-degree relationships, as shown in the diagram on the next page:

---

*There is a triad based on the *diatonic* seventh scale degree in minor ($\hat{7}$/*te*). It is sometimes called the subtonic triad, and it plays a role in applied harmonies and modulations (see Chapters 58, 61, and 70).

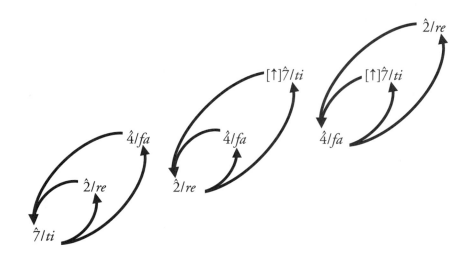

Listening for Leading-Tone Triads

We will now add vii° and vii°⁶ to the triads in our listening repertory. This means that when $\hat{2}$/*re* is in the bass, vii°⁶ is now a possibility (rather common), and when [↑]$\hat{7}$/*ti* is in the bass, vii° is now a possibility (rare by comparison).

When [↑]$\hat{7}$/*ti* in the bass supports a chord in root position the result is the leading-tone triad (vii°), although diminished triads rarely appear in root position. When [↑]$\hat{7}$/*ti* in the bass supports a chord in first inversion, the result is a dominant triad ($\underline{V}^6$). The two triads differ in terms of quality and voice leading. Listen especially for $\hat{4}$/*fa* or $\hat{5}$/*sol* in some upper voice. This small chart will help you distinguish between the two:

	With $\hat{7}$/*ti* in the bass	
$\frac{5}{3}$	[↑]$\hat{7}$/*ti*–$\hat{2}$/*re*–$\hat{4}$/*fa*	vii° (diminished)
$\frac{6}{3}$	[↑]$\hat{7}$/*ti*–$\hat{2}$/*re*–$\hat{5}$/*sol*	$\underline{V}^6$ (major)

The leading-tone triad functions as a dominant chord does, so it is often found in progressions leading directly to the tonic.

EXERCISES

1. Be able to sing skips from any pitch to any other within the leading-tone triad.

2. In each of these preliminary exercises for chord arpeggiation, sing each chord one after the next. Think of these as symbol-reading, solmization, and singing exercises, not as actual chord progressions.

   a. I vii° $\underline{V}^6$ I

   b. I $\underline{V}^6$ vii° I

   c. i vii° $\underline{V}^6$ i

   d. i $\underline{V}^6$ vii° i

3. Learn to arpeggiate the following chord progressions.

a. I I⁶ vii°⁶ I

c. I IV vii°⁶ I V⁶ I

b. i i⁶ vii°⁶ i

d. i vii°⁶ i⁶ iv V i

4. Learn to play the above progressions on the piano (or similar keyboard).

LISTENING

Melodic Dictation

Listen to excerpts 40.1–40.4 and write out the pitches and rhythms for each, following the given instructions.

Exercise	Clef	Tonic	Bottom number in meter sign
40.1	treble	A	4
40.2	bass	B	2
40.3	alto	G	4
40.4	tenor	D♭	4

Harmonic Dictation

Listen to excerpts 40.5–40.10 and write out the bass line for each. Then supply the appropriate Roman numerals and figured bass symbols to represent each chord. Your instructor may also choose to have you write out the top ("soprano") voice as well.

Exercise	Tonic	Bottom number in meter sign
40.5	A♭	8
40.6	B	4
40.7	A	8
40.8	C	2
40.9	D	4
40.10	B♭	4

READING AND SIGHT SINGING

Prepare the following melodies, singing on syllables while conducting. Some of these melodies clearly outline leading-tone chords, whereas others merely emphasize skips to [↑]$\hat{7}$/ *ti,* $\hat{2}$/ *re,* or $\hat{4}$/ *fa.* Some of these might even have been harmonized in their original contexts by other chords (for example, a skip to $\hat{4}$/ *fa* harmonized by a subdominant triad). Nonetheless, all these melodies offer opportunities to practice skips to these scale degrees.

Excerpts for reading and sight singing
from the
Anthology for Sight Singing
456–485

THE SUPERTONIC TRIAD

The triad whose root is the second scale degree ($\hat{2}$/ *re*) is called the supertonic triad. The supertonic triad occurs frequently as a preparation for the dominant, as in the ii–$\underline{V}$ or ii^6–$\underline{V}$ progression.

The Triad with $\hat{2}$/*re* as Root

In the major mode, the supertonic triad is a minor triad, which consists of a minor 3rd ($\hat{2}$/ *re*–$\hat{4}$/ *fa*) and a major 3rd ($\hat{4}$/ *fa*–$\hat{6}$/ *la*). In the example below, the circled pitches in measure 2 (A–C–E) form a supertonic triad ($\hat{2}$/ *re*–$\hat{4}$/ *fa*–$\hat{6}$/ *la*), which is a minor triad.

Sehr mässig.   Robert Schumann, *Lieder-Album für die Jugend*, Op. 79, No. 4, "Frühlingsgruss," mm. 1–4 (1849)

So sei ge - grüsst viel tau - sent - mal,   hol - der, hol - der Früh - ling!

In the minor mode, the supertonic triad is diminished because it consists of two minor 3rds ($\hat{2}$/ *re*–$\hat{4}$/ *fa* and $\hat{4}$/ *fa*–$\hat{6}$/ *le*). In the excerpt below, the supertonic chord (E–G–B♭) is circled, and it is a diminished triad ($\hat{2}$/ *re*–$\hat{4}$/ *fa*–$\hat{6}$/ *le*).

Jean-Philippe Rameau, *Platée,* Act II, 2nd Minuet, mm. 1–10 (1745)

Skips within the Supertonic Triad

The diagram on the next page illustrates the scale-degree combinations of the skips smaller than an octave you might encounter when music outlines the supertonic triad.

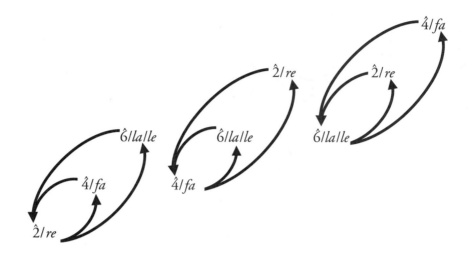

Listening for Supertonic Triads

The supertonic chord occurs frequently in both root position (above $\hat{2}$/*re*) and first inversion (above $\hat{4}$/*fa*). For both, it is important to listen for voice leading and the quality of the triad.

When $\hat{2}$/*re* in the bass supports a $\frac{5}{3}$ chord the result is the supertonic triad—ii or ii°. However, when $\hat{2}$/*re* in the bass supports a $\frac{6}{3}$ chord the result is the leading-tone triad in first inversion—vii°⁶. Listen especially for $\hat{6}$/*la*/*le* or $\hat{7}$/*ti* in an upper voice and for the quality of the chord. The chart below summarizes the differences between the two:

	With $\hat{2}$/*re* in the bass	
$\frac{5}{3}$	Major mode: $\hat{2}$/*re*–$\hat{4}$/*fa*–$\hat{6}$/*la*	Major mode: ii (minor)
	Minor mode: $\hat{2}$/*re*–$\hat{4}$/*fa*–$\hat{6}$/*le*	Minor mode: ii° (diminished; rare)
$\frac{6}{3}$	Both modes: $\hat{2}$/*re*–$\hat{4}$/*fa*–[↑]$\hat{7}$/*ti*	Both modes: vii°⁶ (diminished)

When $\hat{4}$/*fa* in the bass supports a $\frac{5}{3}$ chord the result is the subdominant triad—IV or iv. However, when $\hat{4}$/*fa* in the bass supports a $\frac{6}{3}$ chord the result is the supertonic triad in first inversion—ii⁶ or ii°⁶. Listen especially for $\hat{1}$/*do* or $\hat{2}$/*re* in an upper voice and for the quality of the chord (major, minor, or diminished). The differences are summarized below:

	With $\hat{4}$/*fa* in the bass	
$\frac{5}{3}$	Major mode: $\hat{4}$/*fa*–$\hat{6}$/*la*–$\hat{1}$/*do*	Major mode: IV (major)
	Minor mode: $\hat{4}$/*fa*–$\hat{6}$/*le*–$\hat{1}$/*do*	Minor mode: iv (minor)
$\frac{6}{3}$	Major mode: $\hat{4}$/*fa*–$\hat{6}$/*la*–$\hat{2}$/*re*	Major mode: ii⁶ (minor)
	Minor mode: $\hat{4}$/*fa*–$\hat{6}$/*le*–$\hat{2}$/*re*	Minor mode: ii°⁶ (diminished)

1. Be able to sing skips from any pitch to any other within the supertonic triad.

2. In each of these preliminary exercises for chord arpeggiation, sing each chord one after the next. Think of these as symbol-reading, solmization, and singing exercises, not as actual chord progressions.

   a. I ii vii°⁶ I⁶   c. i ii° vii°⁶ i⁶
   b. I IV ii⁶ V I   d. i iv ii°⁶ V i

3. Learn to arpeggiate the following chord progressions.

   a. I I⁶ ii⁶ V I
   b. i i⁶ ii°⁶ V i
   c. I V⁶ I ii⁶ V I
   d. i V⁶ i ii°⁶ V i
   e. I IV⁶ ii⁶ V I V⁶ I
   f. i i⁶ ii°⁶ V i vii°⁶ i⁶ iv V i

4. Learn to play the above progressions on the piano (or similar keyboard).

Melodic Dictation

Listen to excerpts 41.1–41.4 and write out the pitches and rhythms for each, following the given instructions.

Exercise	Clef	Tonic	Bottom number in meter sign
41.1	bass	E♭	8
41.2	treble	E	4
41.3	tenor	G♭	2
41.4	alto	D	8

Harmonic Dictation

Listen to excerpts 41.5–41.12 and write out the bass line for each. Then supply the appropriate Roman numerals and figured bass symbols to represent each chord. Your instructor may also choose to have you write out the top ("soprano") voice as well.

Exercise	Tonic	Bottom number in meter sign
41.5	D	4
41.6	B	8
41.7	D♭	2
41.8	A	4
41.9	F	2
41.10	E	8
41.11	C	2
41.12	A	4

READING AND SIGHT SINGING

Prepare the following melodies, singing on syllables while conducting. Some of these melodies clearly outline supertonic chords, whereas others merely emphasize skips to $\hat{2}$/ *re,* $\hat{4}$/ *fa,* or $\hat{6}$/ *la*/ *le.* Some of these might even have been harmonized in their original contexts by other chords (for example, a skip to $\hat{4}$/ *fa* harmonized by a subdominant triad). Nonetheless, all these melodies offer opportunities to practice skips to these scale degrees.

**Excerpts for reading and sight singing
from the
Anthology for Sight Singing
486–523**

42 THE SUBMEDIANT TRIAD

The triad whose root is the sixth scale degree (6̂/ *la*/ *le*) is called the submediant triad. It appears frequently as a preparation for the supertonic, as in the circle-of-fifths progression: ⅵ–ⅱ̄–V̄–Ⅰ̄. In addition, the submediant can substitute for the tonic, as in the deceptive cadence: V̄–ⅵ.

The Triad with 6̂/ *la*/ *le* as Root

In the major mode, the submediant triad is built on 6̂/ *la* and it is minor. A submediant triad (6̂/ *la*–1̂/ *do*–3̂/ *mi*) is outlined in measure 7 of the excerpt below:

Ludwig van Beethoven, String Quartet Op. 135, mvt. 3, mm. 3–10 (1826)

Lento assai, cantante e tranquillo.

In the minor mode, the submediant triad is built on 6̂/ *le* and it is major. A submediant triad (6̂/ *le*–1̂/ *do*–3̂/ *me*) is outlined in measures 4 and 8 of the excerpt below:

Andante   Peter Ilich Tchaikovsky, *Swan Lake,* Op. 20, No. 9, Finale, mm. 2–9 (1876)

Skips within the Submediant Triad

The diagram below presents an inventory of the skips smaller than an octave you might encounter when music outlines the submediant triad.

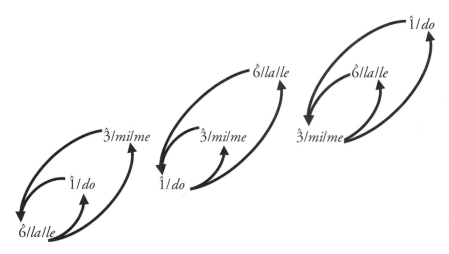

Listening for Submediant Triads

The submediant chord occurs frequently in root position (above $\hat{6}$/*la*/*le*) and, less often, in first inversion (above $\hat{1}$/*do*). For both, you will want to listen for voice leading and chord quality.

When $\hat{6}$/*la*/*le* in the bass supports a $\frac{5}{3}$ chord the result is the submediant triad—vi or VI. However, when $\hat{6}$/*la*/*le* in the bass supports a $\frac{6}{3}$ chord the result is the subdominant triad in first inversion—IV^6 or iv^6. Listen especially for $\hat{3}$/*mi*/*me* or $\hat{4}$/*fa* in an upper voice and for the quality of the chord. The chart below summarizes the differences:

	With $\hat{6}$/*la*/*le* in the bass	
$\frac{5}{3}$	Major mode: $\hat{6}$/*la*–$\hat{1}$/*do*–$\hat{3}$/*mi*	Major mode: vi (minor)
	Minor mode: $\hat{6}$/*le*–$\hat{1}$/*do*–$\hat{3}$/*me*	Minor mode: VI (major)
$\frac{6}{3}$	Major mode: $\hat{6}$/*la*–$\hat{1}$/*do*–$\hat{4}$/*fa*	Major mode: IV^6 (major)
	Minor mode: $\hat{6}$/*le*–$\hat{1}$/*do*–$\hat{4}$/*fa*	Minor mode: iv^6 (minor)

A first inversion triad—vi^6 or VI^6—can occur above $\hat{1}$/*do* in the bass, but this is less common. A root-position I or i is much more common above $\hat{1}$/*do*. Listen especially for $\hat{5}$/*sol* or $\hat{6}$/*la*/*le* in an upper voice and for the chord quality. The chart below summarizes the differences:

	With $\hat{1}$/*do* in the bass	
$\frac{5}{3}$	Major mode: $\hat{1}$/*do*–$\hat{3}$/*mi*–$\hat{5}$/*sol*	Major mode: I (major)
	Minor mode: $\hat{1}$/*do*–$\hat{3}$/*me*–$\hat{5}$/*sol*	Minor mode: i (minor)
$\frac{6}{3}$	Major mode: $\hat{1}$/*do*–$\hat{3}$/*mi*–$\hat{6}$/*la*	Major mode: vi^6 (minor)
	Minor mode: $\hat{1}$/*do*–$\hat{3}$/*me*–$\hat{6}$/*le*	Minor mode: VI^6 (major)

EXERCISES

1. Be able to sing skips from any pitch to any other within the submediant triad.

2. In each of these preliminary exercises for chord arpeggiation, sing each chord one after the next. Think of these as symbol-reading, solmization, and singing exercises, not as actual chord progressions.

   a. I vii° vi V̲ I   c. i ↘ V̲ V̲I̲ V̲ i

   b. I vi⁶ vii°⁶ I⁶   d. i V̲I⁶ vii°⁶ i⁶

3. Learn to arpeggiate the following chord progressions.

   a. I ↘ V̲ vi I̲V̲⁶ V̲ ↗ I

   b. i ↘ V̲ V̲I iv⁶ V̲ ↗ i

   c. I ↘ vi I̲V̲ V̲ I V̲⁶ I

   d. i ↘ V̲I iv V̲ i V̲⁶ i

   e. I I⁶ vi I̲V̲⁶ ii⁶ V̲ I

4. Learn to play the above progressions on the piano (or similar keyboard).

LISTENING

Melodic Dictation

Listen to excerpts 42.1–42.4 and write out the pitches and rhythms for each, following the given instructions.

Exercise	Clef	Tonic	Bottom number in meter sign
42.1	bass	F	8
42.2	treble	B♭	4
42.3	alto	F♯	4
42.4	tenor	F	2

Harmonic Dictation

Listen to excerpts 42.5–42.12 and write out the bass line for each. Then supply the appropriate Roman numerals and figured bass symbols to represent each chord. Your instructor may also choose to have you write out the top ("soprano") voice as well.

Exercise	Tonic	Bottom number in meter sign
42.5	A	4
42.6	G	8
42.7	A	2
42.8	F	4
42.9	G	4
42.10	C♯	2
42.11	A♭	4
42.12	B	4

READING AND SIGHT SINGING

Prepare the following excerpts, singing on syllables while conducting. Some of these melodies clearly outline submediant chords, whereas others merely emphasize skips to $\hat{6}$/ *la*/ *le*, $\hat{1}$/ *do,* or $\hat{3}$/ *mi*/ *me.* Some of these might even have been harmonized in their original contexts by other chords (for example, a skip to $\hat{6}$/ *la* harmonized by a subdominant triad). Nonetheless, all these melodies offer opportunities to practice skips to these scale degrees.

Excerpts for reading and sight singing
from the
Anthology for Sight Singing
524–553

Any triad whose root is the third scale degree (3̂/*mi*/*me*) is called a mediant triad. It appears frequently as a preparation for the submediant, as in the circle-of-fifths progression iii–VI–ii–V̲–I, and it occasionally substitutes for a first-inversion tonic chord.

The Triad with 3̂/*mi*/*me* as Root

In the major mode, the mediant triad is built on 3̂/*mi* and it is a minor triad. The excerpt below features a mediant triad (3̂/*mi*–5̂/*sol*–7̂/*ti*) in the opening measure.

Sergei Rachmaninoff, "How fair this spot!" Op. 21, No. 7, mm. 1–5 (1902)

How fair this spot! I gaze to where The gold-en brook runs by. The fields are all...

In the minor mode, the mediant is built on 3̂/*me* and it is major. A mediant triad (3̂/*me*–5̂/*sol*–7̂/*te*) is outlined in measures 4–5 of the melody below.

Martin Luther, chorale melody, "Von Himmel kam der Engel Schar" (1543)

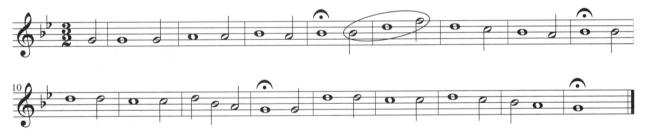

Notice that the fifth of this triad in the minor mode is formed by the *diatonic* seventh scale degree (7̂/*te*) and not the raised seventh (↑7̂/*ti*).

The mediant triad provides an important connection between the minor mode and its *relative major*. The pitches of the mediant triad (3̂/*me*–5̂/*sol*–7̂/*te*) are the same as those of the tonic triad (1̂/*do*–3̂/*mi*–5̂/*sol*) in the relative major. Indeed, the second phrase of the chorale melody above could be harmonized in the relative major (B♭) rather than G minor.

Review Chapter 17, where we defined relative keys as keys that share the same diatonic collection and, therefore, the same key signature. Keep this relationship in mind, particularly when we study modulation in future chapters.

Skips within the Mediant Triad

The diagram below presents an inventory of the skips smaller than an octave you might encounter when music outlines the mediant triad.

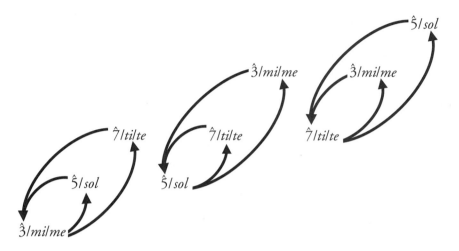

Listening for Mediant Triads

The mediant chord occurs frequently in root position (above $\hat{3}$/*mi*/*me*) and, less often, in first inversion (above $\hat{5}$/*sol*). For both, you will want to listen for voice leading and chord quality.

When $\hat{3}$/*mi*/*me* in the bass supports a $\frac{5}{3}$ chord the result is the mediant triad—iii or III. However, when $\hat{3}$/*mi*/*me* in the bass supports a $\frac{6}{3}$ chord the result is the tonic triad in first inversion—I⁶ or i⁶. Listen especially for $\hat{7}$/*ti*/*te* or $\hat{1}$/*do* in an upper voice and for the chord quality. The chart below summarizes the differences:

	With $\hat{3}$/*mi*/*me* in the bass	
$\frac{5}{3}$	Major mode: $\hat{3}$/*mi*–$\hat{5}$/*sol*–$\hat{7}$/*ti*	Major mode: iii (minor)
	Minor mode: $\hat{3}$/*me*–$\hat{5}$/*sol*–$\hat{7}$/*te*	Minor mode: III (major)
$\frac{6}{3}$	Major mode: $\hat{3}$/*mi*–$\hat{5}$/*sol*–$\hat{1}$/*do*	Major mode: I⁶ (major)
	Minor mode: $\hat{3}$/*me*–$\hat{5}$/*sol*–$\hat{1}$/*do*	Minor mode: i⁶ (minor)

When $\hat{5}$/*sol* in the bass supports a $\frac{5}{3}$ chord the result is the dominant triad—V. However, $\hat{5}$/*sol* in the bass will occasionally support a $\frac{6}{3}$ chord. The result is the mediant triad in first inversion—iii⁶ or III⁶. Listen for $\hat{2}$/*re* or $\hat{3}$/*mi*/*me* in an upper voice and for the chord quality.

	With $\hat{5}$/*sol* in the bass	
$\frac{5}{3}$	Both modes: $\hat{5}$/*sol*–[↑]$\hat{7}$/*ti*–$\hat{2}$/*re*	Both modes: V (major)
$\frac{6}{3}$	Major mode: $\hat{5}$/*sol*–$\hat{7}$/*ti*–$\hat{3}$/*mi*	Major mode: iii⁶ (minor)
	Minor mode: $\hat{5}$/*sol*–$\hat{7}$/*te*–$\hat{3}$/*me*	Minor mode: III⁶ (major)

EXERCISES

1. Be able to sing skips from any pitch to any other within the mediant triad.

2. Learn to arpeggiate the following chord progressions.

   a. I I^6 iii ii^6 V I
   b. i i^6 III ii^{o6} V i
   c. I iii vi IV^6 V I
   d. i III VI iv^6 V i
   e. I iii IV I^6 ii^6 V I
   f. i III ii^{o6} V i
   g. I IV^6 iii^6 ii^6 I^6 IV V I
   h. i ii^{o6} III VI ii^{o6} V i

3. Learn to play the above progressions on the piano (or similar keyboard).

LISTENING

Melodic Dictation

Listen to excerpts 43.1–43.4 and write out the pitches and rhythms for each, following the given instructions.

Exercise	Clef	Tonic	Bottom number in meter sign
43.1	bass	B	4
43.2	treble	C♯	2
43.3	tenor	D	4
43.4	alto	C♭	8

Harmonic Dictation

Listen to excerpts 43.5–43.12 and write out the bass line for each. Then supply the appropriate Roman numerals and figured bass symbols to represent each chord. Your instructor may also choose to have you write out the top ("soprano") voice as well.

Exercise	Tonic	Bottom number in meter sign
43.5	C	4
43.6	A	4
43.7	A	4
43.8	G	2
43.9	B♭	4
43.10	A♭	8
43.11	C	2

READING AND SIGHT SINGING

Prepare the following excerpts, singing on syllables while conducting. Some of these melodies clearly outline mediant chords, whereas others merely emphasize skips to $\hat{3}$/ *mi*/ *me*, $\hat{5}$/ *sol*, or $\hat{7}$/ *ti*/ *te*. Some of these might even have been harmonized in their original contexts by other chords (for example, a skip to $\hat{7}$/ *ti* harmonized by a dominant triad). Nonetheless, all these melodies offer opportunities to practice skips to these scale degrees.

Excerpts for reading and sight singing
from the
Anthology for Sight Singing
554–572

THE DOMINANT SEVENTH CHORD IN HARMONIC CONTEXTS

In Chapter 32, we encountered the concept of seventh chords—built by stacking 3rds to form a root, third, fifth, and seventh—and we explored some melodic characteristics of the dominant seventh chord, the most common seventh chord of all. In this chapter, we will explore some of its harmonic characteristics.

Inversions of the Dominant Seventh Chord

A dominant seventh chord can appear in root position and three different inversions, depending upon which chord member is in the bass voice, as shown below. The upper voices may contain the various members of the chord in myriad spacings and arrangements, but the member of the chord in the *bass voice* determines the inversion of the chord.

	Root position	1st inversion	2nd inversion	3rd inversion
Chord member in bass	root	third	fifth	seventh
Scale degree in bass	$\hat{5}$/*sol*	[↑]7/*ti*	$\hat{2}$/*re*	$\hat{4}$/*fa*
Intervals above bass	$\begin{smallmatrix}7\\5\\3\end{smallmatrix}$	$\begin{smallmatrix}6\\5\\3\end{smallmatrix}$	$\begin{smallmatrix}6\\4\\3\end{smallmatrix}$	$\begin{smallmatrix}6\\4\\2\end{smallmatrix}$
Roman-numeral and figured-bass symbol	$\underline{V}^7$	$\underline{V}^6_5$	$\underline{V}^4_3$	$\underline{V}^4_2$ or $\underline{V}^2$

Arpeggiating the Dominant Seventh Chord

In Chapter 32, you practiced arpeggiating the dominant seventh chord in root position in simple I–$\underline{V}^7$–I progressions. You can now practice arpeggiating it in its inversions as well. The table on the next page shows the dominant seventh chord in root position and its three inversions. Above each chord symbol are the pitches you will sing to arpeggiate the chord. The syllables stacked vertically represent 3rds. The step between $\hat{4}$/*fa* and $\hat{5}$/*sol* is offset to remind you that this is the only interval in the dominant seventh chord that is not a 3rd but a whole step. Think of the motion from $\hat{4}$/*fa* to $\hat{5}$/*sol* not as something harmonic, but rather as a melodic step.

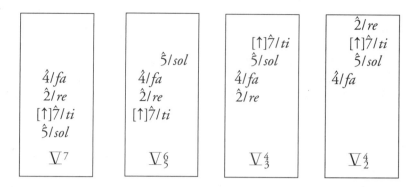

When you arpeggiate seventh chords, keep in mind that the four members of these chords require a longer rhythmic pattern (♩♩♩♩♩♩♩𝄽). In progressions, you will alternate these longer patterns with the usual triad pattern. For example, when presented with the progression I–V⁶₅–I–IV–V⁴₂–I⁶, you would sing the following:

Listening for Dominant Seventh Chords

By adding the dominant seventh chord in root position and three inversions to our array of chords, we increase the number of chord possibilities supported by certain scale degrees. You must now pay extra attention to listen for some form of the dominant seventh chord when any one of its members—$\hat{5}/sol$, $[\uparrow]\hat{7}/ti$, $\hat{2}/re$, or $\hat{4}/fa$—appears in the bass.

When $\hat{5}/sol$ appears in the bass, it could support a triad (V) or a seventh chord (V⁷). The presence or absence of $\hat{4}/fa$ in an upper voice makes the difference. Although iii⁶ (in major) or III⁶ (in minor) are possible, they are much less likely.

When $[\uparrow]\hat{7}/ti$ appears in the bass, it could support a first-inversion dominant triad (V⁶), a dominant seventh chord (V⁶₅), or a leading-tone triad (vii°). The presence or absence of $\hat{4}/fa$ in an upper voice will help distinguish the first two, and the presence or absence of $\hat{5}/sol$ will help distinguish the latter two.

When $\hat{2}/re$ appears in the bass, it could support a dominant seventh chord in second inversion (V⁴₃) in addition to the various triads we have studied (ii, ii°, and vii°⁶). The presence or absence of $\hat{5}/sol$ and the chord quality will be primary clues to making this distinction.

When $\hat{4}/fa$ appears in the bass, it could support a dominant seventh chord in third inversion (V⁴₂) in addition to the triads we have encountered (IV, iv, ii⁶ and ii°⁶). Listen in particular for $\hat{5}/sol$ in an upper voice as well as the chord quality to determine the chord.

These possibilities are summarized in the tables below:

	In the major mode						
Scale degree in bass	$\hat{1}/do$	$\hat{2}/re$	$\hat{3}/mi$	$\hat{4}/fa$	$\hat{5}/sol$	$\hat{6}/la$	$\hat{7}/ti$
Possible chords	I	ii	iii	IV	V	vi	vii°
	vi⁶	vii°⁶	I⁶	ii⁶	iii⁶	IV⁶	V⁶
		V⁴₃		V⁴₂	V⁷		V⁶₅

In the minor mode							
Scale degree in bass	$\hat{1}$/*do*	$\hat{2}$/*re*	$\hat{3}$/*me*	$\hat{4}$/*fa*	$\hat{5}$/*sol*	$\hat{6}$/*le*	↑$\hat{7}$/*ti*
Possible chords	i	ii°	III	iv	V	VI	vii°
	$\underline{VI}^6$	vii°⁶	i⁶	ii°⁶	III⁶	iv⁶	$\underline{V}^6$
		$\underline{V}{}^4_3$		$\underline{V}{}^4_2$	$\underline{V}^7$		$\underline{V}{}^6_5$

The harmonic progression and voice leading also help to clarify the function of the chord. The dominant seventh chord frequently leads to the tonic ($\underline{V}^7$–I), and in this progression $\hat{4}$/*fa* has a strong tendency to resolve down to $\hat{3}$/*mi*/*me*, and $\hat{7}$/*ti* tends to resolve up to $\hat{1}$/*do*. In the resolution of $\underline{V}{}^4_2$, $\hat{4}$/*fa* in the bass voice will always resolve to $\hat{3}$/*mi*/*me*, usually supporting I⁶ (in major) or i⁶ (in minor).

EXERCISES

1. In each of these preliminary exercises for chord arpeggiation, sing each chord one after the next. Think of these as symbol-reading, solmization, and singing exercises, not as actual chord progressions.

   a. I↘$\underline{V}$ vii° $\underline{V}^7$ I
   b. i↘$\underline{V}$ vii° $\underline{V}^7$ i
   c. I↘$\underline{V}$ $\underline{V}^7$ $\underline{V}{}^6_5$ $\underline{V}{}^4_3$ $\underline{V}{}^4_2$ I⁶
   d. i ↘$\underline{V}$ $\underline{V}^7$ $\underline{V}{}^6_5$ $\underline{V}{}^4_3$ $\underline{V}{}^4_2$ i⁶
   e. I↘$\underline{V}^7$ I $\underline{V}{}^6_5$ I $\underline{V}{}^4_3$ I⁶ $\underline{V}{}^4_2$ I⁶ (and in retrograde)
   f. i↘ $\underline{V}^7$ i $\underline{V}{}^6_5$ i $\underline{V}{}^4_3$ i⁶ $\underline{V}{}^4_2$ i⁶ (and in retrograde)
   g. I $\underline{V}^6$ vii° $\underline{V}{}^6_5$ I vii°⁶ $\underline{V}{}^4_3$ I

2. Learn to arpeggiate the following chord progressions.

   a. I $\underline{IV}^6$ $\underline{V}^7$ I $\underline{IV}$ $\underline{V}{}^4_3$ I
   b. i $\underline{V}{}^6_5$ i i⁶ iv $\underline{V}{}^4_2$ i⁶ $\underline{V}{}^4_3$ i
   c. I $\underline{V}{}^6_5$ I $\underline{IV}$ ii $\underline{V}{}^4_3$ I
   d. i $\underline{V}{}^4_2$ i⁶↗VI $\underline{V}{}^4_2$ i⁶ iv $\underline{V}^7$ i
   e. I iii $\underline{V}{}^4_2$ I⁶↘vi $\underline{V}{}^6_5$ I
   f. i iv $\underline{V}{}^4_2$ i⁶ $\underline{V}{}^4_3$ i⁶ ii°⁶ $\underline{V}^7$ i

3. Learn to play the above progressions on the piano (or similar keyboard).

Harmonic Dictation

Listen to excerpts 44.1–44.8 and write out the bass line for each. Then supply the appropriate Roman numerals and figured bass symbols to represent each chord. Your instructor may also choose to have you write out the top ("soprano") voice.

Exercise	Tonic	Bottom number in meter sign
44.1	G	4
44.2	C	2
44.3	B♭	8
44.4	E	4
44.5	A	4
44.6	C	4
44.7	B	4
44.8	A	8

45 VOICE-LEADING TECHNIQUES

Just as individual voices can move to form specific chords, individual voices can move *against* this harmonic context as well. These voice-leading techniques serve to *embellish* rather than change the prevailing harmony. The dissonance created by these techniques can be produced either through melodic motion (moving up or down in a melody) or through rhythmic displacement.

Neighbor and Passing Tones

There are two basic types of dissonance that arise from the melodic motion of a voice: **neighbor tones,** which occur stepwise *above* or *below* a single consonant pitch, and **passing tones,** which occur stepwise *between* two different consonant pitches.

We encountered neighbor notes in Chapter 14, where we learned that they can form a complete figure, in which the neighbor note is preceded and followed by the pitch it embellishes, or an incomplete figure, in which this sandwich effect does not appear. In either case, we hear neighbor tones as upper or lower appendages to chord tones.

> A **neighbor tone** is one step above or below a chord tone. Complete neighbors depart from and return to the chord tone; incomplete ones only depart or return.

> A **passing tone** connects one chord tone to another by step.

Ludwig van Beethoven, Piano Sonata No. 25, Op. 79, mvt. 3, mm. 1–4 (1809)

The excerpt above features a string of complete neighbor-note figures. The dissonant pitches (circled) are all sandwiched between two iterations of the consonant pitch.

The excerpt below features two incomplete neighbors. In beat 2 the F is an incomplete upper neighbor to the consonant E, and in beat 3 the E is an incomplete upper neighbor to the consonant D. This specific kind of incomplete neighbor is also called an *escape tone.*

Joseph Haydn, Piano Sonata in C
(Hob. XVI:35), mvt. 3, mm. 1–2 (c. 1780)

A neighbor note is subordinate to the chord tone it embellishes. The motion involved in such neighboring figures does not change the prevailing harmony. You'll notice that lower neighbors do not occur as frequently as upper neighbors.

Passing tones are non-chord tones that connect one chord tone to another. They are approached and left by step in the same direction. Passing tones are subordinate to the chord tones that they connect. Like neighbor tones, they don't change the prevailing harmony.

In the first four notes of the top voice in the excerpt below, the pitch A connects the two tonic-chord tones G and B♭, and the C connects that B♭ to the dominant-chord tone D in the next measure. Look at and listen to the rest of this short excerpt and determine which of the other pitches are passing tones.

J. S. Bach, Suite in G minor, BWV 822, mvt. 3, mm. 1–2

Gavotte en Rondeau

Diminutions (such as neighbor tones and passing tones) are notes shorter than the prevailing harmonic rhythm that embellish notes or chords.

Neighbor notes, passing notes, and similar figures are sometimes called **diminutions** because they are created by rhythmic values shorter than the prevailing harmonic rhythm. This concept is very important to you as a listener and performer because, as you listen and think harmonically, it is the harmonic rhythm that governs the chord changes. Diminutions do not usually create new chords, but rather embellish the prevailing ones. As you identify the chords you hear, try not to be distracted by diminutions, but recognize them as sounding against a slower harmonic background.

Suspensions and Anticipations

Suspensions and anticipations are also produced by voices that create dissonances against a prevailing harmony. They are products not of melodic motion but of rhythmic displacement.

A suspension is a pitch held over from one chord to form a dissonance with the next chord.

A **suspension** is a pitch held over from a previous harmony to form a dissonance with the new harmony. This pitch may be sustained (through a tie or the use of a longer note value) or rearticulated (struck again with the pitches of the new harmony). Both types of suspension occur in measure 12 of the excerpt below: in the alto voice, the A is rearticulated on the downbeat, and the G is sustained into the first half of beat 3.

J. S. Bach, Chorale No. 1, "Aus meines Herzens Grunde," mm. 10–13

As shown in the example above, suspensions are labeled with figured bass numbers (which, as you know, represent intervals above the bass). These numbers come in a pair: the first represents the suspended note that creates the dissonance and the second represents the consonance to which it resolves. Musicians identify a suspension by this pair of figured bass numbers, referring, for instance, to a 7–6 suspension or a 4–3 suspension. In all cases, suspensions form a delay in the voice leading, so that a voice reaches its destination *after* the harmony changes.

In a similar but opposite manner, an **anticipation** is a pitch that arrives at its voice-leading destination *before* the harmony changes. In measure 7 of the excerpt below, a dissonance is created by the last eighth note in the top voice, which does not belong to the dominant chord sustained from beat 2. This C is an anticipation of the chord-tone C that comes on the downbeat of the next measure.

> An **anticipation** is a pitch from the next chord that is reached early, creating a dissonance with the present chord.

Johann Kuhnau, Biblical Sonata No. 1, *The Battle Between David and Goliath,*
"Victory Dance and Festival," mm. 5–8 (1700?)

The 4–3 Suspension over the Dominant

One important suspension is the 4–3 suspension as it occurs over the dominant pitch. It is one of the most common suspensions, and it can be thought of as a kind of decoration of the third of the dominant chord. This suspension has important consequences for your understanding of $^6_4$ chords (introduced in the next chapter).

In the following excerpt, Bach suspends the pitch C in the tenor voice from the last beat of measure 12 through the downbeat of measure 13 (remember, this is a suspension even though the pitch has been rearticulated).

J. S. Bach, Chorale No. 254, "Treuer Gott, ich mus dir klagen"
["Weg, mein Herz, mit dem Gedanken"], mm. 12–13

The salient voice leading in the 4–3 suspension over the dominant is $\hat{1}$/*do*–$\hat{7}$/*ti*. When you hear $\hat{1}$/*do* moving to $\hat{7}$/*ti* above the dominant pitch, this can either be a 4–3 suspension (if the other voices stay on $\hat{5}$/*sol* and $\hat{2}$/*re*) or it can serve as part of the $^{6-5}_{4-3}$ figure (see next chapter).

5–6 Motion

Voice leading and harmony are intimately tied up with one another. Indeed, harmony is a *product* of the way voices move. One of the clearest examples of this occurs when an upper voice moves from a 5th to a 6th above a bass note.

Franz Schubert, "Du bist die Ruh," Op. 59, No. 3, D. 776, mm. 8–11 (1823)

In the excerpt above, the chord in measure 8 is in $\frac{5}{3}$ position—a tonic chord in root position. Then the 5th (B♭) moves to a 6th (C) in measure 9, creating a chord in $\frac{6}{3}$ position—a submediant chord in first inversion. The voice-leading motion is 5–6, but we recognize the two verticalities as two different harmonies. They are distinct but related through a common bass note and third above that bass. You might simply consider the second measure to be an expansion of the tonic harmony of the previous measure.

Context is extremely important, and you will sometimes hear 5–6 motion not as an expansion of the previous harmony but as motion that creates a new chord with a new function.

J. S. Bach, Chorale No. 248, "Meine Augen schließ' ich jetzt," mm. 1–2

In this Bach chorale, the last beat of measure 1 would be a supertonic chord if your ear accounted for the motion to the 6th (F♯) as simply an expansion of the first half of the beat. But this would create a "cadence" from ii to I, which is neither functional nor the way our ears hear this cadence. In fact, the 6th is a crucial part of the voice leading and harmony because it forms a vii°6 chord that progresses harmonically to the tonic. You might even hear the 5th (E) merely as an accented passing tone on its way to the 6th.

The 5–6 motion also brings into focus yet again the difference between $\frac{5}{3}$ and $\frac{6}{3}$ chords. If you have internalized the differences in scale degrees and chords produced by 5ths and 6ths above various bass pitches, then you are well positioned to listen for the special effects produced by 5–6 motion.

Motion in the Bass Voice

The bass voice can also participate in these types of motion. In your listening, pay attention to whether or not the bass voice moves in a rhythm identical to the harmonic rhythm. When the bass voice moves faster than the harmonic rhythm, listen especially for whether it is arpeggiating through other chord tones or forming passing or neighbor notes. The bass voice can also create suspensions against the other voices, and on rare occasions creates anticipations. A rearticulated 2–3 suspension occurs in the bass of the excerpt below:

George Frideric Handel, Keyboard Suite HWV 430,
mvt. 4, Air ("Harmonious Blacksmith"), mm. 1–2 (1720)

2— 3

Less frequently, the rhythm of the bass voice proceeds more slowly than the harmonic rhythm. This condition is usually associated with $\frac{6}{4}$ figures and the pedal bass, which we will discuss in later chapters.

Keep in mind that there are many other types of voice-leading techniques, particularly those involving combinations of the paradigms discussed in this chapter.

LISTENING

A. Listen to excerpts 45.1–45.3 and write out the harmonic rhythm for each (but don't label the chords). Then listen specifically for voice-leading techniques of the variety discussed in this chapter. Mark them above the harmonic rhythm in a clear, appropriate manner.

B. Listen to excerpts 45.4–45.6. For each, write out the bass line and identify the chords using Roman numerals and figured bass. Then listen specifically for the voice-leading techniques discussed in this chapter. Mark suspensions and 5–6 motion by adding figured bass symbols beneath the bass line. Mark others with appropriate abbreviations (PT, N, etc.).

Exercise	Tonic	Bottom number in meter sign
45.4	G	4
45.5	B	4
45.6	C	2

Triads in root position ($\frac{5}{3}$) and first inversion ($\frac{6}{3}$) account for the vast majority of triads you will encounter in Western music. However, you will also encounter certain triads in second inversion ($\frac{6}{4}$). For the most part, $\frac{6}{4}$ chords are used only in certain contexts with specific kinds of voice leading. For this reason, we will examine four basic contexts for $\frac{6}{4}$ chords and the specific voice leading associated with each.*

The $\frac{6}{4}$ as Cadential Dissonance

One special type of voice leading identified in the last chapter was 4–3 motion. Although the 4–3 embellishes many different chords, it is frequently used to intensify the dominant harmony at cadences.

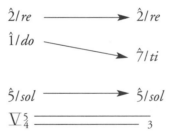

In the example above, the dominant-chord tone $\hat{7}$/*ti* has been displaced by $\hat{1}$/*do*, creating a dissonant 4th above the bass that resolves down by step to $\hat{7}$/*ti*. The chord tone $\hat{2}$/*re* can also be displaced by $\hat{3}$/*mi,* thereby intensifying the 4–3 embellishment of $\underline{\text{V}}$ with the addition of 6–5 motion, as shown below:

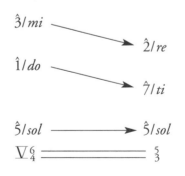

---

*This chapter is meant not as a comprehensive investigation of all possible $\frac{6}{4}$ figures (your harmony textbook should cover them much more thoroughly), but as an introduction to the basic types you will hear and how to approach them aurally. All the generic examples in this chapter are written in the major mode for the sake of simplicity and consistency. Nonetheless, the principles discussed here apply equally in the minor mode.

The 6th and the 4th embellish the dominant harmony and resolve to a 5th and 3rd above the dominant pitch in the bass. Another variation on this figure adds a seventh to the arrival on the second verticality, creating the following voice leading: $\begin{smallmatrix}8-7\\6-5\\4-3\end{smallmatrix}$.

The following Bach chorale illustrates this $\begin{smallmatrix}6-5\\4-3\end{smallmatrix}$ embellishment of the dominant. Note how the bass voice drops an octave between its two statements of $\hat{5}$/*sol.* You will encounter many pieces that use this device, and many others that simply repeat or sustain $\hat{5}$/*sol* in the same octave.

J. S. Bach, Chorale No. 107, "Herzlich lieb hab'ich dich, o Herr," mm. 12–13

E♭: $\underset{}{V^{6}_{4}} \longrightarrow {}^{5}_{3}$ I

In a **cadential $^6_4$**, the bass note $\hat{5}$/*sol* is embellished by $\begin{smallmatrix}6-5\\4-3\end{smallmatrix}$ motion, in which $\hat{3}$/*mi*/*me* moves to $\hat{2}$/*re* and $\hat{1}$/*do* moves to $\hat{7}$/*ti* at a cadence.

Composers have used this $\begin{smallmatrix}6-5\\4-3\end{smallmatrix}$ motion very frequently as an approach to the dominant chord in a *cadence* (as in the chorale, above), so the $^6_4$ in this context has come to be called a **cadential $^6_4$.**

The symbol V^{6-5}_{4-3} does not indicate that the first chord is V^6_4 ($\hat{2}$/*re*–$\hat{5}$/*sol*–$\hat{7}$/*ti*). The notes that create the 6th and 4th in the cadential $^6_4$ are embellishments of the dominant. It is a V^5_3 chord with two auxiliary pitches ($^6_4$) that resolve into the root-position dominant, all over $\hat{5}$/*sol* in the bass.

Some musicians label this as shown above: a dominant harmony with 6th resolving to 5th, and 4th resolving to 3rd. Others identify the first verticality as a different chord whose root is $\hat{1}$/*do*, a tonic chord in second inversion, which moves to another chord, a dominant chord in root position: I^6_4–V. The first chord, however, does not *function* as a tonic. This is part of the special character of the $^6_4$ at a cadence—no matter how you label it, it has a dominant function.

Others combine both main features—the tonic root of the first verticality and the dominant function of the entire figure—in a single set of labels:

$$\underbrace{I^6_4 \quad V}_{V}$$

However you label the cadential $^6_4$, the salient voice leading remains the same: $\hat{3}$/*mi*/*me* descends to $\hat{2}$/*re* and $\hat{1}$/*do* descends to $\hat{7}$/*ti* over $\hat{5}$/*sol* in the bass.

This manual will use all three kinds of symbols for the cadential $^6_4$.

The $^6_4$ as Neighbor Notes

When the fifth and third of a triad move up to a sixth and fourth while the bass voice remains on the root of the chord, the upper notes function as neighbor notes, and the $^6_4$ verticality is often referred to as the **neighboring $^6_4$**. These neighboring notes almost always resolve back to the fifth and third. In measures 1–2 of the excerpt below, the C and E move briefly to their upper neighbors D and F, and then resolve back. This forms $\begin{smallmatrix}5-6-5\\3-4-3\end{smallmatrix}$ voice leading.

Robert Schumann, *Album for the Young*, Op. 68, No. 8, "The Wild Rider," mm. 1–4 (1848)

This figure is also referred to as the **pedal** $^6_4$, so named for the bass note sustained through the entire figure, known as a pedal point.

Although any chord may be embellished in this way, embellishments of the tonic and dominant occur most frequently. The diagram below illustrates the basic models of $^{5-6-5}_{3-4-3}$ motion embellishing each of these chords. These $^6_4$ verticalities may also be thought of as having their own roots, so they may be labeled with separate Roman numerals (for example, I–IV$^6_4$–I).

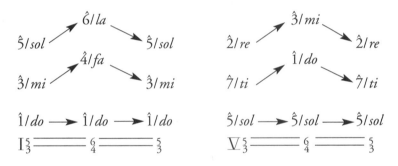

Listen for the following characteristic sounds in the neighboring $^6_4$: the upper-neighbor motion in the upper voices, the repeated or sustained note in the bass voice, and the feeling of a subordinate chord "sandwiched" between two statements of the more structural chord.

The $^6_4$ as Passing Chord

The $^6_4$ verticality can also appear over the middle note of a three-note stepwise motion in the bass voice. The middle note in the bass functions as a passing tone between the two outer notes, even though it does support a separate chord in $^6_4$ position. Therefore, we often refer to this chord as a **passing** $^6_4$.

Ludwig van Beethoven, Piano Sonata No. 3, Op. 2, No. 3, mvt. 3, Trio, mm. 1–3 (1795)

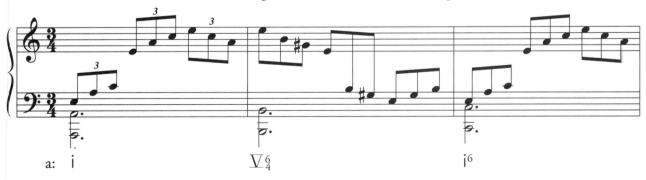

Your first clue indicating a passing $^6_4$ is the presence of three bass notes moving stepwise in the same direction, either ascending (as in the Beethoven sonata, above) or descending. Passing $^6_4$ chords occur most often above scale degrees $\hat{2}(\text{V}^6_4)$ and $\hat{5}(\text{I}^6_4)$, and they often connect two different inversions of the same harmony (for example, IV^6–I^6_4–IV).

The $^6_4$ as a Result of Arpeggiation in the Bass

Motion in the bass voice while a chord is being sustained can also produce a $^6_4$ verticality at least momentarily. This occurs when the bass-voice motion strikes the fifth of the chord, as shown in the first two measures of the excerpt below.

Franz Schubert, Ländler, D. 734 [Op. 67], No. 16, mm. 1–4 (c. 1822)

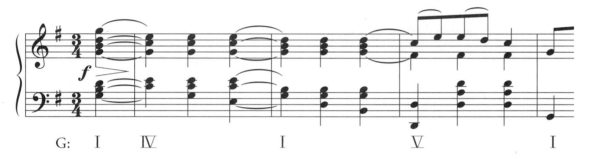

G: I   IV   I   V   I

In measure 1, the IV chord appears in root position at the beginning of the measure, but the bass arpeggiation (C–G–E) creates a momentary second inversion at beat 2. The same thing happens in measure 2 during the arpeggiation through the pitches of the I chord. You hear these $^6_4$s merely as arpeggiations through the pitches of the chord.

EXERCISES

1. In each of these preliminary exercises for chord arpeggiation, sing each chord one after the next. Think of these as symbol-reading, solmization, and singing exercises, not as actual chord progressions.

   a. I I⁶ I$^6_4$ IV IV⁶ IV$^6_4$ V V⁶ V$^6_4$ I

   b. i i⁶ i$^6_4$ iv iv⁶ iv$^6_4$ V V⁶ V$^6_4$ i

2. Prepare the following arpeggiations in the manner presented in previous chapters.

   a. I I⁶ ii⁶ V$^{6-5}_{4-3}$ I

   b. i↘V VI iv⁶ i$^6_4$ V i

   c. I V$^6_4$ I⁶ ii⁶ I$^6_4$ V$^4_2$ I⁶ (What happens to the cadential $^6_4$ in this progression?)

d. i iv$^6_4$ i III VI ii$^{°6}$ $\underbrace{\text{i}^6_4\ \ \text{V}}_{\text{V}}$ i

e. I V^6 IV^6 I$^6_4$ IV I^6 V$^4_2$ I^6

f. I V I$^6_4$ V vi ii^6 V^7 I

LISTENING

Harmonic Dictation

Listen to excerpts 46.1–46.8 and write down the bass voice for each. Then supply Roman numerals and figured bass symbols to represent the chords that you hear above those bass notes. Your instructor may also choose to have you write out the top ("soprano") voice as well.

Exercise	Tonic	Bottom number in meter sign
46.1	C	4
46.2	D	4
46.3	D	8
46.4	E	2
46.5	C	4
46.6	A	4
46.7	B♭	4
46.8	F	4

47 OTHER SEVENTH CHORDS

Thus far we have examined only dominant seventh chords, but there are seventh chords built on other scale degrees as well. This chapter will introduce these seventh chords, and focus on the most common—those built on the leading tone and supertonic scale degrees.

Harmonically, seventh chords can be understood as extensions of the triads on which they are based (for example, the leading-tone seventh chord sounds and behaves similar to the leading-tone triad). The distinction between the sounds of certain triads and seventh chords is a subtle one: the presence or absence of one extra chord tone. Melodically, the new challenge introduced with seventh chords is the interval formed between the root and seventh.

Seventh Chord Qualities

There are several different qualities of seventh chords used in Western tonal music. Each has a distinct sound based on the intervals between its pitches. Particularly important are the quality of the triad formed by the root, third, and fifth, and the quality of the interval formed by the root and seventh.

The diagram below shows the most common types of seventh chords, written in root position, with the third, fifth, and seventh printed directly above each root as a stack of 3rds. To the left of each stack of 3rds, the qualities of the 3rds are shown. To the right of each stack, the quality of the triad and the 7th above the root are shown. You should also become familiar with the alternative names that appear in parentheses below the chord names.

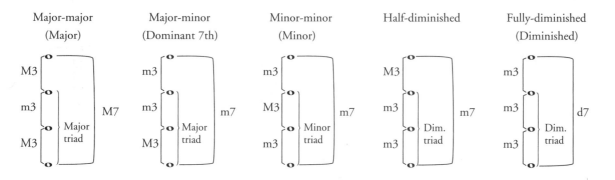

Of these five types of seventh chords, the major-minor seventh is found most frequently in tonal music. Note that the major-minor seventh chord is sometimes called the dominant seventh, but this name should properly be reserved for the chord's *function* and not its quality. The minor-minor, half-diminished, and fully-diminished seventh chords are also prevalent (although not as prevalent as the major-minor). Major-major seventh chords are found much less frequently, mostly as a byproduct of voice-leading events.

Two other types of seventh chords are theoretically possible but rarely used: the augmented seventh chord (an augmented triad with a major 7th above the root), and the minor-major seventh chord (a minor triad with a major 7th above the root). These two structures are typically the illusory products of voice leading and rarely function as chords themselves.

The Leading-Tone Seventh

Leading-tone seventh chords have a dominant function similar to that of leading tone triads—they often lead harmonically to the tonic. It occurs most frequently in the minor mode as a fully-diminished seventh chord.

In the minor mode, the leading-tone seventh chord (↑$\hat{7}$/*ti*–$\hat{2}$/*re*–$\hat{4}$/*fa*–$\hat{6}$/*le*) is built on a chromatically raised pitch (↑$\hat{7}$/*ti*). All 3rds formed by this seventh chord are minor, and the triad (↑$\hat{7}$/*ti*–$\hat{2}$/*re*–$\hat{4}$/*fa*) and the 7th ($\hat{7}$/*ti*–$\hat{6}$/*le*) are both diminished.

In the major mode, the diatonic leading-tone seventh chord ($\hat{7}$/*ti*–$\hat{2}$/*re*–$\hat{4}$/*fa*–$\hat{6}$/*la*) has a half-diminished quality due to the diminished triad ($\hat{7}$/*ti*–$\hat{2}$/*re*–$\hat{4}$/*fa*) and the minor 7th ($\hat{7}$/*ti*–$\hat{6}$/*la*). This chord is relatively rare compared to the form of the leading-tone seventh found in the minor mode. The fully-diminished seventh chord is sometimes borrowed from the minor into the major mode. Thus, you will occasionally hear $\hat{7}$/*ti*, $\hat{2}$/*re*, $\hat{4}$/*fa*, and ↓$\hat{6}$/*le*—with a chromatically lowered sixth scale degree—in the major mode.

The leading-tone seventh chord shares three pitches with the dominant seventh chord ($\hat{7}$/*ti*, $\hat{2}$/*re*, and $\hat{4}$/*fa*), and it also shares a similar function. Because of this, you should be particularly mindful of chords with $\hat{7}$/*ti*, $\hat{2}$/*re*, or $\hat{4}$/*fa* as a bass note. Listen very carefully to voice leading, the intervals formed by the voices above the bass, and the chord qualities. For example, if you heard $\hat{2}$/*re* in the bass in the major mode, it could be a leading-tone seventh chord in $\frac{6}{5}$ position ($\hat{2}$/*re*–$\hat{4}$/*fa*–$\hat{6}$/*la*–$\hat{7}$/*ti*) or a dominant seventh chord in $\frac{4}{3}$ position ($\hat{2}$/*re*–$\hat{4}$/*fa*–$\hat{5}$/*sol*–$\hat{7}$/*ti*). Listen for $\hat{6}$/*la* or $\hat{5}$/*sol* in an upper voice, the intervals above the bass ($\frac{6}{5}$ or $\frac{4}{3}$), and chord quality (half-diminished vs. major-minor).

The Supertonic Seventh

The supertonic seventh chord can be thought of as the product of adding the pitch $\hat{1}$/*do* to the supertonic triad. This results in the syllables $\hat{2}$/*re*–$\hat{4}$/*fa*–$\hat{6}$/*la*–$\hat{1}$/*do* in the major mode and $\hat{2}$/*re*–$\hat{4}$/*fa*–$\hat{6}$/*le*–$\hat{1}$/*do* in the minor mode. In the major mode, this is a minor-minor seventh chord. In the minor mode, it is half diminished.

You can also think of the supertonic seventh chord as a kind of supertonic/subdominant hybrid. The root, third, and fifth form a supertonic triad and the third, fifth, and seventh form a subdominant triad.* The supertonic seventh chord shares the characteristics of these two triads. The diagram below shows how the two overlap in the major mode (the minor mode substitutes $\hat{6}$/*le* for $\hat{6}$/*la*):

$$\text{ii} \left[\begin{array}{l} \hat{1}/do \\ \hat{6}/la \\ \hat{4}/fa \\ \hat{2}/re \end{array} \right. \hspace{-0.5em} \left] \text{IV} \right.$$

---

*It is also possible to think of the dominant seventh chord in this same way—as V and vii° overlapping.

Other Seventh Chords

In addition to $\underline{V}^7$, vii^7, and ii^7, you will occasionally encounter seventh chords built on other scale degrees. Although these chords occur from time to time in common-practice period music, they are much more common in jazz and popular music. Be prepared to hear and sing seventh chords built on various scale degrees.

The Seventh as Non-Chord Tone

As we saw in Chapter 32, the seventh of a chord can be heard as a passing tone in an upper voice. This is particularly apparent when the triad is struck first, followed by the addition of the seventh, as shown in the Bach chorale below:

J. S. Bach, Chorale No. 14, "O Herre Gott, dein göttlich Wort," mm. 1–2

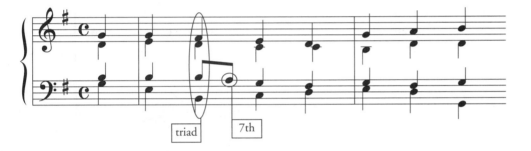

However, if the seventh is struck with the rest of the chord, we usually tend to call the entire verticality a seventh chord. Nonetheless, such sevenths reveal their origins as a passing tone when they resolve down by step.

Some sevenths originate as suspensions. In the following example, the A in the top voice is suspended into the chord on the downbeat of measure 10. Even though this note is rearticulated, we still hear it as a voice-leading suspension.

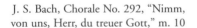

J. S. Bach, Chorale No. 292, "Nimm, von uns, Herr, du treuer Gott," m. 10

Another appearance of a seventh as a voice-leading event occurs when the ii^4_2 chord follows a root-position tonic chord. The upper voices move while the bass voice stays on $\hat{1}/do$, so the bass voice in this second verticality can be thought of as a suspension, which resolves in the following harmony. The voice leading of this motion is illustrated in the diagram below (shown in the major mode).

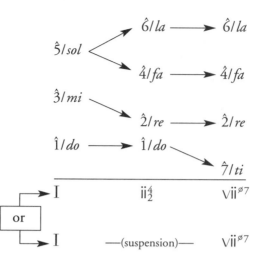

The middle chord in the diagram can be interpreted as a ii$^4_2$ or a suspension. This progression can also move to a V$^6_5$ chord instead of vii^{ø7} by substituting $\hat{5}$/*sol* for $\hat{6}$/*la* in the final chord.

1. List all the diatonic seventh chords in the major mode and identify each by its quality. Memorize these. Repeat this exercise in the minor mode.

2. Identify the seventh chords whose quality is affected by changing the natural minor to the harmonic minor. Identify these changes in quality. What changes would melodic minor cause?

3. When given a pitch, be able to arpeggiate any of the five common seventh-chord qualities in root position starting with the given pitch. For example, if given an F♯ and told to arpeggiate a minor-minor seventh chord, you would sing F♯–A–C♯–E.

4. Once you have established a key, be able to arpeggiate a root-position seventh chord from any given scale degree. Be able to name the quality of each of these chords.

5. Learn to identify the qualities of seventh chords by listening to seventh chords played melodically (heard as separate pitches) and harmonically (with all pitches sounded at once). Work on them in two ways:

   • Sing the pitches that make up the seventh chord and identify the component intervals;

   • Listen to the overall effect and affect of each seventh chord and learn to recognize each seventh-chord quality as a whole.

6. Listen to a variety of compositions, particularly those that are homophonic in texture (chorales, pop music, etc.), and identify the quality of seventh chords at any given point. Be aware that context can be very deceptive. Some listen-

ers who can identify seventh chord qualities in isolation have difficulties when those seventh chords are surrounded by other chords and function within a key.

7. Prepare the following arpeggiations in the manner presented in previous chapters.

a. I V^7 vii^{ø7} I ii vii$^{ø6}_5$ V^4_3 I

b. i vii^{o7} i V^6_5 vii$^{o4}_3$ V^4_2 i^6

c. I ii^7 V I ii$^6_5$ V^7 I

d. i iv ii^{ø7} V^4_3 i^6 ii^{o6} V^7 i

e. I ii$^4_2$ V^6 I vi^7 ii$^4_3$ V^7 I

f. i ii$^{ø4}_2$ vii^{o7} i V^4_2 i^6 iv^7 V i

g. I IV^7 V I^7 iii^7 vi^7 ii^7 V^7 I

h. i i$^4_2$ VI^7 i$^6_4$ V^7 i

LISTENING

Listen to excerpts 47.1–47.12 and write out the bass line for each. Then supply the appropriate Roman numerals and figured bass symbols to represent each chord. Your instructor may also choose to have you write out the top ("soprano") voice as well.

Harmonic Dictation

Exercise	Tonic	Bottom number in meter sign
47.1	C	2
47.2	A♭	8
47.3	F	4
47.4	B	8
47.5	C	Use ¢ as the meter sign
47.6	G	4
47.7	D	4
47.8	D	4
47.9	E♭	4
47.10	B	4
47.11	D	Use $\frac{12}{8}$ meter (first note = ♩.)
47.12	G	4

(What is unusual about the use of the seventh chord in this excerpt?)

READING AND SIGHT SINGING

Prepare the following excerpts, singing on syllables while conducting. Some of these melodies clearly outline specific seventh chords, whereas others merely emphasize particular skips within certain seventh chords (for example, $\hat{7}$/*ti* up to $\hat{6}$/*la* from the leading-tone seventh). Some of these skips might even have been harmonized in their original contexts by other chords (for example, a skip to $\hat{7}$/*ti* harmonized by a dominant triad). Nonetheless, all these melodies offer opportunities to practice skips among these scale degrees.

**Excerpts for reading and sight singing
from the
Anthology for Sight Singing
573–608**

48 TRANSPOSITION

In Chapter 11, when we moved the major scale from C to other pitches, we saw
that the tonic and all the intervals in the diatonic collection could be transferred
to a new pitch level—a process called **transposition.** This chapter will investigate
more about transposition, with special attention to the knowledge and skills necessary for transposing at sight.

> Transferring music with all its
> intervals to a new pitch level is
> called **transposition.**

Moving Music to a New Pitch Level

Any music can be replicated—interval by interval—at a different pitch level. When
music is transposed, all the pitch structures, relationships, and functions are transferred to the new pitch level. For example, consider the following melody by
Schumann, presented below in its original key and transposed to a lower key:

Ziemlich langsam.   Robert Schumann, *Myrthen*, Op. 25, No. 7, "Die Lotosblume," mm. 1–5 (1840)

Die Lo - tos-blu – me äng - stigt   sich vor der Son - ne   Pracht,

Ziemlich langsam.   Robert Schumann, *Myrthen*, Op. 25, No. 7, "Die Lotosblume," mm. 1–5 (1840)

Die Lo - tos-blu – me äng - stigt   sich vor der Son - ne   Pracht,

Every pitch has been lowered by a major 3rd—C in the original becomes A♭ in
the transposed version, B♭ becomes G♭, and so on. In addition, *every relationship*
having to do with pitch has been lowered by this same distance. For example, the
overall tonic has moved from F to D♭ and the raised $\hat{2}$ in measure 2 has moved from
G♯ to E♮. In fact, the entire system of scale-degree functions has been shifted down
to the new pitch level.

Concert Pitch

An essential means by which we understand transposition is the point of reference
known as **concert pitch.** This is the standardized system for naming pitches as they
sound or as they are notated for non-transposing instruments (C instruments, such
as the piano). Concert pitch serves as our absolute point of reference, by which we
understand transposing instruments and music that is transposed to other keys.

> **Concert pitch** is the standard-
> ized system of naming pitches
> as they sound or as they are
> notated for non-transposing
> instruments.

The Need for Transposition

Musicians are called upon to perform different kinds of transpositions in a variety of situations. Among the more common kinds of situations are the following: (1) moving a piece from one key to another; (2) reading from instrumental scores; (3) playing a transposing part on a C instrument (or on an instrument with yet another transposition); and (4) composing or arranging music for transposing instruments.

The Basic Transposition Tasks

Transposition tasks that you may be called upon to perform can be categorized into one of five different types, as outlined below (with each type followed by a couple of representative tasks):

1. Transpose the given music from one key to another key
   - Sing this melody—originally in E—in the key of G
   - Transpose "The Star-Spangled Banner" from D major down to B♭ major

2. Transpose the given music up or down by a specific interval
   - Play this melody a major 3rd higher
   - Transpose "Für Elise" down a perfect 4th

3. Perform, at concert pitch, a part written for a transposing instrument
   - Play the E♭-clarinet part from the last movement of Berlioz's *Symphonie Fantastique* on piano at concert pitch
   - Sing a B♭-tenor-saxophone part on letter names at concert pitch

4. Perform, on a transposing instrument, a part written at concert pitch
   - Sing the pitches, on letter names, you would finger on a D trumpet in order to play written concert pitches
   - Perform, on an A clarinet, the melody from Chopin's Piano Prelude in E minor, Op. 28, No. 4, so that it sounds at concert pitch

5. Perform, on a transposing instrument, a part written for an instrument with a different transposition
   - Sing the pitches, on letter names, you would finger on an A clarinet in order to play pitches written for B♭ clarinet
   - Perform, on a French horn in F, the part for cornet in A at the opening of Stravinsky's *L'histoire du soldat*

Interval of Transposition

The interval between one pitch level and the transposed pitch level is known as the **interval of transposition.**

Before transposing, you must be certain of the proper **interval of transposition**—that is, the exact interval (including direction) to move from one pitch level to another. In the first type of transposition above, this information is easily deduced, and in the second type, it is given overtly as part of the task.

The other three types demand a bit more attention on your part, because they involve at least one transposing instrument. Before proceeding with any task involving a transposing instrument, you must know the interval of transposition for that instrument (see "Transposing Instruments," below). For instance, you must know that an English horn is a transposing instrument in F, sounding a perfect 5th lower than its notated pitches.

Once you know the key of a transposing instrument (horn in F, clarinet in B♭, etc.), you need to understand the relationship between (1) the notated pitch for (or fingered and played on) that instrument, and (2) concert pitch, or sounding pitch.

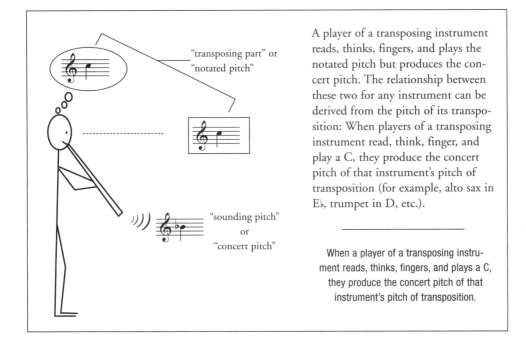

A player of a transposing instrument reads, thinks, fingers, and plays the notated pitch but produces the concert pitch. The relationship between these two for any instrument can be derived from the pitch of its transposition: When players of a transposing instrument read, think, finger, and play a C, they produce the concert pitch of that instrument's pitch of transposition (for example, alto sax in E♭, trumpet in D, etc.).

When a player of a transposing instrument reads, thinks, fingers, and plays a C, they produce the concert pitch of that instrument's pitch of transposition.

In the drawing above, the B♭-clarinet player reads, fingers, and plays a C in order to produce concert B♭. This kind of relationship is true for all transposing instruments. For example, an E♭-clarinet player fingers and plays a C to produce a concert E♭, and a player of the modern French horn (in F) fingers and plays a C to produce the concert pitch F.

You must also pay special attention to the *direction* of transposition. For example, the B♭ clarinet sounds a whole step *below* the notated pitch. This works both ways. The B♭-clarinet player must play a whole step *above* concert pitch in order to sound at concert pitch. This relationship can be rendered graphically:

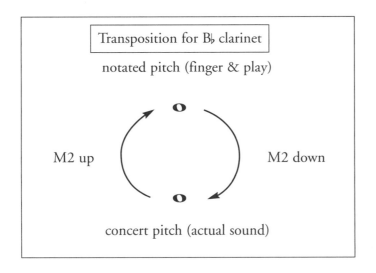

Transposing Instruments

Some instruments include their transposition in their names, particularly when there are two or more transposing versions of the same instrument, such as the B♭ clarinet and A clarinet. Others, such as the English horn and alto saxophone, do not bear a label that telegraphs their transposition. To help you memorize the transpositions of all transposing instruments, the following chart has been organized by letter name of transposition. It groups all descending step transpositions together, all descending 3rds together, and so on, regardless of octave. In this way, you can use a similar method for transposing all instruments in a single group. For example, all A and A♭ instrument parts can be read at concert pitch by sighting down a 3rd; all E♭ parts can be read by substituting bass clef, and so on. (See the following section for these and other strategies.)

Instrument	Written C4* sounds as	Interval of transposition (from written to concert pitch)
B♭ Piccolo Trumpet	B♭4	up m7
B♭ Clarinet	B♭3	down M2
Soprano Saxophone	B♭3	down M2
B♭ Trumpet	B♭3	down M2
Cornet	B♭3	down M2
Flugelhorn	B♭3	down M2
Bass Clarinet	B♭2	down M9
Tenor Saxophone	B♭2	down M9
Euphonium (in treble clef only)	B♭2	down M9
Bass Saxophone	B♭1	down M16 (15ma + M2)
A Piccolo Trumpet	A4	up M6
Oboe d'Amore	A3	down m3
A Clarinet	A3	down m3
Sopranino Clarinet	A♭4	up m6
Alto Flute	G3	down P4
French Horn (modern)	F3	down P5
English Horn	F3	down P5
Basset Horn	F3	down P5
E♭ Clarinet	E♭4	up m3
E♭ Trumpet	E♭4	up m3
Alto Clarinet	E♭3	down M6
Alto Saxophone	E♭3	down M6
Baritone Saxophone	E♭2	down M13 (8va + M6)
D Trumpet	D4	up M2

*This book uses the International Standards Organization (ISO) system of octave designation. In this system, each octave (beginning with each C) is labeled with a number. C0 is four octaves below middle C. Middle C is C4. Therefore, the D immediately above middle C is D4, and the B immediately below middle C is B3, and so on.

You may also encounter other transposing instruments, but—with the exception of a few very unusual ones—they should all be labeled with the pitch of transposition (for example, "Horn in D"). For further reference, most good books on orchestration or notation include information on instruments and their transpositions.

Strategies for Transposition

There are various methods for transposing. What follows is a discussion of the most widely used ones.

Transposition by Sighting

One strategy for transposition is known as sighting. Its procedure is outlined below:

- Determine the target key and visualize the new key signature
- Determine the number of lines and/or spaces between the written music and that to be performed (in other words, determine the interval *number* of transposition—2nd, 3rd, etc.)
- Perform pitches at this fixed distance *ex tempore* (using the new visualized key signature)
- Adjust for accidentals using the interval method (see "Transposition by Interval," below) or the perfect 5ths method (see "Adjusting for Accidentals," below).

Ludwig van Beethoven, Symphony No. 3, Op. 55
("Eroica"), mvt. 1, mm. 631–638 (1803)

In order to transpose the Beethoven excerpt above to concert pitch using sighting, you should imagine the appropriate key signature at the beginning of each system, and see the actual notation but perform pitches a 3rd above (as indicated on the following staff by Xs):

Because the horn in E♭ transposes *down,* the necessary octave adjustment has to be made as well.

In practice, sighting is generally easiest for transpositions involving 2nds or 3rds. Many musicians find it much more difficult to transpose by 4ths and 5ths via sighting.

Transposition by Interval

The strategy of transposing by interval requires that you calculate transposed pitches by constructing the exact interval of transposition from each notated pitch. Thus, you would look at the excerpt from Beethoven's Third Symphony above and transpose each pitch down a major 6th (or up a minor 3rd and down an octave).

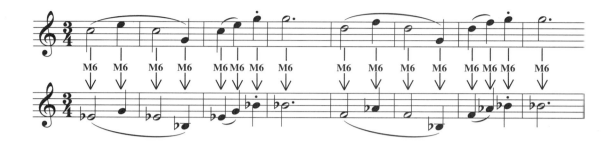

In practice, transposition by interval alone requires constant calculation on the part of the reader, and is best reserved for (1) adjusting for accidentals when transposing tonal music by sighting and (2) transposing atonal music.

Transposition by Tonal Function

One of the most effective strategies for transposing tonal music takes advantage of the fact that all of the tonal functions remain intact and are transferred to the new key. Therefore, if you know the tonal functions of the pitches as notated, you can reproduce those functions in the new key. In the excerpt from Beethoven's Third Symphony, the E♭-horn part contains the following scale degrees (as notated in the key of C):

If you transfer those scale degrees to concert pitch—the key of E♭ major—then you will have made this transposition using tonal function.

This strategy goes well beyond transferring mere scale degrees from key to key. Your ability to recognize configurations such as scalar passages, sequences, triadic outlines, harmonic function, chromatics, and the like will bear directly on your fluency in using features of the tonal system itself as a tool for transposition.

With its reliance on tonal function, this strategy is not really suitable for music that is tonally vague or ambiguous, or for atonal music.

Transposition by Clef

This strategy for transposition takes advantage of your facility in reading or thinking in several different clefs. Because a change in clef appears to "rename" the lines and spaces, it is possible to transpose by substituting a different clef for the original one. To transpose by clef, use the following procedure:

- Determine the target key and visualize the clef that will cause the notated pitches to appear on the appropriate transposed letter names
- Visualize the new key signature

- Read in that new clef and key signature, making appropriate octave adjustments as necessary
- Adjust for accidentals using the interval method (see "Transposition by Interval," above) or the perfect 5th method (see "Adjusting for Accidentals," below).

Using the horn part from Beethoven's Third Symphony, you would look at the original notation, knowing that your target key is E♭ major. Then you would ask yourself which clef, when substituted for the notated treble clef, would allow you to read the letter names E–G–E–B, etc.

Ludwig van Beethoven, Symphony No. 3, Op. 55
("Eroica"), mvt. 1, mm. 631–638 (1803)

The answer is bass clef. Visualize the bass clef, along with the key signature of the new key, and you can read the original printed notes as if they were in that new clef and key (adjusting the octave as necessary).

Imagine this clef and key signature

All seven vocal clefs—treble, bass, alto, tenor, soprano, mezzo-soprano, and baritone—will cover the seven possible letter-name conversions that transpositions require. (Look ahead to Chapter 64, which presents all clefs in detail.) To account for all transpositions from any clef (not just from treble clef), you should memorize the following "circle of clefs":

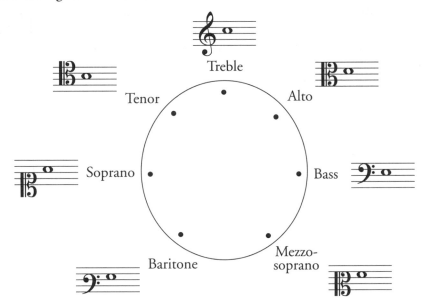

The following process will help you determine the appropriate clef for any transposition:

- Determine the number (but not quality) and direction of the interval of transposition
- Observe the printed clef in the music you are to transpose
- Find that clef on the circle of clefs
- Counting that clef as "1," count the number of the interval of transposition —clockwise for ascending intervals, counterclockwise for descending intervals—to arrive at the appropriate transposing clef.

The horn part from Beethoven's Third Symphony requires a transposition down a 6th, and it is written in the treble clef. Begin counting there on the circle of clefs and move counterclockwise (to transpose down) six clefs to arrive at the bass clef, the appropriate clef to transpose treble clef down a 6th.

The circle of clefs will account for transpositions from *any* starting clef, not just treble clef. Just remember to count your starting clef as "1" (just as we count the starting note of an interval) and to move clockwise to transpose up and counterclockwise to transpose down.

Although changing the clef produces the appropriate letter names, you must also change the key signature to adjust for sharps or flats, thereby fixing the quality of the interval of transposition. For example, if you substituted alto clef for treble to transpose up a *major* 2nd from C major, you would need a key signature of two sharps (D major), but to transpose up a *minor* 2nd, you would need a signature of five flats (D♭ major).

This strategy requires extensive prior study of clefs, but once you have learned all the necessary clefs, this method of transposition is by far the most effortless of all.

Adjusting for Accidentals

In order to transpose by either sighting or clef, you must have some way to account for accidentals. One way is to revert to the interval method, as described above. A slightly quicker method is to note whether the accidental raises or lowers the pitch and by how much. Then apply that same adjustment in the new key.

Another method that systematically accounts for all accidentals in all transpositions in both tonal and nontonal music is sometimes called the "perfect 5ths method" because it relies on calculating the interval of transposition in terms of perfect 5ths. It seems complicated at first, but, once you learn it, you will find it to be completely reliable. Here is how it works.

B♯
E♯
A♯
D♯
G♯
C♯
F♯
B
E
A
D
G
C
F
B♭
E♭
A♭
D♭
G♭
C♭
F♭

First, visualize the new key signature and transpose letter names by sighting or substituting another clef.

Second, calculate the interval of transposition by using the column of perfect 5ths (shown to the left), where every pitch is a perfect 5th above the one below it. To calculate any interval of transposition in terms of perfect 5ths, find the original pitch or key and then find the transposed pitch or key in the column. Then count from the original pitch to the transposed pitch. The result is the number (and direction) of perfect 5ths in that interval.

For example, to transpose from the key of E major to the key of B♭ major, you start with E and count six perfect 5ths *down* the column.

You can also use this for a general interval of transposition, not restricted to any particular pitches or keys. For example, if you know that you want to transpose something down a minor 3rd, you can pick *any* two pitches a minor 3rd apart—C and A, for example—and calculate that this transposition goes up three perfect 5ths. This is the same for any minor 3rd. (Try it.)

Third, take that number and direction and find its corresponding column in the following chart in order to discover which accidentals must be altered and how they should be altered.

transposing *down* this many P5s

7	6	5	4	3	2	1

is the same as transposing these intervals

7	6	5	4	3	2	1
↓A1	↓A4	↑m2	↓M3	↑m3	↓M2	↑P4
↑d8	↑d5	↓M7	↑m6	↓M6	↑m7	↓P5

and yields these "altered" letter names

7	6	5	4	3	2	1
B	B	B	B	B	B	B
E	E	E	E	E	E	
A	A	A	A	A		
D	D	D	D			
G	G	G				
C	C					
F						

Accidentals that appear before any of these "altered" notes must be read as one half step *lower:*

turn 𝄪 into ♯

turn ♯ into ♮

turn ♮ into ♭

turn ♭ into 𝄫

transposing *up* this many P5s

1	2	3	4	5	6	7

is the same as transposing these intervals

1	2	3	4	5	6	7
↓P4	↑M2	↓m3	↑M3	↓m2	↑A4	↑A1
↑P5	↓m7	↑M6	↓m6	↑M7	↓d5	↓d8

and yields these "altered" letter names

1	2	3	4	5	6	7
F	F	F	F	F	F	F
	C	C	C	C	C	C
		G	G	G	G	G
			D	D	D	D
				A	A	A
					E	E
						B

Accidentals that appear before any of these "altered" notes must be read as one half step *higher:*

turn 𝄫 into ♭

turn ♭ into ♮

turn ♮ into ♯

turn ♯ into 𝄪

If you were transposing something from C to A, you would find the appropriate column (*up* three perfect 5ths), and you would know that if you saw any alterations of F, C, or G in the transposed version, you would have to read them one half step higher (for example, an F♯ would become an F×). All other accidentals remain unaltered.

Franz Schubert, German Dance D. 89, Trio II, mm. 1–4 (1813)

Let's try this on the excerpt printed above. To transpose it up a major 3rd, first visualize the new clef (bass) and key signature (four sharps). Then calculate that transposing up a major 3rd is the same as transposing up four perfect 5ths. Using the accidentals chart find that this transposition requires you to alter accidentals before the new pitches F, C, G, and D by reading them one half-step higher. This results in the following transposition:

The sharp on the fourth note must be read as a double sharp when transposed because it falls on an F in the new key (one of the four "altered" notes), but the sharp on the note in measure 2 remains unaltered because it falls on an E (not one of the "altered" notes).

READING AND SIGHT SINGING

Follow the transposition instructions for each of the following exercises. Be sure to understand which type of transposition task is required before you begin each exercise.

Excerpts for reading and sight singing
from the
Anthology for Sight Singing
609–615

Continue to study transposition in various ways. Some suggestions:

1. Return to various melodies you've already sung in this *Manual* and from the *Anthology for Sight Singing*. Transpose and sing them using various criteria (for example—up a major 3rd, or as from a part for B♭ trumpet, etc.).

2. Transpose music at sight on your instrument.

3. Transpose music at sight on the piano.

49 THE MODES: RELATIVE APPROACH

Although this manual focuses on tonal music, and therefore the major and minor modes, you should have some experience working with other modes as well. These other modes (Dorian, Phrygian, Lydian, and Mixolydian) originated in Medieval and Renaissance music, long before the development of the major and minor modes. You can, however, apply the tonal aural skills you have already developed to these older modes as well.

Relative Modes

There is an entire complex of modes—each with its own name—related to one another by specific intervallic distances within any diatonic collection. The following figure shows all the modes in any given diatonic collection, along with the intervallic distance from the major mode to each of the other modes:

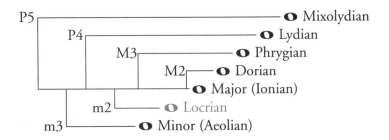

In scalar structure, Ionian is identical to the major scale, and Aeolian is identical to the natural minor scale, but the use of these names is usually reserved for Medieval and Renaissance music.* For music of the common practice period and beyond, we use the names "major" and "minor." In addition, the Locrian mode, which has been dimmed in this figure, appears so rarely that we will not cover it in any detail in this text.

This complex of modes can be moved into any diatonic collection. Let's begin with the no-sharp/no-flat collection, in which the major mode tonic falls on C and the minor mode tonic falls on A. In addition to those two tonics, other diatonic pitches can serve as finals, which for now we will define as the modal equivalent to tonics. The diagram below shows how these tonics and finals project across the no-sharp/no-flat collection.

---

*Medieval and Renaissance music does not behave in the functional ways we associate with major and minor keys and is therefore more appropriately labeled with these old modal names.

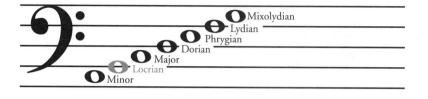

Because the modes in any given diatonic collection all share the same key signature, they are called **relative modes.** Thus—in the same way that we know C major and A minor are relative major and minor keys—D Dorian, E Phrygian, F Lydian and G Mixolydian are also relatives of C major and A minor because they all share the no-sharp/no-flat key signature.

Relative modes share the same diatonic collection, and therefore the same key signature.

White-Key Modes

A lot of modal music is written using the no-sharp/no-flat diatonic collection, which is frequently referred to as the white-key collection because its pitches correspond to the white keys on the piano. Modes written using only the white keys are often called white-key modes or church modes (because of their use in Medieval church music).

Transposed Modes

Early music primarily used the white-key or untransposed church modes. However, music from later eras and folk music transcriptions often use modes that are transposed through the use of key signatures. A new key signature creates a new diatonic collection. If the diatonic collection changes, all of the modes move to new locations, but they retain their positions relative to one another. For example, when we change from the white-key collection to the three-sharp diatonic collection, all of the tonics and finals shift down a minor 3rd:

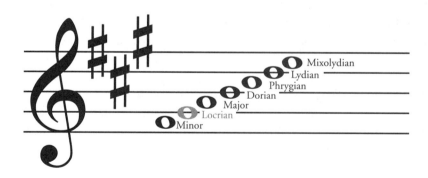

Just as you can calculate a relative minor key signature or tonic by referring to its relative major, you can calculate modal signatures and finals. The complex of keys and modes can be transposed to any of fifteen different diatonic collections through the use of key signatures. As long as you remember the distances between the major tonic and the various relative modal finals, you'll be able to calculate the transposed modes and their corresponding "key" signatures.*

Relative Solmization

Since relative modes share the same diatonic collection, we can simply leave the syllables on the pitches to which they apply in the major mode and recognize a final on a pitch other than *do* (in a manner similar to the relative-minor solmization we used in Chapter 17). Using a relative approach, the major tonic rests on *do,* the minor tonic rests on *la,* and each of the other modes rests on a unique syllable as its final. Leaving *do* where the major tonic would be in any given diatonic collection leaves the two diatonic semitones on *mi–fa* and *ti–do.* The chart below shows the seven modes and their tonic or final syllables in relative solmization:

Modes and tonic or final syllables (relative approach)

Mode	Tonic or final syllable
Mixolydian	*sol*
Lydian	*fa*
Phrygian	*mi*
Dorian	*re*
Major	*do*
Locrian	*ti*
Minor	*la*

The two melodies below are written in the two-sharp collection with relative syllables. *Do* remains where the major tonic would be (on D), leaving all other syllables in their relative positions (note in particular that *mi–fa* remains on F♯–G and *ti–do* remains on C♯–D). The first excerpt is in the major mode because it tonicizes *do,* but the second excerpt is in the Dorian mode with a final on *re* (using the relative approach).

"Old King Cole," English folk song

do do sol sol sol la la la sol sol sol do do do re ti do do

mi mi mi do do do mi mi mi do mi mi sol sol sol fa re do

---

*"Key" is determined by both diatonic collection *and* tonic. The term "key" signature is somewhat of a misnomer since a key signature determines only diatonic collection, not tonic or final.

"The Rocky Road to Dublin," Irish folk song, chorus

la   la   sol   mi   re   la   re   re   re   mi   fa   sol   la   do   ti   re   do   la

sol   do   do   re   mi   fa   sol   la   la   sol   mi   re

With relative solmization, each mode will require you to associate the scale degrees with different sets of syllables. The first note of the Dorian scale is $\hat{1}$/*re*, the first note of the Phrygian scale is $\hat{1}$/*mi*, the first note in the Lydian scale is $\hat{1}$/*fa*, and the first note of the Mixolydian scale is $\hat{1}$/*sol*.

EXERCISES

In order to learn to read, hear, and think in the various modes using a relative approach, you should practice modal scales on relative syllables and memorize certain pitch patterns in each mode.

1. Sing each modal scale, starting and ending on its final syllable. Learn each scale at a brisk pace, ascending and descending, from bottom to top and back, and from top to bottom and back.

    Dorian $\hat{1}$/*re*–$\hat{1}$/*re*
    Phrygian $\hat{1}$/*mi*–$\hat{1}$/*mi*
    Lydian $\hat{1}$/*fa*–$\hat{1}$/*fa*
    Mixolydian $\hat{1}$/*sol*–$\hat{1}$/*sol*

2. Learn the following pitch patterns by heart. Be able to sing them at any time, in any order.

Dorian			
1a. $\hat{1}$/*re* $\hat{2}$/*mi* $\hat{3}$/*fa* $\hat{1}$/*re*		1b. $\hat{1}$/*re* $\hat{3}$/*fa* $\hat{1}$/*re*	
2a. $\hat{1}$/*re* $\hat{2}$/*mi* $\hat{3}$/*fa* $\hat{4}$/*sol* $\hat{5}$/*la* $\hat{1}$/*re*		2b. $\hat{1}$/*re* $\hat{5}$/*la* $\hat{1}$/*re*	
3a. $\hat{1}$/*re* $\hat{7}$/*do* $\hat{6}$/*ti* $\hat{5}$/*la* $\hat{1}$/*re*		3b. $\hat{1}$/*re* $\hat{5}$/*la* $\hat{1}$/*re*	
4a. $\hat{3}$/*fa* $\hat{2}$/*mi* $\hat{1}$/*re* $\hat{3}$/*fa*		4b. $\hat{3}$/*fa* $\hat{1}$/*re* $\hat{3}$/*fa*	

5a. $\hat{5}$/la $\hat{4}$/sol $\hat{3}$/fa $\hat{2}$/mi $\hat{1}$/re $\hat{5}$/la	5b. $\hat{5}$/la $\hat{5}$/la ($\hat{1}$/re)
6a. $\hat{5}$/la $\hat{4}$/sol $\hat{3}$/fa $\hat{5}$/la	6b. $\hat{5}$/la $\hat{5}$/la ($\hat{3}$/fa)
7a. $\hat{3}$/fa $\hat{4}$/sol $\hat{5}$/la $\hat{3}$/fa	7b. $\hat{3}$/fa ($\hat{5}$/la) $\hat{3}$/fa
8a. $\hat{5}$/la $\hat{6}$/ti $\hat{7}$/do $\hat{1}$/re $\hat{5}$/la	8b. $\hat{5}$/la ($\hat{1}$/re) $\hat{5}$/la

Phrygian

1a. $\hat{1}$/mi $\hat{2}$/fa $\hat{3}$/sol $\hat{1}$/mi	1b. $\hat{1}$/mi ($\hat{3}$/sol) $\hat{1}$/mi
2a. $\hat{1}$/mi $\hat{2}$/fa $\hat{3}$/sol $\hat{4}$/la $\hat{5}$/ti $\hat{1}$/mi	2b. $\hat{1}$/mi ($\hat{5}$/ti) $\hat{1}$/mi
3a. $\hat{1}$/mi $\hat{7}$/re $\hat{6}$/do $\hat{5}$/ti $\hat{1}$/mi	3b. $\hat{1}$/mi $\hat{1}$/mi ($\hat{5}$/ti)
4a. $\hat{3}$/sol $\hat{2}$/fa $\hat{1}$/mi $\hat{3}$/sol	4b. $\hat{3}$/sol $\hat{1}$/mi $\hat{3}$/sol
5a. $\hat{5}$/ti $\hat{4}$/la $\hat{3}$/sol $\hat{2}$/fa $\hat{1}$/mi $\hat{5}$/ti	5b. $\hat{5}$/ti $\hat{5}$/ti ($\hat{1}$/mi)
6a. $\hat{5}$/ti $\hat{4}$/la $\hat{3}$/sol $\hat{5}$/ti	6b. $\hat{5}$/ti ($\hat{3}$/sol) $\hat{5}$/ti
7a. $\hat{3}$/sol $\hat{4}$/la $\hat{5}$/ti $\hat{3}$/sol	7b. $\hat{3}$/sol ($\hat{5}$/ti) $\hat{3}$/sol
8a. $\hat{5}$/ti $\hat{6}$/do $\hat{7}$/re $\hat{1}$/mi $\hat{5}$/ti	8b. $\hat{5}$/ti ($\hat{1}$/mi) $\hat{5}$/ti

Lydian

1a.	$\hat{1}$/fa $\hat{2}$/sol $\hat{3}$/la $\hat{1}$/fa	1b.	$\hat{1}$/fa $\hat{3}$/la $\hat{1}$/fa
2a.	$\hat{1}$/fa $\hat{2}$/sol $\hat{3}$/la $\hat{4}$/ti $\hat{5}$/do $\hat{1}$/fa	2b.	$\hat{1}$/fa $\hat{5}$/do $\hat{1}$/fa
3a.	$\hat{1}$/fa $\hat{7}$/mi $\hat{6}$/re $\hat{5}$/do $\hat{1}$/fa	3b.	$\hat{1}$/fa $\hat{5}$/do $\hat{1}$/fa
4a.	$\hat{3}$/la $\hat{2}$/sol $\hat{1}$/fa $\hat{3}$/la	4b.	$\hat{3}$/la $\hat{1}$/fa $\hat{3}$/la
5a.	$\hat{5}$/do $\hat{4}$/ti $\hat{3}$/la $\hat{2}$/sol $\hat{1}$/fa $\hat{5}$/do	5b.	$\hat{5}$/do $\hat{5}$/do $\hat{1}$/fa
6a.	$\hat{5}$/do $\hat{4}$/ti $\hat{3}$/la $\hat{5}$/do	6b.	$\hat{5}$/do $\hat{3}$/la $\hat{5}$/do
7a.	$\hat{3}$/la $\hat{4}$/ti $\hat{5}$/do $\hat{3}$/la	7b.	$\hat{3}$/la $\hat{5}$/do $\hat{3}$/la
8a.	$\hat{5}$/do $\hat{6}$/re $\hat{7}$/mi $\hat{1}$/fa $\hat{5}$/do	8b.	$\hat{5}$/do $\hat{1}$/fa $\hat{5}$/do

Mixolydian

1a.	$\hat{1}$/sol $\hat{2}$/la $\hat{3}$/ti $\hat{1}$/sol	1b.	$\hat{1}$/sol $\hat{3}$/ti $\hat{1}$/sol
2a.	$\hat{1}$/sol $\hat{2}$/la $\hat{3}$/ti $\hat{4}$/do $\hat{5}$/re $\hat{1}$/sol	2b.	$\hat{1}$/sol $\hat{5}$/re $\hat{1}$/sol
3a.	$\hat{1}$/sol $\hat{7}$/fa $\hat{6}$/mi $\hat{5}$/re $\hat{1}$/sol	3b.	$\hat{1}$/sol $\hat{5}$/re $\hat{1}$/sol
4a.	$\hat{3}$/ti $\hat{2}$/la $\hat{1}$/sol $\hat{3}$/ti	4b.	$\hat{3}$/ti $\hat{1}$/sol $\hat{3}$/ti

5a. $\hat{5}/re$ $\hat{4}/do$ $\hat{3}/ti$ $\hat{2}/la$ $\hat{1}/sol$ $\hat{5}/re$	5b. $\hat{5}/re$ $\hat{5}/re$ $\hat{1}/sol$
6a. $\hat{5}/re$ $\hat{4}/do$ $\hat{3}/ti$ $\hat{5}/re$	6b. $\hat{5}/re$ $\hat{3}/ti$ $\hat{5}/re$
7a. $\hat{3}/ti$ $\hat{4}/do$ $\hat{5}/re$ $\hat{3}/ti$	7b. $\hat{3}/ti$ $\hat{5}/re$ $\hat{3}/ti$
8a. $\hat{5}/re$ $\hat{6}/mi$ $\hat{7}/fa$ $\hat{1}/sol$ $\hat{5}/re$	8b. $\hat{5}/re$ $\hat{1}/sol$ $\hat{5}/re$

LISTENING

Melodic Dictation

Listen to excerpts 49.1–49.8 and write out the pitches and rhythms for each, following the given instructions.

Exercise	Clef	Final or tonic	Bottom number in meter sign
49.1	treble	C	4
49.2	bass	B	4
49.3	bass	C	2
49.4	treble	E♭	2
49.5	bass	D	2
49.6	treble	C	4
49.7	tenor	E	2
49.8	alto	D	2

READING AND SIGHT SINGING

Prepare the following melodies, using relative solmization syllables while conducting. Determine the mode or key of each melody, and be prepared to explain your conclusion using your knowledge of key signatures, diatonic collections, tonics, and finals.

Excerpts for reading and sight singing
from the
Anthology for Sight Singing
616–642

50 THE MODES: PARALLEL APPROACH

Parallel Modes

Modes that use different diatonic collections but share the same tonic or final are known as **parallel modes.** The two melodies below have the same tonic or final (C), but their key signatures, and thus their diatonic collections, are different.

> **Parallel modes** share the same tonic or final, but not the same diatonic collection.

J. S. Bach, Chorale No. 239, "Den Vater dort oben," mm. 5–8

"Hajtják a fekete kecskét," Hungarian folk song, mm. 1–6

The Bach chorale has a tonic of C, and uses no sharps or flats—it is in C major. The Hungarian folk song has a final of C, but uses the one-flat collection—it is in C Mixolydian.

It is helpful to compare scale degrees in parallel modes (just as we did with parallel major and minor keys). Comparing the parallel major and Mixolydian modes above, we see that scale degrees $\hat{1}$, $\hat{2}$, $\hat{3}$, $\hat{4}$, $\hat{5}$, and $\hat{6}$ (C, D, E, F, G, and A) are the same in both modes, but scale degree $\hat{7}$ is a half-step lower in the Mixolydian mode (Bb) when compared to the major mode (Bﾑ). This difference in the seventh scale degree is true of all parallel major and Mixolydian scales.

Modal Types

Musicians classify modes according to the quality of the interval formed between the tonic or final and third scale degree. This creates two broad categories of modes: those with a *major* 3rd above their tonic or final, and those with a *minor* 3rd. We shall refer to the first as "major-type" modes, and the second as "minor-type" modes:

Major-type	Minor-type
Major	Minor
Lydian	Dorian
Mixolydian	Phrygian

You can view these categories by placing the corresponding common-practice mode—major or minor—in between the other two parallel modes in each category. As shown in the diagram below, the parallel modes radiate outward in opposite directions in the circle of fifths, adding or subtracting one sharp or flat in each direction. (Review the circle-of-fifths arrangement of the key signatures in Chapter 11.)

Add one flat or subtract one sharp	←	Common-practice mode	→	Add one sharp or subtract one flat
Mixolydian	←	Major	→	Lydian
Phrygian	←	Minor	→	Dorian

These relationships are demonstrated below, using the modes that share the tonic or final C (major-type modes) and A (minor-type modes).

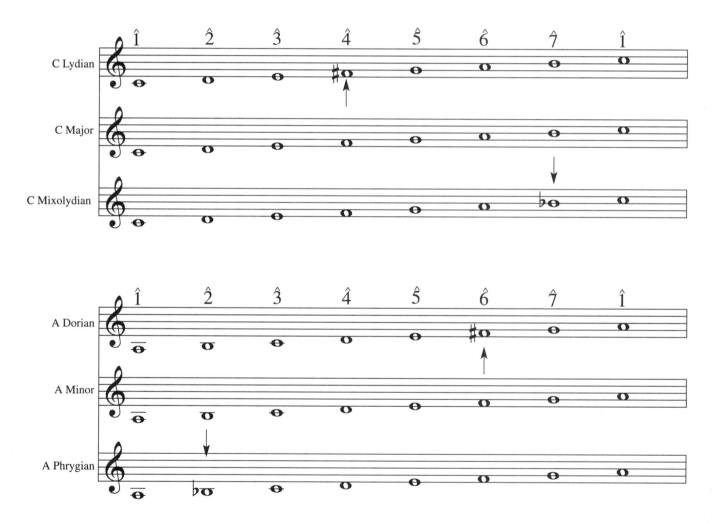

You can also view parallel modes by comparing specific scale degrees in the common-practice modes and each of their parallel category members. Referring to the modes as they are notated above, you can isolate the differences by looking at the arrows. In the major-type category, Lydian differs from the major mode in having a raised fourth scale degree, while Mixolydian differs from the major mode in having a lowered seventh. In minor-type modes, Dorian is like the natural minor mode with a raised sixth, and Phrygian is like minor with a lowered second scale degree.

Major-Type Modes

Lydian is like the *major* mode with a raised $\hat{4}$
Mixolydian is like the *major* mode with a lowered $\hat{7}$

Minor-Type Modes

Dorian is like the *minor* mode with a raised $\hat{6}$
Phrygian is like the *minor* mode with a lowered $\hat{2}$

Parallel Solmization

Parallel modes share the same tonic or final and other scale-degree functions, all of which can be represented by using parallel solmization. If you label the tonic or final in all parallel modes as $\hat{1}$/ *do*, similar syllables will reflect similar functions. For instance, $\hat{1}$/ *do*–$\hat{5}$/ *sol* will represent the tonic dominant or final-dominant relationship in all parallel modes.

The chart below shows the syllables for the major-type modes. Syllables that are altered from the major mode appear in bold:

	$\hat{1}$	$\hat{2}$	$\hat{3}$	$\hat{4}$	$\hat{5}$	$\hat{6}$	$\hat{7}$	$\hat{8}$
parallel Lydian	do	re	mi	**fi**	sol	la	ti	do
Major	do	re	mi	fa	sol	la	ti	do
parallel Mixolydian	do	re	mi	fa	sol	la	**te**	do

A similar chart shows the minor-type modes. Note the introduction of a new syllable for the second scale degree in the Phrygian mode—$\hat{2}$/ *ra* (pronounced "RAH"), which is a half step lower than $\hat{2}$/ *re*.

	$\hat{1}$	$\hat{2}$	$\hat{3}$	$\hat{4}$	$\hat{5}$	$\hat{6}$	$\hat{7}$	$\hat{8}$
parallel Dorian	do	re	me	fa	sol	**la**	te	do
Minor	do	re	me	fa	sol	le	te	do
parallel Phrygian	do	**ra**	me	fa	sol	le	te	do

Modes Notated with Accidentals

One way of notating modal music has developed from these two categories—major-type and minor-type modes. This method uses the key signature of the mode's corresponding major or minor key, and then uses accidentals to make the alterations necessary for that particular mode (raised $\hat{4}$, lowered $\hat{7}$, etc.).

For example, Bartók used the one-sharp signature (associated with G major) for the Mixolydian melody below, and he lowered all seventh scale degrees by writing in an accidental, in this case, a natural.

Béla Bartók, *First Term at the Piano,* No. 16, "Peasant's Dance" (1913)

Allegro moderato. (♩ = 60)

EXERCISES

1. Learn to sing each modal scale starting and ending on 1̂/*do.* Perform each scale at a brisk pace, ascending and descending, from bottom to top and back, and from top to bottom and back.

2. Learn the following pitch patterns by heart. Be able to sing them at any time, in any order. Note that the patterns printed in **bold** are those that deviate from the common-practice mode for that mode's type.

Lydian			
1a. 1̂/*do* 2̂/*re* 3̂/*mi* 1̂/*do*		1b. 1̂/*do* 3̂/*mi* 1̂/*do*	
2a. **1̂/*do*** 2̂/*re* 3̂/*mi* **4̂/*fi*** 5̂/*sol* 1̂/*do*		2b. 1̂/*do* 5̂/*sol* 1̂/*do*	
3a. 1̂/*do* 7̂/*ti* 6̂/*la* 5̂/*sol* 1̂/*do*		3b. 1̂/*do* 1̂/*do* 5̂/*sol*	
4a. 3̂/*mi* 2̂/*re* 1̂/*do* 3̂/*mi*		4b. 3̂/*mi* 1̂/*do* 3̂/*mi*	
5a. 5̂/*sol* **4̂/*fi*** 3̂/*mi* 2̂/*re* **1̂/*do*** 5̂/*sol*		5b. 5̂/*sol* 1̂/*do* 5̂/*sol*	
6a. 5̂/*sol* **4̂/*fi*** 3̂/*mi* 5̂/*sol*		6b. 5̂/*sol* 3̂/*mi* 5̂/*sol*	

7a. $\hat{3}$/**mi** $\hat{4}$/**fi** $\hat{5}$/**sol** $\hat{3}$/**mi** | 7b. $\hat{3}$/mi $\hat{5}$/sol $\hat{3}$/mi

8a. $\hat{5}$/sol $\hat{6}$/la $\hat{7}$/ti $\hat{1}$/do $\hat{5}$/sol | 8b. $\hat{5}$/sol $\hat{1}$/do $\hat{5}$/sol

Mixolydian

1a. $\hat{1}$/do $\hat{2}$/re $\hat{3}$/mi $\hat{1}$/do | 1b. $\hat{1}$/do $\hat{3}$/mi $\hat{1}$/do

2a. $\hat{1}$/do $\hat{2}$/re $\hat{3}$/mi $\hat{4}$/fa $\hat{5}$/sol $\hat{1}$/do | 2b. $\hat{1}$/do $\hat{5}$/sol $\hat{1}$/do

3a. $\hat{1}$/**do** $\hat{7}$/**te** $\hat{6}$/**la** $\hat{5}$/**sol** $\hat{1}$/**do** | 3b. $\hat{1}$/do $\hat{5}$/sol $\hat{1}$/do

4a. $\hat{3}$/mi $\hat{2}$/re $\hat{1}$/do $\hat{3}$/mi | 4b. $\hat{3}$/mi $\hat{1}$/do $\hat{3}$/mi

5a. $\hat{5}$/sol $\hat{4}$/fa $\hat{3}$/mi $\hat{2}$/re $\hat{1}$/do $\hat{5}$/sol | 5b. $\hat{5}$/sol $\hat{1}$/do $\hat{5}$/sol

6a. $\hat{5}$/sol $\hat{4}$/fa $\hat{3}$/mi $\hat{5}$/sol | 6b. $\hat{5}$/sol $\hat{3}$/mi $\hat{5}$/sol

7a. $\hat{3}$/mi $\hat{4}$/fa $\hat{5}$/sol $\hat{3}$/mi | 7b. $\hat{3}$/mi $\hat{5}$/sol $\hat{3}$/mi

8a. $\hat{5}$/**sol** $\hat{6}$/**la** $\hat{7}$/**te** $\hat{1}$/**do** $\hat{5}$/**sol** | 8b. $\hat{5}$/sol $\hat{1}$/do $\hat{5}$/sol

Dorian

1a. $\hat{1}$/do $\hat{2}$/re $\hat{3}$/me $\hat{1}$/do | 1b. $\hat{1}$/do $\hat{3}$/me $\hat{1}$/do

2a. $\hat{1}$/do $\hat{2}$/re $\hat{3}$/me $\hat{4}$/fa $\hat{5}$/sol $\hat{1}$/do | 2b. $\hat{1}$/do $\hat{5}$/sol $\hat{1}$/do

3a. $\hat{1}$/do $\hat{7}$/te $\hat{6}$/la $\hat{5}$/sol $\hat{1}$/do

3b. $\hat{1}$/do $\hat{5}$/sol $\hat{1}$/do

4a. $\hat{3}$/me $\hat{2}$/re $\hat{1}$/do $\hat{3}$/me

4b. $\hat{3}$/me $\hat{1}$/do $\hat{3}$/me

5a. $\hat{5}$/sol $\hat{4}$/fa $\hat{3}$/me $\hat{2}$/re $\hat{1}$/do $\hat{5}$/sol

5b. $\hat{5}$/sol $\hat{1}$/do $\hat{5}$/sol

6a. $\hat{5}$/sol $\hat{4}$/fa $\hat{3}$/me $\hat{5}$/sol

6b. $\hat{5}$/sol $\hat{3}$/me $\hat{5}$/sol

7a. $\hat{3}$/me $\hat{4}$/fa $\hat{5}$/sol $\hat{3}$/me

7b. $\hat{3}$/me $\hat{5}$/sol $\hat{3}$/me

8a. $\hat{5}$/sol $\hat{6}$/la $\hat{7}$/te $\hat{1}$/do $\hat{5}$/sol

8b. $\hat{5}$/sol $\hat{1}$/do $\hat{5}$/sol

Phrygian

1a. $\hat{1}$/do $\hat{2}$/ra $\hat{3}$/me $\hat{1}$/do

1b. $\hat{1}$/do $\hat{3}$/me $\hat{1}$/do

2a. $\hat{1}$/do $\hat{2}$/ra $\hat{3}$/me $\hat{4}$/fa $\hat{5}$/sol $\hat{1}$/do

2b. $\hat{1}$/do $\hat{5}$/sol $\hat{1}$/do

3a. $\hat{1}$/do $\hat{7}$/te $\hat{6}$/le $\hat{5}$/sol $\hat{1}$/do

3b. $\hat{1}$/do $\hat{5}$/sol $\hat{1}$/do

4a. $\hat{3}$/me $\hat{2}$/ra $\hat{1}$/do $\hat{3}$/me

4b. $\hat{3}$/me $\hat{1}$/do $\hat{3}$/me

5a. $\hat{5}$/sol $\hat{4}$/fa $\hat{3}$/me $\hat{2}$/ra $\hat{1}$/do $\hat{5}$/sol

5b. $\hat{5}$/sol $\hat{1}$/do $\hat{5}$/sol

6a. $\hat{5}$/sol $\hat{4}$/fa $\hat{3}$/me $\hat{5}$/sol

6b. $\hat{5}$/sol $\hat{3}$/me $\hat{5}$/sol

7a.	$\hat{3}$/me $\hat{4}$/fa $\hat{5}$/sol $\hat{3}$/me		7b.	$\hat{3}$/me $\hat{5}$/sol $\hat{3}$/me	
8a.	$\hat{5}$/sol $\hat{6}$/le $\hat{7}$/te $\hat{1}$/do $\hat{5}$/sol		8b.	$\hat{5}$/sol $\hat{1}$/do $\hat{5}$/sol	

LISTENING

Melodic Dictation

Use the dictation exercises from Chapter 49 (49.1–49.8), but apply the parallel approach you learned in this chapter. Write out the pitches and rhythms for each, following the given instructions. Write some using the parallel major or minor key signature, inserting accidentals to make the necessary alterations for the appropriate mode.

READING AND SIGHT SINGING

Prepare the following melodies (same as those for Chapter 49), using parallel solmization syllables while conducting.

**Excerpts for reading and sight singing
from the
Anthology for Sight Singing
616–642**

51 ADVANCED TRIPLETS

We have studied the one-beat triplet, which divides the beat into three parts in simple meters. This same principle can be used to divide durations other than the beat into three parts. Two kinds of triplets appear frequently in simple meters: half-beat triplets and two-beat triplets.

Half-Beat Triplets

In simple meters the half beat is usually divided into halves itself, which creates quadruple beat divisions. However, it is possible to divide the beat into three parts using a half-beat triplet.

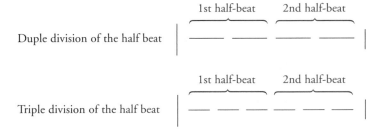

Triple division of successive half beats results in sextuple division of the beat similar to that we have observed in compound meters. The Takadimi syllables for sextuple division that we learned in Chapter 28 (Ta-va-ki-di-da-ma), can also be used in simple meters.

In order to squeeze three notes in the place of two, half-beat triplets are written using the note value that normally represents *quadruple* division of a beat. For example, in the excerpt by Tchaikovsky below, the sixteenth note normally represents a quadruple division of the beat, so the half-beat triplet is notated with three sixteenth-note triplets.

Peter Ilich Tchaikovsky, Symphony No. 4, Op. 36, mvt. 1, mm. 1–2 (1878)

The excerpt above also illustrates the underlying feel of the half-note divisions. You must feel this division first in order to perform half-beat triplets. This is particularly important when the triple divisions of the half beat are not immediately preceded by half-beat divisions. Practice "turning on" this internal sense of half-beat divisions any time half-beat triplets occur. You should also practice dividing each half beat into threes and switching between duple and triple divisions of the half beat.

Two-Beat Triplets

It is also possible to divide a *two-beat* span in simple meters into three equal parts. The symbol for this is the two-beat triplet, which is written using the note value that normally represents *one* beat, but squeezing three of those in the place of two, as illustrated below.

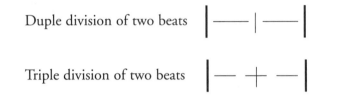

Duple division of two beats

Triple division of two beats

Since two-beat triplets divide two beats into three equal parts, each of those triplets lasts two-thirds of a beat (2 divided by 3). In order to perform two-beat triplets, you must feel the underlying subdivisions of each *beat* into three parts (or, *one*-beat triplets).

Hugo Wolf, "Harfenspieler II," mm. 5–6 (1888)

Each two-beat triplet lasts as long as two notes of the one-beat triplet, as illustrated in the diagram below.

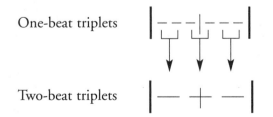

One-beat triplets

Two-beat triplets

Once you feel the underlying one-beat triplets, you achieve the *two*-beat triplets by tying together pairs of those one-beat triplets:

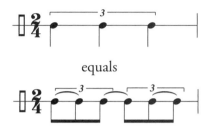

equals

You can practice easing into two-beat triplets in much the same way we approached syncopation (see Chapter 31). Let's walk through this process using the two measures from Wolf's "Harfenspieler II" (shown above). First, articulate each of the one-beat triplets:

Then sing only a soft articulation (such as "haa") on the second of each pair of one-beat triplets:

Finally, perform the passage without rearticulating the second note of each pair. This will yield the original two-beat triplet rhythms.

When a two-beat triplet is preceded by *duple* division of the beat, it makes preparing for the triplet more difficult. You must develop your ability to switch to triple-beat divisions immediately when needed to execute two-beat triplets.

EXERCISES

1. Set a metronome at 60. Conduct each click using any conducting pattern (repeat this exercise with several different patterns). Pretend that each beat is a quarter note, and chant eighth notes. Change to chanting sixteenth notes and then back to eighth notes and then to sixteenth-note triplets. Finally, practice changing directly from sixteenth notes to sixteenth-note triplets and back again.

2. Set a metronome at 90. Conduct each click using any conducting pattern (repeat this exercise with several different patterns). Pretend that each beat is

a quarter note and chant quarter notes. Change to chanting eighth-note triplets and then back to quarter notes. Change to quarter-note triplets, then back to quarter notes, and then to eighth notes. Finally, practice changing directly from eighth notes to quarter-note triplets and back again.

LISTENING

Melodic Dictation

Listen to excerpts 51.1–51.8 and write out the pitches and rhythms for each, following the given instructions.

Exercise	Clef	Tonic	Bottom number in meter sign
51.1	treble	G	4
51.2	bass	D♭	8
51.3	treble	E	2
51.4	bass	C♯	4
51.5	treble	B	4
51.6	bass	B	2
51.7	alto	F	8
51.8	tenor	E♭	4

READING AND SIGHT SINGING

Prepare the following melodies, singing on syllables while conducting. As you prepare, think of the appropriate beat divisions (and subdivisions) necessary for each triplet rhythm.

**Excerpts for reading and sight singing
from the
Anthology for Sight Singing
643–656**

52 CHROMATIC PASSING TONES

In addition to the chromatic pitches we have encountered in the major and minor modes—lower chromatic neighbors, and ↑6̂/*la* and ↑7̂/*ti* in the minor mode (as borrowed from major)—chromatic pitches are also used as passing tones.

Chromatic Connections between Diatonic Pitches

Joseph Haydn, *Lo Speziale (Der Apotheker)*, Act I, scene 4,
"Per quel che ha mal di stomaco," mm. 17–20 (1768)

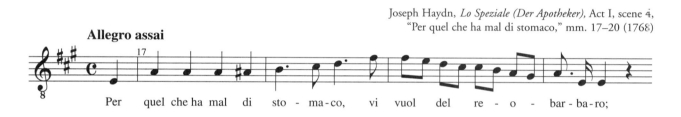

Allegro assai

Per quel che ha mal di sto - ma - co, vi vuol del re - o - bar - ba - ro;

In the excerpt above, the A♯ at the end of measure 17 serves as a connector between two diatonic pitches, A and B. We call this a **chromatic passing tone**.

Structurally, a chromatic passing tone is subordinate to the two diatonic pitches on either side of it. You can get a good sense of the pitch structure of a passage with chromatic passing tones by singing only its diatonic pitches. Pay careful attention to the intonation of the diatonic pitches surrounding any chromatic passing tone since they are the anchors between which the chromatic pitches pass.

The figure on the next page shows the syllables used to represent both diatonic and chromatic pitches. The left-hand column shows the major mode. The middle column shows the minor mode using a parallel approach. The right-hand column shows the minor mode using a relative approach. The diatonic pitches are printed in heavy boxes (to indicate their status as "anchors") and the chromatics are printed between them (with enharmonic equivalents occupying the same horizontal space).

If you follow the ascending arrows up the left side of each column, you'll see the spellings and functions for ascending chromatics. If you follow the descending arrows on the right side of each column, you'll see the spellings and functions for descending chromatics.

Not all composers, arrangers, and editors are consistent in chromatic spellings, particularly in spelling descending chromatic passing tones. The most common exception is a nearly universal one: The chromatic passing tone from 5̂/*sol* down to 4̂/*fa* is usually spelled as a raised 4̂/*fa* instead of a lowered 5̂/*sol*.

In the parallel approach, some musicians think of the upper **tetrachord** in minor (the notes between 5̂/*sol* and 1̂/*do*) as an exact replication of that in the parallel major—with 6̂/*la* and 7̂/*ti* as *diatonic* pitches and ↓6̂/*le* and ↓7̂/*te* as *chromatic* ones. In this case, the upper tetrachord of the center column would be identical to the major-mode one in the left column.

Major mode	Parallel minor	Relative minor

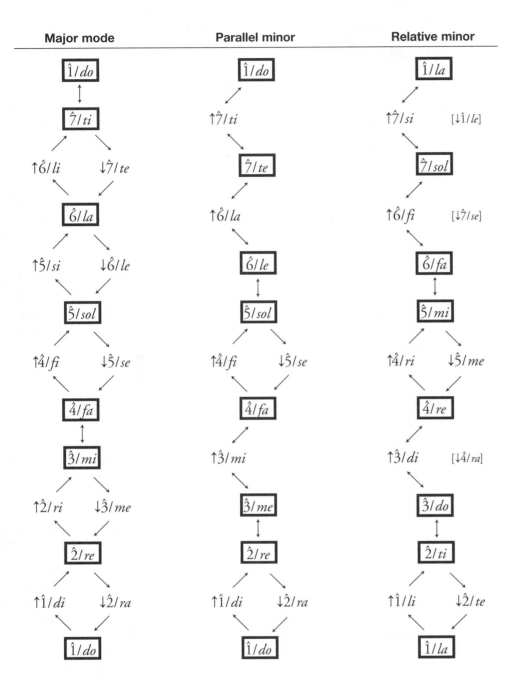

Some of these chromatics are used more frequently than others. In the relative-minor column, the syllables written in brackets are rarely found in music. In the parallel-minor column, no syllables are given for a lowered $\hat{1}$/do, $\hat{7}$/te, and $\hat{4}$/fa because they rarely occur. Chromatic passing tones below these notes take the form of the enharmonic ascending note. For example, the passing tone from $\hat{1}$/do to $\hat{7}$/te is ↑$\hat{7}$/ti, not ↓$\hat{1}$/de. If you find yourself trying to apply the syllables ↓$\hat{1}$/de, ↓$\hat{7}$/ta, or ↓$\hat{4}$/fe, you've almost certainly misinterpreted the functions of the notes, or the music has modulated to another key.

The most common chromatic passing tones, both ascending and descending, are shown in the table below:

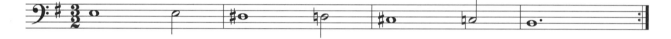

Ascending	Descending
$\hat{1}$/ *do*—↑$\hat{1}$/ *di*—$\hat{2}$/ *re*	$\hat{7}$/ *ti*—↓$\hat{7}$/ *te*—$\hat{6}$/ *la*
$\hat{2}$/ *re*—↑$\hat{2}$/ *ri*—$\hat{3}$/ *mi*	$\hat{6}$/ *la*—↓$\hat{6}$/ *le*—$\hat{5}$/ *sol* [sometimes: $\hat{6}$/ *la*—↑$\hat{5}$/ *si*—$\hat{5}$/ *sol*]
$\hat{4}$/ *fa*—↑$\hat{4}$/ *fi*—$\hat{5}$/ *sol*	$\hat{5}$/ *sol*—↑$\hat{4}$/ *fi*—$\hat{4}$/ *fa* [rarely: $\hat{5}$/ *sol*—↓$\hat{5}$/ *se*—$\hat{4}$/ *fa*]
$\hat{5}$/ *sol*—↑$\hat{5}$/ *si*—$\hat{6}$/ *la*	

At first, practice singing music that contains a single chromatic passing tone between two diatonic pitches. After you master singing such isolated chromatic passing tones, you can progress to music that strings several of them in a row, such as the bass line below, which connects the diatonic pitches in the descent from $\hat{1}$ to $\hat{5}$ with chromatic passing tones:

The Chromatic Scale

> A **chromatic scale** is a series of pitches spanning an octave wherein all adjacent pitches are separated by half steps.

If you string a series of half steps together, all moving in the same direction spanning an octave, the result is called a **chromatic scale.** An ascending chromatic scale beginning and ending on C is shown in the example below. Since we are still dealing with chromatics in the context of tonal music, the tonic and other diatonic pitches should remain important points of reference in your singing and listening. For this reason, the diatonic pitches (in the major mode) have been connected by stems and beams, while the chromatic ones that pass between them have been left as stemless noteheads.

EXERCISES

1. For each of the following familiar tunes, determine the scale degrees of its pitches so that you can sing each tune on its proper syllables. Do the work entirely *in your mind,* without the aid of any instrument or writing.

   Be especially sensitive to where chromatic passing tones occur in these melodies. Identify unequivocally the scale degrees surrounding any chromatic passing tones, then work out the syllable of the chromatic pitch between them.

• Rubber Ducky (first twenty-five notes)
• White Christmas
• Scott Joplin, "The Entertainer" (first eighteen notes)

Memorize each of these tunes on the proper syllables.

2. Learn the following chromatic passing-tone sequentials on syllables. Memorize the *pattern* for each, then learn it without looking at the notation. Imagine these sequentials in various keys as you sing them.

The descending part of the major-mode version has been written entirely with descending chromatics for the sake of consistency and to familiarize you with all the descending syllables. You will encounter many pieces that descend 5̂/*sol*–↑4̂/*fi*–4̂/*fa* and 6̂/*la*–↑5̂/*si*–5̂/*sol*, so you should practice the major-mode chromatic passing tone sequential with those syllables as well. You should also practice the minor-mode version with 5̂/*sol*–↑4̂/*fi*–4̂/*fa*.

Major mode:

Minor mode:

3. Give yourself a starting pitch on the piano or other instrument and sing an ascending chromatic scale. Pay careful attention to the intonation of the diatonic pitches (especially 1̂ and 5̂). When you reach the octave, check yourself against the starting pitch. If you have difficulty ending on the proper pitch, try singing the chromatic scale from 1̂ up to 5̂, then check yourself against 5̂. Once you can do that, then work on singing up from 5̂ up to 1̂ in the same manner. Then finally piece the two scale segments together.

Repeat this procedure with a descending chromatic scale.

LISTENING

Melodic Dictation

Listen to excerpts 52.1–52.11 and write out the pitches and rhythms for each. Listen closely for chromatic passing tones. Focus on the diatonic pitches surrounding these chromatics, especially the notes to which they resolve. Notate ascending chromatics as raised pitches and descending chromatics as lowered pitches (except ↓$\hat{5}$, which you should write as ↑$\hat{4}$). Note that some of these require a grand staff for two- and three-part dictation.

Exercise	Clef	Tonic	Bottom number in meter sign
52.1	bass	B	8
52.2	alto	A♭	2
52.3	treble	E	8
52.4	treble	F	4
52.5	vocal tenor*	F	4
52.6	bass	B♭	4
52.7	bass	A	4
52.8	bass	D	4
52.9	grand staff (2 voices)	B	4
52.10	grand staff (2 voices)	B♭	4
52.11	grand staff (3 voices)	A	2

READING AND SIGHT SINGING

Prepare the following excerpts, singing on syllables while conducting. Sing them first replacing the chromatic passing tones with rests, and then reintroduce the chromatic pitches. Pay special attention to the intonation of the diatonic pitches on either side of the chromatic ones.

Excerpts for reading and sight singing
from the
Anthology for Sight Singing
657–707

---

*Vocal tenor clef (review Chapter 8) looks similar to the treble clef but sounds one octave lower than written.

53 SKIPS TO CHROMATIC PITCHES AS PREFIX NEIGHBORS

We have encountered diatonic pitches that function as incomplete prefix neighbors to other diatonic pitches, as when a skip to $\hat{7}$/*ti* is a prefix neighbor to $\hat{1}$/*do*. (Review Chapters 14 and 27.) *Chromatic* pitches can also function as prefix neighbors, and skips to various chromatic pitches can be understood as prefix neighbor notes that resolve to diatonic pitches. The most common chromatic prefix neighbor notes are lower neighbors, but you will occasionally find upper chromatic prefix neighbors as well.

Chromatic Prefix Neighbors

In previous discussions of neighboring notes, we found it useful to rethink prefix neighbors in two ways: (1) as a complete neighboring note; and (2) by eliminating the prefix neighbor entirely. These two approaches can also be used for skips to chromatic pitches as prefix neighbors.

In measure 4 of the following excerpt, the second note—the chromatic pitch $\hat{\uparrow 4}$/*fi*—is approached by skip from $\hat{2}$/*re*.

Gesangvoll, mit innigster Empfindung
Andante molto cantabile ed espressivo

Ludwig van Beethoven, Piano Sonata No. 30, Op. 109, mvt. 3, mm. 1–4 (1820)

We can recompose this as a complete neighbor, so that the chromatic pitch is surrounded by $\hat{5}$/*sol,* a pitch you know quite well.

After having learned this recomposed version—internalizing $\hat{\uparrow 4}$/*fi* as a complete lower neighbor to $\hat{5}$/*sol*—try singing the original.

We can also recompose this measure by eliminating the chromatic prefix neighbor altogether, which focuses our attention on the target note at its point of arrival. Once again, learn the passage this way, then return to the original.

As in our earlier work on prefix neighbors, you will find that certain contexts demand only one or the other of these two approaches depending on the specific pitches and rhythms they employ.

Embellished Chromatic Passing Tones

When a leap to a chromatic prefix neighbor occurs closely following the diatonic version of that pitch, the chromatic pitch functions as part of an embellished chromatic-passing-tone figure. Two such instances occur in the following excerpt:

Johannes Brahms, Serenade No. 1, Op. 11, Minuet I, mm. 1–8 (1853)

The G♯ at the downbeat of measure 2 can be heard as a chromatic passing tone between the G in measure 1 and the A in measure 2. A similar figure appears in measures 3–4, connecting A and B using A♯. A simplified version of this process might be written this way:

Chromatic Prefix Neighbors in Apparently Linear Contexts

A chromatic prefix neighbor can occur in what appears to be a linear (stepwise) context, but which is nonetheless heard more appropriately as only a prefix neighbor to the diatonic pitch to which it resolves. For instance, in the example below, the C♯ at the end of measure 11 would seem to be part of a stepwise progression from B♭ to D.

Adolphe Adam, *Si J'etais roi*, Act II, "Vous m'aimez, dites-vous," mm. 11–15 (1852?)

However, no matter what linear connection we might feel (if any) between $\hat{1}$/*do* and ↑$\hat{2}$/*ri*, it is most musical and practical to think of ↑$\hat{2}$/*ri* as a prefix chromatic neighbor to $\hat{3}$/*mi*. This is similar to the motion $\hat{6}$/*le*–↑$\hat{7}$/*ti*–$\hat{1}$/*do* in the minor mode, for which we found it useful to think of ↑$\hat{7}$/*ti* as a prefix neighbor to $\hat{1}$/*do*. No matter what note precedes a chromatic prefix neighbor, you should think of it as appended to the diatonic pitch to which it resolves.

Sequentials

Learn the following major-mode sequentials on syllables. Memorize the *pattern* for each, then learn it without looking at the notation. Imagine these sequentials in various keys as you sing them.

Construct similar sequentials for the minor mode.

↑6̂/ *li* (This one is especially difficult because the lower chromatic neighbor to 7̂/ *ti* tends to efface the original tonic)

↓2̂/ *ra*

↓6̂/ *le*

↓7̂/ *te* (This one is especially difficult because the repetition of ↓7̂/ *te* tends to efface the original tonic)

Melodic Dictation

Listen to excerpts 53.1–53.8 and write out the pitches and rhythms for each. Listen closely for chromatic pitches. Focus on the diatonic pitches surrounding these chromatics, especially the notes to which they resolve.

Exercise	Clef	Tonic	Bottom number in meter sign
53.1	bass	E	4
53.2	treble	A♭	4
53.3	treble	G	8
53.4	treble	E♭	4
53.5	treble	G	4
53.6	treble	B	8
53.7	treble	F	4
53.8	treble (two staves)	G	2

Melodic Transcription

Transcribe excerpts 53.9–53.10. Take as many listenings and as much time between them as necessary, but be certain to write down as many aspects of the performances as you can, including timbre, tempo, articulation, rubato, and so forth.

Exercise	Clef	Tonic	Bottom number in meter sign
53.9	vocal tenor*	C	2
53.10	treble & bass (two staves) Write out melody and bass line.	A	4

READING AND SIGHT SINGING

Prepare the following excerpts, singing on syllables while conducting. Practice them using one or both of the approaches we have learned: (1) using a complete neighbor figure, and (2) eliminating the chromatic pitches approached by skip. Then, reintroduce the skips to chromatic pitches while paying special attention to the intonation of the diatonic pitches on either side of the chromatic ones.

Which of the chromatics in these excerpts can be heard as embellished chromatic passing tones?

Excerpts for reading and sight singing
from the
Anthology for Sight Singing
708–746

---

*Vocal tenor clef (review Chapter 8) looks similar to the treble clef but sounds one octave lower than written.

54 CHORDS APPLIED TO THE DOMINANT

Chromatic pitches occur not only in the melodic contexts we have studied (as embellishments to diatonic pitches), but also in harmonic contexts, when the chromatic pitch becomes part of a *chord*. The origins and functions of chromatic harmony are examined in great detail in your harmony textbook. *This* book will focus primarily on the aspects of chromatic harmony specific to sight reading and listening.

The Applied Leading Tone

The raised fourth scale degree (↑4̂/*fi*) has appeared thus far in this book in three different melodic contexts: (1) as a lower chromatic neighbor to 5̂/*sol*, (2) as part of the chromatic passing-tone figure 4̂/*fa*–↑4̂/*fi*–5̂/*sol*, and (3) as an incomplete prefix neighbor to 5̂/*sol*. (See the example below.*)

lower neighbor   passing tone   incomplete prefix neighbor

In all of these, ↑4̂/*fi* leads directly to 5̂/*sol* by half step. Because of this, we can see and hear ↑4̂/*fi* as a kind of *leading tone* to 5̂/*sol*. A leading tone that is created through being chromatically raised to within a half-step of another pitch is called an **applied leading tone**.

> An **applied leading tone** is a note raised chromatically to serve as a temporary leading tone to the diatonic note a half step above it.

Chords Applied to the Dominant

> An **applied leading-tone chord** is a chord with an applied leading tone as its root.

In the same way that the diatonic leading tone (7̂/*ti*) can serve as the root of a leading-tone chord, an applied leading tone can serve as the root of an **applied leading-tone chord** (also called a **secondary leading-tone chord**). Thus, ↑4̂/*fi* can become the root of the chord ↑4̂/*fi*–6̂/*la*–1̂/*do*. Occasionally, 3̂/*mi* or ↓3̂/*me* will be added to this, creating a seventh chord.

---

*For the sake of simplicity, generic examples will be printed in the key of C.

244

In the same way that the diatonic leading tone ($\hat{7}$/*ti*) can serve as the third of a dominant chord, an applied leading tone can also serve as the third of an **applied dominant chord** (also called a **secondary dominant chord**). Thus, ↑$\hat{4}$/*fi* can become the third of a chord built on $\hat{2}$/*re*: $\hat{2}$/*re*–↑$\hat{4}$/*fi*–$\hat{6}$/*la* (with the option of adding $\hat{1}$/*do* to create a seventh chord).

The root of this chord ($\hat{2}$/*re*) functions as the dominant of the root of the chord to which it is applied ($\hat{5}$/*sol*). An applied dominant is a pitch a perfect 5th above (or a perfect 4th below) the pitch to which it is applied. An applied dominant chord (or secondary dominant chord) is a chord whose root is an applied dominant and whose quality is the same as a dominant chord—a major triad or major-minor seventh chord. Although you could think of this chord built on $\hat{2}$/*re* as a supertonic chord with a raised third (II♯), this does not account for its function as an applied chord.

To fully represent the function of an applied chord and its relationship to the chord to which it is applied, we label it with two symbols separated by a slash. The first symbol represents the kind of chord it is (V̲ for applied dominant, vii° for applied leading tone). The second symbol represents the chord to which it is applied. Both types of applied chords are shown below:

C: I   V̲   I   V̲/V̲   V̲   vii°⁶/V̲   V̲⁷   I

Here are the chords applied to the dominant:

V̲/V̲ . . . . $\hat{2}$/*re*–↑$\hat{4}$/*fi*–[↑]$\hat{6}$/*la*

V̲⁷/V̲ . . . . $\hat{2}$/*re*–↑$\hat{4}$/*fi*–[↑]$\hat{6}$/*la*–$\hat{1}$/*do*

vii°/V̲ . . . . ↑$\hat{4}$/*fi*–[↑]$\hat{6}$/*la*–$\hat{1}$/*do*

vii°⁷/V̲ . . . . ↑$\hat{4}$/*fi*–[↑]$\hat{6}$/*la*–$\hat{1}$/*do*–$\hat{3}$/*mi*

vii°⁷/V̲ . . . . ↑$\hat{4}$/*fi*–[↑]$\hat{6}$/*la*–$\hat{1}$/*do*–[↓]$\hat{3}$/*me*

In all these chords, the characteristic tendency tone is ↑$\hat{4}$/*fi*, which resolves up and by step to $\hat{5}$/*sol*. In the vii°⁷/V̲, another tendency tone is [↓]$\hat{3}$/*me*, which resolves down by step to $\hat{2}$/*re*

An **applied dominant** is a pitch a perfect 5th above (or a perfect 4th below) the pitch to which it is applied.

An **applied dominant chord** is a chord whose root is an applied dominant and whose quality is the same as a dominant chord.

Some texts use the term **"secondary"** (as in **"secondary dominant"**) instead of "applied." Do not confuse this with the term "secondary triad," which is used to distinguish the supertonic, mediant, submediant, and leading-tone triads from the so-called "primary triads" —tonic, subdominant, and dominant.

Although only *one* chromatic pitch (↑4̂/*fi*) is needed for all these chords in the major mode, *two* chromatic pitches (↑4̂/*fi* and ↑6̂/*la*) are needed in the minor mode. The pitch ↓3̂/*me* is chromatic in the major mode.

Implications for Reading and Singing

We have encountered skips *to* ↑4̂/*fi*, which all resolved immediately to 5̂/*sol*. We will now begin to encounter skips *away* from ↑4̂/*fi*, particularly to other members of the V/V and vii°/V chords. For example, in measure 74 of the following excerpt, the skip to and from F♯ forms part of a V/V chord:

Allegretto tranquillo, poi più agitato   Edvard Grieg, "Ausfahrt," Op. 9, No. 4, mm. 72–75 (1866)

Er - fül - lung nun ward ih-rem höch-sten Be - gehr,_ sie soll - te die Schön-heit er - schaun,_

As the arrow indicates, the resolution of ↑4̂/*fi* (F♯) to 5̂/*sol* (G) is delayed until after the entire V/V chord has been arpeggiated.

Implications for Listening

The only new material for melodic dictation presented here will involve skips away from ↑4̂/*fi*. However, the addition of V/V and vii°/V introduces quite a few new possibilities for chords above certain scale degrees in harmonic dictation. The chart below shows the bass notes above which chords applied to the dominant may appear and discusses the inversion of each chord associated with each bass note. Keep in mind that you are adding these chords to all the harmonic possibilities you have learned in previous chapters.

2̂/*re*   When you hear 2̂/*re* in the bass voice, it could now also be the root of a V/V chord (2̂/*re*–↑4̂/*fi*–6̂/*la*) or V⁷/V (2̂/*re*–↑4̂/*fi*–6̂/*la*–1̂/*do*). The presence or absence of 1̂/*do* in some upper voice makes the difference.

↑4̂/*fi*   When you hear a chord supported by ↑4̂/*fi*, it could point to a first-inversion applied dominant chord (V⁶/V or V⁶₅/V). Listen for the presence or absence of 1̂/*do* in an upper voice. It could also be an applied leading-tone chord (vii°/V, which is rare, or vii°⁷/V). The presence or absence of 3̂/*mi*(ø) or [↓]3̂/*me*(°) in an upper voice makes the difference. Note that vii°⁷/V is not used in the minor mode.

6̂/*la*   When you hear a chord supported by 6̂/*la*, it could be an applied dominant (V⁶₄/V, which is rare, or V⁴₃/V). Listen for the presence or absence of 1̂/*do* in an upper voice. It could also be an applied leading-tone to V (vii°⁶/V or vii°⁶₅/V). The presence or absence of 3̂/*mi* (ø) or [↓]3̂/*me*(°) in an upper voice makes the difference. Note that vii°⁶₅/V is not used in the minor mode.

1̂/*do*   When you hear a chord supported by 1̂/*do*, it could be a V⁴₂/V, which typically resolves to V⁶, due to voice leading in the bass. It could also be an applied leading-tone to $\underline{V}$ ($\text{vii}^{\circ 6}_{4}/\underline{V}$, which is rare, or $\text{vii}^{\circ 4}_{3}/\underline{V}$). Listen for $\hat{3}/mi$ ($^{\emptyset}$) or $[\downarrow]\hat{3}/me$ ($^{\circ}$) in an upper voice. Note that $\text{vii}^{\emptyset 4}_{3}/\underline{V}$ is not used in the minor mode.

$\hat{3}/mi$ On very rare occasions, $\hat{3}/mi$ or $[\downarrow]\hat{3}/me$ might support a leading-tone sev-
$\downarrow\hat{3}/me$ enth chord in $^{4}_{2}$ position applied to the dominant.

The most important voice-leading event to listen for involves the resolution of the chromatic tendency tone $\uparrow\hat{4}/fi$. If you hear $\uparrow\hat{4}/fi$ in one chord resolving to $\hat{5}/sol$ in the next, you are probably hearing an applied chord resolving to the dominant.

Chords applied to the dominant are frequently used to intensify the approach to a half cadence. One typical but striking implementation of this involves the use of $\uparrow\hat{4}/fi$ to approach $\hat{5}/sol$ in the bass.

EXERCISES

1. Be able to sing skips from any pitch to any other within applied leading-tone and dominant of $\underline{V}$.

2. Practice singing stepwise to $\uparrow\hat{4}/fi$ and then skipping to various other diatonic scale degrees.

3. In each of the following preliminary exercises for chord arpeggiation, sing each chord one after the next. Think of these as symbol-reading, solmization, and singing exercises, not as actual chord progressions.

 a. I ii $\underline{V}/\underline{V}$ $\underline{V}$ I b. i ii$^{\circ}$ $\underline{V}/\underline{V}$ $\underline{V}$ i
 c. I ii^6 $\underline{V}^6/\underline{V}$ $\underline{V}$ I d. i ii$^{\circ6}$ $\underline{V}^6/\underline{V}$ $\underline{V}$ i
 e. I $\underline{IV}$ vii$^{\circ}/\underline{V}$ $\underline{V}$ I f. i iv vii$^{\circ}/\underline{V}$ $\underline{V}$ i
 g. I ii^7 $\underline{V}^7/\underline{V}$ $\underline{V}$ I h. i ii$^{\emptyset7}$ $\underline{V}^7/\underline{V}$ $\underline{V}$ i
 i. I ii$^6_5$ $\underline{V}^6_5/\underline{V}$ $\underline{V}$ I j. i ii$^{\emptyset6}_5$ $\underline{V}^6_5/\underline{V}$ $\underline{V}$ i

4. Learn to arpeggiate the following chord progressions.

 c. i i^6 $\underline{V}/\underline{V}$ $\underline{V}$ i
 e. I $\underline{IV}^6$ vii$^{\circ6}/\underline{V}$ $\underline{V}$ I
 i. I $\underline{V}^6$ $\underline{V}^4_3/\underline{V}$ $\underline{V}$ I
 j. I $\underline{V}^4_2/\underline{V}$ $\underline{V}^6$ I ii$^6_5$ $\underline{V}^7$ I
 k. I I^6 ii^6 $\underline{V}^6_5/\underline{V}$ $\underline{V}^{6-5}_{4-3}$ I
 l. i III VI i$^6_4$ $\underline{V}^4_3/\underline{V}$ $\underline{V}$ $\underline{V}^4_2$ i^6

5. Learn to play the above progressions on the piano (or similar keyboard).

In the following dictations and transcriptions, pay special attention to the appearances of chords applied to the dominant, and work at hearing not only the individual pitches that make up these harmonies but also the holistic result they produce. (For example, can you hear a $\underline{V}/\underline{V}$ in real time and immediately sense "Aha! The old $\underline{V}/\underline{V}$!"?)

Melodic Dictation

Listen to excerpts 54.1–54.4 and write out the pitches and rhythms for each, following the given instructions.

Exercise	Clef	Tonic	Bottom number in meter sign
54.1	treble	D	4
54.2	treble	D	4
54.3	treble	E♭	4
54.4	treble	C	4

Melodic Transcription

Listen to excerpts 54.5–54.8 and write out the pitches and rhythms for each. Also supply any other appropriate performance indications.

Exercise	Clef	Tonic	Bottom number in meter sign
54.5	treble	G	4
54.6	treble	D♭	4
54.7	treble	E♭	4
54.8	treble	F	4

Harmonic Dictation

Listen to excerpts 54.9–54.13 and write out the bass line for each. Then supply the appropriate Roman numerals and figured bass symbols to represent each chord. Your instructor may also choose to have you write out the top ("soprano") voice as well.

Exercise	Tonic	Bottom number in meter sign
54.9	A	4
54.10	A	4
54.11	E	4
54.12	G	4
54.13	C	4

Harmonic Transcription

Listen to excerpts 54.14–54.16 and write out the bass line for each. Then supply the appropriate Roman numerals and figured bass symbols to represent each chord. Your instructor may also choose to have you write out the top ("soprano") voice as well.

Exercise	Tonic	Bottom number in meter sign
54.14	E	4
54.15	G	4
54.16	G	4

READING AND SIGHT SINGING

Prepare the following excerpts, singing on syllables while conducting. Pay special attention to areas that state or imply chords applied to the dominant. Work at internalizing the sound and feel of each entire chord as you sing its pitches. Spend half your practice time accompanying yourself with block chords on the piano or other chord-producing instrument, so that the sounds of applied harmonies become part of your inner hearing.

Some of these excerpts clearly outline chords applied to the dominant, whereas others merely emphasize skips to $\hat{4}$/fi. Some of these appearances of $\hat{4}$/fi might even have been harmonized in their original contexts by other chords. Nonetheless, all these excerpts offer opportunities to practice skips to and from $\hat{4}$/fi in various guises.

Excerpts for reading and sight singing
from the
Anthology for Sight Singing
747–759

55 CHORDS APPLIED TO THE SUBDOMINANT

Dominant and leading-tone chords can be applied to the subdominant in both the major and minor modes.

Chords Applied to IV in the Major Mode

A dominant of the subdominant is built on $\hat{1}$/*do,* but, in the major mode, a major triad built on $\hat{1}$/*do* would simply be a tonic chord. Therefore, to give it a non-tonic or applied function, this chord must become a major-minor seventh chord. The chromatically altered seventh ($\downarrow\hat{7}$/*te*) turns the tonic triad into a V^7/IV.

The leading-tone chord applied to the subdominant can appear as a triad (vii°/IV) or a seventh chord (vii^{ø7}/IV or vii$^{°7}$/IV).

Here are the chords applied to the subdominant in the major mode:

V^7/IV . . . . . $\hat{1}$/*do*–$\hat{3}$/*mi*–$\hat{5}$/*sol*–$\downarrow\hat{7}$/*te*

vii°/IV . . . . $\hat{3}$/*mi*–$\hat{5}$/*sol*–$\downarrow\hat{7}$/*te*

vii^{ø7}/IV . . . . $\hat{3}$/*mi*–$\hat{5}$/*sol*–$\downarrow\hat{7}$/*te*–$\hat{2}$/*re*

vii$^{°7}$/IV . . . . $\hat{3}$/*mi*–$\hat{5}$/*sol*–$\downarrow\hat{7}$/*te*–$\downarrow\hat{2}$/*ra*

In all these chords, the characteristic tendency tone is $\downarrow\hat{7}$/*te*. It resolves down and by step to $\hat{6}$/*la*. In the vii$^{°7}$/IV, $\downarrow\hat{2}$/*ra* is also an important tendency tone, which resolves down by step to $\hat{1}$/*do*. The diatonic pitch $\hat{3}$/*mi* functions in all these chords as the secondary leading tone to $\hat{4}$/*fa*.

Chords Applied to iv in the Minor Mode

In the minor mode, the only alteration needed to change a tonic triad into a dominant of the subdominant is raising the third from $\hat{3}$/*me* to ↑$\hat{3}$/*mi*, thereby changing the quality of the triad from minor to major ($\hat{1}$/*do*–↑**$\hat{3}$/*mi**–$\hat{5}$/*sol*). However, this chromatically altered triad built on $\hat{1}$ can also serve as a tonic chord with a Picardy third (see Chapter 39), which you will hear as a cadential point of arrival at the end of a harmonic progression. On the other hand, if it leads harmonically and rhythmically to a subdominant chord, then you will recognize it as a V/iv.

In the minor mode, the applied dominants and leading-tone chords are identical to those in the major mode, with two important distinctions. In the minor mode, ↑3̂/*mi* is a *chromatically raised* pitch (from the diatonic 3̂/*me*), and 7̂/*te* is a *diatonic* pitch.

Here are the chords applied to the subdominant in the minor mode:

V̲/iv . . . . . 1̂/*do*–↑3̂/*mi*–5̂/*sol*

V̲⁷/iv . . . . 1̂/*do*–↑3̂/*mi*–5̂/*sol*–7̂/*te*

vii°/iv . . . . ↑3̂/*mi*–5̂/*sol*–7̂/*te*

vii°⁷/iv . . . . ↑3̂/*mi*–5̂/*sol*–7̂/*te*–↓2̂/*ra*

There are several characteristic tendency tones in these chords. In all of them, ↑3̂/*mi* resolves up by step to 4̂/*fa*. In all but V̲/iv, 7̂/*te* resolves down and by step to 6̂/*le*. And in vii°⁷/iv, ↓2̂/*ra* resolves down by step to 1̂/*do*.

Implications for Reading and Singing

We will now begin to encounter some applied harmonies containing skips to and from ↓7̂/*te*. For instance, in measures 23–24 below, D♭ (↓7̂/*te*) is approached and left by skip. As we observed with ↑4̂/*fi*, the resolution of such tendency tones can be delayed. Here, ↓7̂/*te* (D♭) resolves to 6̂/*la* (C) on the downbeat of measure 25.

J. S. Bach, Cantata No. 102, "Herr, deine Augen sehen nach dem Glauben," No. 4, Arioso, mm. 23–27 (1726)

Ver - ach - test du den Reich - tum sei - ner Gna - de,

In the minor mode, we will also now encounter skips to and from ↑3̂/*mi*, which is a chromatic pitch. It tends to resolve up to 4̂/*fa*, the root of the subdominant chord.

Implications for Listening

The only new material for melodic dictation presented here will involve skips away from ↓7̂/*te*. However, the addition of chords applied to the subdominant introduces quite a few new possibilities for chords above certain scale degrees in harmonic dictation. The chart below shows the bass notes above which chords applied to the subdominant may appear and discusses the inversion of each chord associated with each bass note. Add these chords to all the harmonic possibilities you have learned in previous chapters.

$\hat{1}/do$ When you hear $\hat{1}/do$ in the bass voice, it could now also be the root of a $\underline{V}^7/\underline{IV}$ chord ($\hat{1}/do$–[↑]$\hat{3}/mi$–$\hat{5}/sol$–[↓]$\hat{7}/te$) or $\underline{V}/\underline{IV}$ ($\hat{1}/do$–↑$\hat{3}/mi$–$\hat{5}/sol$) in minor.

$\hat{3}/mi$ When you hear a chord supported by $\hat{3}/mi$, your choices depend slightly on the mode of the music in which it appears. In the major mode, it could support $\underline{V}^6_5/\underline{IV}$. It could also support an applied leading-tone chord as a triad, vii°/$\underline{IV}$, which is rare, or seventh chord, vii°⁷/$\underline{IV}$ or vii°⁷/$\underline{IV}$. Listen for $\hat{2}/re$ or ↓$\hat{2}/ra$ in an upper voice. In the minor mode, ↑$\hat{3}/mi$ (now a chromatic pitch) can also support the simple triad $\underline{V}^6/iv$. Listen for the presence or absence of $\hat{7}/te$ to distinguish between $\underline{V}^6/iv$ and $\underline{V}^6_5/iv$. If ↓$\hat{2}/ra$ is present in minor, the chord will be vii°⁷/iv. Note that vii°⁷/iv is not used in the minor mode.

$\hat{5}/sol$ When you hear a chord supported by $\hat{5}/sol$, it could be $\underline{V}^6_4/\underline{IV}$, which is rare, or $\underline{V}^4_3/\underline{IV}$. The presence or absence of [↓]$\hat{7}/te$ in an upper voice makes the difference. It could also be an applied leading-tone to $\underline{IV}$ (vii°⁶/$\underline{IV}$, vii°⁶₅/$\underline{IV}$, or vii°⁶₅/$\underline{IV}$). Listen for $\hat{2}/re$ or ↓$\hat{2}/ra$ in an upper voice to determine the quality of the seventh chord. The parallel harmonies applied to iv are possible in the minor mode, but note that vii°⁶₅/iv is not used in minor.

$\hat{7}/te$ When you hear a chord supported by [↓]$\hat{7}/te$, it could be $\underline{V}^4_2/\underline{IV}$, which typically resolves to $\underline{IV}^6$, due to voice leading in the bass. It could also be an applied leading-tone to $\underline{IV}$ (vii°⁶₄/$\underline{IV}$, which is rare, vii°⁴₃/$\underline{IV}$, or vii°⁴₃/$\underline{IV}$). Listen for $\hat{2}/re$ or ↓$\hat{2}/ra$ in an upper voice. The parallel harmonies applied to iv are possible in the minor mode, but note that vii°⁴₃/iv is not used in minor.

$\hat{2}/re$ On very rare occasions, $\hat{2}/re$ or ↓$\hat{2}/ra$ might support a leading-tone seventh
↓$\hat{2}/ra$ chord in $^4_2$ position applied to the subdominant. Note that vii°⁴₂/iv is not used in minor.

The most important voice-leading events to listen for involve the resolutions of the two tendency tones [↓]$\hat{7}/te$ (resolving to $\hat{6}/la/le$) and [↑]$\hat{3}/mi$ (resolving to $\hat{4}/fa$). In the major mode, the chromatic pitch ↓$\hat{7}/te$ is particularly important. If you hear ↓$\hat{7}/te$ in one chord resolving to $\hat{6}/la$ in the next, you are probably hearing an applied chord resolving to the subdominant. In minor, listen for the chromatic pitch ↑$\hat{3}/mi$. If you hear it resolve to $\hat{4}/fa$, it is probably functioning as part of an applied chord resolving to the subdominant.

EXERCISES

1. Be able to sing skips from any pitch to any other within the applied leading-tone and applied dominant of $\underline{IV}$. Pay particular attention to skips to and from [↓]$\hat{7}/te$ (in major and minor modes) and ↑$\hat{3}/mi$ (in the minor mode).

2. In each of these preliminary exercises for chord arpeggiation, sing each chord one after the next. Think of these as symbol-reading, solmization, and singing exercises, not as actual chord progressions.

a. I V^7/IV IV V I
b. I iii vii°/IV IV V I
c. i V/iv iv V i
d. i III vii°/iv iv V i

e. I I⁶ iii V^6_5/IV IV V I
f. I ii⁶ iii⁶ vii°⁶/IV IV V I

3. Learn to arpeggiate the following chord progressions.
   a. I V^4_3/V V I V^7/IV IV V^7 I
   b. I V V^4_3/IV IV I⁶ ii⁶ V^7 I
   c. I V^4_2/IV IV⁶ V^4_3/V V^7 I
   d. i V^6_5/iv iv V^7/V V i
   e. i VI V^4_3/iv iv i^6_4 V i
   f. i V^4_2/iv iv⁶ ii°⁶ V^4_2 i⁶

4. Learn to play the above progressions on the piano (or similar keyboard).

LISTENING

In the following dictations and transcriptions, pay special attention to the appearances of chords applied to the subdominant, and work at hearing not only the individual pitches that make up these harmonies but also the holistic result they produce.

Melodic Dictation

Listen to excerpts 55.1–55.4 and write out the pitches and rhythms for each.

Exercise	Clef	Tonic	Bottom number in meter sign
55.1	treble	G	4
55.2	bass	F	2
55.3	tenor	D♭	4
55.4	treble	E	4

Melodic Transcription

Listen to excerpts 55.5–55.6 and write out the pitches and rhythms for each. Also supply any other appropriate performance indications.

Exercise	Clef	Tonic	Bottom number in meter sign
55.5	treble	D	4
55.6	treble	G	4

Harmonic Dictation

Listen to excerpts 55.7–55.12 and write out the bass line for each. Then supply the appropriate Roman numerals and figured bass symbols to represent each chord. Your instructor may also choose to have you write out the top ("soprano") voice as well.

Exercise	Tonic	Bottom number in meter sign
55.7	F	4
55.8	F	4
55.9	C	4
55.10	C	4
55.11	C	4
55.12	A	4

Harmonic Transcription

Listen to excerpts 55.13–55.14 and write out the bass line for each. Then supply the appropriate Roman numerals and figured bass symbols to represent each chord. Your instructor may also choose to have you write out the top ("soprano") voice as well.

Exercise	Tonic	Bottom number in meter sign
55.13	A♭	4
55.14	A♭	4

READING AND SIGHT SINGING

Prepare the following excerpts, singing on syllables while conducting. Analyze the implied or outlined harmonies, and pay close attention to applied harmonies, particularly those applied to the subdominant. Work at internalizing the sound and feel of each entire chord as you sing its pitches. Spend half your practice time accompanying yourself with block chords on the piano or other chord-producing instrument, so that the sounds of applied harmonies become part of your inner hearing.

Some of these excerpts clearly outline chords applied to the subdominant, whereas others merely emphasize skips to and from ↓$\hat{7}$/*te* and ↑$\hat{3}$/*mi*. Some of these pitches might even have been harmonized in their original contexts by other chords. Nonetheless, all these excerpts offer opportunities to practice skips to these pitches.

Excerpts for reading and sight singing
from the
Anthology for Sight Singing
760–769

56 CHORDS APPLIED TO THE SUPERTONIC

Chords other than the dominant and subdominant may take applied dominant and leading tone chords. One such chord is the supertonic.

Chords Applied to ii—Only in the Major Mode

Composers apply chords to the supertonic almost exclusively in the major mode, since the supertonic is a *diminished* triad in the minor mode and diminished triads rarely take applied harmonies. Therefore, we will examine these chords only in the major mode.

Here are the chords applied to the supertonic:

V/ii . . . $\hat{6}$/ *la*–↑$\hat{1}$/ *di*–$\hat{3}$/ *mi*

V^7/ii . . . $\hat{6}$/ *la*–↑$\hat{1}$/ *di*–$\hat{3}$/ *mi*–$\hat{5}$/ *sol*

vii°/ii . . . . ↑$\hat{1}$/ *di*–$\hat{3}$/ *mi*–$\hat{5}$/ *sol*

vii°^{7}/ii . . . . . . ↑$\hat{1}$/ *di* –$\hat{3}$/ *mi* –$\hat{5}$/ *sol*–↓$\hat{7}$/ *te*

In all these chords, the characteristic tendency tone is ↑$\hat{1}$/ *di*. It resolves up by step to $\hat{2}$/ *re*. In vii°^{7}/ii, ↓$\hat{7}$/ *te* is another important tendency tone, which resolves down by step to $\hat{6}$/ *la*.

Implications for Reading and Singing

Chapter 53 introduced skips to ↑$\hat{1}$/ *di,* but they all resolved immediately to $\hat{2}$/ *re*. Even when implying chords applied to the supertonic, many instances of ↑$\hat{1}$/ *di* in Western music still resolve immediately to $\hat{2}$/ *re*. We will now begin to encounter some applied harmonies containing skips to and from ↑$\hat{1}$/ *di*. In the example below, D♮ (↑$\hat{1}$/ *di*) in measure 3 is approached and left by skip. As the dotted arrow suggests, its resolution to E♭ ($\hat{2}$/ *re*) is only *implied* (as shown by the X). As A♭ ($\hat{5}$/ *sol*) resolves to G♭ ($\hat{4}$/ *fa*), you can auralize D♮ (↑$\hat{1}$/ *di*) resolving up to E♭ ($\hat{2}$/ *re*).

Robert Schumann, *Twelve Pieces for Piano Four Hands,*
Op. 85, No. 12, "Abendlied," mm. 1–6 (1849)

Ausdrucksvoll und sehr gehalten.

Implications for Listening

The only new material for melodic dictation presented here will involve skips away from ↑1̂/*di*. In harmonic dictation, the addition of V/ii and vii°/ii introduces quite a few new possibilities for chords above certain scale degrees. The chart below shows the bass notes above which chords applied to the dominant may appear and discusses the inversion of each chord associated with each bass note. Add these chords to all the harmonic possibilities you have learned in previous chapters.

6̂/*la*   When you hear 6̂/*la* in the bass voice, it could be the root of a V/ii chord (6̂/*la*–↑1̂/*di*–3̂/*mi*) or V⁷/ii (6̂/*la*–↑1̂/*di*–3̂/*mi*–5̂/*sol*). The presence or absence of 5̂/*sol* in an upper voice makes the difference.

↓1̂/*di*   When you hear a chord supported by ↑1̂/*di*, it will be a chord applied to ii. It could be an applied dominant chord (V⁶/ii or V⁶₅/ii). Listen for the presence or absence of 5̂/*sol* in an upper voice. It could also be an applied leading-tone chord (vii°/ii, which is rare, or vii°⁷/ii). The presence or absence of ↓7̂/*te* in an upper voice makes the difference. Note that vii°⁷/ii is not used.

3̂/*mi*   When you hear a chord supported by 3̂/*mi*, it could be an applied dominant to ii (V⁶₄/ii, which is rare, or V⁴₃/ii). Listen for the presence or absence of 5̂/*sol* in an upper voice. It could also be an applied leading-tone to ii (vii°⁶/ii or vii°⁶₅/ii). The presence or absence of ↓7̂/*te* in an upper voice makes the difference. Note that vii°⁶₅/ii is not used.

5̂/*sol*   When you hear a chord supported by 5̂/*sol,* it could be a V⁴₂/ii, which typically resolves to ii⁶ due to voice leading in the bass. It could also be an applied leading-tone to ii (vii°⁶₄/ii, which is rare, or vii°⁴₃/ii). Listen for ↓7̂/*te* in an upper voice. Note that vii°⁴₃/ii is not used.

↓7̂/*te*   On very rare occasions, ↓7̂/*te* might support a leading-tone seventh chord in ⁴₂ position applied to the supertonic.

The most important voice-leading event to listen for involves the resolution of the chromatic tendency tone ↑1̂/*di*. If you hear ↑1̂/*di* in one chord resolving to 2̂/*re* in the next, this is a good indication of an applied chord resolving to the supertonic.

EXERCISES

1. Be able to sing skips from any pitch to any other within the applied leading-tone and applied dominant of ii. Pay particular attention to skips to and from ↑1̂/*di*.

2. In each of these preliminary exercises for chord arpeggiation, sing each chord one after the next. Think of these as symbol-reading, solmization, and singing exercises, not as actual chord progressions.

   a. I   vii°/ii   ii   V⁶₅   I   c. I   V⁶₅/ii   ii   V⁴₃   I
   b. I   vi   V/ii   ii   V   I   d. I   V⁶/ii   ii⁷   V⁶₅   I

3. Learn to arpeggiate the following chord progressions.

a. I $\quad$ V^6 $\quad$ V^7/ii $\quad$ ii $\quad$ V$^6_5$ $\quad$ I

b. I $\quad$ V$^6_4$ $\quad$ I^6 $\quad$ V$^4_3$/ii $\quad$ ii $\quad$ V$^4_2$ $\quad$ I^6

c. I $\quad$ V$^6_4$ $\quad$ I^6 $\quad$ vii°^{6}/ii $\quad$ ii^6 $\quad$ V$^6_5$/IV $\quad$ IV $\quad$ V^7 $\quad$ I

d. I $\quad$ V $\quad$ V$^4_2$/ii $\quad$ ii^6 $\quad$ V$^4_3$/V $\quad$ V $\quad$ I

e. I $\quad$ vii°^{6}/ii $\quad$ ii $\quad$ V^6/V $\quad$ V $\quad$ V$^4_2$ $\quad$ V$^4_3$/ii $\quad$ ii $\quad$ V^7 $\quad$ I

f. I $\quad$ I^6 $\quad$ V^7/ii $\quad$ ii $\quad$ V$^4_2$/ii $\quad$ V$^4_2$ $\quad$ I^6 $\quad$ vii°^{6}/ii $\quad$ ii^7 $\quad$ V$^4_3$ $\quad$ I

4. Learn to play the above progressions on the piano (or similar keyboard).

LISTENING

In the following dictations and transcriptions, pay special attention to the appearances of chords applied to the supertonic, and work at hearing not only the individual pitches that make up these harmonies but also the holistic result they produce.

Melodic Dictation

Listen to excerpts 56.1–56.4 and write out the pitches and rhythms for each.

Exercise	Clef	Tonic	Bottom number in meter sign
56.1	bass	B♭	8
56.2	treble	F♯	4
56.3	tenor	D	8
56.4	alto	A♭	2

Melodic Transcription

Listen to excerpt 56.5 and write out the pitches and rhythms. Also supply any other appropriate performance indications.

Exercise	Clef	Tonic	Bottom number in meter sign
56.5	treble	E♭	8

Harmonic Dictation

Listen to excerpts 56.6–56.9 and write out the bass line for each. Then supply the appropriate Roman numerals and figured bass symbols to represent each chord. Your instructor may also choose to have you write out the top ("soprano") voice as well.

Exercise	Tonic	Bottom number in meter sign
56.6	D	2
56.7	B♭	4
56.8	C	4
56.9	C	8

Harmonic Transcription

Listen to excerpt 56.10 and write out the bass line and supply the appropriate Roman numerals and figured bass symbols to represent each chord. Your instructor may also choose to have you write out the top ("soprano") voice as well.

Exercise	Tonic	Bottom number in meter sign
56.10	C	2

READING AND SIGHT SINGING

Prepare the following excerpts, singing on syllables while conducting. Analyze implied or outlined harmonies and pay close attention to applied harmonies, particularly those applied to the supertonic. Work at internalizing the sound and feel of each entire chord as you sing its pitches. Spend about half of your practice time accompanying yourself with block chords on the piano or other chord-producing instrument, so that the sounds of applied harmonies become part of your inner hearing.

Some of these excerpts clearly outline chords applied to the supertonic, whereas others merely emphasize skips to and from ↑1̂/*di*. Some of these appearances of ↑1̂/*di* might even have been harmonized in their original contexts by other chords. Nonetheless, all these excerpts offer opportunities to practice skips involving ↑1̂/*di*.

**Excerpts for reading and sight singing
from the
Anthology for Sight Singing
770–783**

57 CHORDS APPLIED TO THE SUBMEDIANT

Another chord that may take applied dominant and leading tone chords is the submediant. We must examine these chords separately in the major and minor modes, because their roots and tendency tones are different.

Chords Applied to vi in the Major Mode

Here are the chords applied to the submediant in the major mode:

$\underline{\text{V}}$/vi . . . . $\hat{3}$/ *mi*–↑$\hat{5}$/ *si*–$\hat{7}$/ *ti*

$\underline{\text{V}}^7$/vi . . . $\hat{3}$/ *mi*–↑$\hat{5}$/ *si*–$\hat{7}$/ *ti*–$\hat{2}$/ *re*

vii°/vi . . . . ↑$\hat{5}$/ *si*–$\hat{7}$/ *ti*–$\hat{2}$/ *re*

vii°^{7}/vi . . . . . . ↑$\hat{5}$/ *si*–$\hat{7}$/ *ti*–$\hat{2}$/ *re*–$\hat{4}$/ *fa*

In all these chords, the characteristic tendency tone is ↑$\hat{5}$/ *si*. It resolves up by step to $\hat{6}$/ *la*. In the vii°^{7}/vi, $\hat{4}$/ *fa* also functions as an important tendency tone, which resolves down by step to $\hat{3}$/ *mi*.

Chords Applied to $\underline{\text{VI}}$ in the Minor Mode

In the minor mode, a dominant of the submediant must be built on $\hat{3}$/ *me*. However, a major triad built on $\hat{3}$/ *me* would simply be a diatonic mediant chord, so to give it a dominant function requires an added seventh (↓$\hat{2}$/ *ra*). This turns the mediant triad into a $\underline{\text{V}}^7$/$\underline{\text{VI}}$.

The leading-tone chord applied to the submediant in minor can appear as a triad (vii°/$\underline{\text{VI}}$) or as a seventh chord, usually only in the half-diminished form (vii^{ø7}/$\underline{\text{VI}}$).

Here are the chords applied to the submediant in the minor mode:

$\underline{\text{V}}^7$/$\underline{\text{VI}}$ . . . $\hat{3}$/ *me*–$\hat{5}$/ *sol*–$\hat{7}$/ *te*–↓$\hat{2}$/ *ra*

vii°/$\underline{\text{VI}}$ . . . . $\hat{5}$/ *sol*–$\hat{7}$/ *te*–↓$\hat{2}$/ *ra*

vii^{ø7}/$\underline{\text{VI}}$ . . . . . . $\hat{5}$/ *sol*–$\hat{7}$/ *te*–↓$\hat{2}$/ *ra*–$\hat{4}$/ *fa*

vii°^{7}/$\underline{\text{VI}}$ . . . . $\hat{5}$/ *sol*–$\hat{7}$/ *te*–↓$\hat{2}$/ *ra*–↓$\hat{4}$/ *fe*

In all these chords, $\hat{5}$/ *sol* is the applied leading tone, which resolves up to $\hat{6}$/ *le*. On occasion, you may find vii°^{7}/$\underline{\text{VI}}$, but it is usually associated with modulation to another key. Its lowered seventh (↓$\hat{4}$) has never been given a standardized name in movable-*do* solmization. We will call it ↓$\hat{4}$/ *fe*. In the vii°^{7}/$\underline{\text{VI}}$, ↓$\hat{4}$/ *fe* is also an important tendency tone, which resolves down by step to $\hat{3}$/ *me*.

Implications for Reading and Singing

Harmonic motion applied to the submediant introduces the possibility of skips to and from ↑5̂/*si* in the major mode, and ↓2̂/*ra* (and occasionally ↓4̂/*fe*) in the minor mode. The following example features skips to and from ↑5̂/*si*:

Ludwig van Beethoven, Symphony No. 5, Op. 67, mvt. 2, mm. 1–6 (1808)

The E♮ (↑5̂/*si*) at the downbeat of measure 4 is the first note in a three-note arpeggiation of E♮–G–C (↑5̂/*si*–7̂/*ti*–3̂/*mi*): a V/vi chord. The applied leading tone E♮ does eventually resolve to F in the following measure. This F is not part of vi but of V/ii (a chromatically altered vi), which creates a chain of applied dominants.

Implications for Listening in the Major Mode

The only new material for melodic dictation in the major mode presented here will involve skips away from ↑6̂/*si*. However, the addition of chords applied to the submediant introduces several new possibilities for chords above certain scale degrees in harmonic dictation. The chart below shows the bass notes above which chords applied to the submediant may appear in the major mode, and discusses the inversion of each chord associated with each bass note. Add these chords to all the harmonic possibilities you have already learned.

3̂/*mi*   When you hear 3̂/*mi* in the bass voice, it could be the root of a V/vi chord (3̂/*mi*–↑5̂/*si*–7̂/*ti*) or V⁷/vi (3̂/*mi*–↑5̂/*si*–7̂/*ti*–2̂/*re*). The presence or absence of 2̂/*re* in an upper voice makes the difference.

↑5̂/*si*   When you hear a chord supported by ↑5̂/*si*, it will be a chord applied to vi. It could be an applied dominant chord (V⁶/vi or V⁶₅/vi). Listen for the presence or absence of 2̂/*re* in an upper voice. It could also be an applied leading-tone chord (vii°/vi, which is rare, or vii°⁷/vi). The presence or absence of 4̂/*fa* in an upper voice makes the difference. Note that vii⌀⁷/vi is not used.

7̂/*ti*   When you hear a chord supported by 7̂/*ti*, it could be an applied dominant (V⁶₄/vi, which is rare, or V⁴₃/vi). Listen for the presence or absence of 2̂/*re* in an upper voice. It could also be an applied leading-tone (vii°⁶/vi or vii°⁶₅/vi). The presence or absence of 4̂/*fa* in an upper voice makes the difference. Note that vii⌀⁶₅/vi is not used in the major mode.

2̂/*re*   When you hear a chord supported by 2̂/*re*, it could be V⁴₂/vi, which typically resolves to vi⁶ due to voice leading in the bass. It could also be an applied leading-tone (vii°⁶₄/vi, which is rare, or vii°⁴₃/vi). Listen for 4̂/*fa* in an upper voice. Note that vii⌀⁴₃/vi is not used in the major mode.

4̂/*fa*   On very rare occasions, 4̂/*fa* might support a leading-tone seventh chord in ⁴₂ position applied to the submediant.

The most important voice-leading event to listen for involves the resolution of the chromatic tendency tone ↑$\hat{6}$/*si*. If you hear ↑$\hat{6}$/*si* in one chord resolving to $\hat{6}$/*la* in the next, this is a good indication of an applied chord resolving to the submediant.

Implications for Listening in the Minor Mode

The only new material for melodic dictation in the minor mode presented here will involve skips away from ↓$\hat{2}$/*ra*. However, you will encounter several new possibilities for chords above certain scale degrees in harmonic dictation. The chart below shows the bass notes above which chords applied to the submediant may appear in the minor mode and discusses the inversion of each chord associated with each bass note. Add these chords to all the harmonic possibilities you have learned in previous chapters.

$\hat{3}$/*me* When you hear $\hat{3}$/*me* in the bass voice, it could be the root of a V^7/VI chord ($\hat{3}$/*me*–$\hat{5}$/*sol*–$\hat{7}$/*te*–↓$\hat{2}$/*ra*).

$\hat{5}$/*sol* When you hear a chord supported by $\hat{5}$/*sol,* it could be a first-inversion applied dominant seventh (V^6_5/VI). It could also be an applied leading-tone (vii°/VI, which is rare, or vii^7/VI); listen for $\hat{4}$/*fa*($^\varnothing$) or ↓$\hat{4}$/*fe*(°) in an upper voice.

$\hat{7}$/*te* When you hear a chord supported by $\hat{7}$/*te,* it could be an applied dominant (V^4_3/VI) or an applied leading-tone (vii°^{6}/VI or vii$^6_5$/VI); listen for $\hat{4}$/*fa*($^\varnothing$) or ↓$\hat{4}$/*fe*(°) in an upper voice.

↓$\hat{2}$/*ra* When you hear a chord supported by ↓$\hat{2}$/*ra,* it could be V^4_2/VI, which typically resolves to VI^6. It could also be vii°$^6_4$/VI, which is rare, or vii$^4_3$/VI. The presence or absence of $\hat{4}$/*fa* ($^\varnothing$) or ↓$\hat{4}$/*fe* (°) in an upper voice makes the difference.

$\hat{4}$/*fa* On very rare occasions, $\hat{4}$/*fa* or ↓$\hat{4}$/*fe* might support a leading-tone seventh
↓$\hat{4}$/*fe* chord in $^4_2$ position applied to the submediant.

In the minor mode, the most important voice-leading event to listen for involves the resolution of the chromatic tendency tone ↓$\hat{2}$/*ra*. If you hear ↓$\hat{2}$/*ra* in one chord resolving to $\hat{1}$/*do* in the next, this is a good indication of an applied chord resolving to the submediant.

EXERCISES

1. Be able to sing skips from any pitch to any other within the applied leading-tone and applied dominant of the submediant. Pay particular attention to skips to and from ↑$\hat{5}$/*si* and ↓$\hat{2}$/*ra*.

2. In each of these preliminary exercises for chord arpeggiation, sing each chord one after the next. Think of these as symbol-reading, solmization, and singing exercises, not as actual chord progressions.

a. I   iii $\underline{V}$/vi   vi $\underline{IV}^6$ $\underline{V}^7$ I

b. i   III $\underline{V}^7$/VI   VI   iv^6 $\underline{V}^7$ i

3. Learn to arpeggiate the following chord progressions.

a. I   vi $\underline{V}^6$/vi   vi   ii^6 $\underline{V}^7$ I

b. I   ii^6 $\underline{V}^7$/vi   vi $\underline{V}^4_3$/$\underline{V}$ $\underline{V}$ I

c. I   vi $\underline{V}^6_5$/vi   vi $\underline{V}$/ii   ii $\underline{V}^4_3$ I

d. I $\underline{V}^4_3$/vi   vi $\underline{V}^4_2$/$\underline{IV}$ $\underline{IV}^6$ I$^6_4$ $\underline{V}$ I

e. I $\underline{V}^4_2$/vi   vi^6 $\underline{V}^4_2$/$\underline{V}$ $\underline{V}^6$ I

f. I   vii$^{\circ 6}$/vi   vi $\underline{V}^6_5$/ii   ii $\underline{V}^7$ I

g. i $\underline{V}^6_5$/iv   iv $\underline{V}^6_5$/$\underline{VI}$ VI   ii$^{\varnothing 6}_5$ $\underline{V}$ i

h. i $\underline{V}^6$ i $\underline{V}^4_3$/$\underline{VI}$ VI   i$^6_4$ $\underline{V}^7$ i

i. i $\underline{V}$ vii$^{\circ 6}$/$\underline{VI}$ VI $\underline{V}^4_2$/iv   iv^6 $\underline{V}^7$ i

j. i $\underline{V}^4_2$/$\underline{VI}$ VI^6 $\underline{V}^6_5$ i

4. Learn to play the above progressions on the piano (or similar keyboard).

LISTENING

In the following dictations and transcriptions, pay special attention to the appearances of chords applied to the submediant, and work at hearing not only the individual pitches that make up these harmonies but also the holistic result they produce.

Melodic Dictation

Listen to excerpts 57.1–57.4 and write out the pitches and rhythms for each.

Exercise	Clef	Tonic	Bottom number in meter sign
57.1	bass	B	4
57.2	treble	F♯	8
57.3	tenor	E♭	4
57.4	alto	B♭	2

Melodic Transcription

Listen to excerpt 57.5 and write out the pitches and rhythms. Also supply any other appropriate performance indications.

Exercise	Clef	Tonic	Bottom number in meter sign
57.5	treble	E	4

Harmonic Dictation

Listen to excerpts 57.6–57.9 and write out the bass line for each. Then supply the appropriate Roman numerals and figured bass symbols to represent each chord. Your instructor may also choose to have you write out the top ("soprano") voice as well.

Exercise	Tonic	Bottom number in meter sign
57.6	C	4
57.7	F	4
57.8	A	4
57.9	B♭	4

Harmonic Transcription

Listen to excerpts 57.10–57.13 and write out the bass line for each. Then supply the appropriate Roman numerals and figured bass symbols to represent each chord. Your instructor may also choose to have you write out the top ("soprano") voice as well.

Exercise	Tonic	Bottom number in meter sign
57.10	C	2
57.11	E♭	4
57.12	A	4
57.13	D♭	8

READING AND SIGHT SINGING

Prepare the following excerpts, singing on syllables while conducting. Analyze the implied or outlined harmonies and pay close attention to applied harmonies, particularly those applied to the submediant. Work at internalizing the sound and feel of each entire chord as you sing its pitches. Spend half your practice time accompanying yourself with block chords on the piano or other chord-producing instrument, so that the sounds of applied harmonies become part of your inner hearing.

Some of these excerpts clearly outline chords applied to the submediant, whereas others merely emphasize skips to and from ↑5̂/*si* or ↓2̂/*ra*. Some of these pitches might even have been harmonized in their original contexts by other chords. Nonetheless, these excerpts offer opportunities to practice these skips.

**Excerpts for reading and sight singing
from the
Anthology for Sight Singing
784–788**

58 CHORDS APPLIED TO THE MEDIANT

The mediant chord also may take applied dominant and leading tone chords. As with chords applied to the submediant, we must examine these chords separately in the major and minor modes, because their roots and tendency tones are different.

Chords Applied to iii in the Major Mode

Although chords are only rarely applied to the mediant in the major mode, we will explore the theoretical possibilities of these chords.

Here are the chords applied to the mediant in the major mode:

V/iii . . . $\hat{7}$/ ti–↑$\hat{2}$/ ri–↑$\hat{4}$/ fi

V^7/iii . . . $\hat{7}$/ ti–↑$\hat{2}$/ ri–↑$\hat{4}$/ fi–$\hat{6}$/ la

vii°/iii . . . . . . ↑$\hat{2}$/ ri–↑$\hat{4}$/ fi–$\hat{6}$/ la

vii°⁷/iii . . . . . ↑$\hat{2}$/ ri–↑$\hat{4}$/ fi–$\hat{6}$/ la–$\hat{1}$/ do

In all these chords, the characteristic tendency tone is ↑$\hat{2}$/ ri, which resolves up by step to $\hat{3}$/ mi. In the vii°⁷/iii, $\hat{1}$/ do is also an important tendency tone, which resolves down by step to $\hat{7}$/ ti.

Chords Applied to III in the Minor Mode

In the minor mode, the diatonic third scale degree is $\hat{3}$/ me. A major triad built on its dominant, $\hat{7}$/ te ($\hat{7}$/ te–$\hat{2}$/ re–$\hat{4}$/ fa), would be the diatonic subtonic chord (VII). The subtonic often functions as an applied dominant of the mediant in the minor mode. Adding a seventh ($\hat{6}$/ le) to this chord turns the triad into the V^7/III.

The vii°/III is actually a diatonic supertonic triad. Although it sometimes functions as a vii°/III, we almost always label it as a ii°. The same is true for the applied leading-tone half-diminished seventh of III ($\hat{2}$/ re–$\hat{4}$/ fa–$\hat{6}$/ le–$\hat{1}$/ do). It does indeed progress to III from time to time, but we usually label it as a ii°⁷.

Here are the chords applied to the mediant in the minor mode:

V/III . . . . $\hat{7}$/ te–$\hat{2}$/ re–$\hat{4}$/ fa

V^7/III . . . . $\hat{7}$/ te–$\hat{2}$/ re–$\hat{4}$/ fa–$\hat{6}$/ le

ii° ("vii°/III") . . . . . . $\hat{2}$/ re–$\hat{4}$/ fa–$\hat{6}$/ le

ii°⁷ ("vii°⁷/III") . . . . $\hat{2}$/ re–$\hat{4}$/ fa–$\hat{6}$/ le–$\hat{1}$/ do

vii°⁷/III . . . . $\hat{2}$/ re–$\hat{4}$/ fa–$\hat{6}$/ le–↓$\hat{1}$/ de

In all these chords, $\hat{2}$/*re* is the applied leading tone, which resolves up to $\hat{3}$/*me*. On occasion, you may find Vii°⁷/III. This is usually associated with modulation to another key, so its lowered seventh (↓$\hat{1}$) has never been given a standardized name in movable-*do* solmization. We will call it ↓$\hat{1}$/*de*. In the Vii°⁷/III, ↓$\hat{1}$/*de* is also an important tendency tone, which resolves down by step to $\hat{7}$/*te*.

Implications for Reading and Singing

Harmonic motion applied to the mediant introduces the possibility of skips to and from ↑$\hat{2}$/*ri* in the major mode, although these are very rare. In the minor mode, skips to and from $\hat{7}$/*te* are commonly associated with V̲/III, as shown in the following excerpt:

"Do Not Scold Me and Do Not Reproach Me," Russian folk song

The C ($\hat{7}$/*te*) in measure 4 begins an arpeggiation of C–E–G–B♭ ($\hat{7}$/*te*–$\hat{2}$/*re*–$\hat{4}$/*fa*–$\hat{6}$/*le*): a V̲⁷/III chord. Note how this chord projects a powerful sense of dominant function applied to III, even though the melody only briefly touches on the mediant pitch A in measure 6, before the E at the end of that measure makes III an impossibility. Sing this excerpt, being careful to make the skip to $\hat{7}$/*te* from measure 3 to measure 4, and to arpeggiate the V̲⁷/III with the proper syllables and pitches.

Implications for Listening in the Major Mode

Keep in mind that chords applied to iii in the major mode are relatively rare. The only new material for melodic dictation in the major mode presented here will involve skips away from ↑$\hat{2}$/*ri*. In harmonic dictation, the addition of V̲/iii and Vii°/iii introduces quite a few new possibilities for chords above certain scale degrees. The chart below shows the bass notes above which chords applied to the mediant may appear in the major mode and discusses the inversion of each chord associated with each bass note. Add these chords to all the harmonic possibilities you have already learned.

$\hat{7}$/*ti*   When you hear $\hat{7}$/*ti* in the bass voice, it could be the root of a V̲/iii chord ($\hat{7}$/*ti*–↑$\hat{2}$/*ri*–↑$\hat{4}$/*fi*) or of V̲⁷/iii ($\hat{7}$/*ti*–↑$\hat{2}$/*ri*–↑$\hat{4}$/*fi*–$\hat{6}$/*la*). The presence or absence of $\hat{6}$/*la* in an upper voice makes the difference.

↑$\hat{2}$/*ri*   When you hear a chord supported by ↑$\hat{2}$/*ri*, it will be a chord applied to iii. It could be an applied dominant chord (V̲⁶/iii or V̲⁶₅/iii). Listen for the presence or absence of $\hat{6}$/*la* in an upper voice. It could also be an applied leading-tone chord (Vii°/iii, which is rare, or Vii°⁷/iii). The presence or absence of $\hat{1}$/*do* in an upper voice makes the difference. Note that Vii°⁷/iii is not used in the major mode.

↑$\hat{4}$/*fi*   When you hear a chord supported by ↑$\hat{4}$/*fi*, it could be V^6_4/iii, which is rare, or V^4_3/iii. Listen for the presence or absence of $\hat{6}$/*la* in an upper voice. It could also be an applied leading-tone (vii°⁶/iii or vii°⁶₅/iii). Listen for $\hat{1}$/*do* in an upper voice. Note that vii°⁶₅/iii is not used in the major mode.

$\hat{6}$/*la*   When you hear a chord supported by $\hat{6}$/*la,* it could be V^4_2/iii, which typically resolves to iii⁶. It could also be vii°⁶₄/iii, which is rare, or vii°⁴₃/iii. Listen for $\hat{1}$/*do* in an upper voice, which makes the difference. Note that vii°⁴₃/iii is not used in the major mode.

$\hat{1}$/*do*   On very rare occasions, $\hat{1}$/*do* might support a leading-tone seventh chord in $^4_2$ position applied to the mediant.

The most important voice-leading event to listen for involves the resolution of the chromatic tendency tone ↑$\hat{2}$/*ri*. If you hear ↑$\hat{2}$/*ri* in one chord resolving to $\hat{3}$/*mi* in the next, you are probably hearing an applied chord resolving to the mediant.

Implications for Listening in the Minor Mode

The only new material for melodic dictation in the minor mode presented here will involve skips to and from $\hat{7}$/*te*. However, the addition of V/III and vii°/III introduces several new possibilities for harmonic dictation. The chart below shows the bass notes above which chords applied to the mediant may appear in the minor mode and discusses the inversion of each chord associated with each bass note. Add these chords to all the harmonic possibilities you have learned in previous chapters.

$\hat{7}$/*te*   When you hear $\hat{7}$/*te* in the bass voice, it could be the root of a V/III chord ($\hat{7}$/*te*–$\hat{2}$/*re*–$\hat{4}$/*fa*) or V⁷/III chord ($\hat{7}$/*te*–$\hat{2}$/*re*–$\hat{4}$/*fa*–$\hat{6}$/*le*). The presence or absence of $\hat{6}$/*le* in an upper voice makes the difference.

$\hat{2}$/*re*   When you hear a chord supported by $\hat{2}$/*re*, it could be an applied dominant (V⁶/III or V⁶₅/III). Listen for $\hat{6}$/*le* in an upper voice, which makes the difference. It could also be an applied leading-tone chord (vii°⁷/III). You should also be aware of the possibility of ii° or ii°⁷.

$\hat{4}$/*fa*   When you hear a chord supported by $\hat{4}$/*fa*, it could be V^6_4/III, which is rare, or V^4_3/III. It could also be vii°⁶₅/III, but be aware of the possibility of ii°⁶ or ii°⁶₅.

$\hat{6}$/*le*   When you hear a chord supported by $\hat{6}$/*le*, it could be V^4_2/III, which typically resolves to III⁶, or it could be vii°⁴₃/III. Be aware of the possibility of ii°⁶₄ (rare) or ii°⁴₃.

$\hat{1}$/*do*   On very rare occasions, $\hat{1}$/*do* or ↓$\hat{1}$/*de* might support a leading-tone seventh
↓$\hat{1}$/*de*   chord in $^4_2$ position applied to the mediant.

EXERCISES

1. Be able to sing skips from any pitch to any other within the chords applied to the mediant. Pay particular attention to skips to and from $\hat{7}$/*te* and ↑$\hat{2}$/*ri*.

2. Learn to arpeggiate the following chord progressions.

a. i V^7/III III ii°⁶ i⁶₄ V i

b. i ii°⁷ V^6_5/III III VI iv V^4_3 i

c. i ii°⁶ V^4_3/III III V^4_2 i⁶

d. i V^4_2/iv iv⁶ V^4_2/III III⁶ VI ii°⁶₅ V^7 i

e. i V^4_3/iv iv V^4_3/III III i⁶ V^4_3 i

f. i VI V^4_2/III III⁶ VI i⁶₄ V^7 i

g. i vii°⁷/III III VI ii°⁶ V^7 i

h. I V^6 V/iii iii IV V^4_2 I⁶

i. I I⁶ V^6_5/iii iii vi V^4_3/V V^7 I

3. Learn to play the above progressions on the piano (or similar keyboard).

LISTENING

In the following dictations and transcriptions, pay special attention to the appearances of chords applied to the mediant, and work at hearing not only the individual pitches that make up these harmonies but also the holistic result they produce.

Melodic Dictation

Listen to excerpts 58.1–58.4 and write out the pitches and rhythms for each.

Exercise	Clef	Tonic	Bottom number in meter sign
58.1	treble	D♭	8
58.2	tenor	F	2
58.3	bass	E	4
58.4	alto	B♭	8

Harmonic Dictation

Listen to excerpts 58.5–58.8 and write out the bass line for each. Then supply the appropriate Roman numerals and figured bass symbols to represent each chord. Your instructor may also choose to have you write out the top ("soprano") voice as well.

Exercise	Tonic	Bottom number in meter sign
58.5	F	8
58.6	B	4
58.7	D	4
58.8	D	4

Harmonic Transcription

Listen to excerpts 58.9–58.10 and write out the bass line for each. Then supply the appropriate Roman numerals and figured bass symbols to represent each chord. Your instructor may also choose to have you write out the top ("soprano") voice as well.

Exercise	Tonic	Bottom number in meter sign
58.9	C	2
58.10	A	4

READING AND SIGHT SINGING

Prepare the following excerpts, singing on syllables while conducting. Pay special attention to the areas that state or imply chords applied to the mediant. Work at internalizing the sound and feel of the entire chord as you sing its pitches. Spend half your practice time accompanying yourself with block chords on the piano or other chord-producing instrument, so that the sounds of applied harmonies become part of your inner hearing.

Some of these excerpts clearly outline chords applied to the mediant, whereas others merely emphasize skips to and from $\hat{3}$/ *me* and $\hat{7}$/ *te*. Some of these pitches might even have been harmonized in their original contexts by other chords. Nonetheless, all these excerpts offer opportunities to practice skips to these pitches.

Excerpts for reading and sight singing
from the
Anthology for Sight Singing
789–796

59 THE NEAPOLITAN CHORD

In addition to applied dominants and applied leading-tone chords, several other chromatic chords appear frequently in tonal music. One of these chords involves the lowered second scale degree (↓$\hat{2}$/*ra*). It is known as the Neapolitan chord because of its association with the so-called Neapolitan school, a group of 18th-century composers from Naples.

↓$\hat{2}$/*ra* and the Neapolitan

The following excerpt features a Neapolitan chord in measure 3. Sing the right-hand part (transpose it up a 5th or 6th) and pay special attention to the appearance of D♮ (↓$\hat{2}$/*ra*) in measure 3.

Ludwig van Beethoven, Piano Sonata No. 14, Op. 27,
No. 2 ("Moonlight"), mvt. 1, mm. 1–5 (1801)

The triad that includes the D♮ in the second half of measure 3 is an example of the Neapolitan chord. Note the following three things about this triad:

- It is supported by $\hat{4}$/*fa* (F♯) in the bass
- ↓$\hat{2}$/*ra* (D♮) may be thought of (and heard) as the root
- The triad is a *major* triad—↓$\hat{2}$/*ra*–$\hat{4}$/*fa*–$\hat{6}$/*le* (D♮–F♯–A)

The Neapolitan chord is a major triad with $\downarrow\hat{2}$/*ra* as its root. It often appears in first inversion, with $\hat{4}$/*fa* in the bass, when it is called the **Neapolitan sixth chord.**

The Neapolitan chord is almost always found in first inversion. In fact, it is frequently referred to as the **Neapolitan sixth chord** because of the 6th between $\hat{4}$/*fa* in the bass voice and $\downarrow\hat{2}$/*ra* in some upper voice.

Some textbooks focus on $\downarrow\hat{2}$/*ra* as the root of the chord and label it as $\downarrow\text{II}^6$ (or $\flat\text{II}^6$ or $\natural\text{II}^6$). On the other hand, the strong presence of $\hat{4}$/*fa* as the supporting bass, coupled with its tendency to move to V (just as IV and ii^6 do), make this harmony feel more like a subdominant-type chord. To acknowledge the distinctive function of this chord, we will give it a unique label: N^6 (for Neapolitan 6th).

The Neapolitan in the Minor Mode

In the minor mode, the Neapolitan chord involves the use of only one chromatic pitch: $\downarrow\hat{2}$/*ra*. In the minor mode, $\downarrow\hat{2}$/*ra* is a closely related chromatic, created by moving once in the "flat" direction on the circle of fifths—by adding one flat or removing one sharp. (Review the circle-of-fifths arrangement of the key signatures in Chapter 11.) We have encountered $\downarrow\hat{2}$/*ra* previously as part of chords applied to VI in the minor mode (for example, $\text{V}^7/\text{VI} = \hat{3}$/*me*–$\hat{5}$/*sol*–$\hat{7}$/*te*–$\downarrow\hat{2}$/*ra*).

The Neapolitan in the Major Mode

In the major mode, the Neapolitan chord consists of the exact same pitches as in the parallel minor: $\hat{4}$/*fa* in the bass and what are now *two* chromatic pitches—$\downarrow\hat{6}$/*le* (a lowered $\hat{6}$/*la*) and $\downarrow\hat{2}$/*ra*. Both $\downarrow\hat{6}$/*le* and $\downarrow\hat{2}$/*ra* are *not* closely related to the major key in which they occur. For this reason, the appearance of the Neapolitan chord in the major mode is a less frequent occurrence.

Implications for Reading and Singing

In close position, with $\hat{4}$/*fa* as the supporting bass pitch, the members of the Neapolitan sixth chord are as follows:

$$\downarrow\hat{2}/ra$$
$$[\downarrow]\hat{6}/le$$
$$\hat{4}/fa$$

In singing arpeggiations, when you see the symbol N^6, you will arpeggiate those pitches from the bottom up: $\hat{4}$/*fa*–$\hat{6}$/*le*–$\downarrow\hat{2}$/*ra*–$\hat{6}$/*le*–$\hat{4}$/*fa*.

In melodies, you will encounter $\downarrow\hat{2}$/*ra* as a chromatic upper neighbor to $\hat{1}$/*do,* in stepwise passages between $\hat{1}$/*do* and $\hat{3}$/*me,* and in a variety of skips implying or outlining the Neapolitan chord. In the major mode, you will also need to watch for $\downarrow\hat{6}$/*le* as a chromatic pitch in addition to $\downarrow\hat{2}$/*ra*.

Implications for Listening

In listening harmonically, you must now become aware of the Neapolitan 6th as a possibility above $\hat{4}$/*fa* in the bass. The Neapolitan typically functions as a predominant harmony, in a manner similar to IV and ii^6. In fact, the principal harmonic possibilities when you hear $\hat{4}$/*fa* approach $\hat{5}$/*sol* in the bass will now be IV, ii⁶, and N⁶ (leading to some kind of dominant harmony). To hear the differences among these three chords, listen for the presence of $\hat{1}$/*do*, $\hat{2}$/*re*, or $\downarrow\hat{2}$/*ra*, respectively, in an upper voice. If it is the Neapolitan, you can usually trace a voice from $\hat{1}$/*do* or $\hat{2}$/*re* in the preceding harmony, to $\downarrow\hat{2}$/*ra* in the Neapolitan, and then to [↑]$\hat{7}$/*ti* or $\hat{2}$/*re* in the dominant.

In rare cases, you may hear the Neapolitan chord in root position—with $\downarrow\hat{2}$/*ra* in the bass. Although atypical, this occurrence is a dead giveaway since the Neapolitan's characteristic pitch appears clearly in the bass.

Another harmonic relationship involving the Neapolitan in the minor mode is the function of $\overline{VI}$ as a kind of applied dominant to the Neapolitan, preceding and leading to it. (In rare cases, $\downarrow\overline{VI}$ serves this same function in the major mode.)

EXERCISES

1. Be able to sing skips from any pitch to any other within the Neapolitan chord. Pay particular attention to skips to and from $\downarrow\hat{2}$/*ra* in both major and minor modes and to $\downarrow\hat{6}$/*le* in the major mode.

2. In each of these preliminary exercises for chord arpeggiation, sing each chord one after the next. Think of these as symbol-reading, solmization, and singing exercises, not as actual chord progressions.

   a. i iv N⁶ i$^6_4$ $\overline{V}$ i   c. i ii$^{ø6}_5$ N⁶ i$^6_4$ $\overline{V}$ i

   b. i ii°⁶ N⁶ i$^6_4$ $\overline{V}$ i   d. I $\overline{IV}$ N⁶ I$^6_4$ $\overline{V}$ I

3. Learn to arpeggiate the following chord progressions.

   a. i $\overline{V}^7/\overline{VI}$ $\overline{VI}$ N⁶ $\overline{V}$ i

   b. i N⁶ $\overline{V}^4_2$ i⁶ ii$^{ø6}_5$ $\overline{V}$ i

   c. i $\overline{V}^6_5/\overline{III}$ $\overline{III}$ N⁶ i$^6_4$ $\overline{V}^7$ i

   d. I I⁶ N⁶ $\overline{V}$ $\overline{V}^6_5$/vi vi ii⁶ $\overline{V}^7$ I

4. Learn to play the above progressions on the piano (or similar keyboard).

LISTENING

Melodic Dictation

Listen to excerpts 59.1–59.4 and write out the pitches and rhythms for each.

| | | | Bottom number |
Exercise	Clef	Tonic	in meter sign
59.1	bass	F	8
59.2	treble	C♯	4
59.3	alto	A	2
59.4	treble	C	4

Melodic Transcription

Listen to excerpt 59.5 and write out the pitches and rhythms. Also supply any other appropriate performance indications.

Exercise	Clef	Tonic	Bottom number in meter sign
59.5	treble	C♯	2

Note: The tempo in this excerpt is very slow.

Harmonic Dictation

Listen to excerpts 59.6–59.9 and write out the bass line for each. Then supply the appropriate Roman numerals and figured bass symbols to represent each chord. Your instructor may also choose to have you write out the top ("soprano") voice as well.

Exercise	Tonic	Bottom number in meter sign
59.6	G	8
59.7	C	4
59.8	F	4
59.9	A	4

Harmonic Transcription

Listen to excerpt 59.10 and write out the bass line. Then supply the appropriate Roman numerals and figured bass symbols to represent each chord. Your instructor may also choose to have you write out the top ("soprano") voice as well.

Exercise	Tonic	Bottom number in meter sign
59.10	C♯	2

READING AND SIGHT SINGING

Prepare the following excerpts, singing on syllables while conducting. Pay special attention to the areas that state or imply Neapolitan chords. Spend half your practice time accompanying yourself with block chords on the piano or other chord-producing instrument.

Some of these excerpts clearly outline the Neapolitan chord, whereas others merely emphasize skips to and from $\hat{4}$/*fa*, [↓]$\hat{6}$/*le,* or ↓$\hat{2}$/*ra*. Some of these pitches might even have been harmonized in their original contexts by other chords. Nonetheless, all these excerpts offer opportunities to practice skips to these scale degrees and the use of ↓$\hat{2}$/*ra* in various guises.

Excerpts for reading and sight singing
from the
Anthology for Sight Singing
797–814

60 THE AUGMENTED SIXTH CHORDS

There is a family of chromatic chords that derive their function from two simultaneous voice leading events: (1) [↓]6̂/*le* moving to 5̂/*sol*, and (2) ↑4̂/*fi* moving to 5̂/*sol*. When [↓]6̂/*le* in the bass voice combines with ↑4̂/*fi* in some upper voice, they span the interval of an augmented sixth. Therefore, such chords are called **augmented sixth chords.**

> **Augmented sixth chords** are formed when [↓]6̂/*le* in the bass voice combines with ↑4̂/*fi* in some upper voice.

[↓]6̂/*le* and ↑4̂/*fi* as Tendency Tones

The following excerpt illustrates the approach to and resolution of an augmented sixth chord. Sing each of the outer voices separately, then play the two outer voices together on the piano. Sing one outer voice while someone else sings the other, and finally, sing all the voices with a group.

W. A. Mozart, String Quartet K. 465, mvt. 4, mm. 13–16 (1785)

The first half of measure 14 forms a IV⁶ chord (6̂/*la*–1̂/*do*–4̂/*fa*). In the second half of the measure, the outer voices are both chromaticized: in the bass voice, 6̂/*la* becomes ↓6̂/*le*, and in the top voice, 4̂/*fa* becomes ↑4̂/*fi*. These voices expand chromatically outward toward 5̂/*sol*, which they reach in the next harmony. The pitches ↓6̂/*le* and ↑4̂/*fi* are sometimes referred to as "tendency tones" because of their strong tendency to resolve. Note that in the major mode, both ↓6̂/*le* and ↑4̂/*fi* are chromatic pitches, whereas in the minor mode, ↑4̂/*fi* is chromatic and 6̂/*le* is diatonic.

Three Types: Italian, German, and French Sixth Chords

There are three different types of augmented sixth chords. In all three types, the tendency tone [↓]6̂/*le* nearly always appears in the bass voice. The other tendency tone

↑4̂/*fi* may appear in any upper voice, not just in the top one. The type of augmented sixth chord depends on which note or notes are added to ↓6̂/*le* and ↑4̂/*fi*.

The Italian Sixth Chord

Adding 1̂/*do* to [↓]6̂/*le* and ↑4̂/*fi* results in a three-note chord commonly referred to as the Italian sixth chord, abbreviated as It+6. The Italian sixth contains [↓]6̂/*le* in the bass voice, with some combination of 1̂/*do* and ↑4̂/*fi* in the upper voices. In close voicing, starting with [↓]6̂/*le* in the bass, we arpeggiate the Italian sixth chord as [↓]6̂/*le*–1̂/*do*–↑4̂/*fi*.

In the minor mode, 6̂/*le* and 1̂/*do* are diatonic pitches and ↑4̂/*fi* is chromatic. In the major mode, only 1̂/*do* is diatonic, while both ↓6̂/*le* and ↑4̂/*fi* are chromatic. Note the tritone formed between 1̂/*do* and the tendency tone ↑4̂/*fi*.

The German Sixth Chord

Adding 1̂/*do* and either [↓]3̂/*me* or ↑2̂/*ri* to the tendency tones [↓]6̂/*le* and ↑4̂/*fi*, creates a four-note chord commonly known as the German sixth chord, abbreviated as Gr+6. Note that [↓]3̂/*me* and ↑2̂/*ri* are enharmonically equivalent spellings of the same pitch. Although German augmented sixth chords can be spelled either way, the spelling that uses [↓]3̂/*me* is more common.

The German sixth contains [↓]6̂/*le* in the bass voice, with some combination of 1̂/*do*, [↓]3̂/*me* or ↑2̂/*ri*, and ↑4̂/*fi* in the upper voices. In close voicing, starting with [↓]6̂/*le* in the bass, we arpeggiate the German sixth chord as [↓]6̂/*le*–1̂/*do*–[↓]3̂/*me*–↑4̂/*fi* or [↓]6̂/*le*–1̂/*do*–↑2̂/*ri*–↑4̂/*fi*.

In the minor mode, 6̂/*le*, 1̂/*do* and 3̂/*me* are diatonic pitches (they form the submediant triad) and ↑4̂/*fi* is chromatic. In the major mode, only 1̂/*do* is diatonic while ↓6̂/*le*, ↓3̂/*me* and ↑4̂/*fi* are chromatic. In both modes, ↑2̂/*ri* is a chromatic pitch (although it appears extremely rarely in the minor mode because it is enharmonically equivalent to the diatonic pitch 3̂/*me*).

An interesting feature of the German augmented sixth chord is that its structure is enharmonically equivalent to a major-minor seventh chord (the dominant-seventh-type chord). For example, compare the pitches of the Gr+6 chord in C major with those of the V7 in D♭ major:

Gr+6 in C major   V7 in D♭ major

Nonetheless, the German sixth chord functions and resolves differently from a dominant seventh chord. In particular, compare the two tendency tones of the German sixth ([↓]6̂/*le* and ↑4̂/*fi*) to their enharmonic equivalents, the root and seventh (5̂/*sol* and 4̂/*fa*) of a dominant seventh chord:

C: Gr+6   V   D♭: V7   I

The French Sixth Chord

When $\hat{1}$/*do* and $\hat{2}$/*re* are added to the tendency tones [↓]$\hat{6}$/*le* and ↑$\hat{4}$/*fi*, the result is a four-note chord commonly referred to as the French sixth chord, abbreviated as Fr^{+6}.

The French sixth contains [↓]$\hat{6}$/*le* in the bass voice, with some combination of $\hat{1}$/*do*, $\hat{2}$/*re*, and ↑$\hat{4}$/*fi* in the upper voices. In close voicing, starting with [↓]$\hat{6}$/*le* in the bass, we arpeggiate the French sixth chord as [↓]$\hat{6}$/*le*–$\hat{1}$/*do*–$\hat{2}$/*re*–↑$\hat{4}$/*fi*.

In the minor mode, $\hat{6}$/*le*, $\hat{1}$/*do*, and $\hat{2}$/*re* are diatonic pitches and ↑$\hat{4}$/*fi* is chromatic. In the major mode, $\hat{1}$/*do* and $\hat{2}$/*re* are diatonic while ↓$\hat{6}$/*le* and ↑$\hat{4}$/*fi* are chromatic.

The Augmented Sixth Family

All of these augmented sixth chords are based on the interval of the augmented 6th formed between [↓]$\hat{6}$/*le* and ↑$\hat{4}$/*fi*. Other similarities are shown in the following figure:

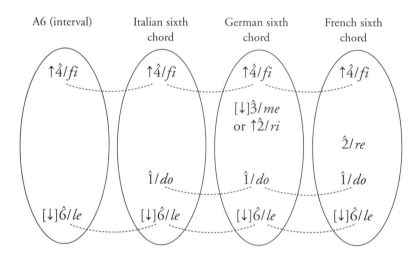

The ↓$\overline{\text{VI}}$ Triad in the Major Mode

The submediant triad in the minor mode ($\overline{\text{VI}}$: $\hat{6}$/*le*–$\hat{1}$/*do*–$\hat{3}$/*me*) shares three of the four pitches in the German augmented sixth chord (Gr^{+6}: $\hat{6}$/*le*–$\hat{1}$/*do*–$\hat{3}$/*me*–↑$\hat{4}$/*fi*). If you hear the submediant in minor, don't confuse it with the German sixth, because the key tendency tone ↑$\hat{4}$/*fi* is missing.

However, composers sometimes borrow this chord into the major mode, creating a major triad built on the lowered sixth scale degree. (↓$\overline{\text{VI}}$: ↓$\hat{6}$/*le*–$\hat{1}$/*do*–↓$\hat{3}$/*me*). If this chord does not contain ↑$\hat{4}$/*fi*, we will label it ↓$\overline{\text{VI}}$. (You might see it labeled ♭$\overline{\text{VI}}$, but $\hat{6}$ can be lowered by accidentals other than the flat sign.) Once ↑$\hat{4}$/*fi* is added, it becomes a Gr^{+6}.

Implications for Reading and Singing

Melodies rarely outline the pitches of an augmented sixth chord. Instead, they emphasize the relationship between [↓]$\hat{6}$/*le* and ↑$\hat{4}$/*fi*, or feature ↓$\hat{6}$/*le* or ↓$\hat{3}$/*me* in the major mode. Pay particular attention to melodic skips between [↓]$\hat{6}$/*le* and ↑$\hat{4}$/*fi* in both modes, and to ↓$\hat{6}$/*le* or ↓$\hat{3}$/*me* in the major mode. Skips from ↑$\hat{4}$/*fi* up to [↓]$\hat{6}$/*le* or from [↓]$\hat{6}$/*le* down to ↑$\hat{4}$/*fi* are particularly important. These pitches form the interval of a diminished 3rd (the inversion of an augmented 6th), which is enharmonically equivalent to a whole step, both pitches of which surround $\hat{5}$/*sol* by half steps.

Since the German augmented sixth chord is enharmonically equivalent to a major-minor seventh chord, you may want to think about forming a structure similar to $\underline{V}^7$ when practicing arpeggiation. Keep in mind the different syllables, functions, and resolutions of these two chords.

Implications for Listening

All augmented sixth chords share three common pitches and a similar function as chromatic chords that lead to the dominant. You may be asked to label all augmented sixth chords with a generic label, such as A⁶ or Aug⁶, or to make the distinction among It⁺⁶, Gr⁺⁶, and Fr⁺⁶. In any case, you must learn to recognize augmented sixth chords as a generic type (hearing the peculiar pull of the tendency tones [↓]$\hat{6}$/*le* and ↑$\hat{4}$/*fi*), and then to make distinctions among the three types.

If you hear [↓]$\hat{6}$/*le* in the bass, you must now consider whether it supports an augmented sixth chord. In the minor mode, $\hat{6}$/*le* could be part of the diatonic chords $\underline{VI}$ or iv⁶, so you must learn to distinguish between the particular sound, voice leading, and quality of those in contrast to the augmented sixth chords. In the major mode, the only chords we've encountered containing ↓$\hat{6}$/*le* are the augmented sixth chords, so—at present—the appearance of ↓$\hat{6}$/*le* in the bass should be a dead giveaway.

EXERCISES

1. Be able to sing skips from any pitch to any other within the augmented sixth chords. Pay particular attention to skips to and from and [↓]$\hat{6}$/*le* and ↑$\hat{4}$/*fi* in both major and minor modes and to ↓$\hat{3}$/*me* in the major mode.

2. In each of these preliminary exercises for chord arpeggiation, sing each chord one after the next. Think of these as symbol-reading, solmization, and singing exercises, not as actual chord progressions.

   a. i $\underline{VI}$ Gr⁺⁶ It⁺⁶ Fr⁺⁶ $\underline{V}$ i

   b. i iv⁶ It⁺⁶ Fr⁺⁶ Gr⁺⁶ i$^6_4$ $\underline{V}^7$ i

   c. I $\underline{IV}^6$ vii°⁶/$\underline{V}$ It⁺⁶ $\underline{V}$ I

   d. I $\underline{V}^4_3$/$\underline{V}$ Fr⁺⁶ $\underline{V}^7$ I

3. Learn to arpeggiate the following chord progressions.

   a. i $\underline{V}^6_4$ i⁶ ii°⁶ $\underline{III}$ Gr⁺⁶ i$^6_4$ $\underline{V}$ i

   b. I vi Gr⁺⁶ I$^6_4$ $\underline{V}$ I

   c. i $\underline{V}^6_5$ i It⁺⁶ i$^6_4$ $\underline{V}^7$ i

   d. I ii⁶ Gr⁺⁶ $\underline{V}$ $\underline{V}^6_5$/vi vi $\underline{V}^4_2$ I⁶

4. Learn to play the above progressions on the piano (or similar keyboard).

Harmonic Dictation

Listen to excerpts 60.1–60.4 and write out the bass line for each. Then supply the appropriate Roman numerals and figured bass symbols to represent each chord. Your instructor may also choose to have you write out the top ("soprano") voice as well.

Exercise	Tonic	Bottom number in meter sign
60.1	E	4
60.2	G	4
60.3	C	4
60.4	C♯	8

Harmonic Transcription

Listen to excerpts 60.5–60.8 and write out the bass line for each. Then supply the appropriate Roman numerals and figured bass symbols to represent each chord. Your instructor may also choose to have you write out the top ("soprano") voice as well.

Exercise	Tonic	Bottom number in meter sign
60.5	E♭	4
60.6	C	4
60.7	E	2
60.8	C	2

Where you hear only single pitches, mark no chords. What harmonies are *implied* at these spots?

Prepare the following excerpts, singing on syllables while conducting. Pay special attention to the areas that emphasize [↓]$\hat{6}$/*le* and ↑$\hat{4}$/*fi*.

In the multi-voice excerpts, note the places where the confluence of the voices creates augmented sixth chords. Label these chords by type.

Although few melodies blatantly outline any of the augmented sixth chords, you will find places where [↓]$\hat{6}$/*le* and ↑$\hat{4}$/*fi* occur either next to one another or are closely juxtaposed. The skip from [↓]$\hat{6}$/*le* directly to ↑$\hat{4}$/*fi* is particularly characteristic. The single-voice excerpts that follow feature this juxtaposition.

Excerpts for reading and sight singing
from the
Anthology for Sight Singing
815–822

61 OTHER CHORDS

This chapter introduces a few of the more common chords that don't fit neatly into the categories we've studied so far.

Borrowed iv and ii°⁷ in the Major Mode

Two chords may be thought of as borrowed from the minor mode into the major mode by chromatically lowering $\hat{6}$/*la* to ↓$\hat{6}$/*le*: iv and ii°⁷. The diatonic subdominant triad in the major mode is major: $\hat{4}$/*fa*–$\hat{6}$/*la*–$\hat{1}$/*do* (IV). Lowering the third chromatically changes it to minor: $\hat{4}$/*fa*–↓$\hat{6}$/*le*–$\hat{1}$/*do* (iv). This chord appears frequently in the progression IV–iv–I, in which the salient voice leading is $\hat{6}$/*la*–↓$\hat{6}$/*le*–$\hat{5}$/*sol*. The pitch $\hat{6}$/*la* can also be chromatically lowered to ↓$\hat{6}$/*le* as the fifth of the supertonic seventh chord, changing the quality of this chord from minor-minor (ii⁷) to half-diminished (ii°⁷).

V of VII (on $\hat{7}$/*te*) in the Minor Mode

One applied chord we have not covered is the dominant of the diatonic seventh scale degree in the minor mode. The triad built on $\hat{7}$/*te* is a major triad labeled VII, sometimes called the subtonic (review Chapters 19 and 58). The applied dominant of this chord (V/VII or V⁷/VII) is a major triad or major-minor seventh chord built on $\hat{4}$/*fa* ($\hat{4}$/*fa*–↑$\hat{6}$/*la*–$\hat{1}$/*do*–[$\hat{3}$/*me*]) and it resolves to the subtonic triad, $\hat{7}$/*te*–$\hat{2}$/*re*–$\hat{4}$/*fa*.

Harmonically, the V/VII creates a very "major" feel similar to that created by V/III and V/VI. Melodically, it tends to emphasize the relationship between $\hat{4}$/*fa* and $\hat{7}$/*te* (the applied dominant to the subtonic), and between ↑$\hat{6}$/*la* and $\hat{7}$/*te* (the applied leading tone to the subtonic).

The Minor v in the Minor Mode

So much Western tonal music in the minor mode uses the *major* dominant—with its chromatically raised third ↑$\hat{7}$/*ti*—that it can be easy to overlook the diatonic version of this triad. When the third of the dominant in the minor mode is left unaltered (as $\hat{7}$/*te*), the strong tonal function of ↑$\hat{7}$/*ti* is missing, which results in a more "modal" feel. We label this triad with a lower-case Roman numeral (v) and call it a minor dominant, although it does not have the strong dominant function of the major dominant.

The minor dominant appears most frequently in first inversion as part of the following progression: i–v⁶–iv⁶–V. This is a harmonization of the descending bass line $\hat{1}$/*do*–$\hat{7}$/*te*–$\hat{6}$/*le*–$\hat{5}$/*sol*, a common pattern in the passacaglia, chaconne, and ground bass.

When it appears in root position, especially when directly juxtaposed with the tonic, the minor dominant often seems very modal. (Note that the subtonic $\hat{7}/te$ appears not only in the minor dominant, but also in Dorian, Phrygian, Mixolydian, and Aeolian modes). Because of this, some composers have used the minor dominant to evoke a primitive mood.

EXERCISES

1. Be able to sing skips from any pitch to any other within iv, ii⌀7, V/VII, and v. Pay particular attention to skips to and from ↓6̂/le in the major mode, and 7̂/te and ↑6̂/la in the minor mode.

2. Learn to arpeggiate the following chord progressions.
   a. I IV iv I⁶ V I
   b. I ii⁷ ii⌀⁷ V⁴₃ I
   c. I V⁶₄ I⁶ iv I⁶₄ V I
   d. I ii⌀⁶₅ V I V⁶₅/IV IV V⁷ I
   e. i i⁶ iv V⁷/VII VII V⁶₅ i V⁷ i
   f. i V V⁶₅/VII VII V⁷/III III VI ii⌀⁶₅ V i
   g. i v⁶ iv⁶ V i
   h. i v VI ii°⁶ V⁶⁻⁵₄₋₃ i

3. Learn to play the above progressions on the piano (or similar keyboard).

LISTENING

Melodic Dictation

Listen to excerpts 61.1–61.6 and write out the pitches and rhythms for each.

Exercise	Clef	Tonic	Bottom number in meter sign
61.1	bass	D	8
61.2	vocal tenor*	B♭	4
61.3	treble	E	4
61.4	treble	C	4
61.5	alto	A	2
61.6	tenor	C♯	8

Melodic Transcription

Listen to excerpts 61.7–61.8 and write out the pitches and rhythms for each. Also supply any other appropriate performance indications.

---

*Vocal tenor clef (review Chapter 8) looks similar to the treble clef but sounds one octave lower than written.

Exercise	Clef	Tonic	Bottom number in meter sign
61.7	treble	G	2
61.8	treble	G	8

Harmonic Dictation

Listen to excerpts 61.9–61.12 and, for each, write out the bass line, then supply the appropriate Roman numerals and figured bass symbols to represent each chord. Your instructor may also choose to have you write out the top ("soprano") voice as well.

Exercise	Tonic	Bottom number in meter sign
61.9	E	2
61.10	F	4
(Note: This excerpt begins on an upbeat.)		
61.11	B	4
61.12	F	4

Harmonic Transcription

Listen to excerpts 61.13–61.14 and, for each, write out the bass line, then supply the appropriate Roman numerals and figured bass symbols to represent each chord. Your instructor may also choose to have you write out the top ("soprano") voice as well.

Exercise	Tonic	Bottom number in meter sign
61.13	E	4
61.14	G	4

Harmonic and Melodic Transcription

Listen to excerpts 61.15–61.16 and, for each, write out the bass line *and the melody*, then supply the appropriate Roman numerals and figured bass symbols to represent each chord.

Exercise	Clef	Tonic	Bottom number in meter sign
61.15	grand staff	C	4
(Try to account for the fermata toward the end of this excerpt.)			
61.16	grand staff	C	4

Prepare the following excerpts, singing on syllables while conducting. Pay special attention to the use of ↓6̂/*le* in the major mode and 7̂/*te* in the minor mode. Look for instances of iv and ii°⁷ in the major mode and for v and V/VII in the minor mode.

Excerpts for reading and sight singing
from the
Anthology for Sight Singing
823–836

62 MELODIC SEQUENCE

You have already worked with melodic sequences in the singing exercises called sequentials. Composers use sequences in many ways, and understanding sequences can help your music reading and listening.

Melodic Sequence as a Compositional Device

> A **melodic sequence** repeats the contour and rhythms of a pattern on a series of scale degrees.

A **melodic sequence** repeats the step-and-skip contour and rhythms of a melodic pattern on a series of scale degrees. There are many types of sequences. Some sequences use simple patterns and others use more complex ones; some repeat the pattern on adjacent scale degrees and others skip to different pitch levels; some follow the precise contour of the pattern and others make slight alterations; some repeat the exact rhythms of the pattern and others undergo rhythmic changes.

The sequential passage below is based on a six-note ascending scale pattern, which is repeated on successive ascending scale degrees. Notice that the sequence breaks off after the first note in measure 82. Composers break most sequences at some point in order to move the music in some other direction, often to a cadence.

Arcangelo Corelli, Concerto Grosso Op. 6, No. 12, Giga, mm. 78–83

Underlying the first five measures of this passage is a simple linear structure that moves from F in measure 78 to B♭ in measure 82, shown by the circled notes. Regardless of how complex a sequential passage is, it can always be reduced to its underpinning scale degrees.

The example above moves to a new scale degree at each new measure, but some sequences are based on longer patterns. For example, in the following excerpt the pattern is four measures long. It begins with the last two notes in measure 1, and it is sequenced down a step beginning with the last two notes in measure 5.

W. A. Mozart, Symphony No. 40, K. 550, mvt.1, mm. 1–9 (1788)

Other sequences are based on much shorter patterns, as in the example below. Also notice that this passage is based on an *ascending* sequence. Many sequences descend, but some ascend and others use both types of motion.

George Frideric Handel, *Samson*, HWV 57, Act I, "Why Does the God of Israel Sleep?" mm. 4–5 (1742)

Not all sequences repeat on adjacent scale degrees. The example below moves by descending 3rd:

George Frideric Handel, *Israel in Egypt*, HWV 54, Part III, "Thou Did'st Blow," mm. 1–2 (1738)

Composers often use separate sequences as a means of constructing different parts of a passage. The following excerpt contains two distinct sequences, as shown by the brackets and arrows.

William Boyce, Symphony No. 3 (Op. 2, No. 3), mvt. 3, mm. 1–8

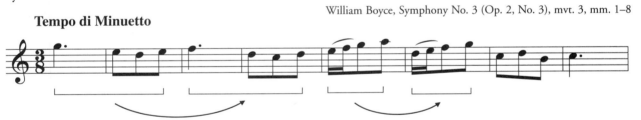

A sequence can create a compound melody when it suggests two or more concurrent lines (review Chapter 38). For example, sing through the following excerpt (transpose it, if necessary):

George Frideric Handel, Concerto Grosso Op. 6, No. 7, HWV 325, mvt. 1, mm. 1–4 (1739)

The compound melody comprises two lines in parallel 6ths for the first three measures. Play these parallel 6ths on the piano while you sing the melody. Listen to how these lines underpin the structure of the music.

Remember that **voice leading** follows the abstract lines formed by the smoothest possible melodic motion from one harmony to the next.

Understanding sequence and **voice leading** (review Chapter 38) can often help you to negotiate what might seem at first like extremely difficult passages. For instance, if you wanted to sing the excerpt below (transpose it down a 5th), you would first observe the sequence in descending 3rds in the upper voice (indicated by brackets).

Joseph Haydn, String Quartet Op. 20, No. 6 (Hob. III:36), mvt. 4, mm. 1–5 (1772)

Further examination reveals that each measure in this sequence is actually based on two pitches, the second of which fills in each 3rd in the sequence creating a smooth stepwise descent. This stepwise descent is supported by the lower voice as notated below. Sing these two stepwise voices as a duet.

By reducing this passage to its underlying pitches, you can see and hear that it is simply a series of 2–3 suspensions (review Chapter 45). As long as you can aurally keep track of the linear underpinnings of the top part, you should be able to stay on course, even if you make a mistake or two with the octave leaps and triad arpeggiations. Play the reduction on the piano while you and a friend sing the actual music.

Finally, you should note that even this reduction is an embellishment of a simpler structure—a series of parallel 3rds:

Implications for Sight Reading

As you read music—and particularly as you read *ahead*—you will find it helpful to look for sequences. If you notice that a passage is based on sequence, you will have drastically reduced the amount of information you must take in to perform the passage. As you sing the first segment in the sequence, try to keep its pattern—its contour and rhythm—in your memory. Scan ahead with your eyes and take in each segment of the sequence, looking closely for any alterations in the contour and rhythm.

Look from one segment of the sequence to the next (from beat to beat, measure to measure, or whatever the segment length) and determine the interval and direction by which it proceeds. If you are practicing (as opposed to sight singing), make a point of singing the underlying structure (as in the excerpts above) and then keep that structure in mind when you sing the actual music.

When reading a passage based on sequence, you must stay particularly vigilant for the place (or places) where the sequence is broken. Some passages are particularly subtle in this regard. For example, where and how is the sequence broken in the following passage?

J. S. Bach, Chorale Prelude, "Nun freut euch, lieben Christen gmein," BWV 734, mm. 1–2

At the downbeat of measure 2, the skip of a 4th from D to G (5̂/*sol*–1̂/*do*) breaks the sequence. An inattentive reader might mistakenly sing a 3rd here as an unbroken continuation of the sequence.

Implications for Listening

In dictation and transcription, once you write down the first statement of a sequence, you need only sketch out each of the series of scale degrees on which it appears so that you can then go back and fill in each segment of the sequence later. If you follow the pattern underlying the sequence, you can greatly increase the limits of your short-term musical memory by treating each successive segment as a single memorable chunk.

In listening, as in reading, pay particular attention to any alterations to the sequenced pattern and to the place where the sequence finally breaks.

1. Review all of the sequentials you have sung up to this point. Be able to sing any of them after having been given only the initial pattern and an underlying repetition structure (for example, "up by step" or "down by 3rds").

2. Invent at least two different sequentials. Share them with your classmates. How quickly can they learn them to sing them from memory?

3. Compose an easily singable eight-measure melody based on sequence. Share it with your classmates for them to sing at sight.

4. Take a segment from one of your favorite melodies and write a sequential passage based on it. Play this for your classmates for dictation or transcription practice.

5. Find at least one excerpt from real music (not found in this chapter) based on sequence. Write out its initial pattern and the underlying structure.

LISTENING

Melodic Dictation

Listen to excerpts 62.1–62.6 and write out the pitches and rhythms for each.

Exercise	Clef	Tonic	Bottom number in meter sign
62.1	bass	C	8
62.2	treble	F	4
62.3	treble	A	4
62.4	treble	C	4
62.5	alto	F♯	8
62.6	tenor	G♭	2

Melodic Transcription

Listen to excerpts 62.7–62.10 and write out the pitches and rhythms for each. Also supply any other appropriate performance indications.

Exercise	Clef	Tonic	Bottom number in meter sign
62.7	bass	A	4
62.8	bass	B♭	2
62.9	treble	G	4
62.10	bass	C♯	4

READING AND SIGHT SINGING

Prepare the following excerpts, singing on syllables while conducting. Pay close attention to the sequences, noting the length of each sequenced segment, its rhythm, and contour. Observe the underlying structure that connects one segment to the next, being sure to keep this broader motion in your mind's ear. Notice any alterations to the sequenced pattern and watch out for the place where the sequence is finally broken.

Excerpts for reading and sight singing
from the
Anthology for Sight Singing
837–881

63 HARMONIC SEQUENCE

Just as melodies can be based on sequence, so too can harmonic progressions. A **harmonic sequence** is typically built on a pair of chords (occasionally more) sequenced at a repeating interval, or on a series of root movements—usually by 4th or 5th (circle of fifths motion), occasionally by 3rd.

> A **harmonic sequence** is based on a group of chords sequenced at a repeating interval or on a series of root movements.

Harmonic Sequence as a Compositional Device

The famous *Canon and Gigue* (often called "Canon in D") by Pachelbel is based on a harmonic sequence. The I–V progression of the first two chords is sequenced down a 3rd for the next two chords to become vi–iii, then sequenced down again to form IV–I.

Johann Pachelbel, Canon and Gigue, mm. 1–2

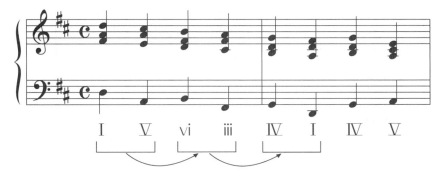

I   V   vi   iii   IV   I   IV   V

Play this progression on a piano, then arpeggiate the chords by singing. Sing this passage with at least three friends as if it were a four-voice composition. Notice how the sequence controls harmonic motion so that we accept the sound of vi moving to iii and iii moving to IV due to their role in the overall sequence. Otherwise, this progression does not follow traditional patterns of harmonic motion.

Here are some chord progressions based on sequences. What is the pattern that underlies each one?

1. iii vi ii V I
2. I vi IV ii
3. I V⁶ vi iii⁶ IV I⁶
4. i⁶ iv V⁶/III III VI⁶ ii° V⁶ i

The first progression follows the circle of fifths, and the second moves by descending 3rds. The third and fourth are based on chord pairs. The third takes the I–V⁶ pair and sequences it by descending 3rd, and the fourth takes the i⁶–iv pair and sequences it by descending 2nd. Composers often use chromatic harmonies in harmonic sequences, as in the last progression which incorporates an applied dominant.

A significant consequence of circle-of-fifths motion is the fact that alternate pitches in the bass line of such progressions produce linear motion. Sing or play through the following setting of the French folk song, "Vive la compagnie."

"Vive la compagnie," French-Canadian folk song, chorus

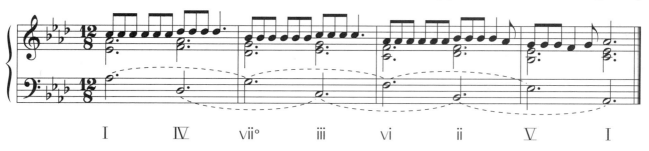

Notice how the bass pitches on successive downbeats form a descending scale from A♭ (1̂/do) to E♭ (5̂/sol), shown by the dotted slurs above the staff. The *other* bass pitches—the notes on beat 3 in each measure—also form a descending scale from D♭ (4̂/fa) to A♭ (1̂/do), shown by the dotted slurs below the staff. Although both of these lines are important, in such circle-of-fifths passages one of these lines can be thought of as more prominent or structurally significant. In this case, since the goal of the passage is the tonic chord on A♭ at the cadence, you might choose to focus on the lower line, which descends from D♭ to A♭.

Recognizing such linear connections can help you as you listen and as you perform. Listening for these lines can help to organize what you hear into cohesive, meaningful structures that are easier to remember. Performing with such connections in mind can help you to communicate the same cohesiveness to your listeners.

Implications for Listening

When you hear that a passage employs harmonic sequence, you can use this knowledge to increase the limits of your short-term musical memory. If the sequence is based on a segment of chords, write down the first segment and then treat each successive segment as a single chunk to remember. If the sequence is based on a single repeated interval (the circle of fifths or thirds), sketch the beginning of this pattern and listen for the point at which it ends. Listen for the underlying linear structure created by many sequences and sketch this on the staff, leaving the details to fill in later. Be particularly alert for any alterations to the basic sequence pattern and for the spot when the sequence is finally broken.

EXERCISES

1. Learn to arpeggiate the following chord progressions.

   a. I iii vi ii V̲ I
   b. i iv VII III VI ii°⁶ V̲ i
   c. I V̲ ii vi IV̲ V̲ I

d. I V^6 vi iii^6 IV I^6 V I
e. i v^6 VI III^6 iv i^6 V$^4_3$ i
f. I V^7/vi vi V^7/V V I
g. I vi IV ii V I
h. I V vi iii IV I IV V I
i. i V VI III iv i V i
j. i i^6 iv V^6/III III VI ii^{o6} V i

LISTENING

Harmonic Dictation

Listen to excerpts 63.1–63.5 and, for each, write out the bass line, then supply the appropriate Roman numerals and figured bass symbols to represent each chord. Your instructor may also choose to have you write out the top ("soprano") voice as well.

Exercise	Tonic	Bottom number in meter sign
63.1	D	4
63.2	D	4
63.3	F	8
63.4	C	2
63.5	F	8

Harmonic Transcription

Listen to excerpts 63.6–63.10 and, for each, write out the bass line, then supply the appropriate Roman numerals and figured bass symbols to represent each chord. Your instructor may also choose to have you write out the top ("soprano") voice as well.

Exercise	Tonic	Bottom number in meter sign
63.6	B♭	4
63.7	G	2
63.8	E	4
63.9	F	4
63.10	E	4

Y ou have gained some fluency in the four modern clefs (treble, bass, alto, and tenor) as well as the vocal tenor clef, all of which are still used by composers, arrangers, and editors today. In Chapter 26, you also learned about the role of C clefs in accommodating instruments or voices in a variety of registers. There are other clefs that function in the same way, which were used in earlier centuries.

Clef Families and the Grand Staff

We have already encountered members of the three clef "families." Each family uses a single symbol that represents a specific pitch. G clefs use the symbol &, which curls around the G-line (G4). C clefs use the symbol ⷺ, which centers on the C-line (C4). F clefs use the symbol 𝄢, whose two dots surround the F-line (F3).*

Within each family, the clef never moves. It is the lines and spaces which surround it that change. No matter where each clef is placed on a staff, the G clef always curls around the G4 line, the C clef always centers on the C4 line, and the two dots of the F clef always surround the F3 line. Seeing each clef and staff as a five-line segment of the grand staff will help you become fluent in reading and writing in all clefs. The following diagram shows the nine clefs in these three families, each printed on a different segment of the grand staff:

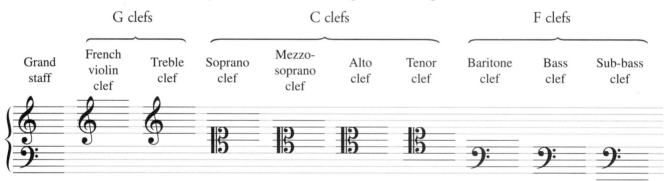

Clefs do give the illusion of moving when shown on a single staff. For example, consider what happens when each of the four C clefs is printed in succession on one continuous staff:

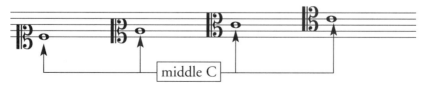

*This book uses the International Standards Organization (ISO) system of octave designation. In this system, each octave (beginning with each C) is labeled with a number. C0 is four octaves below middle C. Middle C is C4. Therefore, the next G above middle C is G4, and the next F below middle C is F3.

The C-clef above might at first appear to move to a higher note with each incarnation. In fact, the C-clef always stays centered on middle C. Therefore, it is the notes indicated by the lines and spaces that change as the clef is moved up or down on the staff.

In fact, any note can be made to appear on any line or space through the use of different clefs. For example, the single note C can be made to appear on successive lines and spaces through the use of the following clefs. (Obviously, the C falls in different octaves, from C3 to C5.)

Two clef-pairs produce identical line and space names (but in different octaves). The bass and French violin clefs both place C (C3 and C5 respectively) on the second space. The treble and sub-bass clefs both place C (C5 and C3 respectively) on the third space. This makes reading in these clefs a snap. To read French violin clef, think bass clef up two octaves. To read sub-bass clef, think treble clef down two octaves.

Reasons for Studying "Older" Clefs

For hundreds of years, music was written down using the variety of clefs discussed in this chapter. During the nineteenth and twentieth centuries, common practice coalesced around the use of the four modern clefs, which are now used almost exclusively.

The older clefs (French violin, soprano, mezzo-soprano, baritone, and sub-bass) remain valuable to us as we encounter music that has not been transcribed into modern clefs. It is also helpful to consult original sources even when they have been transcribed. In addition, seeing and understanding the complete system of clefs can give you a deeper and more facile mastery of the four modern clefs as part of this larger system. Finally, for those wishing to study transposition by clef, fluency in seven unique clefs is mandatory. (Review Chapter 48.)

EXERCISES

1. What clef or clefs will place the following notes on the indicated lines or spaces?
   a. D on the first line
   b. E on the fifth line
   c. B on the first space
   d. C on the first space
   e. A on the fourth space
   f. A on the second line
   g. D on the fifth line

   h. D on the fourth line

   i. E on the third space

   j. F on the third line

2. What clef or clefs will make the following transpositions? (Review Chapter 48.)

   a. up a 3rd from treble clef

   b. down a 4th from bass clef

   c. up a 2nd from bass clef

   d. down a 5th from treble clef

   e. down a 2nd from alto clef

L I S T E N I N G

Melodic Dictation

Listen to excerpts 64.1–64.8 and write out the pitches and rhythms for each. Be sure to observe the indicated clefs.

Exercise	Clef	Tonic	Bottom number in meter sign
64.1	mezzo-soprano	C	4
64.2	mezzo-soprano	D	2
64.3	soprano	A♭	4
64.4	soprano	B	2
64.5	baritone	C	8
64.6	baritone	G	4
64.7	sub-bass	G	2
64.8	French violin	E	4

R E A D I N G   A N D   S I G H T   S I N G I N G

Prepare the following excerpts on both syllables and letter names while conducting. Learn the individual lines of each of these excerpts on the piano. Be able to play them on at least one other instrument as well.

**Excerpts for reading and sight singing
from the
Anthology for Sight Singing
882–893**

65 HEMIOLA

O nce a composition has established a regular pattern of metric grouping between levels of pulses, it is possible for that pattern to change—creating what feels like a change in meter. One of the most common of these changes involves a temporary shift between duple and triple groupings within a passage, a device known as *hemiola*.

Hemiola across Two or More Measures

The following excerpt from an opera by Handel is written in simple triple meter ($\frac{3}{8}$). You will notice a change in the feeling of meter towards the end of the passage, as represented in the pulse-graph written directly below the music.

George Frideric Handel, *Giulio Cesare,* HWV 17, Act III, scene 4, "Aure, deh, per pietà spirate," mm. 143–148 (1724) [piano reduction]

The normative triple grouping in $\frac{3}{8}$ changes in measures 146–147 to a 2 + 2 + 2 grouping. (This change is particularly apparent in the rhythm of the upper two voices, but is also reinforced by the contour of the lower voices.) In a sense, the prevailing $\frac{3}{8}$ meter has been replaced for these six beats. You may think of the replacement meter as three measures of $\frac{2}{8}$ or as one measure of $\frac{3}{4}$:

Hemiola is a metric condition that regroups 3 + 3 as 2 + 2 + 2, or vice versa.

This metric change is known as **hemiola,** which (from Greek) means "the half and the whole" or "one and a half times." This proportion (3:2 or 1½:1) reflects the relationship between two different groupings of six pulses: 3 + 3 and 2 + 2 + 2. The normative metric grouping of two measures (six beats) in simple triple meter is 3 + 3, but during hemiola they are grouped as 2 + 2 + 2.

Hemiola can occur in ⅜ meter, as in the excerpt above, but it also appears in other simple triple meters, most notably ¾ and 3/2. In addition, you will find passages that continue the hemiola for more than just two measures.

This kind of hemiola—carving the equivalent of three duple measures out of two triple ones—became a kind of signal in Baroque music announcing the approach of a cadence. Later composers explored this, as well as longer spans of hemiola in various contexts.

Hemiola within a Single Measure

A hemiola can also regroup six pulses *within* a single measure. This usually takes place in either compound duple or simple triple meter. You have probably noticed that a measure of 6/8 and a measure of ¾ contain the same number of eighth notes. This type of hemiola highlights this relationship.

Sing the following excerpt from the Mexican folk song "Macario Romero":

"Macario Romero," Mexican folk song, mm. 1–8

The prevailing meter in this song is compound duple (6/8), which normally groups six pulses in each measure into groups of 3 + 3. But in measure 2 this shifts momentarily to 2 + 2 + 2, so it seems like a measure of simple triple meter (¾). The pulse-graph for the first four measures of this song illustrates the three levels of pulse at work in this short passage:

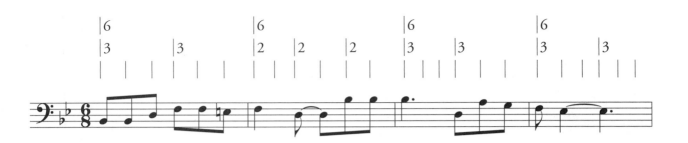

Now sing the Honduran folk song below. You will notice that the first full measure is grouped in compound duple even though the meter is $\frac{3}{4}$. In a sense, this excerpt is the opposite of the previous one: the hemiola shifts the normative simple triple meter (2 + 2 + 2) to compound duple (3 + 3) for one measure.

"El sapo," Honduran folk song, mm. 1–8

Some pieces exhibit isolated cases of this kind of hemiola, whereas others make frequent switches between simple triple and compound duple.

Implications for Sight Reading

When you are reading music and you encounter hemiola, you will want to bring it out through your performance. You will need to address hemiola across measures differently than that within measures.

The excerpt from Handel's *Giulio Cesare,* which we discussed at the beginning of this chapter, features hemiola across measures. At the very least, you could communicate the metric shift by stressing groups of twos during the hemiola. You could also change your conducting pattern from simple triple meter (conducting each eighth note) to a *broad three* for the two-measure hemiola (conducting every other eighth note, as if changing from $\frac{3}{8}$ to $\frac{3}{4}$). Be certain that the underlying pulse does not change.

When interpreting hemiola *within* a measure, there are some passages that change between compound duple and simple triple so forcefully that it is practically incumbent on you to change your conducting pattern with every metric shift brought on by hemiola. This is particularly common in some Spanish and Latin American folk music. To effect this conducting change properly, you must be certain to maintain a steady underlying pulse. For example, conduct the first measure of "Macario romero" with a two pattern (representing compound duple) but change to a three pattern for the second measure. Keep the eighth-note pulse steady. You may want to practice this with a metronome set to click on every eighth note pulse.

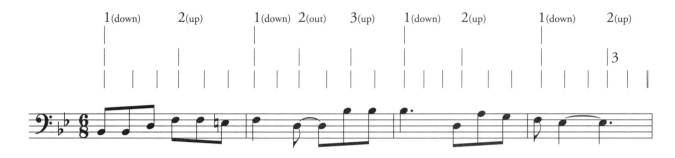

One of the most striking things about passages with hemiola is the many different ways that composers, editors, and arrangers notate them. Some use a compound duple meter sign and some use simple triple, but the notation within each meter sign can vary. For example, compare the second measure of the Mexican folk song "Macario Romero" as it appears earlier in this chapter with the version below:

This notational grouping clearly expresses the metric regrouping caused by hemiola, making the second measure look like ¾ (in contrast with the prevailing ⅜ meter). Some editions and transcriptions regroup notes, stems, and beams this way; others do not. In addition, some use a "double" meter sign (either ⅜¾ or ¾⅜), which means that the music alternates (regularly or not) between the two meters. In all cases, it is up to you—the reader—to recognize hemiola and to take it into account in your reading and performance.

Implications for Listening

At the very essence of hemiola is metric ambiguity. Even though listeners can hear *any* group of six pulses as 3 + 3 or 2 + 2 + 2, most music gives a rather clear sense of which grouping is predominant. However, when hemiola enters a passage listeners can become disoriented with regard to where the different levels of pulse fall, and they may become confused about the meter and, consequently, the rhythms.

You must now incorporate hemiola as a possibility when listening to meter and rhythm in music. If you are careful to attend to the common underlying pulse (for example, the eighth note in "Macario Romero") and allow for the possibility of regrouping by twos and threes, then you should be well prepared to deal with the aural curve ball thrown by hemiola.

EXERCISES

1. Set a metronome to 120 and imagine that each click is an eighth note. First, conduct quarter notes in ¾ (♩ = *60*). Then, change to conducting dotted quarter notes in ⅜ (♩. = *40*). Change the metronome's speed to 180 and repeat the process. What new tempi result for ¾ and ⅜? Repeat this process again at 240.

2. Set a metronome to 120 and imagine that each click is a quarter note. Conduct quarter notes in ¾ (♩ = *120*), then change to conducting half notes in 3/2 (♩ = *60*). Repeat this process at several other metronome settings.

Melodic Dictation

Listen to excerpts 65.1–65.4 and write out the pitches and rhythms for each, following the instructions.

	Clef	Tonic	Meter	Additional notes
65.1	Alto	C	¾	Rewrite it in 2/4. Which meter do you think the composer used? Compare to the original.
65.2	Treble	C	6/8	
65.3	Treble	F♯		This is a waltz. Choose an appropriate meter.
65.4	Treble	B♭		Metronome mark is ♩. = 100

Melodic Transcription

Listen to excerpt 65.5 and write out the pitches and rhythms following the instructions. Also supply any other appropriate performance indications.

	Tonic	Beat unit	Additional notes
65.5	G	♩	Try using several different meters and starting on downbeats and other beats before settling on an answer. Compare your version with those of your classmates, and finally with the original notation.

Pulse-Graph Transcription

Listen to excerpts 65.6–65.9. For each, write out a pulse-graph representing the fastest tappable pulse and two levels of pulse above that. Be sure to adjust your graph to accommodate any hemiola you hear.

Rhythm Transcription

Listen to excerpt 65.10. Write out the rhythm of the melody in 30 measures of ¾ meter, starting with a quarter-note rest. Use ties or slurs as needed to indicate hemiola.

Prepare the following excerpts, singing on syllables while conducting. As you prepare these excerpts, look for instances of hemiola. Try performing some of these by changing your conducting pattern to accommodate and bring out the hemiola.

Excerpts for reading and sight singing
from the
Anthology for Sight Singing
894–909

66 STEPWISE CHROMATIC ALTERATIONS

We have encountered chromatic pitches in melodic contexts as passing tones, neighboring tones, and leaps to prefix chromatic passing tones. We have also heard and sung them in arpeggiations of chromatic chords. Another melodic context in which you will hear, read, and perform chromatic pitches involves stepwise chromatic alterations.

Four Types of Chromatic Alteration

The following excerpt features all four types of chromatic alteration in a melodic context, each one involving the pitch D♯ (↑1̂/*di*).

Franz Schubert, Symphony No. 8 ("Unfinished"), D. 759, mvt. 1, mm. 258–267 (1822)

In the first instance, the D♯ functions as a chromatic passing tone (1̂/*do*–↑1̂/*di*–2̂/*re*). (Review Chapter 52.) The second bracket marks the figure E–D♯–E (2̂/*re*–↑1̂/*di*–2̂/*re*), where D♯ serves as a lower chromatic neighboring tone. (Review Chapter 19.) The fourth bracket marks the figure [B–]D♯–E ([6̂/*la*–]↑1̂/*di*–2̂/*re*), or a leap to a prefix chromatic neighboring tone. (Review Chapter 53.)

The *third* bracket marks the figure C♯–D♯–E (7̂/*ti*–↑1̂/*di*–2̂/*re*), where C♯ and E are diatonic pitches in D major and D♯ is chromatic. This chromatic pitch functions differently than a chromatic passing or neighboring tone. In a sense, the D♯ has replaced the diatonic D♮ in a scalar connection between C♯ and E. We shall refer to this type of condition as a **stepwise chromatic alteration.**

What makes stepwise chromatic alterations *stepwise* is that they connect two pitches using one half step and one whole step. Stepwise connections involving only one chromatic alteration can occur only immediately above or below one of the two diatonic half steps. For example, in the white-key diatonic collection (C major or A minor), stepwise chromatic alterations can occur only at the two diatonic half steps, E–F and B–C. To appreciate the stepwise nature of these changes, we must put each chromatic alteration in the middle of a three-note stepwise segment. The following chart shows the diatonic and then chromatic versions of each of these three-note groups.

> A **stepwise chromatic alteration** raises or lowers by a half step the middle note in a three-note stepwise segment of a diatonic scale, turning one of the half steps into a whole step and the adjacent whole step into a half step.

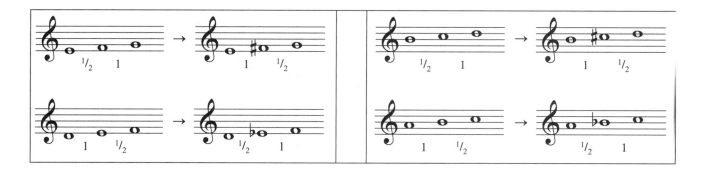

Stepwise Chromatic Alteration in the Major Mode

In the major mode, the diatonic half steps occur at $\hat{3}/mi–\hat{4}/fa$ and $\hat{7}/ti–\hat{1}/do$. The $\hat{3}/mi–\hat{4}/fa$ half step can be expanded by either raising $\hat{4}/fa$ to ↑$\hat{4}/fi$ or lowering $\hat{3}/mi$ to ↓$\hat{3}/me$. The $\hat{7}/ti–\hat{1}/do$ half step can be expanded by either raising $\hat{1}/do$ to ↑$\hat{1}/di$ or lowering $\hat{7}/ti$ to ↓$\hat{7}/te$.

The following list of scales shows each of the chromatic alterations in relation to the C-major diatonic scale. The half steps are marked with angle brackets:

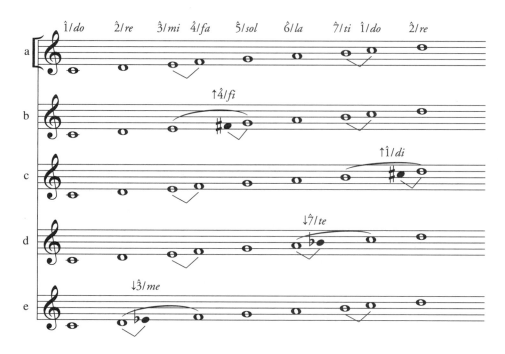

Composers have frequently used the alterations shown in (b), (c), and (d). The lowered third scale degree found in (e) is typically associated with a change in mode from major to minor (which we will cover in Chapter 71).

Stepwise Chromatic Alteration in the Minor Mode

In the minor mode, the diatonic half steps occur at $\hat{2}/re–\hat{3}/me$ and $\hat{5}/sol–\hat{6}/le$. The $\hat{2}/re–\hat{3}/me$ half step can be expanded by either raising $\hat{3}/me$ to ↑$\hat{3}/mi$ or lowering $\hat{2}/re$ to ↓$\hat{2}/ra$. The $\hat{5}/sol–\hat{6}/le$ half step can be expanded by either raising $\hat{6}/le$ to ↑$\hat{6}/la$ or lowering $\hat{5}/sol$ to ↓$\hat{5}/se$.

For the sake of comparing scale degrees, let's look at these diatonic half steps in the *parallel* minor scale. The list of scales below shows each of these chromatic alterations in relation to the C-minor diatonic scale. The half steps are again marked with angle brackets:

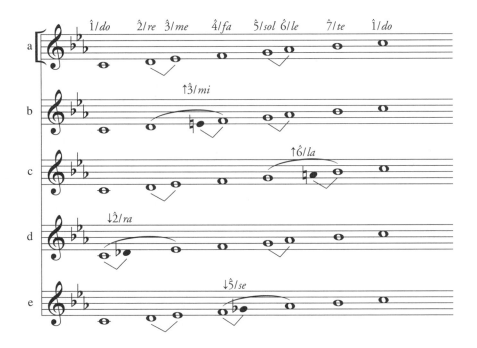

Composers have frequently used the alterations shown in (b), (c), and (d). The lowered fifth scale degree found in (e) is rarely used, usually in modulations.

Larger Implications

Stepwise chromatic alterations often have at least one of several larger implications. Let's look a little more closely at each of these.

The modes: The chromatic alteration of a single scale degree, while retaining the same tonic/final, can turn a major or minor scale into a modal one. (Return to Chapters 49 and 50 and review these relationships.)

Chromatic harmony: The applied chords and other chromatic harmonies we have studied have all been achieved through the chromatic alteration of certain pitches. Some of these can be introduced as stepwise chromatic alterations. For example, ↑4̂/fi is part of V/V and ↓2̂/ra is part of the Neapolitan sixth. Review Chapters 54–61 and determine how many of these chromatic harmonies can be achieved through stepwise chromatic alterations.

Modulation: Many of the modulations we'll encounter in the following chapters will be effected in part by the stepwise chromatic alteration of one diatonic collection to create yet another diatonic collection. Keep the concepts and skills you learn in this chapter in mind as we explore various modulations in future chapters.

EXERCISES

1. Practice singing stepwise patterns created by stringing together one half step (H) with one whole step (W). This will create four patterns: two ascending (beginning with H, then with W) and two descending (beginning with H, then with W) as shown in the example below:

H W W H   W H H W   H W W H   W H H W

Sing these patterns on a neutral syllable, all starting on the same pitch, in the given order. Then, practice them in various orders. Finally, practice them in various orders with each pattern beginning on a different starting pitch.

2. Write "The Star-Spangled Banner" from memory in the treble clef, in the key of C♯, using a **4** as the bottom number in meter sign. What accidentals do you need to use? Why?

LISTENING

Melodic Dictation

Listen to excerpts 66.1–66.7 and write out the pitches and rhythms for each.

Exercise	Clef	Tonic	Bottom number in meter sign
66.1	treble	C	4
66.2	treble	C	4
66.3	treble	E	4
66.4	treble	A	4
66.5	bass	B	4
66.6	alto	D♭	2
66.7	tenor	F♯	2

Melodic Transcription

Listen to excerpts 66.8–66.10 and write out the pitches and rhythms for each. Also supply any other appropriate performance indications.

Exercise	Clef	Tonic	Bottom number in meter sign
66.8	treble	G	4
66.9	treble	A	4
66.10	treble	A♭	4

Prepare the following excerpts, singing on syllables while conducting. Pay special attention to the stepwise chromatic alterations, making whole- and half-step adjustments as necessary. Do any of these imply other modes? Chromatic harmonies? Modulation?

Excerpts for reading and sight singing
from the
Anthology for Sight Singing
910–934

READING IN KEYS OTHER THAN THE NOTATED KEY SIGNATURE

The diatonic collections we have studied so far have all been established entirely by the key signature printed at the beginning of each staff, and accidentals have functioned as chromatic alterations to the diatonic pitches given by the key signature. However, accidentals can also create *diatonic* pitches and establish a diatonic collection that differs from the one indicated by the key signature. This chapter explores the specific kinds of contexts that give rise to contradictions between key signature and prevailing diatonic collection and explains how to read and write such passages.

Accidentals That Create Diatonic Pitches

Key signatures make it unnecessary to write accidentals repeatedly before notes that are consistently sharp or flat in a given diatonic collection. However, composers, arrangers, and editors sometimes use accidentals to create diatonic collections, as Bartók does in the example below.

Béla Bartók, *For Children,* Part I, No. 27, "My Sheep Are Lost," mm. 5–16 (1909)

Although the excerpt is printed without a key signature, sharps have been added to every F and C to create an actual diatonic collection with two sharps. In addition, the configuration of the pitches in this passage establishes D the tonic. Therefore, this excerpt is in D major even though it is printed without a key signature.

Diatonic Collections That Contradict the Key Signature

Accidentals can also alter a passage so that the actual prevailing diatonic collection becomes some combination of the key signature and those accidentals. For example, the key signature for the excerpt below contains one sharp (F♯), but sharps have been added to C, G, D, and A as accidentals. The actual diatonic collection contains five sharps, and this is coupled with the strong tonicization of B resulting in B major as the key of this passage.

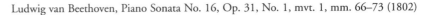

Ludwig van Beethoven, Piano Sonata No. 16, Op. 31, No. 1, mvt. 1, mm. 66–73 (1802)

Accidentals can either increase the number of sharps or flats, or negate sharps or flats in the signature through natural signs. They can also send the diatonic collection from sharps in the signature to flats, or from flats to sharps. Certain accidentals may alter the prevailing diatonic collection, and others may be used in the same passages as local chromatic pitches. You will have to distinguish between these and judge just what is the new prevailing diatonic collection.

Recognizing the Tonic in a New Diatonic Collection

To determine the key of a passage, you must figure out both diatonic collection *and* tonic. You will recall from chapters 18, 20, and 49 that diatonic collection and tonic are separate concepts (for example, both B minor and D major take place in the two-sharp collection). The three principal forces that can tonicize one of the pitches in a diatonic collection are (1) the *dominant-tonic* relationship, (2) the *mediant-tonic* relationship, and (3) the use of the *leading tone*. In addition, the appearance of familiar melodic and harmonic figures can also help tonicize certain pitches in your mind's ear.

Understanding tonicization and the role of accidentals in altering diatonic collections will help you read and write passages that contradict the given key signature. In addition, these concepts are essential in choosing the correct pitch solmization for such passages.

Chromatic Pitches in Diatonic Collections That Contradict the Key Signature

Looking at the notes of a passage and deciding which are consistently natural and which are consistently sharp or flat is a relatively simple process when all pitches in the passage are diatonic. The task becomes a bit more complicated when a passage includes both diatonic and chromatic pitches.

Look at the following excerpt from a symphony by Mozart and determine the prevailing diatonic collection.

W. A. Mozart, Symphony No. 41, K. 551 ("Jupiter"), mvt. 1, mm. 56–62 (1788)

The key signature has no sharps or flats, but there are four F♯s, one C♯, one G♯, and even one D♯. Of those, only the F♯s are applied consistently and structurally. The pitches C♯, G♯, and D♯ are non-structural pitches—in this case, chromatic passing tones. So, we can combine a one-sharp diatonic collection with the tonicization of G to determine that this passage is in G major. Now sing the passage on syllables or scale-degree numbers using G as the tonic.

It is important to distinguish between *accidentals* and *chromatics*. Some accidentals result in chromatic pitches (such as the C♯, G♯, and D♯ in the passage above). Other accidentals result in diatonic pitches (such as the F♯ in the passage above). You may have previously used the word "chromatic" casually to refer to all accidentals, but you must now be more careful to make a clear distinction between these two terms and concepts.

Furthermore, just as some accidentals can result in diatonic pitches, the absence of an accidental can result in a chromatic pitch. Look over the following excerpt, noting in particular the use of added flats, and carefully sing through it:

George Frideric Handel, Chandos anthem *Have Mercy upon Me O God,* HWV 248, No. 2, "Wash Me Throughly from My Wickedness," mm. 1–13 (1718)

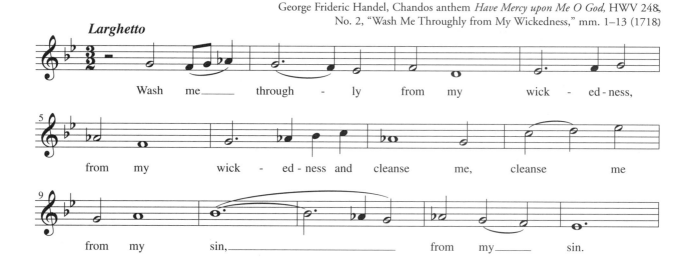

This passage is in E♭ major (with the three-flat collection created by two flats in the signature and one through accidentals). How should you treat the A in measure 9? All the accidentals on A♭ create *diatonic* pitches, but the one chromatic pitch is created through the *absence* of an accidental (the A in measure 9).

The chart below summarizes the relationships between accidentals and diatonic and chromatic pitches:

- some pitches with accidentals are diatonic
- some pitches with accidentals are chromatic
- most pitches without accidentals are diatonic
- some pitches without accidentals are chromatic

"Incomplete" Key Signatures

Some compositions from the Baroque era use what we refer to as "incomplete" key signatures. These key signatures typically contain fewer sharps or flats than required by the diatonic collection. Accidentals are then used to establish the rest of the collection. For instance, the passage below is written with a signature of two flats, but the actual diatonic collection is *three* flats due to the consistent use of accidentals on A♭.

George Frideric Handel, Chandos anthem *Have Mercy upon Me O God*, HWV 248, No. 8, "Then Shall I Teach Thy Ways unto the Wicked," mm. 1–5 (1718)

C is tonicized in this passage, and with a three-flat collection, this means the passage is in the key of C minor, even though the printed signature contains only two flats. The most common incomplete signatures occur when the keys of D, G, and C minor are printed with one flat fewer than we are now accustomed to. Other incomplete signatures include both major and minor keys written with one or (rarely) two fewer flats or sharps.

New Diatonic Collections after Modulation

Many compositions move to new keys after stating their opening materials in the main key. Your ability to recognize those new keys accurately and rapidly will directly affect your ability to read, auralize, and perform such compositions. For example, the following excerpt from J. S. Bach's F-major invention features the main subject in C major here, after it appeared in measure 1 and following in F major.

J. S. Bach, Invention No. 8, BWV 779, mm. 12–14 (c. 1720)

Incomplete Diatonic Collections

In some passages, not all seven pitches of a diatonic collection will appear. If certain pitches are absent, it may be more difficult to determine the new prevailing diatonic collection.

Joseph Haydn, Symphony No. 104, mvt. 4, mm. 55–64 (1795)

In the excerpt above, there are no Fs and Gs, but the consistent use of C♯ implies that F♯ is also diatonic. However, we cannot easily conclude whether the pitch G should be natural (a two-sharp collection, as provided by the key signature) or sharp (a three-sharp collection). So, we must first come to a conclusion about the tonic in this passage. The strong dominant-tonic relationship between E and A clearly makes A feel like the tonic. Once we know this, we can also conclude that G♯ (and not G♮) should be inferred in this passage.

As previously noted, the introduction of chromatic pitches makes this process even trickier. Look at the following excerpt and consider these questions: Which pitches are diatonic and which are chromatic? Should you infer D♮ or D♭? Why?

Pietro Antonio Locatelli, Concerto Grosso Op. 1, No. 6, mvt. 3, mm. 1–6 (1721)

The tonicization of F and the constant appearance of A♭ lead us to hear this passage in F minor and infer the four-flat collection, including D♭. We hear the E-naturals as chromatic pitches.

EXERCISES

1. Pick a familiar tune and write it out using a key signature of two flats, but starting on F♯. Use accidentals as necessary. Write the same tune a second time, this time with a key signature of four sharps, but starting on B♭.

2. Pick one tune from column A and one tune from column B. Write out both tunes using accidentals (no key signature) and a tonic of D. What is different about the two tunes? What accounts for this difference?

Column A	Column B
• When Johnny Comes Marching Home	• We Three Kings of Orient Are (first 31 notes)
• Heigh-ho, Anybody Home? (Food nor Drink nor Money Have We None)	• God Rest Ye Merry Gentlemen

---

LISTENING

Melodic Dictation

Listen to excerpts 67.1–67.4 and write out the pitches and rhythms for each, following the given instructions.

Exercise	Clef	Key signature	Bottom number in meter sign	Starting pitch
67.1	tenor	none	2	E4
67.2	treble	2 flats	4	G5
67.3	bass	3 flats	4	A♭3
67.4	treble	5 sharps	8	C6

Melodic Transcription

Listen to excerpts 67.5–67.8 and write out the pitches and rhythms for each. Also supply any other appropriate performance indications.

Exercise	Clef	Key signature	Bottom number in meter sign	Starting pitch
67.5	treble	1 sharp	8	D4
67.6	treble	4 flats	4	C4
67.7	treble	2 sharps	4	E5
67.8	grand staff (2 voices)	none	4	D3 (1st voice)

READING AND SIGHT SINGING

Prepare the following excerpts, singing on syllables while conducting. As you prepare each of these excerpts, answer the following questions: (1) What is the prevailing diatonic collection? (2) What is the tonic? Then decide how you will interpret the key and what solmization to use.

**Excerpts for reading and sight singing
from the
Anthology for Sight Singing
935–977**

68 INTRODUCTION TO MODULATION

Up until now, we have sung and listened to excerpts that stay in a single key. Now, we will begin to investigate music that moves from one key to another within a single excerpt, a change that we call **modulation.**

Change of Tonic

In all music that modulates, an initial passage tonicizes one pitch, then moves to another passage that tonicizes a different pitch. So far, we have understood tonicization as a single static condition that stayed the same for the entire duration of a musical excerpt. But tonicization also operates as a *dynamic* process, whereby the tonic of an excerpt can change from one passage to the next. You must sharpen your hearing and reading skills in order to identify the tonic at any point in an excerpt and you must be vigilant for possible changes in the tonic at any point in an excerpt.

The following melody is in the one-sharp diatonic collection. The first eight measures and the final four measures tonicize E, resulting in E minor. But the passage in between (measures 9–12) tonicizes G, so this middle passage is in G major—the relative major of E minor. Although you could hear and perform this entire short piece in E minor, it makes more musical sense to think of measures 9–12 in G major.

"A Geneyve," Yiddish folk melody

This excerpt illustrates a modulation between relative keys, which involves a change of tonic without a change of diatonic collection. Although some different pitches are emphasized in each area, they are all still part of the same collection.

Change of Collection

As demonstrated above, modulations between relative keys involve a change in tonic, but not in collection. Other modulations involve a change in collection, but not in tonic (moves between *parallel* keys, which we will examine in greater depth in Chapter 71). However, the vast majority of modulations you will encounter involve a change in both tonic *and* collection.

Franz Schubert, "Kennst du das Land," D. 321, mm. 1–11 (1815)

In the excerpt above, measures 1–5 are clearly in A major; however, the natural signs on F, C, and G beginning in measure 6 create a new diatonic collection with no sharps or flats. The pitch C is tonicized in these measures, so you can see and hear that this passage has modulated from A major to C major.

The Art of Changing Syllables during Performance

In order to use functional solmization (scale-degree syllables or numbers) for music that modulates, you must change from one tonic and scale to another. For example, the first two measures of the following excerpt are in C major, but measures 3–4 are in G major (a precise transposition of the opening). In order to solmize measures 1–2 with a tonic of C and solmize measures 3–4 with a tonic of G, you must change from one scale system to another, and you must determine a point at which to make this change.

J. S. Bach, Concerto for Three Harpsichords, BWV 1064, mvt. 1, mm. 1–4 (c. 1730)

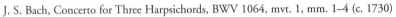

C major is represented in the syllables and scale degree numbers below the notes in the first two measures. At the downbeat of measure 3, the syllable that would be $\hat{5}$/*sol* in the old key changes to $\hat{1}$/*do* in the new key of G major. Of course, you might choose to change on the last pitch in measure 2, singing $\hat{7}$/*ti* instead of $\uparrow\hat{4}$/*fi*, or you might even mumble through a few of the notes in that entire beat before reaching the new $\hat{1}$/*do* on G in measure 3. In any case, you must change soon enough so that the music makes sense in the new key, and you must abandon the old key in your thinking and hearing so that the new key can be firmly established.

You can sometimes take advantage of a rest to change syllables. During the pause in measure 9 of the following excerpt, the pitch C can change from $\hat{5}$/*sol* to $\hat{3}$/*mi*.

Ziemlich langsam.

Robert Schumann, *Myrthen*, Op. 25, No. 7, "Die Lotosblume," mm. 1–13 (1840)

You can also change syllables during a longer note, as in the excerpt below. The chromatic pitch C♯ appears as ↑1̂/*di* in C major but changes function to ↑7̂/*ti* in the new key of D minor. Since this pitch is twice as long as the quarter notes around it, you can begin singing it as ↑1̂/*di* and change to ↑7̂/*ti* during the note.

Henry Purcell, *King Arthur*, z628, Act III, "Thou Doting Fool," mm. 17–32 (1691)

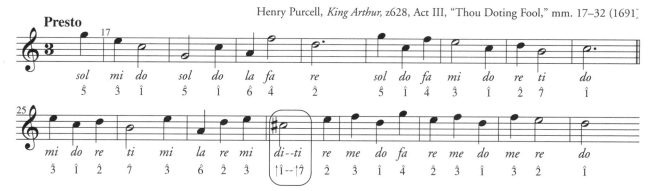

You may also find that you have to fake a few notes in between in order to come out all right on the other side, particularly if it's not clear exactly where the new tonicization will be. For instance, the F♯ at the end of measure 4 in the excerpt below can be thought of as ↑6̂/*la* in the initial key of A minor. The passage seems to move toward G major in measure 5, but it becomes clearer in measure 6 that the ultimate goal is E minor. You could sing measure 5 in this intermediate key of G major, thinking of F♯ as 7̂/*ti*, or you could simply sing on a neutral syllable until the new tonic becomes clear.

J. S. Bach, Sinfonia No. 13, BWV 799, mm. 1–8 (c. 1720)

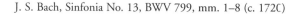

Where and How Does a Modulation Occur?

As you may have discovered in written harmony classes, the question of precisely where (or, more accurately, *when*) a modulation takes place looms large. There is no single "correct" answer to this question. When sight reading or listening to melodies that modulate, you must reorient from the original key to the new one, but the precise point at which you do this can remain flexible.

In sight reading the following excerpt, you can clearly recognize the opening as being in E♭ major. At some point, however, before you reach the cadence in measure 7, you will need to shift the tonic from E♭ to G.

Johannes Brahms, *Lieder und Gesänge*, Op. 57, No. 2, "Wenn du nur zuweilen lächelst," mm. 1–7 (c. 1871)

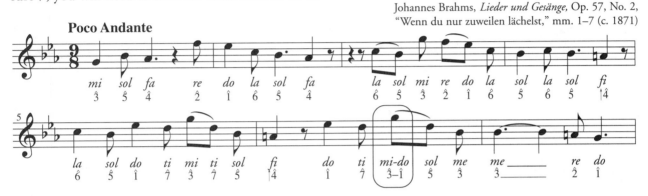

At first, you might not look far enough ahead to realize the role of the A♮ in measure 4 as a cue to the modulation. In this case, you might interpret this passage as shown above, so that the change of tonic and scale occurs in measure 6, where $\hat{3}$/*mi* becomes $\hat{1}$/*do*. If you were singing this passage and wanted to change syllables at this point, you would think of the skip to G as $\hat{3}$/*mi* in E♭ major but sing it as $\hat{1}$/*do* in G minor and continue in that key.

However, you might just as easily make the change earlier, as in the following version:

In fact, you could make the change at *any* point during measures 5–7. In sight reading and listening (as opposed to analysis, for which you have lots of time to consider your decisions and defend them) the idea is to change at *some* time so that you end up working comfortably in the new key.

Types of Modulations

You should familiarize yourself with three types of melodic modulation.

Common-Tone Modulations

A common-tone modulation occurs when a single pitch can be reinterpreted in the move from one key to another. Sight singers need to reinterpret the common tone before leaving it and proceeding in the new key. We have already encountered an example of this in Schumann's "Die Lotosblume" (page 314), in which the pitch C functions as $\hat{5}$/*sol* in the first key and as $\hat{3}$/*mi* in the new key.

Modulations by Leap to a Chromatic Pitch

Modulations introduced by leaps to pitches that are chromatic in the initial key pose one of the more difficult challenges for sight readers. In the following excerpt, the leap to E♮ at the downbeat of measure 9 introduces this type of modulation. You could conceive of this pitch as $\hat{4}$/*fi* in the opening key of B♭, but it functions as $\hat{7}$/*ti* in the new key of F.

Franz Schubert, "Geheimnis," D. 491, mm. 3–12 (1816)

Sag an, wer lehrt dich Lie - der, so schmeich-elnd und so zart?_____

Sie ru - fen ei - nen Him - mel aus trü - ber Ge - gen - wart.

When you sing this excerpt, use the rests in measures 7–8 to rethink the D as $\hat{6}$/*la* in the key of F. Then, the skip down to E♮ is merely a skip to $\hat{7}$/*ti*. (You might also try hearing this E♮ up an octave, moving stepwise from the D, before making the leap to its proper octave.)

In most modulations that are introduced by difficult skips to chromatic pitches, it will help you to begin thinking in the new key a bit earlier than you otherwise might have.

Gradual Modulations

As we have discovered, it is often impossible to point to a single spot and say "the modulation occurs there." Indeed, most modulations involve a *process* in which one key gradually *becomes* another key over time.

Jean Baptiste Loeillet (de Gant), Sonata, Op. 3, No. 4, mvt. 4, mm. 1–22 (1715)

Although it's clear that the excerpt above moves from G major at the opening to E minor at the cadence in measure 22, how and when to make this change is not so clear. The D♯ in measure 14 might lead you to try to move directly to E minor there, but the D♮ in measure 18 and C♯ in measure 19 make this less clear (perhaps momentarily hinting at D major). It's not until the return of D♯ in measure 20 that E minor becomes clear. You could move to E minor as early as measure 14 or as late as measure 20, with or without an excursion to D major in between. There is no single "correct" way to make such a modulation, so you must find a reasonable strategy that works and use it.

Modulations in Harmonic Progressions

Just as melodies modulate from one key to another, so do harmonic progressions.

We will indicate modulations in harmonic progressions by writing the chord symbols in the initial key on one line, then writing the chord symbols in the new key on a line directly below. As illustrated below, the new key will be indicated as an "area" in the initial key represented by a Roman numeral followed by a colon, all enclosed in a box. Where the two keys share a common chord, that chord will be represented by dual chord symbols aligned vertically to show the single chord's function in each key.

$$\text{I} \quad \text{V}^{4}_{3} \quad \text{I}^{6} \quad \text{V}^{6}_{5}/\text{IV} \quad \text{IV}$$
$$\boxed{\text{IV:}}\ \text{I} \quad \text{V}^{4}_{3} \quad \text{I}^{6} \quad \text{ii} \quad \text{vii}^{ø7} \quad \text{I}$$

This progression begins in the major mode and modulates to the key of the subdominant (IV: in the box). A common chord occurs where IV in the initial key on the upper line appears above I in the new key on the lower line.

You might begin to hear this modulation as early as the fourth chord or as late as the sixth chord. When arpeggiating such progressions, it is up to you to decide where you feel and hear the key change and then change your syllables accordingly.

EXERCISES

1. Practice modulating between relative major and minor keys.

   a. Sing pitches that tonicize the major mode, then—without changing the diatonic collection—move to a tonicization of the relative minor. Then return to the original major key. One example of this is shown below.

b. Repeat this process beginning with the minor mode. Move to a tonicization of the relative major without changing the diatonic collection. Then return to the original minor key. One example of this is shown below.

2. Practice singing **stepwise** patterns that will enable you to move from one diatonic collection to another. These patterns are built from linear combinations of half and whole steps (H and W). The following example begins each pattern on the common tone G:

Sing these patterns on a neutral syllable, then choose appropriate functional syllables (such as "$\hat{1}$/do–$\hat{2}$/re–$\hat{3}$/mi" for the first pattern). At first, practice these six patterns in the given order, and then mix them up. Finally, practice them in various orders, beginning each pattern on a different starting pitch.

3. Practice singing **triadic** patterns that will enable you to move from one diatonic collection to another. The following example begins each pattern on the common tone E:

Sing these patterns on a neutral syllable, then choose appropriate functional syllables (such as "$\hat{1}$/do–$\hat{3}$/mi–$\hat{5}$/sol" for the first pattern). At first, practice these twelve patterns in the given order, and then mix them up. Finally, practice them in various orders, beginning each pattern on a different starting pitch.

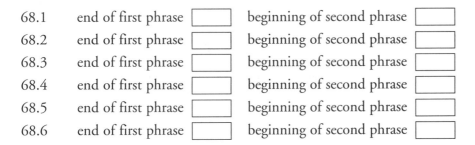

A. Common-Tone Functions

Listen to excerpts 68.1–68.6, each of which contains two short phrases. For each, the second phrase begins on the same pitch that the first phrase ends on. Write the scale-degree function of this pitch in both places.

68.1	end of first phrase ☐	beginning of second phrase ☐
68.2	end of first phrase ☐	beginning of second phrase ☐
68.3	end of first phrase ☐	beginning of second phrase ☐
68.4	end of first phrase ☐	beginning of second phrase ☐
68.5	end of first phrase ☐	beginning of second phrase ☐
68.6	end of first phrase ☐	beginning of second phrase ☐

B. Stepwise Patterns

Return to the stepwise patterns in exercise 2, above.

Your instructor will play these in various orders. You must identify each pattern you hear by its label (a, b, c . . . f), by its intervallic construction (for example, "whole step, whole step"), and by its scale-degree numbers or syllables (for example, "1̂/do–2̂/re–3̂/mi–2̂/re–1̂/do").

C. Triadic Patterns

Return to the triadic patterns in exercise 3, above.

Your instructor will play these in various orders. You must identify each pattern you hear by its label (a, b, c . . . l), by its intervallic construction (for example, "major 3rd, major 3rd"), and by its scale-degree numbers or syllables (for example, "1̂/do–3̂/mi–5̂/sol –3̂/mi–1̂/do").

Although modulations can be categorized in many ways, one of the most common is to classify them according to the relationships between the two keys involved. Under this system, modulations are classified as either "closely related" or "distant." This chapter investigates closely related modulations that begin in the major mode.

Closely Related Keys

The idea of closely related keys is best understood through the circle of fifths, illustrated below with major keys written around the outside of the circle and their relative minor keys written on the inside.

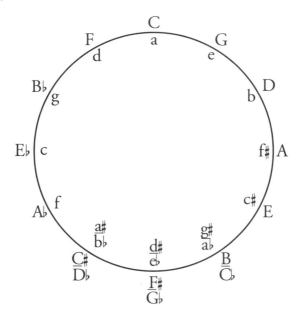

Each of the twelve positions around the circle corresponds to a unique diatonic collection associated with a key signature (with enharmonic equivalents such as F♯ and G♭ occupying the same position). Thus, any one position stands for a key signature and its two relative major and minor keys. For example, the "one o'clock" position stands for the one-sharp collection and the relative keys G major and E minor.

Moving one position in the clockwise direction results in either adding one sharp or removing one flat. For example, moving clockwise from D major to A major adds one sharp (G♯), and moving clockwise from B♭ major to F major removes a flat (E♭). In fact, adding a sharp and removing a flat are the same process.

Similarly, moving one position in the counterclockwise direction results in either adding one flat or removing one sharp. For example, moving counterclockwise from Bb major to Eb major adds one flat (Ab), and moving counterclockwise from D major to G major removes a sharp (C#). In fact, adding a flat and removing a sharp are really the same process.

Closely related keys are those that can be arrived at on the circle of fifths by (1) not changing the diatonic collection, (2) moving once in the clockwise (or "sharp") direction, or (3) moving once in the counterclockwise (or "flat") direction.

For example, if we begin with the key of C major, we could modulate to the following closely related keys:

1. By not changing the diatonic collection, we could modulate to the relative minor:

   • A minor

2. By moving once in the clockwise (or "sharp") direction, we arrive at the one-sharp collection and we could modulate to two keys:

   • G major
   • E minor

3. By moving once in the counterclockwise (or "flat") direction, we arrive at the one-flat collection and we could modulate to two keys:

   • F major
   • D minor

> **Closely related keys** are those keys that have the same diatonic collection or those that can be arrived at through adding or removing one sharp or flat in the circle of fifths.

C major and its five closely related keys form a three-position slice out of the circle-of-fifths pie, as shown below.

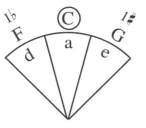

This same slice applies to all of the major keys on the circle. If we rename C major as tonic (I), the relationships can be understood in terms of harmonic function. Thus, the closely related keys to any major-key tonic are its submediant (vi), dominant (V), mediant (iii), subdominant (IV), and supertonic (ii), as shown below.

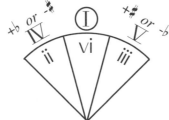

Remember that an apparent change in collection alone is not sufficient to cause a modulation. The new key must be tonicized as well (review Chapters 17, 67, and 68). We will now examine each of these key relationships in greater detail.

No Change of Collection

From Tonic Major to Relative Minor: I → vi

In order to modulate to the submediant (the relative minor), only one change must take place:

1. The tonic must shift from scale degree $\hat{1}$ to $\hat{6}$ (which then becomes a temporary or local $\hat{1}$).

A second signal will often appear since this is a move to a minor mode:

2. The leading tone to the submediant (↑$\hat{5}$/*si*) may occur, to be reinterpreted as ↑$\hat{7}$/*ti* in the new key. This may be accompanied by ↑$\hat{6}$/*la* in the new key.

Bernardo Pasquini, Bizzarria in C major, mm. 1–8

The excerpt above opens in the no-sharp/no-flat collection with a tonic of C. By measures 6–7, we begin to hear A as a new local tonic, which is reinforced by the appearance of G♯, the leading tone to A. As a chromatic pitch, this G♯ does not alter the diatonic collection. The G♯ might appear to be ↑$\hat{5}$/*si* in C major, but can be reinterpreted as $\hat{7}$/*ti* in the new key of the submediant, A minor.

Adding a Sharp or Removing a Flat

A diatonically added sharp or removed flat in the major mode will appear as ↑$\hat{4}$/*fi* in the initial key. In modulations to closely related keys, this pitch can then function as either $\hat{7}$/*ti* in the key of the dominant or $\hat{2}$/*re* in the key of the mediant.

From Tonic Major to Dominant Major: I → V

The modulation to the dominant major is by far the most common modulation found in tonal music. Just as the dominant *chord* is an important harmonic goal (see Chapter 34), so is the dominant *key*. Many compositions that begin in a major key make their first modulation to the dominant.

In order to modulate to the dominant, two changes must take place:

1. The diatonic collection must be altered to shift once in the sharp direction by adding a sharp or removing a flat;

2. The tonic must shift from scale degree $\hat{1}$ to $\hat{5}$ (which then becomes a temporary or local $\hat{1}$).

The change in diatonic collection is effected by the introduction of what appears to be ↑$\hat{4}$/*fi* in the initial key. This will be reinterpreted as $\hat{7}$/*ti* in the new key of the dominant.

George Frideric Handel, Psalm *Laudate pueri Dominum* No. 2, HWV 237, "Suscitans a terra inopem," mm. 13–30 (1707)

The excerpt above opens in the three-sharp collection in the key of A major. In measure 25, D♮ becomes D♯, and this changes the three-sharp collection into the four-sharp collection. In addition, the tonic shifts from A to E. Therefore, the passage has modulated to the key of E major, the dominant of the original key of A.

The D♯ might appear to be ↑$\hat{4}$/*fi* in the opening key of A major, but becomes $\hat{7}$/*ti* in the new key of E major.

From Tonic Major to Mediant Minor: I → iii

The appearance of ↑$\hat{4}$/*fi* as part of a change in collection can also help create a different modulation—to the key of the minor mediant.

In order to modulate to the mediant, two changes must take place:

1. The diatonic collection must be altered to shift once in the sharp direction by adding a sharp or removing a flat;

2. The tonic must shift from scale degree $\hat{1}$ to $\hat{3}$ (which then becomes a temporary or local $\hat{1}$).

A third signal will often appear since this is a move to a minor mode:

3. The leading tone to the mediant (↑$\hat{2}$/*ri*) may occur, to be reinterpreted as ↑$\hat{7}$/*ti* in the new key. This may be accompanied by ↑$\hat{6}$/*la* in the new key.

The change in diatonic collection is effected by the introduction of what appears to be ↑$\hat{4}$/*fi* in the initial key. This will be reinterpreted as $\hat{2}$/*re* in the new key of the mediant. For example, if starting in C major, F♯ (↑$\hat{4}$/*fi*) would become $\hat{2}$/*re* in E minor.

Adding a Flat or Removing a Sharp

A diatonically added flat or removed sharp in the major mode will appear as ↓$\hat{7}$/*te* in the initial key. In modulations to closely related keys, this pitch can then function as either $\hat{4}$/*fa* in the key of the subdominant or as $\hat{6}$/*le* in the key of the supertonic.

From Tonic Major to Subdominant Major: I → IV

In order to modulate to the subdominant, two changes must take place:

1. The diatonic collection must be altered to shift once in the flat direction by adding a flat or removing a sharp;

2. The tonic must shift from scale degree $\hat{1}$ to $\hat{4}$ (which then becomes a temporary or local $\hat{1}$).

The change in diatonic collection is effected by the introduction of what appears to be ↓$\hat{7}$/*te* in the initial key. This will be reinterpreted as $\hat{4}$/*fa* in the new key of the subdominant.

Robert Schumann, Dichterliebe, Op. 48, No. 4, "Wenn ich in deine Augen seh," mm. 1–8 (1840)

The excerpt above opens in the one-sharp collection in the key of G major. In measure 6, the F♯ we have thus far inferred (and would hear in the piano accompaniment) becomes F♮. This changes the one-sharp collection into the no-sharp/no-flat collection. In addition, the tonic shifts from G to C. Therefore, the passage has modulated to the key of C major, the subdominant of the original key of G.

The F♮ might appear to be ↓$\hat{7}$/*te* in the opening key of G major, but becomes $\hat{4}$/*fa* in the new key of C major. No accidental is required to create the leading tone in the subdominant: the diatonic half step $\hat{3}$/*mi*–$\hat{4}$/*fa* becomes $\hat{7}$/*ti*–$\hat{1}$/*do* in the new key.

From Tonic Major to Supertonic Minor: I → ii

In order to modulate to the supertonic, two changes must take place:

1. The diatonic collection must be altered to shift once in the flat direction by adding a flat or removing a sharp;

2. The tonic must shift from scale degree $\hat{1}$ to $\hat{2}$ (which then becomes a temporary or local $\hat{1}$).

A third signal will often appear since this is a move to a minor mode:

3. The leading tone to the supertonic (↑1̂/*di*) may occur, to be reinterpreted as ↑7̂/*ti* in the new key. This may be accompanied by ↑6̂/*la* in the new key.

The change in diatonic collection is effected by the introduction of what appears to be ↓7̂/*te* in the initial key. This will be reinterpreted as 6̂/*le* in the new key of the supertonic. For example, if starting in C major, B♭ (↓7̂/*te*) would become 6̂/*le* in D minor.

Alterations and the New Key

When pitches are altered by adding or removing a sharp or flat, those pitches can act as a signal that a modulation might be underway. Sometimes, however, altered pitches function simply as chromatics and no modulation takes place. But once your eye and ear tell you that a modulation is occurring, knowing the potential functions of altered pitches in various keys can help you make sense out of these notes as the music modulates.

These altered pitches fall into two categories. The first category includes chromatic pitches that become part of the diatonic collection in the new key:

$$↑4̂/fi → \boxed{7̂/ti \text{ in } \underline{\text{V}} \quad | \quad 2̂/re \text{ in } \ddot{\text{iii}}}$$

$$↓7̂/te → \boxed{4̂/fa \text{ in } \underline{\text{IV}} \quad | \quad 6̂/le \text{ in } \ddot{\text{ii}}}$$

The second category includes chromatic pitches that remain chromatic in the new key, but take on roles as raised leading tones:

$$↑5̂/si → \boxed{↑7̂/ti \text{ in } \text{vi}}$$

$$↑2̂/ri → \boxed{↑7̂/ti \text{ in } \ddot{\text{iii}}}$$

$$↑1̂/di → \boxed{↑7̂/ti \text{ in } \ddot{\text{ii}}}$$

EXERCISES

1. Begin singing pitches from the diatonic major mode (tonicizing 1̂/*do*), then—while retaining the same collection—change 6̂/*la* to 1̂/*do* and modulate to the submediant (relative minor).

2. Begin singing pitches from the diatonic major mode (tonicizing 1̂/*do*), then change 4̂/*fa* to ↑4̂/*fi* and proceed to each of the following tonicizations:

   a. Tonicize 5̂/*sol* so that ↑4̂/*fi* becomes 7̂/*ti* and you modulate to the dominant;

   b. Tonicize 3̂/*mi* so that ↑4̂/*fi* becomes 2̂/*re* and you modulate to the mediant.

3. Begin singing pitches from the diatonic major mode (tonicizing 1̂/*do*), then change 7̂/*ti* to ↓7̂/*te* and proceed to each of the following tonicizations:

   a. Tonicize 4̂/*fa* so that ↓7̂/*te* becomes 4̂/*fa* and you modulate to the subdominant;

   b. Tonicize 2̂/*re* so that ↓7̂/*te* becomes 6̂/*le* and you modulate to the supertonic.

4. Learn to arpeggiate the following chord progressions. Change syllables to the new key at the point of modulation.

a. I $\underline{V}^6$ $\underline{V}^4_3/vi$ vi
   $\boxed{vi:}$ i i^6 $\underline{V}^4_2$ i^6

b. I I^6 ii $\underline{V}^7/\underline{V}$ $\underline{V}$
   $\boxed{V:}$ I $\underline{V}^6$ $\underline{IV}^6$ ii^6 $\underline{V}^7$ I

c. I $\underline{V}$ I   iii
   $\boxed{iii:}$ i $\underline{V}^6_5$ i iv^6 $\underline{V}^7$ i

d. I $\underline{V}^4_3$ I^6 $\underline{V}^6_5/\underline{IV}$ $\underline{IV}$
   $\boxed{IV:}$ I $\underline{V}^4_3$ I^6 ii $\underline{V}$ I

e. I I^6 ii^6 $\underline{V}^4_3/ii$ ii
   $\boxed{ii:}$ i $ii^{\varnothing 6}_5$ $\underline{V}^7$ i

5. Learn to play the above progressions on the piano (or similar keyboard).

LISTENING

For each of the following excerpts, look at the music to determine the *initial* tonic. This is the key in which the excerpt begins. Listen carefully and use the cues discussed in this chapter to determine the key to which the excerpt modulates.

Melodic Dictation

The opening measures are provided for excerpts 69.1–69.4. Listen to each excerpt and write out the pitches and rhythms for the remainder of each excerpt.

69.1

J. S. Bach, Suite No. 4 for Cello, BWV 1010, Courante, mm. 1–4

69.2

5

69.3

69.4

Melodic Transcription

Listen to excerpts 69.5–69.8 and write out the pitches and rhythms for each. Also supply any other appropriate performance indications.

Exercise	Clef	Initial tonic	Bottom number in meter sign
69.5	alto	E	8
69.6	treble	D	4
69.7	bass	E♭	8
69.8	grand staff (transcribe 2 voices)	E♭	4

Bass-Line Transcription

Listen to excerpt 69.9 and write out the pitches and rhythms for the bass line only. Also supply any other appropriate performance indications.

Exercise	Clef	Initial tonic	Bottom number in meter sign
69.9	bass	F	4

Harmonic Dictation

The opening measures are provided for excerpts 69.10–69.13. Listen to each excerpt and write out the bass line, then supply the appropriate Roman numerals and figured bass symbols to represent each chord for the remainder of each excerpt. When the music modulates, indicate the new key and chord symbols in that key. Your instructor may also choose to have you write out the top ("soprano") voice as well.

69.10

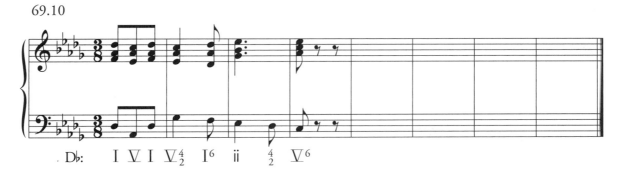

D♭:   I   V   I   V$^4_2$ I^6 ii $^4_2$ V^6

69.11

G: I   V   vi   IV   V^6/V   V

69.12

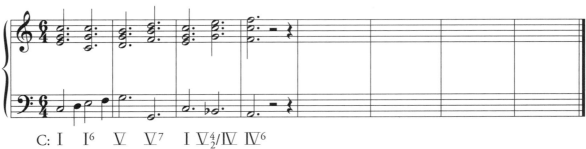

C: I   I^6 V   V^7 I   V$^4_2$/IV   IV^6

69.13

B♭:   I   V^6 I   V$^6_4$ I^6 V$^4_3$/ii   ii   V$^4_2$/V   V^6

Harmonic Transcription

Listen to excerpts 69.14–69.16 and, for each, write out the bass line, then supply the appropriate Roman numerals and figured bass symbols to represent each chord. When the music modulates, indicate the new key and chord symbols in that key. Your instructor may also choose to have you write out the top ("soprano") voice as well.

Exercise	Initial tonic	Bottom number in meter sign
69.14	D	4
69.15	F	2
69.16	A	4

READING AND SIGHT SINGING

Prepare the following excerpts, singing on syllables while conducting. Pay close attention to the cues concerning changes in collection and tonic in order to make decisions about where each passage modulates. Decide where and how you will change syllables and practice each of these spots very carefully and thoroughly.

**Excerpts for reading and sight singing
from the
Anthology for Sight Singing
978–1001**

CLOSELY RELATED MODULATION FROM THE MINOR MODE

In the previous chapter, we took a three-position slice from the circle of fifths and calculated the keys that are closely related to the major key in the center position. Let's return to the circle of fifths and calculate keys that are closely related to the *minor* key in the center position.

If we begin with the key of A minor, we could modulate to the following closely related keys:

1. By not changing the diatonic collection, we could modulate to the relative major:
   • C major

2. By moving once in the clockwise (or "sharp") direction, we arrive at the one-sharp collection and we could modulate to two keys:
   • E minor
   • G major

3. By moving once in the counterclockwise (or "flat") direction, we arrive at the one-flat collection and we could modulate to two keys:
   • D minor
   • F major

The three-position slice out of the circle-of-fifths pie formed by A minor and its five closely related keys is illustrated below.

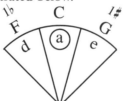

The same diagram applies to all of the minor keys on the circle, just as we observed in Chapter 69 for the major keys. Rename A minor as tonic (i) in order to view the relationships in terms of harmonic function. Thus, the closely related keys to *any* minor-key tonic are its mediant (III), dominant (V), subtonic (VII), subdominant (iv), and submediant (VI), as shown below.

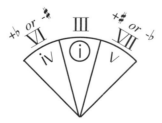

Remember that an apparent change in collection alone is not sufficient to cause a modulation. The new key must be tonicized as well (review Chapters 15, 67, and 68).

No Change of Collection

From Tonic Minor to Relative Major: i → III

As in major keys, the only kind of modulation that requires no change of diatonic collection is one that moves to the relative key. Motion from an initial tonic minor to the relative major is by far the most common modulation found in tonal music in the minor mode.

Only one change is necessary for a modulation from the tonic minor (i) to the mediant (III):

1. The tonic must shift from scale degree $\hat{1}$ to $\hat{3}$ (which then becomes a temporary or local $\hat{1}$).

A second signal will often appear since this is a move from the minor mode:

2. If the chromatic leading tone (↑$\hat{7}$/ti) has appeared in the initial key it will be changed to its diatonic state ($\hat{7}$/te), to be reinterpreted as $\hat{5}$/sol in the new key.

For example, the excerpt below opens in the two-flat collection with a tonic of G—the key of G minor. The pitch G is reinforced as a tonic by the appearance of its chromatic leading tone, F♯. Beginning in measure 6, F♯ is changed to F♮, and we start to hear B♭ as the new tonic. The underlying diatonic collection (two flats) remains the same throughout the passage while the music modulates from the minor tonic of G to its relative minor, B♭.

J. S. Bach, English Suite No. 3, BWV 808, mvt. 5, mm. 1–8

The F♮ might appear to be $\hat{7}$/te in the opening key of G minor, but that pitch can be reinterpreted as $\hat{5}$/sol in the new key of the mediant, B♭ major. Note that no accidental is required to create the leading tone in the mediant: the diatonic half step $\hat{2}$/re–$\hat{3}$/me becomes $\hat{7}$/ti–$\hat{1}$/do in the new key.

Adding a Sharp or Removing a Flat

A diatonically added sharp or removed flat in the minor mode will appear as ↑$\hat{6}$/la in the initial key. In modulations to closely related keys, this pitch can then function as either $\hat{2}$/re in the key of the dominant or $\hat{7}$/ti in the key of the subtonic.

From Tonic Minor to Dominant Minor: i → v

In order to modulate to the dominant, two changes must take place:

1. The diatonic collection must be altered to shift once in the sharp direction by adding a sharp or removing a flat;

2. The tonic must shift from scale degree $\hat{1}$ to $\hat{5}$ (which then becomes a temporary or local $\hat{1}$).

A third signal will often appear since this is a move from the minor mode:

3. If the chromatic leading tone (↑$\hat{7}$/*ti*) has appeared in the initial key it will be changed to its diatonic state, to be reinterpreted as $\hat{3}$/*me* in the new key.

A fourth signal will often appear since this is a move to a minor mode:

4. The leading tone to the dominant (↑$\hat{4}$/*fi*) may occur, to be reinterpreted as ↑$\hat{7}$/*ti* in the new key. This may be accompanied by ↑$\hat{6}$/*la* in the new key.

The change in diatonic collection is effected by the introduction of what appears to be ↑$\hat{6}$/*la* in the initial key. This will be reinterpreted as $\hat{2}$/*re* in the new key of the dominant.

W. A. Mozart, String Quintet K. 406 (516$^\text{b}$), mvt. 4, mm. 1–8 (1783)

For example, the excerpt above opens in the three-flat collection with a tonic of C—the key of C minor. This is reinforced by the appearance of the leading tone, B♮. In measure 6, B♮ is changed to B♭, but this is merely a chromatic pitch returning to its diatonic form. In measure 7, A♭ is changed to A♮, which changes the diatonic collection from three flats to two. Finally, F♮ is changed to F♯ in measure 7 and we begin to hear G as tonic, which—coupled with a move to the two-flat collection—indicates a modulation to the key of G minor, the dominant of the original key of C.

The A♮ might appear to be ↑$\hat{6}$/*la* in the opening key of C minor, but becomes $\hat{2}$/*re* in the new key of G minor. Similarly, B♭ now functions as $\hat{3}$/*me* and F♯ now functions as ↑$\hat{7}$/*ti*.

From Tonic Minor to Subtonic Major: i → VII

The appearance of ↑$\hat{6}$/*la* as part of a change in collection can also help create a different modulation—to the key of the major subtonic. This is perhaps the least common of all the closely related modulations.

In order to modulate to the subtonic, two changes must take place:

1. The diatonic collection must be altered to shift once in the sharp direction by adding a sharp or removing a flat;

2. The tonic must shift from scale degree $\hat{1}$ to $\hat{7}$ (which then becomes a temporary or local $\hat{1}$). Note that this is the *diatonic* seventh scale degree, a whole step below the tonic.

A third signal will often appear since this is a move from the minor mode:

3. If the chromatic leading tone (↑7̂/*ti*) has appeared in the initial key it will be changed to its diatonic state, to be reinterpreted as 1̂/*do* in the new key.

The primary indication of this modulation is still the change in diatonic collection effected by the introduction of what appears to be ↑6̂/*la* in the initial key. This will be reinterpreted as 7̂/*ti* in the new key of the subtonic. For example, if starting in A minor, F♯ (↑6̂/*la*) would become 7̂/*ti* in G major.

Adding a Flat or Removing a Sharp

A diatonically added flat or removed sharp in the minor mode will appear as ↓2̂/*ra* in the initial key. In modulations to closely related keys, this pitch can then function as either 6̂/*le* in the key of the subdominant or as 4̂/*fa* in the key of the submediant.

From Tonic Minor to Subdominant Minor: i → iv

In order to modulate to the subdominant, two changes must take place:

1. The diatonic collection must be altered to shift once in the flat direction by adding a flat or removing a sharp;

2. The tonic must shift from scale degree 1̂ to 4̂ (which then becomes a temporary or local 1̂).

A third signal will often appear since this is a move from the minor mode:

3. If the chromatic leading tone (↑7̂/*ti*) has appeared in the initial key it will be changed to its diatonic state, to be reinterpreted as 4̂/*fa* in the new key.

A fourth signal will often appear since this is a move to a minor mode:

4. The leading tone to the subdominant (↑3̂/*mi*) may occur, to be reinterpreted as ↑7̂/*ti* in the new key. This may be accompanied by ↑6̂/*la* in the new key.

The change in diatonic collection is effected by the introduction of what appears to be ↓2̂/*ra* in the initial key. This will be reinterpreted as 6̂/*le* in the new key of the subdominant. For example, if starting in A minor, B♭ (↓2̂/*ra*) would become 6̂/*le* in D minor.

From Tonic Minor to Submediant Major: i → VI

In order to modulate to the submediant, two changes must take place:

1. The diatonic collection must be altered to shift once in the flat direction by adding a flat or removing a sharp;

2. The tonic must shift from scale degree 1̂ to 6̂ (which then becomes a temporary or local 1̂).

A third signal will often appear since this is a move from the minor mode:

3. If the chromatic leading tone (↑$\hat{7}$/*ti*) has appeared in the initial key it will be changed to its diatonic state, to be reinterpreted as $\hat{2}$/*re* in the new key.

The change in diatonic collection is effected by the introduction of what appears to be ↓$\hat{2}$/*ra* in the initial key. This will be reinterpreted as $\hat{4}$/*fa* in the new key of the subdominant. For example, if starting in A minor, B♭ (↓$\hat{2}$/*ra*) would become $\hat{4}$/*fa* in F major. Note that no accidental is required to create the leading tone in the submediant: the diatonic half step $\hat{5}$/*sol*–$\hat{6}$/*le* becomes $\hat{7}$/*ti*–$\hat{1}$/*do* in the new key.

Alterations and the New Key

As you learned in the previous chapter, you will need to determine if altered pitches signal a modulation or if they function simply as chromatics. Knowing the potential functions of altered pitches in various keys can help you make sense out of these notes as the music modulates.

These altered pitches fall into two categories. The first category includes chromatic pitches that become part of the diatonic collection in the new key:

↑$\hat{6}$/*la* →	$\hat{2}$/*re* in V	$\hat{7}$/*ti* in $\overline{\text{VII}}$
↓$\hat{2}$/*ra* →	$\hat{6}$/*le* in iv	$\hat{4}$/*fa* in $\overline{\text{VI}}$

The second category includes chromatic pitches that remain chromatic in the new key, but take on roles as raised leading tones:

↑$\hat{4}$/*fi* →	↑$\hat{7}$/*ti* in V
↑$\hat{3}$/*mi* →	↑$\hat{7}$/*ti* in iv

In the minor mode, a third category involves a chromatic pitch (↑$\hat{7}$/*ti*) that is returned to its diatonic state ($\hat{7}$/*te*), which can function as a diatonic pitch in five different keys:

$\hat{7}$/*te* →	$\hat{5}$/*sol* in $\overline{\text{III}}$	$\hat{3}$/*me* in V	$\hat{1}$/*do* in $\overline{\text{VII}}$	$\hat{4}$/*fa* in iv	$\hat{2}$/*re* in $\overline{\text{VI}}$

EXERCISES

1. Begin singing pitches from the diatonic minor mode (tonicizing $\hat{1}$/*do*), then—while retaining the same collection—change $\hat{3}$/*me* to $\hat{1}$/*do* and modulate to the mediant (relative major).

2. Begin singing pitches from the diatonic minor mode (tonicizing $\hat{1}$/*do*), then change $\hat{6}$/*le* to ↑$\hat{6}$/*la* and proceed to each of the following tonicizations:

    a. Tonicize $\hat{5}$/*sol* so that ↑$\hat{6}$/*la* becomes $\hat{2}$/*re* and you modulate to the dominant;
    b. Tonicize $\hat{7}$/*te* so that ↑$\hat{6}$/*la* becomes $\hat{7}$/*ti* and you modulate to the subtonic.

3. Begin singing pitches from the diatonic minor mode (tonicizing $\hat{1}$/*do*), then change $\hat{2}$/*re* to $\downarrow\hat{2}$/*ra* and proceed to each of the following tonicizations:

   a. Tonicize $\hat{4}$/*fa* so that $\downarrow\hat{2}$/*ra* becomes $\hat{6}$/*le* and you modulate to the subdominant;

   b. Tonicize $\hat{6}$/*le* so that $\downarrow\hat{2}$/*ra* becomes $\hat{4}$/*fa* and you modulate to the submediant.

4. Learn to arpeggiate the following chord progressions. Change syllables to the new key at the point of modulation.

   a. i   V   i   V⁷/III   III

   III: I   V⁶   IV⁶   V⁷   I

   b. i   V$^4_2$/iv   iv⁶   v

   V: i   V$^6_5$ i   ii°$^6_5$ i$^6_4$ V   i

   c. i   V   i   v⁶   V$^6_5$/VII   VII

   VII: I   V$^4_3$ I⁶   ii⁶   V   I

   d. i   VI   iv   V$^6_5$/iv   iv

   iv: i   III   VI   ii°⁶   V²   i⁶

   e. i   ii°⁶   V⁷/VI   VI

   VI: I   vi   ii⁶   V$^{8-7}_{6-5}_{4-3}$ I

5. Learn to play the above progressions on the piano (or similar keyboard).

LISTENING

For each of the following excerpts, look at the music to determine the *initial* tonic. This is the key in which the excerpt begins. Listen carefully and use the cues discussed in this chapter to determine the key to which the excerpt modulates.

Melodic Dictation

The opening measures are provided for excerpts 70.1–70.4. Listen to each excerpt and write out the pitches and rhythms for the remainder of each excerpt.

70.1

Giuseppi Verdi, *La forza del destino,* Act IV, "Le minacce, i fieri accenti," mm. 13–20

70.2

70.3

70.4   Ludwig van Beethoven, Bagatelle, Op. 126, No. 4, mm. 1–9

Presto

Melodic Transcription

Listen to excerpts 70.5–70.8 and write out the pitches and rhythms for each. Also supply any other appropriate performance indications.

Exercise	Clef	Initial tonic	Bottom number in meter sign
70.5	treble	D	4
70.6	treble	D	8
70.7	grand staff (transcribe 2 voices)	C	4
70.8	grand staff (transcribe 2 voices)	D [Hint: this excerpt does not begin on the tonic harmony]	2

Bass-Line Transcription

Listen to excerpts 70.9–70.10 and write out the pitches and rhythms for the bass line only. Also supply any other appropriate performance indications.

Exercise	Clef	Initial tonic	Bottom number in meter sign
70.9	bass	D	8
70.10	bass	D	4

Harmonic Dictation

The opening measures are provided for excerpts 70.11–70.14. Listen to each excerpt and write out the bass line, then supply the appropriate Roman numerals and figured bass symbols to represent each chord for the remainder of each excerpt. When the music modulates, indicate the new key and chord symbols in that key. Your instructor may also choose to have you write out the top ("soprano") voice as well.

70.11

70.12

70.13

bb: i   V   i   i⁶   iv   V   VI   ii°⁶   V

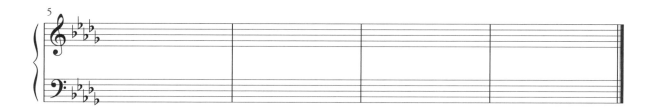

70.14

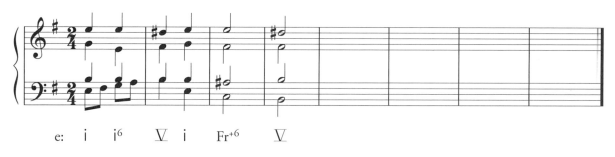

e: i   i⁶   V   i   Fr⁺⁶   V

Harmonic Transcription

Listen to excerpts 70.15–70.16 and, for each, write out the bass line, then supply the appropriate Roman numerals and figured bass symbols to represent each chord. When the music modulates, indicate the new key and chord symbols in that key. Your instructor may also choose to have you write out the top ("soprano") voice as well.

Exercise	Initial tonic	Bottom number in meter sign
70.15	C	4
70.16	C	4

READING AND SIGHT SINGING

Prepare the following excerpts, singing on syllables while conducting. Pay close attention to the cues concerning changes in collection and tonic in order to make decisions about where each passage modulates. Decide where and how you will change syllables and practice each of these spots very carefully and thoroughly.

Excerpts for reading and sight singing
from the
Anthology for Sight Singing
1002–1027

Distant keys (also called **remote** or **foreign** keys) are those arrived at through adding or removing more than one sharp or flat in the circle of fifths.

Keys other than the five closely related keys are referred to as **distant keys.** They are also known as **remote** or **foreign** keys. Similarly, modulations to such keys are called distant (or remote or foreign) modulations. Distant modulations are achieved by adding or removing more than one sharp or flat in the circle of fifths.

Melodic Connections between Distant Keys

Melodic connections between distantly related keys involve either the use of a common tone—a pitch shared between the two keys—or a chromatic pitch that becomes diatonic in the new key.

Common tone connections are often relatively easy to perform and hear, particularly if the common tone is long enough for you to reorient your sense of key. For example, starting in measure 13 in the following excerpt, the pitch A changes function from $\hat{5}$/*sol* to $\hat{3}$/*mi*. Sing through the excerpt and be certain to make this change by the time you reach measure 17.

Franz Schubert, German Dance D. 790 [Op. 171], mm. 1–26 (1823)

A chromatic pitch that becomes diatonic in the new key can be approached by step or by leap. The modulation is usually easier to negotiate when this pitch is approached by step. In measure 17 of the following excerpt, the pitch D♭ appears as if it were ↓$\hat{3}$/*me* in the opening key of B♭ major, but it should be reinterpreted as $\hat{1}$/*do* in the new key of D♭ major.

Robert Schumann, "Mein Wagen rollet langsam," Op. 142, No. 4, mm. 8–23 (1840)

Distant modulations that involve a leap to a chromatic pitch are often more difficult. Readers and listeners must manage the leap and simultaneously reinterpret the chromatic pitch in the new key.

Harmonic Connections between Distant Keys

You will also need to be aware of the harmonic relationships between the two keys in a distant modulation.

A change of mode can turn a closely related connection into a distant one. This kind of modulation shifts the tonic pitch to a diatonic pitch in the original key but alters the mode of the new key. For example, the closely related modulation I → iii becomes distant when it goes to the major mode (III). So, a modulation from C major to E *major* is distant. Look and listen for the diatonically related new tonic coupled with an altered third above it. Even a change of mode between parallel keys, from tonic major to tonic minor or vice versa, might be considered a distant "modulation" since it involves adding or removing three sharps or flats. However, many argue that changes between parallel keys are not modulations at all. From this point of view, a key is a tonic and its associated scale degree functions (1̂, 2̂, 3̂, etc.) and harmonic functions (tonic, dominant, etc.) are all capable of undergoing modal inflection. (See "Parallel Keys" in Chapter 17.)

A chromatically related new tonic occurs when a passage moves to a key whose tonic is not a diatonic member of the original key. For example, a modulation from I to ↓VI (for instance, from C major to A♭ major) would involve moving four positions counterclockwise on the circle of fifths. (Note the use of the symbol ↓ before the Roman numeral to indicate a chord built on a chromatically lowered scale degree. The symbol ↑ can be used similarly to indicate a chromatically raised one.) Look and listen for the chromatically inflected new tonic and any common tones between the two keys.

Common tones reinterpreted in a new key can be quite helpful in determining harmonic connections between distant keys. For example, you can identify the move from C major to A♭ major very quickly if you hear that the pitch C has become the third scale degree of a new major key.

Similarly, common chords can be used to connect distant modulations, especially when such chords are enharmonically reinterpreted. One chord that is commonly reinterpreted in this way is the fully diminished seventh chord. For example, vii°$^{4}_{3}$ in C minor (F–A♭–B♮–D) can be reinterpreted as vii°7 in F♯ minor (E♯–G♯–B–D). Likewise, a German augmented sixth chord can be reinterpreted as a dominant seventh chord. For example, the Gr+6 in C major (A♭–C–E♭–F♯) could become a V̲7 in D♭ major (A♭–C–E♭–G♭). This kind of reinterpretation can also go the other way: a dominant seventh chord could become a German augmented sixth chord.

EXERCISES

Because relationships between distant keys involve altering two or more pitches, the appearance of two or more accidentals usually makes these modulations easier to spot by eye (and by ear). They are, however, often challenging to read and sing in tempo. Review and drill the exercises in Chapter 68 to gain fluency in altering the whole and half steps that make up the diatonic collection (Exercise 2) and in altering the quality and function of the intervals that make up triads in various keys (Exercise 3). Sing these patterns in any order from a variety of starting pitches. As you practice moving from one pattern to another, pick starting pitches that force you to move into distantly related keys. In addition, pick some starting pitches that are chromatic in relation to the pattern you just finished. (For example, after singing a C-major triad start the next pattern on a G♯.)

LISTENING

For each of the following excerpts, look at the music to determine the *initial* tonic. This is the key in which the excerpt begins. You are to determine the key to which the excerpt modulates.

Melodic Dictation

The opening measures are provided for excerpts 71.1–71.4. Listen to each excerpt and write out the pitches and rhythms for the remainder of each excerpt.

71.1

5

71.2

71.3

71.4

Melodic Transcription

Listen to excerpts 71.5–71.8 and write out the pitches and rhythms for each. Also supply any other appropriate performance indications.

Exercise	Clef	Initial tonic	Bottom number in meter sign
71.5	treble	G	4
71.6	treble	D♭	4
71.7	treble	C	2
71.8	treble	A	4

Harmonic Dictation

The opening measures are provided for excerpts 71.9–71.12. Listen to each excerpt and write out the bass line, then supply the appropriate Roman numerals and figured bass symbols to represent each chord for the remainder of the excerpt. When the music modulates, indicate the new key and chord symbols in that key. Your instructor may also choose to have you write out the top ("soprano") voice as well.

71.9

Ab: I   V   I   I⁶   V

71.10

b: i   iv⁶   V   i⁶   III⁶   VI

71.11

B: I   V   iii   vi   ii⁶   V⁷

71.12

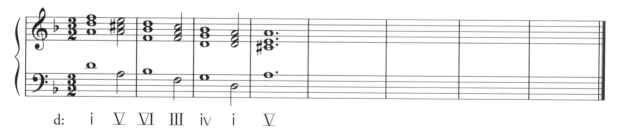

d: i   V   VI   III   iv   i   V

Harmonic Transcription

Listen to excerpts 71.13–71.14 and, for each, write out the bass line, then supply the appropriate Roman numerals and figured bass symbols to represent each chord. When the music modulates, indicate the new key and chord symbols in that key. Your instructor may also choose to have you write out the top ("soprano") voice as well.

Exercise	Initial tonic	Bottom number in meter sign
71.13	E	4
71.14	D♭	4

READING AND SIGHT SINGING

Prepare the following excerpts, singing on syllables while conducting. Pay close attention to the cues concerning changes in collection and tonic in order to make decisions about where each passage modulates. Decide where and how you will change syllables and practice each of these spots very carefully and thoroughly.

**Excerpts for reading and sight singing
from the
Anthology for Sight Singing
1028–1049**

Typically, music that modulates does so several times within a piece. This chapter examines multiple modulations and expands your skills to modulate among various keys in a single excerpt.

You will now need to remain alert for the possibility of several modulations throughout each excerpt in the remaining chapters. You must keep in mind that many subsequent modulations will begin in a key other than that in which the excerpt began. Not only will you have to recognize when a new key is established, but also when it becomes destabilized and what *newer* key then comes into effect. This can happen many times in an excerpt, sometimes in rapid succession.

Tonal Departure and Return

Imagine an excerpt that has modulated from an initial key to a second one. At this point, it can move to yet another new key or return to the original key. Although it is possible to modulate from an initial key and never return, this is rare. Most Western music that modulates returns to the key in which it began, in order to manifest a kind of tonal closure.

One very common key scheme is a three-key structure that begins and ends in the tonic with a middle section in a contrasting key. In the major mode, the contrasting key is often the dominant—creating a I V I structure. In the minor mode, the contrasting key is often the mediant—creating a i III [V] i structure. In minor, the dominant chord or key area often appears after the mediant key in order to allow a smooth return to the tonic.

Take note of the relationships among the various keys in excerpts that you hear and sing. Look for patterns in successive key relationships as well as the relationship of each key to the tonic.

Pay special attention to the departure from and return to the tonic. While listening, this will provide a framework of tonal stability and give you a point of reference from which to calculate the key(s) in between. In singing, you should communicate a sense of stability in the opening key, a feeling of departure as the piece moves away from the tonic, and a sense of return when arriving back in the tonic. Think about how you can use nuances such as tempo, dynamics, articulation, accents, and so forth to communicate these ideas.

For each of the following excerpts, you will be given an *initial* tonic. This is the key in which the excerpt begins. You are to determine the keys to which the excerpt modulates.

Melodic Transcription

Listen to excerpts 72.1–72.6 and write out the pitches and rhythms for each. Also supply any other appropriate performance indications.

Exercise	Clef	Initial tonic	Bottom number in meter sign
72.1	bass	D♭	8
72.2	treble	D	4
72.3	bass	F♯	4
72.4	treble	C	8
72.5	treble	G	4
72.6	tenor	A	2

Harmonic Transcription

Listen to excerpts 72.7–72.12 and, for each, write out the bass line, then supply the appropriate Roman numerals and figured bass symbols to represent each chord. When the music modulates, indicate the new key and chord symbols in that key. Your instructor may also choose to have you write out the top ("soprano") voice as well.

Exercise	Initial tonic	Bottom number in meter sign
72.7	F	2
72.8	G	4
72.9	C	4
72.10	G	4
72.11	B	4
72.12	F♯	4

Note (72.10): Treat the first chord you hear in this excerpt as tonic. (It's also possible to hear the *third* chord as tonic. What changes would this cause?)

Prepare the following excerpts, singing on syllables while conducting. Pay close attention to the cues concerning the changes in collection and tonic in order to make decisions about where each passage modulates. Decide where and how you will change syllables and practice each of these spots very carefully and thoroughly. In excerpts that modulate from an initial tonic and then return to it, find ways to imbue your performance with a sense of departure (tension and instability) when away from the home key and a sense of return (release and stability) when you return to the home key.

Excerpts for reading and sight singing
from the
Anthology for Sight Singing
1050–1085

73 FRAGMENTS OF TONALITY

You have now become accustomed to changing key centers and solmization occasionally during the course of a piece. This skill will also help you deal with the frequent changes that occur when fragments of different diatonic collections are juxtaposed in rapid succession.

Juxtaposition of Diatonic Fragments

The following excerpt presents fragments of several diatonic collections within a brief span of music:

Charles Ives, *Pictures,* mm. 23–30 [The Moor] (1906)

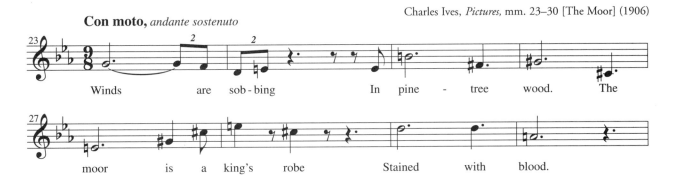

In order to sing this passage, you will need to reorient your tonal bearings at least once. With a minimum of syllable/scale-degree changes, you might begin in the no-sharp-no-flat collection and then change to the three-sharp collection at the pickup to measure 25, as shown below.

Upon further reflection, you might decide that the music following the rests in measure 24 works well in E major for a few notes, after which it seems to slide into the relative minor (c♯), and then to D, as shown in the interpretation below.

The second version is not necessarily more analytically valid than the first one. However, these particular fragments are more immediately workable within this context. In fact, the best analysis would rely at least on investigations of the entire composition, including the preceding and subsequent passages and the accompaniment. But when you are sight reading or taking dictation or transcription, you must act quickly in real time, so you don't have time for detailed analysis.

The approaches you use may differ from those of your classmates and even your instructor. If your approach works, that's an excellent start. Keep honing your skills by comparing your solutions with those of others and discussing what might work best and why.

These challenging passages will often require you to draw on various scale fragments, chords, and other figures from different keys and to change among these rather quickly. When you encounter such a passage, you need to be flexible and fluent enough to reorient your tonal bearings as rapidly as the music does.

Contexts for Juxtaposed Fragments

You will find such juxtaposed fragments from several different diatonic collections in various contexts. Three typical contexts are vocal recitatives, modulatory or developmental sections, and music in a state of tonal flux (such as the excerpt by Ives above).

Recitatives appear in vocal music beginning in the seventeenth century as a means of presenting a relatively great amount of text in a short period of time. Recitatives use a declamatory, syllabic style to achieve this goal, often coupled with a fragmentary approach to tonal materials. You will find it necessary to employ the kinds of frequent tonal shifts we've explored in this chapter in order to navigate through many recitatives.

In some modulations from one key to another, a period of tonal instability may involve materials from keys other than the two main keys involved in the modulation. In such cases, readers and listeners will find it necessary to think of several intervening fragments from different keys. Similarly, the areas of marked tonal instability that characterize many development sections in Western classical music often exploit such fragments. In such passages, you will need to change fluently between several successive tonal orientations before functional stability returns.

Some Romantic and twentieth-century compositions that seem to remain in a constant state of tonal flux, slipping easily from one tonal reference to the next, are best approached by looking for fragments of diatonic collections. You will find that this music challenges your skills in reading, solmization, memory, and understanding pitches in the most taxing ways you have yet experienced. When such excerpts stretch the limits of functional tonality to extremes, you may find that a diatonic-tonal approach is almost nonsensical. Music that has left the realm of tonality is often referred to as post-tonal music, which will be explored a bit further in Chapter 76.

EXERCISES

Return to Chapter 68, Exercises (2) and (3). Sing these stepwise and triadic patterns in any order in rapid succession without pauses between them.

LISTENING

The following melodies use only *fragments* of tonality, so, you will be given a starting pitch rather than a tonic or key for each melody.

Melodic Dictation

Listen to excerpts 73.1–73.5 and write out the pitches and rhythms for each.

Exercise	Clef	Bottom number in meter sign	Starting pitch
73.1	bass	4	A♭2
73.2	alto	8	E3
73.3	treble	2	G4
73.4	treble	4	B4
73.5	treble	4	F♯4

Melodic Transcription

Listen to excerpts 73.6–73.10 and write out the pitches and rhythms for each. Also supply any other appropriate performance indications.

Exercise	Clef	Key signature	Bottom number in meter sign	Starting pitch
73.6	treble	2 flats	4	G4
73.7	treble	2 flats	8	F4
73.8	treble	3 flats	4	C5
73.9	treble	2 sharps	4	A5
73.10	treble	5 sharps	4	A4

READING AND SIGHT SINGING

Prepare the following excerpts, singing on syllables while conducting. Determine where and how you will change syllables and prepare those changes so that they work smoothly. Compare your interpretations with those of your classmates.

**Excerpts for reading and sight singing
from the
Anthology for Sight Singing
1086–1104**

74 ADVANCED METRIC CONCEPTS

In addition to duple, triple, and quadruple meters, you will also encounter meters with five or seven beats per measure and asymmetrical meters in which the beats in each measure are not all the same duration. You must also be prepared for music in which the meter changes during performance.

Quintuple and Septuple Meters

The excerpt below is an example of **quintuple meter.** It has five beats in each measure when you beat quarter notes.

In **quintuple meter,** there are five beats per measure.

Peter Ilich Tchaikovsky, Symphony No. 6, Op. 74 ("Pathétique"), mvt. 2, mm. 1–9 (1893)

The conducting patterns for quintuple meter vary according to how the beats are grouped in the music.* Sometimes, the measure is divided into 2 + 3 beats (Pattern A), and sometimes it is divided into 3 + 2 beats (Pattern B).

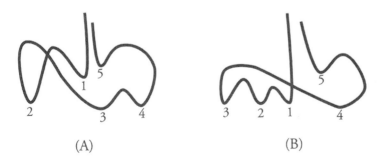

(A)   (B)

For each excerpt in quintuple meter, look to the music to determine which pattern is most appropriate.

---

*You may learn variations on conducting these and other meters from your instructor in this class and in courses on conducting.

Simple quintuple meters have a 5 on top of their meter signs (for example, $\frac{5}{4}$). Compound quintuple meters have a 15 on top of their meter signs (for example, $\frac{15}{8}$). Both kinds should be felt and conducted in a five. As you perform and listen to music in quintuple meter, practice counting fives and develop a comfortable fluency in conducting a five pattern. Perform the excerpt by Tchaikovsky above, singing it while conducting a quintuple pattern (transpose it down a 5th or 6th for singing).

Septuple meter contains seven beats per measure, as shown in the following excerpt:

> In **septuple meter,** there are seven beats per measure.

Edward Elgar, *Caractacus*, Op. 35, Scene 4, "Lament," mm. 1–6 (1898)

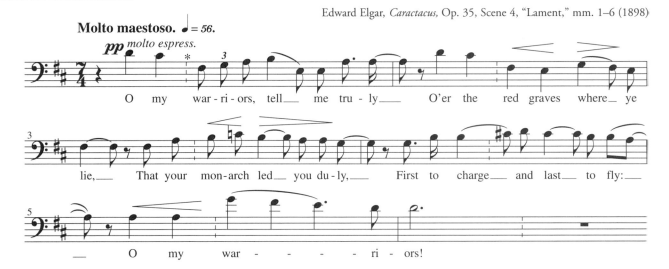

*This division is made for convenience only: there should be no accent, however, on the fourth crochet [♩].

Perform this excerpt while conducting the septuple pattern shown below. As you perform and listen to music in septuple meter, practice counting sevens and develop a comfortable fluency in conducting with a seven pattern.

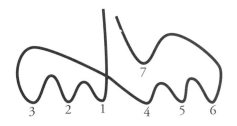

The excerpt above is an example of *simple* septuple meter. Although *compound* septuple meter is possible, it is extremely rare.

Not all meter signs with a 5 or 7 on top are to be felt and conducted as simple meters with as many individual beats. At faster tempi we group the fives and sevens into larger beats containing two or three pulses each. In addition, although other simple meters (11, 13, etc.) are possible, these larger numbers almost always call for grouping into twos and threes as well, as we'll explore in the following section.

Asymmetrical Compound Meters

> In **symmetrical compound meters,** beats of equal duration are produced by divisions of threes.

Compound meters with a multiple of three on the top of the meter sign (such as $\frac{6}{8}$) are called **symmetrical** because their beats are consistently divisible into threes. In this context, the word *symmetrical* refers not to balance around a central point but to equivalence among constituent parts. However, when a meter arises from groupings of *both* twos and threes, the parts are not equivalent and the meter is **asymmetrical.**

Asymmetrical compound meters exist in duple, triple, and quadruple forms depending on the number of broad beats per measure. Conducting these meters requires that you modify the traditional conducting patterns to accommodate the lopsided or unequal parts, with some of the conducting beats lasting for two divisions and some for three.

> In **asymmetrical compound meters,** beats of unequal duration are produced by divisions of both twos and threes.

Asymmetrical Duple Meters

The following folk tune is an example of asymmetrical duple meter. It is to be performed at a rather fast tempo, so the individual eighth notes (**a**) must be grouped into two beats (**b**) in a pattern of 2 + 3:

"Ej, sama moma tsrny ochy," Macedonian folk song

Each measure contains two broad, asymmetrical beats, so we feel and conduct this music using a two pattern. The first beat contains two eighth notes and the second contains three and lasts correspondingly longer. Other excerpts may begin with a group of three followed by a group of two. Some asymmetrical meters shift unpredictably between 2+3 and 3+2. The beaming and other musical features (such as melodic and harmonic grouping) will often guide you as to how to group these passages.

Asymmetrical Triple Meters

An asymmetrical triple meter is conducted using a modified three pattern. In this type of meter, pulses are organized into three asymmetrical beats.

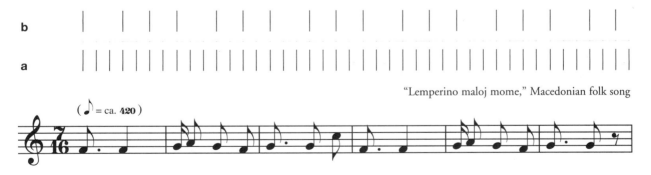

"Lemperino maloj mome," Macedonian folk song

In the excerpt above, groupings of sixteenth notes (the unit on the bottom of the meter sign) combine in a 3+2+2 pattern. Asymmetrical meters with seven as the top number in the meter sign can be grouped in three ways: 3+2+2, 2+3+2, or 2+2+3.

The excerpt below features an asymmetrical triple meter with *eight* beat divisions in each measure:

Béla Bartók, *44 Duos,* No. 19, "A Fairy Tale," mm. 2–7 (1931)

Bartók provides an unorthodox though explicit meter sign as well as dotted lines to show how the eight eighth notes group into 3+3+2. Some composers use meter signs such as ⅜ or ⅝ to represent such meters. In any case, eight fast pulses can be grouped in three different ways: 3+3+2, 3+2+3, or 2+3+3.

Asymmetrical Quadruple Meters

Asymmetrical quadruple meters can be formed from combinations of twos and threes that total nine, ten, or eleven. When you see a meter sign such as ⅒ or ¼, you should look to the music to see how those smaller units are grouped, and feel and conduct them in a four.

For example, in the following excerpt each measure of eleven eighth notes is divided into four beats in the pattern 3+3+3+2.

Roy Harris, Symphony No. 7, rehearsal 32, mm. 8–14 (1955)

Nine fast pulses generally group together as compound triple (as in 9/8 meter). However, on rare occasions nines can be grouped asymmetrically into three groups of 2 plus one group of 3.

Changing Meters

Finally, we must deal with meter changes during the course of a passage. Changes from one simple meter to another or from one compound meter to another are relatively straightforward and easy to follow. The excerpt below illustrates changes between two simple meters:

Igor Stravinsky, *Le cinq doigts,* No. 1, mm. 1–11 (1921)

You must feel and conduct in duple meter for the first eight measures of this passage, change to triple meter for measure 9, then return to duple meter, keeping a steady pulse throughout.

Changes *between* simple and compound meters can be more complicated. In the example below, de Falla prepares you for meter changes with the sign $\frac{3}{4} = \frac{6}{8}$:

Manuel de Falla, *El retablo de maese Pedro,* scene 2, "Melisendra," mm. 1–12 (1923)

When the music changes frequently between simple and compound meters, you should assume that all rhythmic symbols retain their values across each change (♪ = ♪, ♩ = ♩, etc.). If some other metric relationship is intended, composers often accompany changes in meter with a small equation, such as ♪ = ♩., which makes the relationship explicit. The same principles apply to meter changes involving asymmetrical meters.

In music written before the twentieth century, a change from a long section in simple meter to one in compound (or vice versa) was understood in terms of equivalent conducted beats. For example, in changing from $\frac{2}{4}$ to $\frac{6}{8}$ the dotted quarter note in $\frac{6}{8}$ would be equivalent to the quarter note in $\frac{2}{4}$.

EXERCISES

1. Quintuple conducting. Practice using a quintuple conducting pattern while steadily counting fives: 1 2 3 4 5 1 2 3 4 5. Use both patterns A and B.

2. Septuple conducting. Practice using a septuple conducting pattern while steadily counting sevens: 1 2 3 4 5 6 7 1 2 3 4 5 6 7.

3. Asymmetrical duple conducting. Steadily count fives aloud at a fairly rapid speed (at least 144 counts per minute) and then conduct this with a duple pattern. First, use the 2+3 grouping, so that you group 1 and 2 on the downbeat and 3,

4, and 5 on the upbeat. Switch to the 3+2 grouping. Then practice changing from 2+3 to 3+2 and back again between various measures. Be certain that your counting remains steady.

4. Asymmetrical triple conducting. Steadily count sevens aloud at a fairly rapid speed (at least 144 counts per minute) and then conduct this with a triple pattern. First, use the 3+2+2 grouping, then 2+3+2, and finally 2+2+3. Then practice switching among the three. Be certain that your counting remains steady.

    Do the same with eights, using the groupings 2+3+3, then 3+2+3, and finally 3+3+2. Then practice switching among the three. Be certain that your counting remains steady.

5. Asymmetrical quadruple conducting. Practice counting and conducting various possible groupings of twos and threes in asymmetrical meters with nine, ten, and eleven steady beat divisions per measure.

6. Changing meters. Practice conducting while changing—from measure to measure—among duple, triple, and quadruple simple and compound meters. Also work at mixing in quintuple and septuple patterns.

LISTENING

Meter Transcription

Listen to excerpts 71.1–71.4 and write out a pulse-graph for each, showing at least three different levels of pulse for the music. Decide what you think would be the most appropriate meter in which to notate the excerpt. Compare your results with those of your classmates. What accounts for the differences?

Melodic Transcription

Listen to excerpts 74.5–74.8 and determine the most appropriate meter or meters in which to notate each excerpt. Then write out the pitches and rhythms for each.

Exercise	Clef	Tonic	Bottom number in meter sign
74.5	treble	B	4
74.6	bass	G♯	8
74.7	treble	(start on D5)	8
74.8	bass	G♭	4

READING AND SIGHT SINGING

Prepare the following excerpts, singing on syllables while conducting. You must determine the appropriate conducting pattern for each. If the meter changes during an excerpt, prepare changes in your conducting pattern accordingly.

Excerpts for reading and sight singing
from the
Anthology for Sight Singing
1105–1147

In this chapter, we will investigate divisions of the beat into smaller equal values as well as some irregular rhythms that span two or more beats.

Smaller Divisions of the Beat

We have divided the beat equally in twos (for example, ♩♩ in 2/4), in threes (♩♩♩ in 6/8), in fours (♩♩♩♩ in 2/4), and in sixes (♩♩♩♩♩♩ in 6/8).

The beat can also be divided into five, seven, or eight equal parts. The most common of these is the division into eight parts. In the excerpt below, the quarter-note beat divides evenly into eight thirty-second notes.

Carl Stamitz, Duo in F major for Viola and Cello, mvt. 3, mm. 83–88

Perform this excerpt (transpose it up a third) after clearly feeling the duple, then quadruple, and finally octuple divisions of the beat. You may find that you cannot articulate solmization syllables for such small divisions of the beat, so you may prefer to use a neutral syllable, such as *taah*. You may also find it helpful to try articulations used by wind players for double tonguing (*du-gu*, for divisions into multiples of two) and triple tonguing (*du-du-gu*, for divisions into multiples of three).

To use the Takadimi system for octuple division of the beat, you need to shift the syllables Ta-ka-di-mi from the beat to the *half-beat* and divide each half-beat into four equal parts. For instance, you would sing the first measure of Stamitz's Duo as Ta-di-mi Ta-ka-di-mi Ta-ka-di-mi Ta-di.

Divisions of the beat into five and seven equal parts occur less often. They are generally notated with a number, just as triplets are, to reflect the equal division of the beat into five (quintuplets) or seven (septuplets).

Frédéric Chopin, Prelude Op. 28, No. 15, mm. 1–8 (1839)

In the example above, the figure 7 under the group of notes in measure 4 indicates that these seven notes occupy the duration of one beat. You will also occasionally find divisions into other equal parts, such as nine, ten, and so on. Pay special attention to dividing the beat evenly in each case.

Practice intoning rhythms that divide the beat into two to eight equal parts. You may do this on a neutral syllable or use Takadimi syllables. To use Takadimi for quintuplets and septuplets, you extend the quadruple and sextuple patterns by adding the syllable ti. Thus, quintuplets become Ta-ka-di-mi-ti and septuplets become Ta-va-ki-di-da-ma-ti.

Other Irregular Rhythms

Some irregular rhythms involve dividing more than one beat into various equal parts. In measure 282 of the following excerpt, the number 5 indicates that five eighth notes are equally spaced across a two-beat measure.

Béla Bartók, Suite No. 1 for Orchestra, Op. 3, mvt. 3, mm. 279–285 (1905)

In order to perform such rhythms accurately, you must first determine precisely how the rhythms intersect with the beats they span. To do this, you must resort to some simple arithmetic:

1. Find the least common multiple. The least common multiple of any two numbers is the lowest value that is a multiple of both numbers. In the case of five notes in two beats, the least common multiple of 2 and 5 is 10.

2. Divide the total beats spanned into that many equal parts. In the case of five notes in two beats, divide those two beats into ten parts. That would mean dividing each beat into quintuplets.

3. Tie these smaller divisions into groups determined by the number of notes in the tuplet. Here, we tie the sixteenth-note quintuplets in five groups, which represent the five notes spanning two beats.

In the above example, the least common multiple is simply the product of the two numbers (2 x 5 = 10). In some cases, however, the least common multiple is a smaller number than this product. Knowing this will greatly simplify your task. In the example below, you must distribute six notes equally across four beats.

The least common multiple of 4 and 6 is 12 (not 24). Therefore, you must divide all four beats into a total of twelve equal parts, which you can do with eighth-note triplets.

Tie these smaller divisions to arrive at the rhythmic goal of six equal notes over four beats.

As you become familiar with each of these kinds of rhythms, you can begin to recognize and perform it as a unit in a holistic fashion. It takes time, repetition, and effort to develop the fluency necessary to reach this point. Don't expect to be able to perform them accurately by intuition alone. Carefully work out the divisions necessary to perform them properly and work with them repeatedly until you achieve the necessary level of mastery and familiarity.

For Further Study

Learning to read, interpret, perform, hear, understand, and notate many of these advanced rhythms is a subject that could fill another entire manual. The following texts offer further study of performing and hearing advanced rhythms:

Kazez, Daniel. *Rhythm Reading: Elementary through Advanced Training.* 2nd edition. New York: W. W. Norton, 1997.

Hall, Anne C. *Studying Rhythm.* 3rd edition. Upper Saddle River, NJ: Prentice-Hall, 2005.

Hindemith, Paul. *Elementary Training for Musicians.* New York: Associated Music Publishers, 1946.

In addition, you may also wish to consult the best resource on notating various divisions of the beat:

Read, Gardner. *Modern Rhythmic Notation.* Bloomington: Indiana University Press, 1978.

EXERCISES

1. Set a metronome to 60 beats per minute. Practice intoning rhythms (on a neutral syllable, and with double or triple tonguing as necessary) to divide the beat *evenly* into two to eight equal parts. As you divide the beat into eight equal parts, gradually increase the metronome setting to see how fast you can go. Try dividing the beat evenly into nine or more parts.

2. Return the metronome to 60 and practice changing among the various divisions you practiced above. Have a classmate or instructor call out various division numbers for you to change to on the next beat.

3. Practice various beat-rhythm combinations (also known as cross rhythms) by tapping both hands on your knees, a tabletop, or other suitable surface. Begin with 3:2, then progress through various rhythms, such as 4:3, 5:4, 5:2, and so on. First, work out the intersections of the two rhythms as described in the chapter. Then practice each pattern until you have mastered it and can produce it with ease. Each pattern takes time to master (and some more than others) so don't be discouraged at first if this seems challenging.

LISTENING

Melodic Dictation

Listen to excerpts 75.1–75.4 and write out the pitches and rhythms for each. In all of these, the bottom number in the meter sign is **4** and the first duration is a quarter note.

Exercise	Clef	Tonic	Bottom number in meter sign	First duration
75.1	bass	C	4	♩
75.2	tenor	C♯	4	♩
75.3	treble	D♭	4	♩
75.4	bass	E	4	♩

Melodic Transcription

Listen to excerpts 75.5–75.8 and write out the pitches and rhythms for each. Also supply any other appropriate performance indications. Be certain to observe the indicated duration for the first note.

Exercise	Clef	Tonic	Bottom number in meter sign	First duration
75.5	treble	D	4	♪
75.6	treble	G	4	♪.
75.7	treble	A	8	♪.

75.8 The lower voice of a two-voice excerpt is provided below. Write out the upper voice.

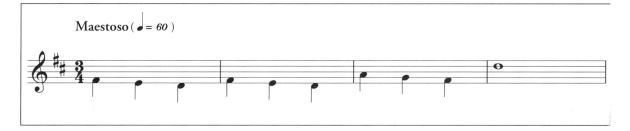

READING AND SIGHT SINGING

Prepare the following excerpts, singing on syllables while conducting. Look for the smaller divisions of the beat and irregular rhythmic proportions and carefully work out and rehearse the proper timings of these rhythms.

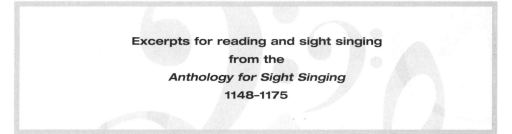
Excerpts for reading and sight singing
from the
Anthology for Sight Singing
1148–1175

76 SOME COMMON NON-DIATONIC PITCH COLLECTIONS

In Chapter 73, we observed that some music lies outside the realm of functional tonality. You can begin to explore some of this post-tonal music by developing your fluency with three of the most common non-diatonic pitch collections: whole-tone, octatonic, and quartal.

All of these collections involve pitch relationships other than those of diatonic harmony, so they present new challenges in aural skills. In both listening and reading, you will now need to determine if a passage is diatonic or not. If it's not, you'll need to determine if it uses one of these three collections, and when—if ever—it deviates from that collection.

The Whole-Tone Collection

The first eight measures of the passage below are clearly in D major (with two non-diatonic pitches introduced in measures 350–351 as part of a chromatic scale). But in measures 357–360, the music has left the domain of the diatonic and uses a new descending scale: D–C♮–B♭–A♭–F♯–E–D. This new scale consists entirely of whole steps between adjacent pitches. For this reason it is called the **whole-tone-scale.**

> The **whole-tone scale** is composed entirely of whole steps between adjacent pitches.

Mikhail Glinka, *Ruslan and Lyudmila*, Overture, mm. 349–360 (1842)

When the pitches of a whole-tone scale are considered not in scalar arrangement but in any order, they are referred to as a whole-tone *collection*. Entire sections of some compositions are based on the whole-tone collection. The composer who is probably the most famous for this is Claude Debussy (although he is highly regarded for much more than whole-tone music). Here is such a passage from one of his compositions:

Claude Debussy, *Six épigraphes antiques*, No. 2,
"Pour un tombeau sans nom," mm. 8–11 (1915)

Although whole-tone *scales* can start on a variety of different pitches, there are only two distinct whole-tone *collections*. One whole-tone collection, beginning arbitrarily on C, contains the pitches C, D, E, F♯, G♯, and A♯ (and their enharmonic equivalents). The other whole-tone collection contains the other unique pitches: C♯, D♯, F, G, A, and B (and their enharmonic equivalents).

Singing whole-tone music can be particularly challenging, so you should practice some preliminary whole-tone exercises. To begin with, relate the whole-tone scale to some skills you already know from your work with diatonic collections and modulations. Sing 1̂/*do*–2̂/*re*–3̂/*mi*, then modulate up a major 3rd by common tone so that 3̂/*mi* becomes a new 1̂/*do*. Then sing 1̂/*do*–2̂/*re*–3̂/*mi* from that *new* 1̂/*do*. Repeat this procedure, modulating up another major 3rd. This results in a complete whole-tone scale spanning one octave, as shown below.

You should leave the syllables behind as quickly as possible, since they serve merely as a crutch here and do not function tonally. One alternative is to sing on letter names. Other exercises that will help build your fluency singing in the whole-tone collection will be found at the end of this chapter.

The Octatonic Collection

The passage below is based on another non-diatonic collection that plays important roles in many twentieth-century compositions (and a few earlier ones).

Igor Stravinsky, *Oedipus Rex*, Act II, rehearsal 158, mm. 1–10 (1927)

Although the accidentals in this excerpt might seem to be randomly placed, they are in fact the product of a systematically constructed scale called the **octatonic scale,** which alternates between half steps and whole steps as shown below.

The **octatonic scale** (or **diminished scale**) is composed of alternating whole and half steps between adjacent pitches.

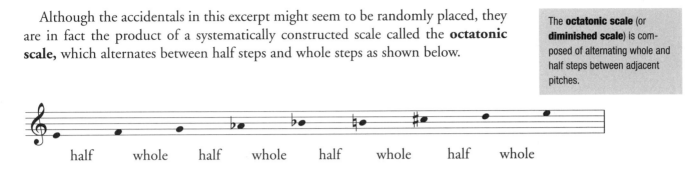

The term *octatonic* recognizes the fact that this scale is composed of eight unique pitches. Jazz and popular musicians sometimes call it the **diminished scale,** due to the diminished chords formed by alternating pitches in the scale.

The octatonic scale appears in two different forms (or modes): one beginning with a half step (as above) and one beginning with a whole step. Although any octatonic scale in either of these two modes can begin on any pitch, there are only three possible octatonic pitch collections (each with its enharmonic equivalents):

- the one containing C, D, E♭, F, G♭, A♭, A, and B
- the one containing C♯, D♯, E, F♯, G, A, B♭, and C
- the one containing D, E, F, G, A♭, B♭, B♮, and C♯

Some preliminary exercises will pave the way toward singing octatonic music. Again, begin by relating the octatonic scale to some skills you already know. Sing 1̂/*do*–2̂/*re*–3̂/*me*, then modulate up a minor 3rd by common tone so that 3̂/*me* becomes a new 1̂/*do*. Then sing 1̂/*do*–2̂/*re*–3̂/*me* from that *new* 1̂/*do*. Repeat this procedure two more times to form a complete octatonic scale spanning one octave, as shown below.

1̂/*do*   2̂/*re*   3̂/*me*   1̂/*do*   2̂/*re*   3̂/*me*   1̂/*do*   2̂/*re*   3̂/*me*   1̂/*do*   2̂/*re*   3̂/*me*

You can use this same approach with the three-pitch fragment 3̂/*mi*–4̂/*fa*–5̂/*sol* in order to produce the other octatonic mode (the one beginning with the half step).

As with the whole-tone scale, you should leave the syllables behind as quickly as possible (perhaps switching to letter names). Other exercises that will help build your fluency singing in the octatonic collection will be found at the end of this chapter.

Quartal Passages

The final non-diatonic collection we will investigate is not as prevalent as whole-tone or octatonic collections, but it does appear in some twentieth-century music. It is also built on a repetitive interval pattern, that of the perfect 4th. Note how the passage below features both melodic and harmonic 4ths.

Charles Ives, "Psalm XXIV," mm. 22–27 (c. 1913)

Quartal music is based on perfect 4ths. **Quartal harmony** is composed of chords built from perfect 4ths.

Any passage that is constructed from a series of perfect 4ths is called **quartal**. Perfect 4ths seem to form the basis of more chords than melodies, so musicians frequently refer to **quartal harmony.**

Quartal music presents listening and singing challenges similar to those of whole-tone and octatonic music. Similarly, you can initially approach singing quartal music by drawing on your tonal training, using a series of progressions from $\hat{5}$/*sol* to $\hat{1}$/*do* as shown below. Once again, abandon these syllable crutches as quickly as you can.

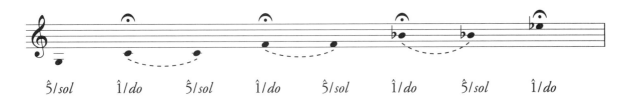

5̂/sol   1̂/do   5̂/sol   1̂/do   5̂/sol   1̂/do   5̂/sol   1̂/do

For Further Study

Although this chapter has made a small excursion into the realm of post-tonal music, a more thorough investigation is far beyond the scope of this manual. If you wish to undertake a more formal and comprehensive study of this music, you should consult the two books below. They take different but musical and usable approaches to aural skills in post-tonal music.

Edlund, Lars. *Modus Novus: Studies in Reading Atonal Melodies.* Stockholm: Nordiska Musikförlaget, 1964.

Friedmann, Michael. *Ear Training for Twentieth-Century Music.* New Haven: Yale University Press, 1990.

EXERCISES

1. Learn to sing the whole-tone scale spanning a single octave. Start slowly, first in the manner described in the chapter, then in steady, even notes. Work up to a tempo of at least 100 notes per minute. Be able to sing the scale from the bottom to the top and back down again, and from the top to the bottom and back up again. Practice starting these scales on different pitches and as you do so, visualize the note names of the pitches you sing. Be prepared to name any pitch you are stopped on while singing.

2. Create sequentials in the whole-tone scale. Here are two examples:

   Learn at least two of these (at least one of which you have invented on your own). Be able to perform them at a steady tempo.

3. Auralize a whole-tone scale. As you do so, sing aloud only every other note. What structure does this create?

4. Repeat exercises 1 through 3 using the octatonic scale.

As you repeat exercise 2, consider the following examples of octatonic sequentials:

At least one of the octatonic sequentials you create should use the other octatonic mode, beginning with the half step.

As you repeat exercise 3, auralize octatonic scales starting with both a whole step and a half step.

5. Sing a pitch near the very bottom of your vocal range. Sing a string of ascending perfect 4ths from that pitch until you reach the top of your range, then descend through those same pitches back to your starting pitch. Repeat this process starting at the *top* of your range and sing down and back up. Work these up to a tempo of at least 100 notes per minute.

6. Start in the lower part of the middle of your range, sing up two perfect 4ths, drop the last pitch down an octave and sing up two more 4ths, drop that last pitch down an octave, and so on. Continue singing this pattern of perfect 4ths to sing a total of seven pitches. What pitch collection results if you sing seven pitches? (Try this by naming a starting pitch and singing on pitch names, accidentals and all.)

7. Use the same process as in 6, but sing a total of thirteen pitches. Where do you end up? (Try this by naming a starting pitch and singing on pitch names, accidentals and all.)

LISTENING

Melodic Dictation

Listen to excerpts 76.1–76.8 and write out the pitches and rhythms for each.

Exercise	Clef	Bottom number in meter sign	Starting pitch
76.1	bass	4	G3
76.2	treble	4	C4
76.3	treble	4	F♯5
76.4	bass	8	A2
76.5	treble	4	F4
76.6	alto	2	D3
76.7	treble	4	G5
76.8	bass	2	E3

READING AND SIGHT SINGING

Prepare the following excerpts, singing while conducting. Look for the kinds of non-diatonic pitch collections discussed in this chapter and apply the skills you learned in the exercises to these passages.

**Excerpts for reading and sight singing
from the
Anthology for Sight Singing
1176–1195**

77 HYPERMETER

We have examined the interactions among various levels of pulse within a measure. This chapter investigates how measures themselves can group into still broader levels of pulse.

Levels of Pulse Broader Than the Measure

In our earliest investigations in this book, we explored the relationships between various levels of pulse and found that meter is a result of pulses being organized into primary and secondary levels. We discovered, for instance, that duple meter is produced by the beat level grouping by twos into the measure level. (See Chapter 1.) We also found that quadruple and compound meters reflect interactions among more than just two levels of pulse. (See Chapters 5 and 16.)

Pulses also combine into groups broader than the measure. Sing the following passage from Schubert's Second Symphony while conducting one beat for each measure using a 1-pattern (review Chapter 23):

Franz Schubert, Symphony No. 2, D. 125, mvt. 4, mm. 5–12 (1815)

Determine how the pulses at level **b** would group into a broader level **c**. Sing the passage again while conducting one beat per measure, but turn your conducting pattern into a duple pattern. Now try it once more, but use a triple pattern. Which one feels more musically appropriate?

A duple pattern is much more fitting, so measure-level pulses (**b**) group by pairs into a broader level **c**:

Franz Schubert, Symphony No. 2, D. 125, mvt. 4, mm. 5–12 (1815)

The way that measures combine metrically into larger groups is called **hypermeter.**

This grouping may extend to even deeper levels, as illustrated below. Here, pulses at level c combine to form a level **d**. Sing the excerpt again and try conducting the level **c** pulses in groups of twos and then in threes. The duple pattern works best at this level as well.

> **Hypermeter** is the way measures combine metrically into larger groups.

Franz Schubert, Symphony No. 2, D. 125, mvt. 4, mm. 5–12 (1815)

A great deal of Western music consists of multiple levels of pulse. Many levels are not made obvious by the meter sign, but involve both smaller divisions of the beat and groupings broader than the measure.

Duple and Triple Groupings

We have focused on groupings of either twos or threes because duple and triple are the two fundamental types of metric organization in Western music. Any other group is produced by some combination of twos and/or threes. For example, simple quadruple meter results from grouping at three three different levels—beats group by twos to form half-measures, which group by twos to form measures. (See Chapter 5.)

Meter and hypermeter, no matter how complicated, can always be conceived of as some product of twos and/or threes. What seems to be a group of five pulses at one level can be felt best as a combination of 2+3 or 3+2. Similarly, a group of seven might be 2+2+3, 2+3+2, or 3+2+2.

Changes in Pulse Grouping

Typically, pulse groupings at one level in a piece are consistent. Thus, once a particular level is perceived as grouping in either twos or threes it will typically continue throughout in that same way. However, a pulse level may change from duple to triple grouping or vice versa. Look at and listen to the following excerpt from the second movement of Beethoven's Ninth Symphony:

Ludwig van Beethoven, Symphony No. 9, Op. 125, mvt. 2, mm. 9–20 (1824) [strings only]

Notice how the fugue subject enters at four-measure intervals. This is a strong indication that some kind of duple-duple grouping is taking place between successive levels of hypermetric pulse. Try conducting one beat per measure in a quadruple pattern.* It should be clear that the measures group into pairs and then pairs of pairs to result in four-measure groups.

This pattern continues for well over a hundred measures. Then, beginning in measure 177, a new pattern emerges:

Ludwig van Beethoven, Symphony No. 9, Op. 125, mvt. 2, mm. 177–188 (1824)

---

*Try this two ways: (1) conducting measure 1 as a downbeat, and (2) conducting measure 1 as an upbeat.

At the opening of this passage, the measures are clearly grouped in *threes,* as indicated by the three-measure spacing of the entries of the fugue subject and Beethoven's marking—*Ritmo di tre battute.* Thus, the hypermeter has changed from duple/quadruple to triple.

Be aware of the possibility that pieces beginning with one type of hypermetric grouping might change to another as they progress and that such changes might occur multiple times throughout a composition.

Elision

Another feature of hypermetric grouping involves the shifting or reinterpretation of primary and secondary pulses after a pattern has been established.

The pulse-graph for the following passage shows five levels of pulse, from the half-note beat through groups of many measures. Listen to this excerpt and think about the relationships between these pulse levels.

Joseph Haydn, Symphony No. 104, mvt. 1, mm. 17–33 (1795)

The relationships between pulse levels are all duple at the outset. Now take a closer look at (and listen to) the relationship between levels **b** and **c**. The measures **b** come in pairs **c**, so that each odd-numbered measure serves as a primary pulse, which is followed by an even-numbered measure as a secondary one. This pattern continues for 31 measures. Then, measure 32, which should be a secondary pulse at level **c**, is reinterpreted as a new *primary* pulse at that level. It is as if the primary pulse that would "normally" appear in measure 33 has been pushed one measure earlier to overlap with the secondary pulse in measure 32. In this way, measure 32 serves two functions: as the end of one primary-secondary pattern and as the beginning of another. This kind of condition is called an **elision.**

An **elision** occurs when a pulse that would ordinarily serve as secondary is reinterpreted as primary.

Now that we have investigated pulse grouping beyond the measure level, the fundamental nature of grouping by twos and threes, changes in pulse grouping, and elision, you are ready to begin work on hypermetric analyses by listening and to incorporate awareness of hypermeter into your performances.

LISTENING

Listen to excerpts 77.1–77.6. Read over the instructions and questions printed for each excerpt before you listen. After repeated listenings, follow the instructions and answer the questions.

77.1

a. Construct a hypermetric graph (like those in the chapter) for this excerpt showing at least six levels of pulse.

b. How many levels of pulse do you think are significant in this excerpt?

c. How do you think this piece might continue?

d. Listen carefully to how the music progresses for the first five notes of the excerpt. Pay special attention to the musical emphasis achieved by the arrival on the fourth note. How does this emphasis align with the sense of pulse (and therefore "stress") shown in your graph?

77.2

a. Construct a hypermetric graph for this piece and compare it to the previous excerpt and its graph.

77.3

a. Construct a hypermetric graph showing at least three levels of pulse for this short piece.

b. What is unusual about the hypermetric structure of this piece? What hypermetric device creates that unusualness?

77.4

a. Construct a hypermetric graph of this excerpt representing at least five levels of pulse.

b. What is unusual about the broader levels of hypermetric pulse in this excerpt?

77.5

a. Construct a hypermetric graph of the first complete phrase, which ends with an authentic cadence.

b. Where does the first downbeat fall? Compare this with the actual notation of the first few measures.

c. Where is the hypermetric middle of this first phrase? How does the rhythmic activity there compare and contrast with the hypermetric grouping?

d. This first phrase is eight measures long. Does this movement consist entirely of eight-measure phrases? If not, where does the hypermetric structure deviate from this eight-measure pattern?

e. How many times does the opening phrase return in this movement?

77.6

  a. What do you feel constitutes the fastest (narrowest) musically significant level of pulse in this piece?

  b. How many levels of pulse are musically significant in this piece?

  c. What meter sign do you think the composer used for this piece? Show how that meter sign represents two or more levels of pulse in your graph.

  d. Construct a graph that represents all significant levels of metric and hypermetric grouping in the piece.

  e. [for extra credit] In what ways does the hypermetric grouping interact with the form? In what ways does it interact with the harmonic structure (key areas, etc.)?

Additional exercise (not recorded on the accompanying CD):

• Elvis Presley, "Hound Dog," RCA compact disc 68079 or 67732 or 66050; or Rhino Records compact disc 70599

• Big Mama Thornton, "Hound Dog," MCA compact disc 10668; or New World Records LP 80261 [Peacock 1612]; or ACE (U.K.) compact disc 940

  a. Listen to Elvis Presley's rendition of "Hound Dog." Write a pulse graph that shows at least five levels of pulse. Why is this type of song called a "12-bar blues"?

  b. Listen to Big Mama Thornton's version of "Hound Dog" (which was recorded a few years before Elvis's version). Construct the same kind of pulse graph that you did for Elvis's version. What are some of the differences between these two performances? Why do you suppose there are differences in hypermeter between the two performances?

READING AND SIGHT SINGING

Prepare the following excerpts, singing on syllables while conducting. Pay special attention to at least two levels of pulse broader than the measure. Practice conducting each excerpt beating only once per measure and grouping those beats into larger hypermeasures. Are there alternative groupings that are also musically valid? In what ways can you incorporate your new awareness of hypermeter into your performances so that this is audible to listeners?

**Excerpts for reading and sight singing
from the
Anthology for Sight Singing
1196–1207**

78 FORM

Form, like many other features of musical compositions, can be comprehended aurally. This chapter introduces some techniques you can use to begin assessing form through listening.

Musical Forms

An adequate study of the many different musical forms in Western music requires much more than a small segment in a course on ear training. For the purposes of this introduction to the aural analysis of form, we will restrict our discussion to the following forms:

- binary
- rounded binary
- ternary
- compound ternary
- rondo
- sonata allegro
- theme and variations

This chapter assumes that you have studied these forms adequately in a separate theory or analysis course.*

Laying Out a Metric Grid

In order to analyze form entirely by ear without recourse to a printed score, you will need to map out where the sections of a piece occur on a grid similar to those we have used to show meter and hypermeter. Form grids need not show the multiple levels that hypermetric grids do but they should show at least the downbeat of every measure you hear. If you hear multiple pulse levels and you are uncertain about what constitutes a measure, you should simply pick a level and move on, just as you have done in dictation. As long as the sections of your grid are in proportion to those of the piece, you'll be fine.

The following demonstration will provide an example of the kind of work you can do beginning with a metric or hypermetric grid and projecting an analysis of form on top of that. The score is included here for the sake of discussion. You will not have access to the printed score for the aural analyses at the end of this chapter.

---

*For a review of these forms, consult any textbook on the subject. Two suggestions: (1) Peter Spencer and Peter Temko, *A Practical Approach to the Study of Form in Music* (Prospect Heights, IL: Waveland Press, 1994) [reissue of the 1988 Prentice-Hall edition]; (2) William Caplin, *Classical Form* (New York: Oxford University Press, 1998).

Robert Schumann, *Album for the Young,* Op. 68, No. 8, "The Wild Rider," (1848)

Imagine now that you are listening repeatedly to a recorded performance of this small piece. Your goal is to create a visual representation of the form of what you hear.

In order to write out a steady stream of pulses—with one pulse for each measure—you will have to choose a particular pulse level to call the measure. Do you hear each group of three as a measure (as if it were in ⅜) or do you move to the next broader metric level and call groups of six a measure (as Schumann did, using ⅝ meter)? Without the score, you may choose either.

For the sake of discussion, let's assume that you choose groups of six (as in Schumann's ⅝), so you would hear a total of 32 measures (including the repeat). Your initial metric grid for your aural analysis would look like this:

| | | | | | | | | | | | | | | | | | | | | | | | | | | | | | | | |

Next, you can begin to group measures into longer units or phrases:

Then you can label the sections according to principles of repetition, contrast, variation, and so forth. You can use the types of labels used in many approaches to form: A for the first section, B for a new section, and so on, reusing labels as needed for repeated sections.

You may find it helpful to include measure numbers in your graph before adding these formal labels. In this way, you can be very specific about just what form you hear in this work (and other works) and where the sections occur. The grid below shows that "The Wild Rider" is in simple ternary form, in which the first section repeats immediately and each section lasts eight measures.

```
1                 9                17                25
A                 A                B                 A
```

For longer works, you will need to extend your grids over several lines or—in a graphically powerful solution—tape multiple sheets together to form a single long timeline for each piece.

As you progress to larger and more complicated pieces with more sophisticated forms, you can use labels you learn in theory and analysis courses, such as second theme, ritornello, recapitulation, and so on.

LISTENING

For excerpts 78.1–78.9, use the following procedure for each excerpt. First, listen to the excerpt once and then write the name of the form you think you hear. Next, listen to the excerpt repeatedly and construct a metric grid on separate paper. Then show the divisions of the piece into formal sections by marking above the grid in the manner discussed in the chapter. Add measure numbers at important places to aid in reading your graph. How (if at all) did repeated listenings and work with the grid change your impression of the form? Finally, answer the questions specific to each excerpt (if any).

78.1 Form: _____

- Does this piece stay in one key or modulate?
- If it modulates, to what key (e.g., "subdominant") does it move?
- Does it return to the tonic?

78.2 Form: _____

- Does this piece stay in one key or modulate?
- If it modulates, to what key (e.g., "subdominant") does it move?
- Does it return to the tonic?
- Does the piece begin on a downbeat or an upbeat?

78.3 Form: _____

78.4 Form: _____

- Do the phrases remain in two-, four-, and eight-measure groupings?
- If not, where do they deviate from this pattern?

78.5 Form: _____

The opening phrase of this piece begins on a downbeat.

- Do all subsequent appearances of this phrase also begin on a downbeat?
- If this phrase also begins on a *hypermetric* downbeat, how can you account for the hypermetric position of the subsequent appearances of this phrase?
- To what key (e.g., "subdominant") does this piece modulate and where does this occur in the form?

78.6 Form: _____

   • How do the lengths of the phrases compare between the A and B sections of this piece?

78.7 Form: _____

78.8 Form: _____

   • What cues help you determine when each new section of the form begins?

78.9 Form: _____

Accidental: a symbol (such as a sharp or flat) placed directly before a note, affecting its pitch

Alto clef: a C clef placed on the third line of a five-line staff

Anacrusis (or **Pickup**): any incomplete measure of music before the first downbeat

Anticipation: a pitch from the next chord that is reached early, creating a dissonance with the present chord

Applied dominant: a pitch a perfect 5th above (or a perfect 4th below) the pitch to which it is applied

Applied dominant chord: a chord whose root is an applied dominant and whose quality is the same as a dominant chord

Applied leading tone: a note raised chromatically to serve as a temporary leading tone to the diatonic note a half step above it

Applied leading-tone chord: a chord with an applied leading tone as its root

Asymmetrical compound meters: meters in which beats of unequal duration are produced by divisions of both twos and threes

Augmentation dot: a dot following a note that increases the note by half its rhythmic value

Augmented sixth chords: chords formed when [↓]$\hat{6}$/*le* in the bass voice combines with ↑$\hat{4}$/*fi* in some upper voice

Baritone clef: the staff in which the F clef places F on the third line of a five-line staff

Bass clef staff: the staff in which the F clef places F on the fourth line from the bottom

Beat: the duration between successive pulses

Beat value (or **Beat unit**): the note value equal to one beat

Cadence: the point of arrival created by the confluence of harmonic motion and metric and rhythmic punctuation

Cadential $\frac{6}{4}$: the instance when the bass note $\hat{5}$/*sol* is embellished by $\frac{6}{4}$—$\frac{5}{3}$ motion and in which $\hat{3}$/*mi*/*me* moves to $\hat{2}$/*re* and $\hat{1}$/*do* moves to $\hat{7}$/*ti* at a cadence

C clef: the clef whose center shows the position of middle C

Chromatic passing tone: a chromatic note that connects two diatonic pitches and is

approached and left by half step all in the same direction

Chromatic pitch: a pitch that is not part of the diatonic collection

Chromatic scale: a series of pitches spanning an octave wherein all adjacent pitches are separated by half steps

Circle of fifths: the arrangement of twelve enharmonically unique keys in a circle, in which each key is separated from the next by one more or one fewer sharp or flat, and in which the tonics of the keys progress around the circle by fifths

Closed (or **Full**) **cadence:** a cadence that ends on the tonic

Closely related keys: keys that have the same diatonic collection or those that can be arrived at through adding or removing one sharp or flat in the circle of fifths

Complete neighbor-note figure: a three-note group that begins with a main pitch, moves to its neighbor, and returns to the main pitch

Compound melody: a melody in which two or more voices seem to progress as equal partners

Compound meter: a meter in which the beat is regularly divided into threes, in which the beat unit is equal to three of the note values represented by the bottom number of the meter sign

Concert pitch: the standardized system of naming pitches as they sound or as they are notated for non-transposing instruments

Conclusive cadence: a cadence that ends on the tonic

Conjunct motion (or **Stepwise motion**): motion to an adjacent scale degree, including repeated notes

Deceptive cadence: a cadence that ends on an unexpected chord

Diatonic collection: all the diatonic pitches from a given key signature

Diatonic pitches: pitches created by a given key signature

Diminished scale (or **Octatonic scale**): a scale composed of alternating whole and half steps between adjacent pitches

Diminutions: notes shorter than the prevailing harmonic rhythm that embellish notes or chords (such as neighbor tones and passing tones)

Disjunct motion (or **Motion by skip or leap**): motion that moves from one scale degree to a non-adjacent scale degree by jumping over the intervening stepwise pitches

Distant keys (or **Remote** or **Foreign keys**): keys arrived at through adding or removing more than one sharp or flat in the circle of fifths

Dominant pitch: the pitch a perfect fifth above (or a perfect fourth below) the tonic

Dominant triad: a triad whose root is $\hat{5}$/*sol*

Downbeat: the first beat of a measure

Duple meter: a meter in which there are two beats per measure

Duplet: two notes of equal duration that fit in the place of three

Elision: the condition in which a pulse that would ordinarily serve as secondary is reinterpreted as primary

Enharmonic pitches: pitches that are spelled differently but occupy the same location on the piano keyboard (and therefore sound the same)

F clef: the clef that surrounds the line representing F with two dots

Foreign keys (or **Distant** or **Remote keys**): keys arrived at through adding or removing more than one sharp or flat in the circle of fifths

French violin clef: the staff in which the G clef places G on the first line of a five-line staff

Full (or **Closed**) **cadence:** a cadence that ends on the tonic

G clef: the clef that curls around the line representing G

Grand staff: a combination of the treble and bass clef staves

Half cadence (or **Open cadence** or **Semicadence**): a cadence that ends on the dominant

Half step: the smaller of the two kinds of steps, equal to half of a whole step; for example $\hat{3}$/*mi* to $\hat{4}$/*fa*

Harmonic rhythm: the durations governed by successive chords

Harmonic sequence: a group of chords sequenced at a repeating interval or on a series of root movements

Hemiola: a metric condition that regroups 3 + 3 as 2 + 2 + 2, or vice versa

Holistic identification: identifying something simply because you know what it is, not because you have analyzed or manipulated it

Hypermeter: the way measures combine metrically into larger groups

Ictus: the point in each beat of a conducting pattern at which the pulse occurs

Incomplete neighbor-note figure: a two-note group that either begins with a neighbor and moves to the main pitch (a **prefix neighbor**), or begins with the main pitch and moves to its neighbor (a **suffix neighbor**)

Inconclusive cadence: a cadence that ends on some other chord than the tonic

Interval: the distance, in terms of pitch, between two notes

Interval of transposition: the interval between one pitch level and the transposed pitch level

Key: the pitch where the tonic lies

Key signature: the sharps and flats at the beginning of a staff that move the pattern of whole and half steps, which allows the tonic to be moved

Leading tone: a pitch one half step below the tonic

Leading-tone triad: a triad whose root is the leading tone

Leap (or **Skip**): an interval larger than a step

Ledger line: a small segment of a staff line used for writing notes too high or too low for a staff

Major scale: the following series of intervals (in steps) ascending from the tonic: 1, 1, ½, 1, 1, 1, ½

Measure: the duration between successive primary pulses

Mediant pitch: the pitch a third above (or a sixth below) the tonic

Mediant triad: a triad whose root is the mediant

Melodic contour: the relative up-and-down motion of pitches in a melody

Melodic sequence: the repetition of the contour and rhythms of a pattern on a series of scale degrees

Meter: the organization of pulses into primary and secondary levels

Meter sign (or **"time signature"**): indicates the number of beats per measure (the top number) and the note value equal to one beat (the bottom number) for simple meters

Mezzo-soprano clef: a C clef placed on the second line of a five-line staff

Middle C: the C between the treble and bass clef staves, near the middle of the piano

Minor tonic: the pitch that lies a minor third below (or a major sixth above) the major tonic within a given diatonic collection

Modal borrowing: the process of borrowing a pitch from one mode and producing it in a parallel mode through chromaticism

Mode: the combination of a tonic and a diatonic collection

Modulation: the change from one key to another within a composition

Motion by skip or leap (or **Disjunct motion**): motion that moves from one scale degree to a non-adjacent scale degree by jumping over the intervening stepwise pitches

Neapolitan sixth chord: the first inversion of the Neapolitan chord (a major triad that has ↓$\hat{2}$/*ra* as its root) with $\hat{4}$/*fa* in the bass

Neighbor note: the scale degree immediately above or below a pitch

Neighbor tone: a tone that is one step above or below a chord tone: complete neighbors depart from and return to the chord tone, while incomplete ones only depart or return

Neighboring $^6_4$ (or **Pedal $^6_4$**): the movement in which the upper voices trace a $^5_3$—$^6_4$—$^5_3$ pattern while the bass voice remains stationary

Octatonic scale (or **Diminished scale**): a scale composed of alternating whole and half steps between adjacent pitches

Open cadence (or **Half cadence** or **Semicadence**): a cadence that ends on the dominant

Parallel keys: keys that share the same tonic but not the same diatonic collection

Parallel modes: modes that share the same tonic or final, but not the same diatonic collection

Part: the notes played or sung from a single printed part

Passing $^6_4$: the motion in which the bass note is approached and left by step, all in the same direction, and the middle bass note supports a $^6_4$ chord sandwiched between two other chords

Passing tone: a tone that connects one chord tone to another by step

Pedal $^6_4$ (or **Neighboring $^6_4$**): the movement in which the upper voices trace a $^5_3$—$^6_4$—$^5_3$ pattern while the bass voice remains stationary

Pickup (or **Anacrusis**): any incomplete measure of music before the first downbeat

Pitch: the characteristic of sound we perceive as being higher or lower

Prefix neighbor: see **Incomplete neighbor-note figure**

Primary pulse: a pulse that regularly contains greater stress

Pulse: a regularly recurring feeling of stress in music

Quadruple meter: a meter in which there are four beats per measure

Quartal harmony: harmony composed of chords built from perfect 4ths

Quartal music: music based on perfect 4ths

Quintuple meter: a meter in which there are five beats per measure

Relative keys: keys that share the same diatonic collection and, therefore, the same key signature

Relative modes: modes that share the same diatonic collection, and therefore the same key signature

Remote keys (or **Distant** or **Foreign keys**): keys arrived at through adding or removing more than one sharp or flat in the circle of fifths

Rest: a duration of silence in music

Rhythm: duration in music

Scale: a list of pitches in ascending and/or descending order

Scale degrees: the unique pitches in a scale (usually referred to by number)

Secondary pulse: a pulse that regularly contains less stress

Semicadence (or **Half cadence** or **Open cadence**): a cadence that ends on the dominant

Septuple meter: a meter in which there are seven beats per measure

Sequential: an exercise in which a pitch pattern is repeated on successive scale degrees

Simple meter: a meter in which the beat is regularly divided in halves

Skip (or **Leap**): an interval larger than a step

Solmization: the discipline of singing syllables that correspond to pitches or rhythms

Soprano clef: a C clef placed on the first line of a five-line staff

Step: the distance between two adjacent scale degrees

Stepwise chromatic alteration: the raising or lowering by a half step of the middle note in a three-note stepwise segment of a diatonic scale, turning one of the half steps into a whole step and the adjacent whole step into a half step

Stepwise motion (or **Conjunct motion**): motion to an adjacent scale degree, including repeated notes

Sub-bass clef: the staff in which the F clef places F on the fifth line of a five-line staff

Subdominant pitch: the pitch a perfect fourth above (or a perfect fifth below) the tonic

Subdominant triad: a triad whose root is the subdominant

Submediant pitch: the pitch a sixth above (or a third below) the tonic

Submediant triad: a triad whose root is the submediant

Subtonic pitch: the pitch a whole step below the tonic

Subtonic triad: a triad whose root is the subtonic

Suffix neighbor: see **Incomplete neighbor-note figure**

Supertonic pitch: the pitch a second above (or a seventh below) the tonic

Supertonic triad: a triad whose root is the supertonic

Suspension: a pitch held over from one chord to form a dissonance with the next chord

Symmetrical compound meters: meters in which beats of equal duration are produced by divisions of threes

Syncopation: the elimination of articulations on a beat or beats, which occurs when the duration of the previous note is cut short

Takadimi: a system of rhythm syllables

Tempo: the speed at which pulses progress

Tenor clef: a C clef placed on the fourth line of a five-line staff

Tetrachord: a stepwise succession of four pitches, usually a four-note segment of a scale

Tie: a curved line that joins the rhythmic values of the notes it connects

Timbre (or **Tone color**): the difference between notes of identical pitch, rhythm, and dynamics produced by different instruments or voices

Time signature: see **Meter sign**

Tone color (or **Timbre**): the difference between notes of identical pitch, rhythm, and dyna-mics produced by different instruments or voices

Tonic: the pitch to which all others seem to want to resolve

Tonicization: the organization of the notes in a particular composition that establishes a pitch as a tonic

Tonic triad: a triad whose root is the tonic

Transposition: the transfer of music with all its intervals to a new pitch level

Treble clef staff: the staff in which the G clef places G on the second line from the bottom

Triple meter: a meter in which there are three beats per measure

Triplet: three notes of equal duration that fit in the place of two

Upbeat: the last beat of a measure

Voice: the abstract line formed by the smoothest possible melodic motion from one harmony to the next

Voice leading: the motion of the abstract lines formed by the smoothest possible melodic motion from one harmony to the next

Whole step: the larger of the two kinds of steps equal to two half steps; for example, $\hat{1}$/*do* to $\hat{2}$/*re*

Whole-tone scale: a scale composed entirely of whole steps between adjacent pitches

INDEX OF EXAMPLES

GENERAL INDEX

2–3 motion, 193
4–3 motion, 191, 194–95
5–6 motion, 192–93

accents, 111
accidentals, 83
    adjusting for in transposition, 212–14
    chromatics distinguished from, 308
    diatonic pitches created by, 306
    modes notated with, 225–26
Aeolian mode, 215–18, 281
"alla breve," 31
alto clef, 119–20, 211–12, 292–93
anacrusis, 23
anticipations, 190–91
applied dominant chord, 245, 250–52, 255, 259, 264–66, 280
applied dominant seventh chord, 245, 250–52, 255, 259, 264–66, 280
applied leading tone, 244
applied leading-tone chord, 244–46, 250–52, 255, 259, 264–66
applied leading-tone seventh chord, 244–46, 250–52, 255, 259, 264–66
arpeggiation
    in bass, 197
    of chord progressions, 158–59
    of dominant seventh chord, 185–86
    of triads, 157–58
articulation markings, 110–11
asymmetrical compound meters, 354–56
asymmetrical duple meters, 355
asymmetrical quadruple meters, 356
asymmetrical triple meters, 355–56
augmentation dot, 31–32, 53, 99
augmented seventh chord, 200
augmented sixth chords, 274–77
augmented triads, 167

baritone clef, 211–12, 292–93
Baroque, "incomplete" key signatures in, 308–9
bass clef, 36, 211–12, 292–93
bass clef staff, 36–37
bass lines
    dictation of, 155
    hearing voice motion of, 161–62
    motion in, 193
beams, 31

beat(s), 2
    dividing notated, 104–7
    duple division of, 21–22, 232
    grouping notated, 103–4
    quadruple division of, 98–101, 230–31
    sextuple division of, 126–28
    smaller divisions of, 360–61
    tempo and, 66
beat value (beat unit), 30
binary form, 378
breve, 29

C clefs, 119–21, 292–93
cadences, 151
    4–3 motion at, 194–95
cadential $^6_4$ chord, 194–95
changing meters, 356–57
chord progressions
    arpeggiating, 158–59
    listening to, 159–60
chords. *See also* seventh chords; triads
    applied to mediant, 264–66
    applied to submediant, 259–61
    applied to the dominant, 244–47
    applied to the subdominant, 250–52
    applied to the supertonic, 255–56
    augmented sixth, 274–77
    borrowed iv and ii°⁷ in major mode, 280
    chromatic alterations to, 303
    names for, 145
    Neapolitan, 269–71
    V of VII in minor mode, 280
chromatic alterations
    accidentals distinguished from, 308
    modulation and, 325, 334
    stepwise, 301–3
    types of, 301–2
chromatic lower neighbors, 82–84, 301
chromatic passing tones, 234–36, 301
    embellished, 240
chromatic pitches, 82, 246, 251
    modulation between distant keys by, 340–41
    modulation by leap to, 316
    reading and writing, 83
chromatic prefix neighbors, 239–40, 301
chromatic scale, 236